THE PRESENCE OF ROME IN MEDIEVAL AND EARLY MODERN BRITAIN

This book explores the cultural and intellectual stakes of medieval and Renaissance Britain's sense of itself as living in the shadow of Rome, a city whose name could designate the ancient, fallen, quintessentially human power that had conquered and colonized Britain, and also the alternately sanctified and demonized Roman Church. Wallace presses medieval texts in a range of languages (including Latin, medieval Welsh, Old English and Old French) into conversation with early modern English and humanistic Latin texts (including works by Gildas, Bede, Chaucer, Shakespeare, Bacon, St Augustine, Dante, Erasmus, Luther, and Montaigne). 'The Ordinary', 'The Self', 'The Word', and 'The Dead' are taken as compass points by which individuals lived out their orientations to, and against, Rome, isolating important dimensions of Rome's enduring ability to shape and complicate the effort to come to terms with the nature of self and the structure of human community.

ANDREW WALLACE is Associate Professor in the Department of English Language and Literature at Carleton University. He studies the Classical tradition and is author of *Virgil's Schoolboys: The Poetics of Pedagogy in Renaissance England* (2010), along with essays on authors and topics ranging from Shakespeare and Spenser to *Lily's Grammar*.

THE PRESENCE OF ROME IN MEDIEVAL AND EARLY MODERN BRITAIN

Texts, Artefacts, and Beliefs

ANDREW WALLACE

CAMBRIDGE
UNIVERSITY PRESS

University Printing House, Cambridge CB2 8BS, United Kingdom

One Liberty Plaza, 20th Floor, New York, NY 10006, USA

477 Williamstown Road, Port Melbourne, VIC 3207, Australia

314–321, 3rd Floor, Plot 3, Splendor Forum, Jasola District Centre, New Delhi – 110025, India

79 Anson Road, #06–04/06, Singapore 079906

Cambridge University Press is part of the University of Cambridge.

It furthers the University's mission by disseminating knowledge in the pursuit of education, learning, and research at the highest international levels of excellence.

www.cambridge.org
Information on this title: www.cambridge.org/9781108496100
DOI: 10.1017/9781108866071

First published 2020

A catalogue record for this publication is available from the British Library.

ISBN 978-1-108-49610-0 Hardback

This book is dedicated to Dana, Harry, and Sasha.

Contents

Figures

Preface

This book takes a long view of Rome's entanglement in the lives of the inhabitants of the island that once constituted the Roman provinces of Britannia. Its emphasis is on texts and phenomena ranging from the early Middle Ages to the late seventeenth century, though in a few cases it reaches beyond those temporal limits in order to establish prehistories and afterlives for the problems under examination.

Medieval and early modern conceptions of *auctoritas* were genuinely transhistorical, transnational, and multilingual. The book, therefore, ranges quite widely. Writers such as Gildas, Bede, Geoffrey Chaucer, Roger Ascham, Sir Thomas Wilson, Edmund Spenser, William Shakespeare, John Donne, Sir Francis Bacon, Sir Thomas Browne, and John Milton are pressed into dialogue with Continental writers who exercised vast influence on the literary and religious cultures of medieval and Renaissance Britain. The latter include, for example, St Augustine, Dante, Petrarch, Erasmus, Martin Luther, Joachim Du Bellay, and Montaigne, each of whom shaped English experiences and understandings of Rome's unnerving persistence.

The book opens by examining some lines from Virgil's 'First Eclogue', a poem in which a goatherd stares down the prospect of a life of exile while his interlocutor rhapsodizes on the subject of a life-altering visit to Rome. It closes by exploring passages from some poems in which Ovid, exiled from Rome, fears that he is losing his Latin. Ovid's poems of exile were popular curriculum texts in the grammar schools of sixteenth- and seventeenth-century England. They therefore provide a final vantage point from which to reframe the book's arguments against the backdrop of humanist pedagogy. This sort of historical and cultural range presents obvious challenges, but the book's examinations of individual texts and writers attend to the historical particularities of their origins, production, and consumption.

A large body of scholarship has, to excellent effect, established that Rome is at once a place and an idea. This double formula, however, risks depicting Rome primarily as a *distant* place (distant, that is, from the perspective of Britain) and as a *mere* idea (that is, as a wholly immaterial concept or notion of that distant place). It needs, therefore, to be supplemented by an acknowledgement that the Roman Empire had left in its wake material remains and cultural practices that ensured that Rome could always be close-to-hand, familiar, and domestic – even a thousand or more miles from the Eternal City. Ruins, roads, the Latin language and the thickets of its grammar, cultural and spiritual institutions, liturgical texts and devotional regimens: these phenomena ensured that Rome could be, even as far away as medieval or Renaissance Britain, experienced as near rather than far, and as a highly complex network of material remains and cultural practices rather than as an abstract idea. I gather these disparate phenomena under the rubric of the 'fact' of Rome (with an eye to the word's derivation from the Latin *factum*) in an effort to show that lives lived in medieval and Renaissance Britain were continually immersed in versions of Rome that oscillated between conspicuousness and invisibility.

Seeking to capture a wide-angle image of the plural legacies of the city's persistence, the book studies how Rome figures in the murky processes by which individuals settled their relation to the world (Chapter 1), in shifting conceptions of the problem of the self (Chapter 2), in the experience of studying, mastering, and being altered by Latin words and the Word of God (Chapter 3), and in the ties that bind the living to the dead (Chapter 4). These chapters are linked by my effort to take seriously a number of metonymic and synecdochic formulas in which the word 'Rome' is made to serve as shorthand for a broad range of material and literary artefacts, linguistic and cultural phenomena, and religious and liturgical debates that bear on understandings of human community and the nature of 'the human' itself.

Although English humanism and the Reformation are rightly credited with having significantly reoriented attitudes to Rome, the enduring scholarly assumption that the sixteenth century marks the moment when English writers initiate critical and self-conscious engagements with a distant city on the banks of the Tiber loses sight of the thoroughness with which Rome had long inhabited the lives of those who lived in its wake. It is still common, for example, to regard the advent of Renaissance humanism and the Reformation as marking moments when a properly historical view of Rome's presence in the island of Britain comes into focus. This book, however, shows that the critical intelligence and casts of mind that scholars of the early modern period associate with sixteenth-century inquiry are already significant components in some influential and widely circulated early medieval English perspectives on Rome. Those early perspectives, in turn, continue to shape experiences and understandings of Rome during the sixteenth and seventeenth centuries.

Acknowledgements

It is a pleasure to have this opportunity to acknowledge guidance and support received in the course of my work. Much of the book's prehistory can be traced to conversations with the late F. T. Flahiff. Those conversations were casual, even directionless, at the time, and they occurred many years before I wrote anything that appears here. I wish that I had benefitted from his wisdom and generosity during the course of the book's composition. I am sorry that he is gone.

I continue to owe longstanding debts of gratitude to Nancy Lindheim and Elizabeth D. Harvey. They were model mentors. I offer special thanks to Paul Stevens. At different stages of my work he provided fruitful suggestions, clarified the implications of those suggestions, and gave me an opportunity to think aloud at the 2012 iteration of his Canada Milton Seminar in Toronto. Finally, he pointed me in the right direction.

I am fortunate to have been able to draw on the expertise and generosity of a number of colleagues at Carleton University. Siobhain Bly Calkin, Robin Norris, and Micheline White read individual chapters and helped me see things that I had not seen. Zeba Crook, Travis DeCook, and Johannes Wolfart answered random questions with detailed and thoughtful answers. In each case, those answers helped me out of jams. John Osborne shared his knowledge on the subject of late antique and medieval Rome. Brian Cummings and Jeanne Shami made decisive contributions at key moments of the project's development. I am certain that they will have little sense of the importance of their interventions. I am delighted to be able to acknowledge them.

Audiences at multiple annual meetings of the Renaissance Society of America and the Modern Language Association helped me to sharpen the arguments on view here. I had the great pleasure of presenting material from Chapter 2 at Julia L. Hairston and Paolo Alei's 'Early Modern Rome 3' conference in 2017, which was held at the University of California's Piazza dell'Orologio Study Center in Rome. Stuart

J. Murray invited me to participate in his 'Research Talks' series in our home department. Shane Hawkins and Carleton University's Department of Greek and Roman Studies offered the same opportunity. I owe special thanks to Mario Erasmo and to the faculty, graduate students, and staff of the Department of Classics at the University of Georgia for having invited me to speak to them about this project.

I thank the staff of Carleton's MacOdrum Library for their expertise and support.

A small portion of this book has appeared in print. Chapter 2 revises several paragraphs from an essay titled 'Education' in Michael Schoenfeldt (ed.), *John Donne in Context* (Cambridge University Press, 2019), 131–8. Chapter 3 revises a small number of paragraphs from 'Spenser's Dead' in Melissa Sanchez and Ayesha Ramachandran (eds.) *Spenser Studies: A Renaissance Poetry Annual* 30 (2016), 255–70.

I am grateful to Emily Hockley, to my two anonymous readers, and to the entire production team at Cambridge University Press. I have benefitted from their guidance and suggestions. The book is stronger for their efforts. Any lingering errors are, of course, my responsibility.

This book was 'first' completed during a sabbatical in Aix-en-Provence with Dana, Harry, and Sasha. My debts to them cannot be repaid.

Go, litel boke, go.
A. W.

Note on Texts and Translations

I have, for ease of reference, cited Classical texts and translations as they appear in the relevant editions of the Loeb Classical Library. Other texts and translations have been chosen on a case-by-case basis and credited in footnotes. Where possible, my goal has been to pair authoritative modern editions in the original language with the most readily available solid English translations. Unattributed translations from Latin, French, Old French, and Old English are mine. Biblical citations are drawn from the following editions: for the Vulgate, *Biblia Sacra iuxta vulgatam versionem*, 4th edn. (Stuttgart: Deutsche Bibelgesellschaft, 1994); for the King James Version, *The Holy Bible: 1611 Edition* (Nashville: Thomas Nelson, 1989). Passages from Shakespeare are from *The Riverside Shakespeare*, ed. G. Blakemore Evans and J. J. M. Tobin, 2nd edn. (Boston: Houghton Mifflin, 1997).

Abbreviations

ASD	*Opera Omnia Desiderii Erasmi Roterodami* (Amsterdam: North-Holland Publishing Company, 1969–).
BT	Martin Heidegger, *Being and Time*, trans. John Macquarrie and Edward Robinson (New York: Harper & Row, 1962).
Conf.	Augustine, *Confessions*, ed. and trans. Carolyn J.-B. Hammond, 2 vols., LCL 26–7 (Cambridge, MA: Harvard University Press, 2014).
CT	Chaucer, *The Canterbury Tales*, in *The Riverside Chaucer*, ed. Larry D. Benson, 3rd edn. (Boston: Houghton Mifflin, 1987).
CWE	*Collected Works of Erasmus* (University of Toronto Press, 1974–).
CPW	John Milton, *Complete Prose Works of John Milton*, ed. Don M. Wolfe, 8 vols. (New Haven: Yale University Press, 1953–82).
HE	Bede, *The Ecclesiastical History of the English People*, ed. Bertram Colgrave and R. A. B. Mynors (1969; Oxford University Press, 2007).
KGW	Friedrich Nietzsche, *Werke: Kritische Gesamtausgabe*, ed. Giorgio Colli and Mazzino Montinari, 9 vols. (Berlin: Walter de Gruyter, 1967–2015).
LCL	Loeb Classical Library.
LW	*Luther's Works*, ed. Jaroslav Pelikan and Helmut T. Lehmann, 56 vols. (Philadelphia: Concordia Publishing House, 1955–1986).
MED	*Middle English Dictionary*, 20 vols. (Ann Arbor: University of Michigan Press, 1952–2001).
OED	*OED Online* (Oxford University Press, 2019).
SKS	*Søren Kierkegaards Skrifter*, ed. Niels Jørgen Cappelørn, Joakim Garff, Jette Knudsen, Johnny Kondrup, Alastair McKinnon, and Finn Hauberg Mortensen (Copenhagen: Gads Forlag, 1997–).

SZ	Martin Heidegger, *Sein und Zeit* (Tübingen: Max Niemeyer Verlag, 2006).
STC	A. W. Pollard and G. R. Redgrave, *A Short-Title Catalogue of Books Printed in England, Scotland, and Ireland, and of English Books Printed Abroad, 1475–1640*, 2nd edn., rev. W. A. Jackson, F. S. Ferguson, and Katharine F. Pantzer, 3 vols. (London: Bibliographical Society, 1976–1993). The print edition has been consulted in conjunction with *English Short Title Catalogue* (Online Database), British Library and North American Center for *ESTC*, 2019. Capitalization in titles follows the latter.
WA	*D. Martin Luthers Werke: Kritische Gesamtausgabe*, 68 vols. (Weimar: Herman Böhlaus Nachfolger, 1883–1999).
WA DB	*D. Martin Luthers Werke: die Deutsche Bibel*, 12 vols. (Weimar: Herman Böhlaus Nachfolger, 1906–61).
Wing	D. G. Wing, *A Short-Title Catalogue of Books Printed in England, Scotland, Ireland, Wales, and British America, and of English Books Printed in Other Countries, 1641–1700*, 2nd edn., rev., 4 vols. (New York: Modern Language Association of America, 1972–98). The print edition has been consulted in conjunction with *English Short Title Catalogue* (Online Database), British Library and North American Center for *ESTC*, 2019. Capitalization in titles follows the latter.
WJM	*The Works of John Milton*, ed. Frank Allen Patterson, 18 vols. (New York: Columbia University Press, 1931–38).

Introduction

At nos hinc alii sitientis ibimus Afros,
pars Scythiam et rapidum cretae veniemus Oaxen
et penitus toto divisos orbe Britannos.

[But we must go hence – some to the thirsty Africans, some to reach Scythia and the chalk-rolling Oaxes, and the Britons, wholly sundered from all the world.]
Virgil, 'First Eclogue'[1]

As Virgil's First Eclogue draws to its close, the goatherd Meliboeus meditates the prospect of an exile that will drive him towards, and then finally beyond, the distant limits (south, north-east, and north-west) of what he takes to be the known world. In the goatherd's eyes, the land of the Britons sits somewhere just beyond the long arm of Rome's civilizing reach. As far as Meliboeus is concerned, that long arm's reach determines what does, and what does not, count as belonging to the world.

The trajectory that will take Meliboeus into exile is definitively contrasted with the 'otium' (leisure) of his interlocutor, the shepherd Tityrus. Meliboeus' land has been seized and bestowed upon a soldier, but Tityrus has managed to retain his own plot through the benevolent intercession of 'a god': 'deus nobis haec otia fecit'.[2] The god is, presumably, the young Octavian, and the First Eclogue has long been regarded as working against the historical backdrop of land confiscations in Cisalpine Gaul after the battle of Philippi (42 BCE). And yet, when Meliboeus asks to be given the name of this god ('sed tamen, iste deus qui sit, da, Tityre, nobis'), Tityrus responds in a manner that epitomizes the elliptical, decidedly off-kilter quality of the poem's exchanges:

[1] Virgil, *Eclogues* in [Works], trans. H. R. Fairclough, rev. G. P. Goold, LCL 63 (Cambridge, MA: Harvard University Press, 1999), Eclogue I, lines 64–6. Subsequent footnotes give eclogue and line numbers.

[2] *Eclogues* I.6.

Urbem quam dicunt Romam, Meliboee, putavi
stultus ego huic nostrae similem, quo saepe solemus
pastores ovium teneros depellere fetus.
sic canibus catulos similes, sic matribus haedos
noram, sic parvis componere magna solebam.
verum haec tantum alias inter caput extulit urbes,
quantum lenta solent inter viburna cupressi.[3]

[The city which they call Rome, Meliboeus, I, foolish one! thought was like this of ours, whither we shepherds are wont to drive the tender younglings of our flocks. Thus I knew puppies were like dogs, and kids like their dams; thus I used to compare great things with small. But this one has reared her head as high among all other cities as cypresses oft do among the bending osiers.]

If we are to take Tityrus at his first words, 'the city which they call Rome' is the god that made possible the leisure in which Meliboeus has found him. Tityrus will later clarify, if that is an appropriate way to describe anything he says in the poem, that it was at Rome that he saw the young man ('hic illum vidi iuvenem'[4]) who spared him from the deprivations of exile. Across an interval of more than twenty lines, however, the answer to Meliboeus' question ('who is this god of yours?') has appeared to be 'the city which they call Rome'. For in this poem the city's name serves as shorthand for networks of power and decision-making, and even for apparently arbitrary distinctions among the forms of life (reclining in the shade; wandering, harried, into exile; observing that it might have been possible to share apples, chestnuts, and pressed cheeses in the waning light) that will be available to those who live under Rome's thumb.

According to Tityrus, Rome is an entity that is capable of disrupting the unspoken calculations and analogies by which individuals make themselves at home in the world. His experience of Rome has taught him that the city unmakes the perspectives and ratios by which like is expected to relate to like. Tityrus has discovered that Rome sets in place new standards by which even the most ordinary relations must be judged. His visit to Rome helped him to secure his land. And yet, the city has altered forever his understanding of the connections that order the world and make it intelligible. Perhaps this is what has stunned Tityrus into the cascading *non sequiturs* that dominate his contributions to the poem's efforts at dialogue. Meliboeus, in turn, can only wonder what occasioned the encounter that has wrought these changes in Tityrus: 'Et quae tanta fuit Romam tibi causa videndi?'.[5] Taken as a whole, these passages establish a series of tentative

[3] *Eclogues* I.18; *Eclogues* I.19–25. [4] *Eclogues* I.42. [5] *Eclogues* I.26.

links between two exceptions: the land of the Britons, wholly sundered from the world ('penitus toto divisos orbe Britannos'), and Rome, which stands apart from other cities as a cypress among osiers.

Notwithstanding Meliboeus' anxieties, Britain was firmly within Rome's imaginative orbit by the years to which the composition of the *Eclogues* is conventionally assigned.[6] During the summers of 55 and 54 BCE, Julius Caesar had landed on the island's south-east shores. Having pulled an at-least-partially credible appearance of victory from the jaws of disasters wrought by bad weather and the hazards of pitched battle, Caesar induced the Britons to promise to pay tribute to Rome.[7] In 43 CE, under Claudius, a Roman invasion (aided, if Dio Cassius 60.21 is to be believed, by what the ancient Britons would have regarded as the spectacular support of war elephants[8]) initiated the conquest of most of the island.[9]

Within a few more decades, the poet Marcus Valerius Martialis would lament in an epigram that even though his verses were sung in distant Britannia, he derived no money from his far-flung literary celebrity.[10] Rome ruled the province of Britannia (and eventually, the twin provinces of 'Britannia Superior' and 'Britannia Inferior': there would be further provincial subdivisions of the conquered territories) until the first years of the fifth century, when the Sack of Rome in 410 by the armies of Alaric put a decisive end to Rome's ability to re-garrison the island.[11] These former

[6] Forms of the name Britannia were used by the Greeks and Romans. When I use the term 'Britain', especially in relation to texts from the early Middle Ages, it is to be understood as designating the territories that once comprised the Roman provinces of Britannia. For a discussion of some of the complexities that attend the term see Alan MacColl, 'The Meaning of "Britain" in Medieval and Early Modern England', *Journal of British Studies* 45 (2006), 248–69.

[7] Scholars see Caesar's two campaigns as having produced 'hard-won but empty victories' (Barri Jones and David Mattingly, *An Atlas of Roman Britain* (Oxford: Blackwell, 1990), 65).

[8] Dio Cassius, *Roman History*, ed. and trans. Earnest Cary, 9 vols., LCL 32, 37, 53, 66, 82–3, 175–7 (Cambridge, MA: Harvard University Press, 1914–27), vol. VII.420–1.

[9] See the useful collection of translated texts assembled in J. C. Mann and R. G. Penman (ed.), *Literary Sources for Roman Britain*, 3rd edn. (London Association of Classical Teachers, 1996).

[10] 'Non urbana mea tantum Pipleide gaudent / otia nec vacuis auribus ista damus, / sed meus in Geticis ad Martia signa pruinis / a rigidio teritur centurione liber, / dicitur et nostros cantare Britannia versus. / quid prodest? nescit sacculus ista meus' ('Not alone does Rome's leisure rejoice in my Pipleis, nor do I give these pieces only to empty ears. My book is thumbed by hard centurions beside Mars' standards in Getic frosts, and Britain is said to recite my verses. What's the use? My purse knows nothing of all that.') See Martial, *Epigrams*, ed. and trans. D. R. Shackleton Bailey, 3 vols., LCL 94, 95, 480 (Cambridge, MA: Harvard University Press, 1993), vol. III, book XI.3.1–6. Martial makes his literary celebrity stretch eastward from Rome to the land in which Ovid had written his poems of exile, and westward to the land named in the opening lines of Virgil's First Eclogue. I take up Ovid's poems of exile in this book's Conclusion.

[11] Dating the end of Roman Britain is a surprisingly challenging undertaking. I am merely designating what was regarded as a point of no return. On these and related issues see James Gerrard, *The Ruin of Roman Britain: An Archaeological Perspective* (Cambridge University Press, 2013); Michael E. Jones,

provinces would only firmly re-enter a new Rome's consciousness towards the end of the sixth century, when Pope Gregory I sent missionaries to convert the pagan kingdom of Æthelberht of Kent. And yet, there are literal and metaphorical senses in which, throughout the fifth and sixth centuries, and indeed for many centuries afterwards, the inhabitants of the island that had been called Britannia lived entangled in versions of Rome that were as near and familiar as they had ever been. Entanglement and familiarity are, therefore, the terms through which this book studies the persistence of Rome.[12]

The Fact of Rome

A recent and insightful collection of essays asserts that the 'uniqueness' of Rome 'resides, *inter alia*, in its double nature of both "place" and "idea"'.[13] To this traditional pairing of place and idea I offer, by way of supplement, the 'fact' of Rome, emphasizing its derivation from the Latin *factum*, a word whose remarkable semantic range encompasses deeds, actions, exploits, happenings, and matters that are judged to be real or true (i.e., factual). Most importantly for this book's purposes, the word designates the results of doing or making. *Factum* is the perfect passive participle of the verb *facere*: to make, fashion, construct, etc. *Facta* are things made, done, built, framed and accomplished. Such *facta* can be encountered, in a further extension, as the givens of the world in which we live. To attend to the 'fact' of Rome is therefore to capture a host of phenomena that can too easily, and altogether too thoroughly, drift from view when 'place' and 'idea' determine the nature and boundaries of an inquiry.

The End of Roman Britain (Ithaca: Cornell University Press, 1996); A. S. Esmonde Cleary, *The Ending of Roman Britain* (Savage, MD: Barnes & Noble, 1990).

[12] Here, and in a few other places where my terminological debt may be obvious, I am drawing on phrases and coinages associated with Martin Heidegger's project in *Sein und Zeit* (*SZ*) (Tübingen: Max Niemeyer Verlag, 2006). Most important, for my purposes here, is Heidegger's sense that we are 'primordially familiar' (*Being and Time* (*BT*), trans. John Macquarrie and Edward Robinson (New York: Harper & Row, 1962), 119; *SZ*, 86 'ursprünglich vertraut') with the world in a non-cognitive manner that underwrites and makes possible our critical and theoretical engagements with things. *Being and Time* thus anchors human beings in a world that they already understand in a 'primordial' sense. My goal in taking recourse to Heidegger's concept of familiarity is to capture a non-cognitive and non-ideological experience of what I am calling the fact of Rome. More broadly, I am invoking Hubert Dreyfus' efforts to establish the relevance to Heidegger of Wittgenstein's conception of the 'background' (*Hintergrund*). See Chapter 1 on this topic.

[13] Claudia Bolgia, 'Introduction', in Claudia Bolgia, Rosamond McKitterick, and John Osborne (eds.), *Rome Across Time and Space: Cultural Transmission and the Exchange of Ideas, c. 500–1400* (Cambridge University Press, 2011), 1.

This is in no sense a denial that place and idea are foundational categories for the study of Rome. They play a key role in organizing any account of the forms in which Rome disclosed itself to inhabitants of the island of Britain during the Middle Ages and Renaissance. Writers during these periods knew that Rome was 'an elsewhere': that is, a specific distant city on the banks of the Tiber in central Italy. But at what point in history could so narrow and so literal an identification have done more than merely begin to sum up what the word Rome was taken to mean and stand for?[14]

Chapter 1 explores the implications of several significant lines of continuity between medieval and so-called Renaissance afterlives of Roman Britain. The chapter moves among texts by authors as different as Gildas (*floruit* from the fifth to the sixth centuries), the Venerable Bede (673/4–735), anonymous Anglo-Saxon poets, and Sir Thomas Browne (1605–82), setting their works within several centuries of quotidian encounters with ancient ruins and other material remains of the Eternal City's dominion. The chapter argues that Rome could be experienced, even across wide expanses of time and from the soil of the island that had been Britannia, as domestic and familiar rather than distant and mysterious. This is so, I argue, because Rome had embedded itself deep within what the philosopher Stanley Cavell calls 'the order of the ordinary', and because it derived from its position within that order an ability to entangle past and present, self and world, in medieval and early modern Britain.[15]

This version of Rome is to be understood not simply as a distant city that is alternately subjected to devotion and then, after the Reformation, heated polemic, but rather, as Browne puts it in his *Hydriotaphia*, as one of the means by which we are prompted to 'make up our selves'.[16] Rather than look for decisive moments, specific authors and texts, or even simply decades capable of marking a point after which engagements with the ancient past become 'properly' critical or self-conscious, as some scholars continue to do when working with materials from the late sixteenth century, I argue that the perception of a break with the past that can, paradoxically, bring that past and one's relationship to it into view, is an

14 For an account of the efforts of Renaissance humanists to recover and generate accurate conceptions of the city's foundation and earliest boundaries see Philip Jacks, *The Antiquarian and the Myth of Antiquity: The Origins of Rome in Renaissance Thought* (Cambridge University Press, 1993).

15 Stanley Cavell, 'Introductory Note to "The *Investigations*' Everyday Aesthetics of Itself"', in John Gibson and Wolfgang Huemer (eds.), *The Literary Wittgenstein* (London: Routledge, 2004), 19.

16 Sir Thomas Browne, *Hydriotaphia, Urne-Buriall, or a Brief Discourse of the Sepulchrall Urnes Lately Found in Norfolk*, in *The Major Works*, ed. C. A. Patrides (London: Penguin, 1977), 265.

epistemological position that was available throughout the centuries that connect the fall of Roman Britain in the early fifth century to the final decades of the seventeenth century.

Chapter 2 studies Rome as it helps constitute, and as it figures within, the problem of the self. The chapter broaches this topic by exploring a series of metaphorical, metonymic, and synecdochic formulas in which 'Rome' can name a metaphysical condition of the educated imagination – regardless of whether that imagination ever finds itself at Rome or not.[17] This Rome is the plight not only of (for example) intrepid Protestants who really did find themselves at, and then escaped from, Rome, but of anyone who has had their mind and body shaped by Rome, and has recognized that they are living in the grip of that word's metaphorical possibilities. Juxtaposing authors such as Edmund Spenser (1552?–1599), John Donne (1572–1631), Thomas Wilson (1523/4–1581), John Milton (1608–1674), and others (chiefly Continental writers whose influence in Renaissance England was considerable, such as Joachim Du Bellay (1522–1560) and Michel Eyquem de Montaigne (1533–1592)), the chapter argues that the encounter with Rome is an encounter with the self 'made strange' (from the Latin *extraneus*, external).[18] Because of this, actual voyages to Rome of the kind ventured by Wilson and Milton can be regarded as especially vexatious encounters not with an exotic, alluring, and finally unknowable other, but rather with an externalized self that disarms precisely because it is utterly familiar.

Chapter 3 yokes together Latin and 'the Word': the former designating a human language whose systematic, prescriptive grammar played a vital role in the processes by which individuals constituted and then reached themselves in speech, writing, and thought; the latter marking a divine incursion into human language and history. The first half of the chapter

[17] I borrow the phrase from the title of Northrop Frye's *The Educated Imagination* (Toronto: Anansi Press, 2002).

[18] It bears emphasizing at the outset that my use of the words 'familiar' and 'strange' is rather different from Catherine Nicholson's recourse to these terms in her excellent *Uncommon Tongues: Eloquence and Eccentricity in the English Renaissance* (Philadelphia: University of Pennsylvania Press, 2014). Nicholson 'situates eccentricity at the paradoxical heart of sixteenth-century pedagogical, rhetorical, and literary culture', and argues that classical conceptions of eloquence had 'as much to do with estrangement as with intimacy and familiarity' (1, 3). By way of contrast, my own suggestion that the encounter with Rome is an encounter with a self that has been 'made strange' refers not to the aesthetics of strangeness (*qua* oddness) persuasively described by Nicholson, but rather to the word's etymological derivation from the Latin *extraneus*. My argument, therefore, focuses not on an encounter between the self and something odd or unaccountable, but rather between the self and an entity that is susceptible to being interpreted as an externalized version of that self. I am using the words 'familiar' and 'strange', therefore, to capture different angles of convergence upon the same phenomenon.

argues that Latin was the medium in which Rome was experienced most intimately by those who received formal schooling. My point of entry into these matters is a puzzling, but extravagantly suggestive, inquiry into the nuances of the Latin case system by the early medieval grammarian Virgilius Maro Grammaticus (*floruit* seventh century). Having established the complexity and vitality of the problem explored by Virgilius, I turn to the scene of instruction in Renaissance humanist pedagogy and to some remarks on Latin prose style by Desiderius Erasmus (1466–1536) and Roger Ascham (1514/5–1568). In each case, I show that the debates in question bear on the problem of the self and thereby enable us to conceive of that entity as a grammatical relation whose complexities swing into and out of view within the structures of Rome's language. The second half of the chapter drives this argument into new territories by exploring the work of Rome within a short sequence of biblical, confessional, and autobiographical accounts of reading, exegesis, and conversion. Examining a seventeenth-century English translation of Martin Luther's 'Vorrede auff die Epistel S. Pauli an die Roemer' ('Preface to Paul's Epistle to the Romans'), I establish a prehistory for the translator's obvious struggles with some of Luther's remarks on the subject of Paul and Rome. This involves framing the translator's efforts against the backdrop of Luther's, St Augustine's, and St Paul's negotiations with Rome. The chapter argues that across this wide range of writers and texts and topics, the Eternal City and its language play a decisive role in breaking down the self and then rebuilding it on a radically new image.

Chapter 4 studies the borders between life and death. Emphasizing that debates about the relationship between the living and the dead involved patrolling, and testing the justice of, borders constructed by (or in polemical response to) Rome, I argue that these debates place Rome at the very centre of a series of unsettling questions about the nature of 'the human' as a category of experience. The chapter's concerns flow through debates concerning the relationship between life, death, and the human voice, and between literary texts and devotional practices, in the course of examining material from Geoffrey Chaucer (*circa* 1340–1400), prayer books and primers, Thomas More (1478–1535), and William Shakespeare (1564–1616).

The book's conclusion follows the fact of Rome east rather than west via a seventeenth-century translation of Ovid's *Tristia* – a collection of poems written by Ovid near the Black Sea during the years following his exile from Rome. These translations see a former grammar-school boy reconstructing, from the temporal distance of manhood and maturity, a popular curriculum text and, by necessary extension, revisiting the scene of his own instruction. Ovid's meditations on the subject of what it means to live apart from Rome, and his expressions of fear that Rome's language is slipping from his grip, provide a final backdrop against which to reframe the book's arguments.

The book's chapters are united by a desire to explore the cultural and intellectual stakes of medieval and Renaissance Britain's sense of itself as living in the shadow of Rome: that is, as forever living in the shadow of a city whose name could designate both the ancient, fallen, quintessentially human power that had once conquered and colonized Britain, and also the alternately sanctified and demonized edifice of the Roman Church. Within that broad area of concern, I argue that 'The Ordinary', 'The Self', 'The Word', and 'The Dead' are compass points by which individuals lived out their orientations to, and against, Rome. Each of these four topics isolates an important dimension of Rome's enduring ability to shape and complicate the effort to come to terms with the nature of the self and the structure of human community. Each, moreover, lets us regard the Middle Ages and Renaissance as having ceaselessly confronted shifting expressions and perceptions of Rome's hold over lived experience.

This description of the book's structure will make it clear that I do not claim to have undertaken anything like a systematic history of Roman Britain and its shifting frontiers, a vision of British and pan-European conceptions of *Romanitas*, an analysis of myths of origins in English poetry, or an account of the growth of antiquarianism.[19] Some great and influential books (William Camden's *Britannia*, for example) figure hardly at all in this study. Instead, the book strives to isolate for discussion a version of Rome that has not figured prominently in the large body of excellent work on the city's plural legacies in Medieval and Renaissance Britain. Scholars have tended, for good reason, to focus on Rome as a distant city that is

[19] For distinguished work on Roman Britain and its frontiers see a pair of studies by Richard Hingley: *The Recovery of Roman Britain 1586–1906: A Colony So Fertile* (Oxford University Press, 2008); and *Hadrian's Wall: A Life* (Oxford University Press, 2012). On the subject of the northern wall, see also R. E. Witcher, Divya P. Tolia-Kelly, and Richard Hingley, 'Archaeologies of Landscape: Excavating the Materialities of Hadrian's Wall', *Journal of Material Culture* 15 (2010), 105–28. For an account of the ways in which late sixteenth- and early seventeenth-century poets sought to re-evaluate 'the relationship between classical literature and English writing, at a time when the humiliation of the Roman Conquest was uppermost in the minds of English writers', see Sean Keilen, *Vulgar Eloquence: On the Renaissance Invention of English Literature* (New Haven: Yale University Press, 2006), 3. For an authoritative study of the growth of antiquarianism see Graham Parry, *The Trophies of Time: English Antiquarians of the Seventeenth Century* (Oxford University Press, 1995). See also Kelsey Jackson Williams, *The Antiquary: John Aubrey's Historical Scholarship* (Oxford University Press, 2016), which sets Aubrey's work within the larger context of the growth of antiquarian scholarship in the wake of Renaissance humanism.

experienced through the lenses of, for example, religious conflict, or the emergence and re-emergence of nationalist and republican discourses, or international power politics.[20] The Reformation has been one of several inevitable touchstones for scholars, since authorized religion in sixteenth- and seventeenth-century England was predisposed to regard Rome and its ways either as foreign and ostentatious, or as strategically concealed and in need of being ferreted out.

What this book offers, instead, is a genealogy of certain significant expressions and experiences of Rome's nearness and familiarity, especially where those expressions and experiences lurk below or outside self-consciously political or ideological polemics. This involves, for example, arguing in Chapter 1 that a proto-phenomenological attunement to Rome's immediate proximity can be discerned in texts ranging from the work of Gildas, in the middle of the sixth century, to writers such as Sir Thomas Browne, in the seventeenth century. Ranging across the span of time that connects Gildas to Browne, the book argues that the longstanding scholarly emphasis on the ways in which the city of Rome was an object of deliberate and highly self-conscious study during the Middle Ages and Renaissance (Rome as ancient power, Rome as foreign authority, Rome as Catholic Church, etc.) needs to be supplemented by a greater awareness of the stakes of that distant city's entanglement in aspects of the ordinary that are mostly experienced in an unconscious manner. This is the version of Rome that is latent in Britain's ancient roads, in lives lived amidst the vestiges of ancient city walls or within view of ancient and even monastic ruins, in shifting conceptions of time and the calendar, in the complexities of the Latin case system, etc. The phenomena that dominate this book, in short, range from dirt, stones, and poems to grammatical nuances and rhetorical tropes. The book's goal, throughout, is to explore configurations

20 On nationalism see Paul Stevens, 'Archipelagic Criticism and Its Limits: Milton, Geoffrey of Monmouth, and the Matter of England', *The European Legacy* 17 (2012), 151–64. See also Yann Coz, 'The Image of Roman History in Anglo-Saxon England', in D. Rollason, C. Leyser, and H. Williams (eds.), *England and the Continent in the Tenth Century: Studies in Honour of Wilhelm Levison (1876–1947)*, Studies in the Early Middle Ages 37 (Turnhout, Belgium: Brepols, 2010), 545–58. On ruins, history, and resistance to Rome see Robert Rouse, 'Arthurian Caerleon and the Untimely Architecture of History', *Arthuriana* 23 (2013), 40–51; Caroline D. Eckhardt, 'The Presence of Rome in the Middle English Chronicles of the Fourteenth Century', *Journal of English and Germanic Philology* 90 (1991), 187–207. On republicanism and the matter of Rome see Freyja Cox Jensen, *Reading the Roman Republic in Early Modern England* (Leiden: Brill, 2012). On public spectacle, ritual display, and politics see Anthony Miller, *Roman Triumphs and Early Modern English Culture* (Houndmills, Basingstoke, Hampshire: Palgrave, 2001). On faith as a lived relation to Rome see the essays collected in Ronald Corthell, Frances E. Dolan, Christopher Highley, and Arthur F. Marotti (eds.), *Catholic Culture in Early Modern England* (Notre Dame: University of Notre Dame Press, 2007).

of texts and phenomena in which Rome is not distant and foreign but rather intimately familiar and, indeed, too ready-to-hand to be understood as something outside the self and susceptible to being assessed dispassionately as an 'other'.[21]

My effort to keep a wide historical range of texts in view proceeds from a desire to call attention to some significant limitations in traditional conceptions of historical periods. Efforts to characterize the sixteenth century as the period that first brought the proper kind of light to the topic of Rome's role in the history of Britain remain common. Richard Hingley, for example, asserts that,

> Before the later sixteenth century, people in Britain had thought and written about the Roman past, but conventional wisdom suggests that it is only from this time that a self-critical and conscious appreciation of the classical writings that addressed Britain emerged. It was also from this time that the value of past objects and sites started to be recognized.[22]

Hingley's formulation is in some ways unobjectionable. The recovery of classical texts clearly played a significant role in altering the terms in which the material remains of Roman Britain were understood on the cusp of the seventeenth century. This is true perhaps even where it is necessary to speak not of the recovery of texts but of a new vogue for writings by authors who had never in any obvious sense gone missing or been lost, authors who had all along been open to view and available. Any list of such authors would have to include Virgil, Horace, and Ovid, but also Lucan, Statius, and Claudian at the very least.[23] Tacitus, whose *Germania* and *Agricola* are especially important with respect to knowledge concerning Roman Britain, is a significant recovery, but Caesar's *Commentarii de bello gallico*

[21] The subject–object relation that Descartes inaugurates is not, according to Heidegger, our foundational experience of the world; we dwell within, and as familiars with, the world. See Heidegger on the sites and phenomena that are relevant to his project: 'In roads, streets, bridges, buildings, our concern discovers nature as having some definite direction' (*BT*, 100); 'In den Wegen, Straßen, Brücken, Gebäuden is durch das Besorgen die Natur in bestimmter Richtung entdeckt' (*SZ*, 71). References to that which is ready-to-hand draw on Heidegger's distinction between *Vorhandenheit* (presence-at-hand) and *Zuhandenheit* (readiness-to-hand). The former designates an abstract and systematic view of entities as merely present, observable, and classifiable substances; the latter describes our non-cognitive access to a totality of things in a world that is capable of meeting our needs. See *BT*, esp. 26–7, 115. See below, Chapter 1, n. 82, on Heidegger's distinction between *Besorgen* (concern) and *Auslegung* (interpretation).

[22] Richard Hingley, *The Recovery of Roman Britain*, 2.

[23] The best guide to these topics is the multi-volume *Oxford History of Classical Reception in English Literature* (Oxford University Press). Volume I (edited by Rita Copeland and published in 2016) covers the years 800–1558; Volume II (edited by Patrick Cheney and Philip Hardie, and published in 2015) covers the years 1558–1660.

(with its account of his two summer campaigns in Britain) were known in multiple manuscripts during the Middle Ages, and the *editio princeps* was printed in 1469.[24] Pliny was circulating widely by the twelfth century. More importantly, it is not clear precisely what is to be understood as constituting 'a self-critical and conscious appreciation' of those writings; nor what it means to imagine smart people in any age as reading without the aid of such casts of mind; nor, finally, is it self-evident that the value of Roman remains had to sit patiently until it could be recognized under the dispensations of humanist inquiry and antiquarianism in late sixteenth-century England. Indeed, the value of past objects and sites related to Rome was being more or less constantly negotiated throughout the Middle Ages.

Hingley's remarks tacitly endorse a tendency that remains surprisingly robust in Renaissance scholarship, whereby Medieval approaches to the remains of Roman rule in Britain are still too frequently viewed as unmethodical, slapdash engagements with matters that really ought to have been appreciated in a more profoundly (or even simply more properly) intellectualized manner that is said, in England at least, to have emerged only during the late sixteenth century. This view, which Hingley is probably accurate in describing as the enduring state of conventional wisdom, simply draws attention to a significant limitation in conventional wisdom. Indeed, the view Hingley describes is perhaps best regarded as a long-lived product of the polemics of sixteenth-century humanists, men who fashioned for themselves intellectual niches by energetically disowning the legacies of their immediate forebears. That this surprisingly durable perception of a stark division between the late Middle Ages and the Renaissance is at least partly the result of sixteenth-century humanist propaganda has been demonstrated both by scholars of English humanism specifically and by those whose work bridges a temporal divide that is still too often, even too easily, viewed as decisive.[25]

24 See Virginia Brown, 'Latin Manuscripts of Caesar's *Gallic War*', in Giulio Battelli (ed.), *Paleographica Diplomatica et Archivistica: Studi in Onore di Giulio Battelli* (Rome: Edizioni di Storia e Letteratura, 1979), 105–58. The text was in wide circulation by the fourteenth and fifteenth centuries. The first English translation of the two relevant books of the *Commentarii de bello gallico* was printed in 1530.

25 A considerable body of scholarship challenging conventional schemes of periodization has developed over the course of the past two decades. A recent contribution is Jacques Le Goff's final work, *Faut-il Vraiment Découper l'Histoire en Tranches?* (Paris: Éditions Seuil, 2014). See also, for example, James Simpson, *Reform and Cultural Revolution, 1350–1547*, The Oxford Literary History vol. II (Oxford University Press, 2002); Brian Cummings and James Simpson (eds.), *Cultural Reformations: Medieval and Renaissance in Literary History* (Oxford University Press, 2010); Margreta de Grazia, 'The Modern Divide: From Either Side', *Journal of Medieval and Early*

To be sure, Polydore Vergil's *Anglica Historia* (1534) exploded many of the fantasies set forth in Geoffrey of Monmouth's *Historia Regum Britanniae* (*circa* 1100). But several of Geoffrey's own medieval contemporaries and successors – William of Malmesbury, Henry of Huntingdon, William of Newburgh, and Gerald of Wales, for example – had already assailed him as a liar and shameless fabricator. Above all, the sixteenth century can in no sense be regarded as the period that first achieved enduring clarity about Rome's work as the island's ancient colonizer. Scholars have shown that Geoffrey's historicity was already being energetically challenged in the twelfth century, and that it was actually during the sixteenth century that writers such as John Leland laboured to defend and rehabilitate Geoffrey's reputation as part of a reaction against the Italian historian.[26] Vergil's insistence on the importance of that history of Roman conquest and rule did strike a new chord within the heated atmosphere of relations between England and Rome at the onset of the English Reformation. But Vergil's 1525 edition of the *De excidio et conquestu Britanniae* of the sixth-century British monk Gildas had already shown that the story of Roman conquest had been known to medieval writers and readers. And Gildas, in turn, exerted a significant influence on the Venerable Bede. Sean Keilen has asserted that English writers of the sixteenth century 'were trying to come to terms with the implications of a new historical dispensation for their vernacular writing – a dispensation under which modern England was not the rightful heir of the Roman Empire, as Geoffrey of Monmouth had claimed, but the victim of a Roman

Modern Studies 37 (2007), 453–67; Greg Walker, 'When Did "the Medieval" End?: Retrospection, Foresight, and the End(s) of the English Middle Ages', in Elaine Treharne and Greg Walker, with William Green (eds.), *The Oxford Handbook of Medieval Literature in English* (Oxford University Press, 2010), 725–38; David Matthews, 'The Medieval Invasion of Early-Modern England', *New Medieval Literatures* 10 (2008), 223–44; Danila Sokolov, *Renaissance Texts, Medieval Subjectivities: Rethinking Petrarchan Desire from Wyatt to Shakespeare* (Pittsburgh: Duquesne University Press, 2017).

[26] Neil Wright notes that Henry of Huntingdon is the earliest authority to cast doubt on Geoffrey's veracity ('The Place of Henry of Huntingdon's *Epistola ad Warinumin* in the Text-History of Geoffrey of Monmouth's *Historia regum Britannie*: A Preliminary Investigation', in Gillian Jondorf and David N. Dumville (eds.), *France and the British Isles in the Middle Ages* (Woodbridge: Boydell & Brewer, 1991), 91). For other examples of early attacks on Geoffrey see Anne Lawrence-Mathers, 'William of Newburgh and the Northumbrian Construction of English History', *Journal of Medieval History* 33 (2007), 339–57; Julia Crick, 'The British Past and the Welsh Future: Gerald of Wales, Geoffrey of Monmouth and Arthur of Britain', *Celtica* 23 (1999), 60–75. On the subject of English defences of Arthur see James P. Carley, 'Polydore Vergil and John Leland on King Arthur: The Battle of the Books', in Edward Donald Kennedy (ed.), *King Arthur: A Casebook* (New York: Garland, 1996), 185–204. See also Victoria Shirley, 'The Galfridian Tradition(s) in England, Scotland, and Wales: Texts, Purpose, Context, 1138–1530', unpublished PhD thesis, Cardiff University, 2017.

Conquest, the bastard progeny of a brutal rape'.[27] The Galfridian tradition, however, had long been a site of contestation, and the historical dispensation to which Keilen gestures was longstanding, persistent, and widely circulated. It was, in short, not new.

In order to make this point, Chapter 1 places considerable emphasis on Bede's *Historia ecclesiastica gentis anglorum* (731). Bede deals at great length with Rome's rule in Britain, its material remains, and the advent of Rome's Church. Bede's *Historia* circulated widely in Latin and (to a lesser extent) Old English before it was translated into early modern English in 1565 by a Catholic exile named Thomas Stapleton. Some 160 complete or nearly complete manuscripts of the immense Latin text (it contains more than 79,000 words) survive, as do many fragmentary manuscripts.[28] It was copied and circulated from the eighth through the fifteenth century. Several of these manuscripts postdate the publication of the late fifteenth-century *editio princeps*.[29] The text was well known in England and on the Continent from the early to the high and late Middle Ages. Bede had become renowned as an historian; this was the work upon which that international reputation rested. Nor was Bede's account of the Roman Conquest, and of the persistence of Rome's colonial footprint in Britain, buried in some dark, unvisited corner of the *Historia*. Following a Preface and a short first chapter that plotted the locations of Britain and Ireland, the story of Roman conquest and rule begins to unfold in the work's second chapter. In short, to read, reproduce, and disseminate Bede's *Historia* was to read, reproduce, and disseminate the story of Rome's conquest and rule in Britain, and of the conspicuousness of the remains it had left in its wake.

Bede's influence and wide circulation help us see that whatever Polydore Vergil achieved in the 1530s cannot be described as having revealed to sixteenth-century readers a story whose contours and details had been unknown to readers during the Middle Ages. And although Keilen describes the sixteenth century as 'the very moment that Roman remains

[27] Keilen, *Vulgar Eloquence*, 19.

[28] The anonymous Old English translation, which transforms and abbreviates Bede's Latin, is much less widely attested. It survives in five manuscript copies and three excerpts. These date from the tenth to the late eleventh centuries. See Sharon M. Rowley, *The Old English Version of Bede's Historia Ecclesiastica* (Cambridge: D.S. Brewer, 2011).

[29] See the 'Textual Introduction' in Bede, *The Ecclesiastical History of the English People*, ed. Bertram Colgrave and R. A. B. Mynors (Oxford University Press, 2007), xxxix–lxxiv. On manuscript copies and their range of circulation see also M. L. W. Laistner and H. H. King, *A Hand-List of Bede Manuscripts* (Ithaca: Cornell University Press, 1943), 139–53. On the reception of Bede see the essays of Rowley ('Bede in Later Anglo-Saxon England') and Allen J. Frantzen ('The Englishness of Bede, From Then to Now'), in Scott DeGregorio (ed.), *The Cambridge Companion to Bede* (Cambridge University Press, 2010), 216–28, 229–40.

were more familiar and desirable than they had ever been', the familiarity of Rome and its material remains in Britain is precisely what Bede's exceptionally influential work had emphasized to English and Continental readers for some eight hundred years.[30]

It will be clear by now that this project (especially its first chapter) has been inspired by certain currents in the field of reception studies. Though the book's temporal reach is long, my goal has been to attend to the historical specificity of the texts, writers, and periods I explore. Charles Martindale is an excellent guide when he insists that an inquiry of this kind can be fuelled not by universalizing aspirations or crude generalizations, but rather by 'the seeking out of often fugitive communalities across history, communalities that emerge only in the processes we may term "reception"'.[31] The great value of Martindale's assertion rests not in the bare fact of his having reached for these 'communalities', but rather in his willingness to characterize them as 'fugitive', for that word captures quite nicely both the inherent challenges of the enterprise and the delicate nature of the links it may uncover. Far from insisting on some sort of impossible uniformity of experience across long stretches of time, I have attempted to isolate moments where specific historical circumstances and rhetorical occasions can be pressed into productive dialogue with each other. As Martindale puts it, 'illumination can come from the friction between different historical moments in our aesthetic perception of, our receptivity to, different objects from the past'.[32] This book is not, then, an experiment in transhistorical inquiry, but rather an attempt to capture some inflections of Rome's persistence that have been insufficiently attested by scholarship on the early modern period.

Roman Soil

To further illustrate the sorts of texts and phenomena that dominate this book, I want briefly to explore an enigmatic tale in which dirt is shipped from Rome to Britain. The transfer occurs in a twelfth-century Welsh prose narrative known as the *Breudwyt Maxen Wledic* (*The Dream of Maxen*

[30] Keilen, *Vulgar Eloquence*, 2.

[31] Martindale, 'Reception – A New Humanism? Receptivity, Pedagogy, the Transhistorical', *Classical Receptions Journal* 5 (2013), 171. Martindale, of course, played a decisive role in naturalizing reception theory to classical studies with his *Redeeming the Text: Latin Poetry and the Hermeneutics of Reception* (Cambridge University Press, 1993). For other foundational work and bibliographies see Charles Martindale and Richard F. Thomas (eds.), *Classics and the Uses of Reception* (Malden, MA: Blackwell, 2006); Lorna Hardwick, *Reception Studies* (Cambridge University Press, 2003).

[32] Martindale, 'Reception', 181.

Wledig). The story views, as though through a glass darkly, scenes from the final decades of Roman Britain. The historical figure (one of them, at least) who hangs behind the story's 'Maxen Wledig' was Magnus Maximus (died 388). Maximus was commander of the Roman forces in Britain. In 383 he was proclaimed Western Emperor by the island's garrison. He returned to the Continent, successfully usurped the position of the actual Western Emperor, Gratian, and consolidated a form of divided authority in the west that was to be shared with Gratian's half-brother, Valentinian II. In his sixth-century *De excidio et conquestu Britanniae*, the British monk Gildas blames Maximus for having drained Britain of its armies and thereby left the island vulnerable to later invaders. Maximus was eventually defeated and executed by the Eastern Emperor Theodosius in 388.

This story of a military commander in Britain who returns to the Continent to wage war, as usurping emperor, against Gratian, is twisted into fantastic shapes in the Welsh tale. In *Breudwyt Maxen Wledic*, Maxen, who is already the legitimate Emperor of Rome, goes hunting in the Tiber river valley. He dreams of a beautiful distant land and of an equally beautiful woman. Upon waking, he is bereft and spends a week or more suffering in his palace at Rome. Finally, his counsellors convince him to reveal to them the cause of his distress. They announce that they will empower messengers to spend three years searching for Maxen's dream. These messengers eventually recognize, in the landscape of the island of Britain, the land that had filled the emperor's dream, and they work their way across the island to Wales and Elen, the beautiful maiden he had seen. When the Emperor Maxen himself finally comes as conqueror to the island, he immediately greets Elen as 'Amperodres Rvuein' (Empress of Rome).[33]

The rest of the story involves a tumbling, rapid-fire sequence of incidents. Maxen weds Elen and settles in Britain. This facilitates the rise of an usurper at Rome. Bent on defending his authority, Maxen returns to the Continent and, with the aid of the men of Britain, conquers France and Burgundy. His army lays siege to Rome for a year. Finally, unbeknownst to Maxen, Elen's brothers and the men of Britain launch a devious attack (it involves ladders and a lunch break) and conquer the city. After three days in the city, Elen's brothers finally yield up Rome to Maxen, reminding him that he owes this victory entirely to the men of Britain. Rome has been restored to its emperor by the men of Britain, and so Maxen promises

[33] Brynley F. Roberts (ed.), *Breudwyt Maxen Wledic* (Dublin Institute for Advanced Studies, 2005), 6.

Elen's brothers, Cynan and Gadeon, that they can conquer any lands they wish:

> Ac yna y kerdassant wynteu, ac y gwerescynnassant gwladoed a chestyll a dinassoed ac y lladassant eu gwyr oll, ac y gadassant y gwraged yn uyw. Ac velly y buant hyny yttoed y gweisson ieueinc a dathoed y gyt ac wynt yn wyr llwydon rac hyt y buassynt yn y gwerescyn hwnnw. Ac yna y dywawt Kynan wrth Adeon y vrawt:
>
> 'Beth a vynny ti,' heb ef, 'ae trigyaw yn y wlat hon, ae mynet y'r wlat yd hanwyt ohonei?'
>
> Sef y kauas yn y gyngor mynet y wlat a llawer y gyt ac ef. Ac yno y trigywys Kynan a rann arall y bresswylaw, ac y kawssant yn eu kyghor llad tauodeu y gwraged rac llygru eu ieith. Ac o achaws tewi o'r gwraged ac eu ieith a dywedut o'r gwyr y gelwit gwyr Llydaw Brytanyeit. Ac odyna y doeth yn vynych o ynys Prydein, ac etwa y daw yr ieith honno.
>
> A'r chwedyl hon a elwir Breudwyt Maxen Wledic, amherawdyr Rufein. Ac yma y mae teruyn arnaw.[34]
>
> [Then they set off and conquered lands and castles and cities, and they killed all their men, but left the women alive. And so they continued until the young lads who had come with them were grey-haired men, for they had been conquering for such a long time. Then Cynan said to Gadeon his brother, 'What do you want,' he said, 'to stay in this country or to return to your native land?'
>
> He decided to return to his own country, along with many others. But Cynan and another group stayed on to settle there. And they decided to cut out the tongues of the women, lest their own language be corrupted. Because the women and their language were silenced, while the men spoke on, the Britons were called Llydaw men. And after that there have often come, and still do come to the Island of Britain, people speaking that language.
>
> And this tale is called The Dream of Maxen Wledig, emperor of Rome. And here it ends.][35]

This savage etiology is designed to explain how the language of the Britons came to be spoken on the Continent in the land that would become known as Brittany. It amounts to a complex – even astonishing – wish-fulfilment fantasy in which the Welsh, living under the thumb of England during the twelfth century, reimagine themselves as both conquerors and restorers of Rome. The story also depicts (in this it follows a precedent set by Virgil's First Eclogue) the transformative power of a journey to Rome in which

[34] Roberts (ed.), *Breudwyt Maxen Wledic*, 10–11.

[35] English citations are from 'The Dream of the Emperor Maxen', in Sioned Davies (ed. and trans.), *The Mabinogion* (Oxford University Press, 2007), 110.

Britain hovers in the distance. So far, so good. The tale can be read to excellent effect in terms of discourses of nationhood, linguistic misogyny, and the depraved violence of conquest and empire. The assertion of a vital connection to Rome is commonly regarded as one of the foundational principles of Welsh historiography during the Middle Ages.[36]

And yet, I am principally interested in how Rome functions as a different sort of cog within the imaginative machinery of *Breudwyt Maxen Wledic*. The episode in question takes place the morning after Maxen spends his first night with Elen:

> A thrannoeth e bore yd erchis e vorwyn y hagwedi am e chaffael en vorwyn. Ac enteu a erchis idi hi nodi y haguedi. Hitheu a'e nodes val hynn: Enys Brydein a nodes y'u that o Vor Vd hyt Vor Ywerdon a'r teir rac enys a'e dale a dan amperauder Ruvein, a gwneithur teir prif gaer idi hitheu en e tri lle a dewissei en enys Brydein. Ac ena e dewissaud wneithur a gaer uchaf en Arvon idi, ac e ducpwyt gweryt Ruvein hyt eno hyt pan vei yachussach e'r amperauder y gysgu ac y eisted ac y orymdeith endi. Odena e gwnaethpwyt idi e dwy gaer ereill, nyt amgen Caer Llion a Chaer Verdin.[37]

> [Early the next day the maiden claimed her maiden fee, since he had found her to be a virgin. He asked her to name her maiden fee. She listed thus: the Island of Britain for her father, from the North Sea to the Irish Sea, and the Three Adjacent Islands to be held under the empress of Rome; and three major forts to be built for her in three locations of her choice in the Island of Britain. Then she asked that the prime fort be built for her in Arfon. And soil from Rome was brought there, so that it would be healthier for the emperor to sleep and sit and walk around. After that the other two forts were built for her, namely Caerllion and Caerfyrddin.][38]

A good deal of time could be spent on this paragraph. It emphasizes Elen's forcefulness in her dealings with the conqueror of her island, so that major Roman forts and lasting roads in Wales are represented as materializations of a woman's desire, rather than as tools of empire. The impositions of conquest, moreover, have been transformed into the products of a virgin bride's right to claim her 'maiden fee'. For the purposes of this study, however, the most interesting detail is the one that risks appearing like a bizarre throwaway: 'And soil from Rome was brought there, so that it would be healthier for the emperor to sleep and sit and walk around' ('Ac e ducpwyt gweryt Ruvein hyt eno hyt pan vei yachussach e'r amperauder

[36] On this topic see A. Joseph McMullen, 'Rewriting History through the Landscape in *Breuddwyd Maxen Wledig*', *Proceedings of the Harvard Celtic Colloquium* 31 (2011), 225–41.

[37] Roberts (ed.), *Breudwyt Maxen Wledic*, 8.

[38] Davies (ed. and trans.), 'The Dream of Emperor Maxen', 108.

y gysgu ac y eisted ac y orymdeith endi'). This detail captures quite precisely the version of Rome that dominates this book: the distant city is literally near, underfoot, domestic, and dirt-deep. The soil that supports and nourishes Maxen is Rome itself made tactile and even ordinary in the landscape of Britain. That soil, and Elen's demands concerning the Roman roads and forts whose origins were utterly familiar to the story's medieval Welsh audiences, establish a Roman genealogy for what counts as ordinary.

The Roman soil that supports the emperor's health in Britain offers a jurisdictional fantasy of continuity and legitimacy for empire. But it is also (and this is the key matter for this study) a chapter in the story of Rome's dispersal among distant regions and facets of lived experience. The passage crafts an origin story for Rome's ability to be here, there, and almost everywhere. It compresses into a single node Rome at its most concentrated and Rome at its most dispersed.

One of the histories of Rome is the history of the processes by which a proper noun was unlaced from the city it named. By the end of the third century the city of Rome was not even the gravitational centre of a single Roman Empire. Divided east and west by Diocletian, the empire's western capital had been moved from Rome to Mediolanum (Milan); the eastern capital was Nicomedia. When Rome was sacked in 410 by Alaric, the western capital of the Roman Empire was no longer even at Mediolanum; it had already drifted to Ravenna. The western empire fell in the last quarter of the fifth century, but this was, in a genuinely vital sense, no end at all for the Roman Empire. This is because although we are in the habit of speaking casually about the fall of the 'Byzantine' Empire to the Turks in 1453, the entity that fell in that year knew itself simply as the Roman Empire. It was, in its own tongue, the 'Βασιλεία Ῥωμαίων', even though it had abandoned west for east, and Latin for Greek, hundreds of years earlier. When Rome itself was sacked again in 1527 (there had been other disasters in the meantime), the incursion was carried out by the troops of the Holy Roman Empire.[39] The *Sacrum Imperium Romanum* is yet another enduring testament to the talismanic power and unsettling mobility of the word Rome. Voltaire's joke about the Holy Roman Empire is worth citing, because it captures something important about the word's history: 'Ce corps qui s'appelait et qui s'appelle encore le saint empire romain n'était en aucune manière ni saint, ni romain, ni empire.'[40]

[39] On the 1527 event see Kenneth Gouwens, *Remembering the Renaissance: Humanist Narratives of the Sack of Rome* (Leiden: Brill, 1998).

[40] Voltaire, *Essai sur les Mœurs et l'Esprit des Nations et sur les Principaux Faits de l'Histoire Depuis Charlemagne Jusqu'à Louis XIII*, ed. René Pomeau, 2 vols. (Paris: Garnier, 1963), vol. I.683 (the body

These considerations supply a series of discrete historical positions from which to assess a sixteenth-century humanist commonplace. In a treatise on Latin prose style titled *Ciceronianus* (1528), Erasmus observed that 'Roma Roma non est, nihil habens præter ruinas ruderaque priscæ calamitatis cicatrices ac vestigia' (Rome is not Rome, having nothing besides ruins and rubble and the scars and vestiges of past calamity).[41] Rome, that specific city on the banks of the Tiber, has lived much of its life with its name articulated out at odd angles from itself. Erasmus roots one reason for believing that 'Roma Roma non est' in the 1527 cataclysm, but there is an even more fundamental reason to feel the truth and enduring power of his remark. 'Roma Roma non est' because so many other places and experiences and phenomena go by that name. To violently wrench from its context a metaphor that occurs in one of John Donne's love poems, we should see the Eternal City as having endured 'not yet / A breach, but an expansïon, / Like gold to aery thinness beat', and as having shaped lives in distant lands with an unexpected intensity, thoroughness, and intimacy.[42]

that called, and still calls itself, the Holy Roman Empire, was neither holy nor Roman nor an empire).

[41] *Ciceronianus*, in Desiderius Erasmus, *Opera Omnia Desiderii Erasmi Roterodami* (*ASD*) (Amsterdam: North-Holland Publishing Company, 1969–), I–2:694. This dialogue is discussed in Chapter 3.

[42] Donne, 'A Valediction Forbidding Mourning', in *The Complete Poems*, ed. Robin Robbins (Harlow: Pearson, 2010), lines 22–4.

CHAPTER I

The Ordinary

Where was Rome? Where is Rome? What is Rome? What was Rome? These questions are almost too broad to be answerable, and they risk seeming too nebulous to serve as incitements to inquiry. They open onto wide expanses of territory and time. And yet, they capture something of the complexity, and even the counterintuitive elusiveness, of an earthly city that is at once eternal and inescapable. These questions, moreover, present several challenges to traditional conceptions of disciplinarity and periodicity. Generated by means of simple adjustments to preposition, tense and pronoun, they indicate how speedily answers can accumulate in response to even minor changes of framing and emphasis when Rome is the topic at hand.

The agglomeration of stories and phenomena that the Middle Ages learned to call 'the matter of Rome' was, by a turn that ought to surprise us, susceptible to being represented as the matter of significance itself. We owe that phrase to the aggressively codifying genius of the medieval French poet Jehan Bodel, who asserted that anything worth saying by a poet could be derived from three *matières*:

Ne sont que .III. matieres a nul home antandant:
De France et de Bretaigne et de Rome la grant;
Et de ces .III. matieres n'i a nule samblant.
Li conte de Bretaigne sont si vain et plaisant,
Cil de Rome sont sage et de san aprenant,
Cil de France de voir chascun jor aparant.[1]

[There are just three matters for all men to know:
Of France and of Britain and of Rome the great;
In no way do these three matters resemble each other.
The stories of Britain are so empty and pleasant;

[1] Jehan Bodel, *La Chanson des Saisnes*, ed. Annette Brasseur, 2 vols. (Geneva: Librairie Droz, 1989), vol. I, §I.6–11.

Those of Rome are wise and instructive;
Those of France are seen to be confirmed daily.]

'Sage' (wise) and 'de san aprenant' (literally, 'sense-' or 'meaning-teaching'), *la matière de Rome* differs in both kind and degree of significance from the matters of Britain and France. Under its most extreme construction, Bodel's formula can be regarded as asserting that meaning itself emerges from the matter of Rome.

The goal of this chapter is to establish something of the range of conditions under which medieval and (to a much lesser extent) early modern texts negotiate their own absorption into the matter of Rome. The chapter pursues at length tenacious habits of attending not so much to the wonders of Rome, but rather to all that is most ordinary, obvious (in the word's etymological reference to that which is encountered 'in the way'), and ubiquitous in what Rome left in its wake when it relinquished its formal, administrative hold on the provinces of Britannia.[2] These preoccupations open onto a wide span of time: from the middle of the sixth to the middle of the seventeenth century.

It will be immediately obvious that an inquiry of this kind cannot produce anything like an exhaustive history of Rome as seen from the perspective of its erstwhile provinces during the Middle Ages and the Renaissance. Instead, the chapter accumulates a collection of miniature case studies drawn from an array of histories, material remains, poems, and antiquarian or proto-archaeological texts, each of which has been chosen to isolate for study different angles of convergence upon the past, present, city, self, and world. The chapter argues that these texts and problems convey expressions of ancient Rome's nearness, familiarity, and availability to those who live in its wake, and that versions of these expressions persist across a remarkably long period of time – even in the midst of a sequence of radical changes to what Rome itself was taken to represent. It argues, moreover, that these texts and problems make it possible to construct something like a phenomenology of Rome's afterlives in the territories that had constituted the Roman provinces of Britannia. My goal here is not to flatten historical specificity, but rather to explore some potential alignments, however delicate, among different historical perspectives on Rome.

[2] Once again, it is in the restrictive, Roman-historical sense of the word that I use the otherwise historically charged term 'Britain'. The book, therefore, does not engage with debates concerning, for example, the Act of Union, which founded the Kingdom of Great Britain.

It is crucial for this project that Rome be regarded, all at once, as place, idea, and fact; that it be understood as the vanishing point of a number of conditions and phenomena with which individuals were unthinkingly familiar, and to which their relations were not ordinarily charged in an intellectual or ideological sense; and finally, that it be regarded, under specific circumstances and historical conditions, as an entity that could suddenly seem to demand of individuals that they settle, and come to terms with, their relation to it. Rome, on this account, could awaken and stir medieval and early modern minds to thoughts concerning the nature and elusive order of human situatedness in the world. It could also rock them to unreflective sleep in a vision of the world's availability to human wants and needs.

Entanglements: Gildas, Bede, and the Anglo-Saxon Rome

Throughout the early and high Middle Ages, a wide array of authorities made it clear to their readers that ancient Rome's *imperium* had been at once real and metaphorical, and that it had encircled the Mediterranean as it stretched across huge sections of Europe, North Africa, and Asia Minor. These writers disseminated considerable knowledge concerning Rome's hold on Britain: for example, that most of the island of Britain had for several centuries been ruled by imperial Rome, and that this imperial power had withdrawn from the island around the time of the sack of Rome by Alaric and his armies in 410, decades before the collapse of the Western Empire.[3] Writers such as the Venerable Bede knew that the city's ancient *imperium* had been both reborn and reconfigured under the aegis of Pope Gregory I in 597.[4] It was in this year that the Benedictine monk Augustine (i.e., Augustine of Canterbury) had initiated his mission to convert the Germanic kingdoms that were ruling the territories that the Romans had once called Britannia. Bede makes it clear that ancient Rome's *imperium* had prepared the ground for the sacred mission of a Church whose origins and oldest stories are in a distant Holy Land, but whose administrative and spiritual centre was Rome.

[3] On the considerable challenges that attend the desire to date the waning of Roman influence in Britain see Ian Wood, 'The End of Roman Britain: Continental Evidence and Parallels', in Michael Lapidge and David Dumville (eds.), *Gildas: New Approaches* (Woodbridge, Suffolk: Boydell, 1984), 1–25.

[4] See, most recently, Paul Hilliard, 'Bede and the Changing Image of Rome and the Romans', in Elina Screen and Charles West (eds.), *Writing the Early Medieval West: Studies in Honour of Rosalind McKitterick* (Cambridge University Press, 2018), 33–48.

These overlapping imperial and ecclesiastical histories ensured that Rome dominated the rhythms and disciplines of daily life, conceptions of holiness, the liturgical calendar, and even the visible signs of a life dedicated to God. In 664, for example, the Synod of Whitby had determined that Oswiu's kingdom in Northumbria would calculate the date of Easter and perform monastic tonsure in accordance with Roman, as opposed to Irish, practices. And Rome would remain central to medieval and early modern imaginations even when those imaginations were in deep error. A longing for imaginative and material entanglements between past and present, near and far, nourished the erroneous medieval and Renaissance belief that the Tower of London had been built by Julius Caesar.[5] Rome is, in these examples, susceptible to being regarded as both 'place' and 'idea'. These same examples, however, should already be understood as moving beyond those categories and as impinging on conceptions of the self by shaping how the 'here and now' of medieval and early modern Britain was inhabited. What I am calling 'the fact of Rome' designates a collection of social practices and cultural inheritances within a built environment whose foundations had been laid, in part, by Rome.

The period between Rome's withdrawal from Britannia, *circa* 400, and the initial stages of Augustine's mission in the final years of the sixth century, was marked by massive cultural and structural upheavals whose rhythms cannot be precisely tracked. This is the so-called 'sub-Roman' period; the term was originally an archaeological designation for pottery found at fifth- and sixth-century sites. It begins as a period in which most of the island of Britain was ruled under the name of Rome – by that time a Christian empire – and concludes as a period in which the former provinces of Roman Britain have been transformed into myriad kingdoms ruled by Germanic pagans. There is, as T.M. Charles-Edwards has noted, a topsy-turvy quality to these metamorphoses: 'The most Romanized areas in 350 were those that, by 550, would be most securely English; the least Romanized areas in 350 were those that two hundred years later would still retain some continuity with the Roman past.'[6]

Few surviving voices in Britain bear witness to these changes. One of them (indeed, almost the only one) was that of a monk named Gildas who is thought to have lived from the late fifth through roughly the first half of the sixth century. Gildas conveys an enduring fascination with the fact of

[5] This tradition is attested by the fourteenth century and later by Shakespeare. See Homer Nearing Jr., 'Julius Caesar and the Tower of London', *Modern Language Notes* 63 (1948), 228–33.

[6] T. M. Charles-Edwards, *Wales and the Britons, 350–1064* (Oxford University Press, 2013), 31–2.

what Rome had done, made, and left in its wake. His *De excidio et conquestu Britanniae* (*Concerning the Destruction and Conquest of Britain*) is a work of almost hypnotic intensity. Gildas is chiefly concerned with the destruction, by the Anglo-Saxons, of what Rome had established in Britain, and with how that destruction was abetted by the depravity and cowardice of his own people, the Britons. His account of instabilities dating to the first decades of Roman rule is instructive for a number of reasons. The passage is long, but it bears quoting in full:

> Quibus statim Romam ob inopiam, ut aiebant, cespitis repedantibus et nihil de rebellione suspicantibus rectores sibi relictos ad enuntianda plenius vel confirmanda Romani regni molimina leaena trucidavit dolosa. Quibus ita gestis cum talia senatui nuntiarentur et propero exercitu vulpeculas ut fingebat subdolas ulcisci festinaret, non militaris in mari classis parata fortiter dimicare pro patria nec quadratum agmen neque dextrum cornu aliive belli apparatus in litore conseruntur, sed terga pro scuto fugantibus dantur et colla gladiis, gelido per ossa tremore currente, manusque vinciendae muliebriter protenduntur, ita ut in proverbium et derisum longe lateque efferretur quod Britanni nec in bello fortes sint nec in pace fideles.
>
> Itaque multis Romani perfidorum caesis, nonnullis ad servitutem, ne terra penitus in solitudinem redigeretur, mancipalibus reservatis, patria vini oleique experte Italiam petunt, suorum quosdam relinquentes praepositos indigenarum dorsis mastigias, cervicibus iugum, solo nomen Romanae servitutis haerere facturos ac non tam militari manu quam flagris callidam gentem maceraturos et, si res sic postulavisset, ensem, ut dicitur, vagina vacuum lateri eius accommodaturos, ita ut non Britannia, sed Romania censeretur et quicquid habere potuisset aeris argenti vel auri imagine Caesaris notaretur.
>
> Interea glaciali frigore rigenti insulae et velut longiore terrarum secessu soli visibili non proximae verus ille non de firmamento solum temporali sed de summa etiam caelorum arce tempora cuncta excedente universo orbi praefulgidum sui coruscum ostendens, tempore, ut scimus, summo Tiberii Caesaris, quo absque ullo impedimento eius propagabatur religio, comminata senatu nolente a principe morte delatoribus militum eiusdem, radios suos primum indulget, id est sua praecepta, Christus.[7]
>
> [The conquerors soon went back to Rome – allegedly for want of land – and had no suspicion of rebellion. A treacherous lioness butchered the governors

[7] I cite the original Latin and English translation of *De excidio et conquestu Britanniae* as they appear in Gildas, *The Ruin of Britain and Other Works*, ed. and trans. Michael Winterbottom (London: Phillimore, 1978), §6–8 (91 / 18–19). Quotations from this work give traditional section numbers and then, between parentheses, page references to the Latin text and Winterbottom's translation. Polydore Vergil was responsible for a 1525 printing of Gildas. Further editions were published in 1567 and 1568. English translations appeared in 1638 and 1652.

who had been left to give fuller voice and strength to the endeavours of Roman rule. On this, the news was reported to the senate, which hastened to send an army with all speed to seek revenge on what were pictured as tricky foxes. But there was no warlike fleet at sea, ready to put up a brave fight for its country; no orderly square, no right wing or other apparatus of war drawn up on the beach. The British offered their backs instead of shields to their pursuers, their necks to the sword. A cold shudder ran through their bones; like women they stretched out their hands for the fetters. In fact, it became a mocking proverb far and wide that the British are cowardly in war and faithless in peace.

So the Romans slaughtered many of the treasonable, keeping a few as slaves so that the land should not be completely deserted. The country now being empty of wine and oil, they made for Italy, leaving some of their own people in charge, as whips for the backs of the inhabitants and a yoke for their necks. They were to make the name of Roman servitude cling to the soil, and torment a cunning people with scourges rather than military force. If necessary they were to apply the sword, as one says, clear of its sheath, to their sides: so that the island should be rated not as Britannia but as Romania, and all its bronze, silver and gold should be stamped with the image of Caesar.

Meanwhile, to an island numb with chill ice and far removed, as in a remote nook of the world, from the visible sun, Christ made a present of his rays (that is, his precepts), Christ the true sun, which shows its dazzling brilliance to the entire earth, not from the temporal firmament merely, but from the highest citadel of heaven, that goes beyond all time. This happened first, as we know, in the last years of the emperor Tiberius, at a time when Christ's religion was being propagated without hindrance: for, against the wishes of the senate, the emperor threatened the death penalty for informers against soldiers of God.]

Gildas, a Briton writing some one hundred and fifty or more years after the late Roman Empire's final withdrawal from the island, commands a difficult and alluring version of Latin. He calls this language 'ours', thereby tracing a linguistic circle around himself and those capable of understanding him, distinguishing himself and that community of readers from the pre-conversion Anglo-Saxons.[8] Latin is to Gildas what the Mediterranean (proverbially, 'mare nostrum') had been to the Romans. Artful, even outlandish, patterns of hyperbaton and subordination drive words and developing thoughts in unexpected directions as Gildas' prose wanders and explores the territories of his culture's past and present.

[8] The phrase occurs in a passage in which Gildas distinguishes between the Saxon and Latin words for longships: 'ut lingua eius exprimitur, cyulis, nostra [lingua] longis navibus' (*De excidio et conquestu Britanniae*, §23.3 (97)).

The stylistic complexity of this passage is an unmistakable sign of what Michael Lapidge calls Gildas' 'first-hand knowledge of Latin as a living language'.[9] The passage has the rhetorical *form* of a statement about what Rome did and did not do in the wake of its decisive victories in Britain, but has the rhetorical *force* of a triumphant demonstration of what Latin can do. It is striking to see a living Latin of this kind brought to bear on a narrative in which Gildas attests again and again to the cataclysms and social collapses that attend Rome's serial, and then finally decisive, withdrawals from Britannia: striking not because his prose fits some badly outdated image of the supposed barbarity of medieval Latin, but rather because it testifies to the surprising ways in which a deeply learned, and indeed treasured, image of Rome shoots through Gildas' assaults on the disorders and perversities of his own day.

To write Latin of this kind is to model for oneself and one's readers an image of what it means to think deeply and adventurously about the relationship between past and present. It seems designed, moreover, to make readers see the thoroughness and intensity with which language shapes our experience of the world. Gildas' sometimes fiendishly difficult prose is no tangled mess, but rather a dream of almost inscrutable order articulated from within the dispositional borders of a language capable of great nuance, sophistication, and condensation.[10] It orders and paces its disclosures, shaping for itself a home within an idiom at once, perhaps, both native and foreign to Gildas himself, thereby making us see that Latin

9 Michael Lapidge, 'Gildas's Education and the Latin Culture of Sub-Roman Britain', in Lapidge and Dumville (eds.), *Gildas: New Approaches*, 37. Lapidge concludes, on stylistic grounds, that 'Gildas was trained at the hands of a *grammaticus* and then a *rhetor* (in the traditional Roman manner) in preparation for a secular administrative career' (48). He adumbrates the implications of this as follows: 'If the conventional dating of Gildas is correct, some recognisable form of Roman government must have existed in Britain in the early years of the sixth century' (49). On stylistic matters see also the essays of Neil Wright ('Gildas' Prose Style and its Origins', 107–28) and Giovanni Orlandi ('*Clausulae* in Gildas' *De Excidio Britanniae*', 129–49) in the same volume. On Latin learning and the Britons see Charles-Edwards, *Wales and the Britons*, 625–50.

10 Gildas' first English translator, the Catholic Thomas Habington, acknowledged his own struggles with the text's corruption and with the idiosyncrasies of Gildas' prose style: 'I found two especiall difficulties, the one he was in many places (through the negligence of them in whose hands he rested) so over-eaten with the rust of time, that I could scarcely discerne his lively Portrature, the other his sentences were so long and obscure, that they would be harsh and disliking to the reader, yet love overcomming all, and pleasure drawing mee forward, I adventured as touching the first, to ayme at this Image, & give a guesse where I could not determine the certainety, and for the last to let himself (as neere as I could) according to his proper fashion, knowing it to be as undecent to turne his grave speeches into idle words, and his long periods into short sentences, as to picture a sad man with a pleasant looke, and to draw the counterfet of a reverent Iudge not in his robes but in some light attire' (*The epistle of Gildas, the most ancient British author: who flourished in the yeere of our Lord, 546. And who by his great erudition, sanctitie, and wisedome, acquired the name of sapiens. Faithfully translated out of the originall Latine.* (London, 1638), A4^{v}-A5^{v} [STC 11895].)

itself had come to the island with something like the meandering force and surprise that mark the coming of Christ's teachings in the extraordinary final sentence of the cited passage. Note that Gildas' 'Christus' is at once the subject of this final sentence and the last of its sixty-seven words, so that the freedom of Latin syntax is made to echo the surprise of Christ's revelation, lending meaning and retrospective order to an historical sequence that had risked seeming meaningless and disordered.

The passage opens with one iteration of Rome's serial withdrawals from Britain: here, a troop movement that Gildas regards as having left Roman interests vulnerable to a *laena*. This 'she-lion' is presumably to be regarded as the wronged British queen Boudicca (though the identification is not entirely secure), leader of an uprising against the Romans *circa* 60 or 61 CE. Gildas lets his readers discover that this withdrawal, and the disorders it engendered, were finally repaired only by the coming of the teachings of Christ. The grand deferral of the name 'Christus' in Gildas' complex final sentence works to reproduce the thrill and surprise with which the teachings of Christ reached Britain. Gildas' syntax, therefore, models for the book's readers a life-altering invasion: just one of many to bring complex images of order to the island. Call it the *adventus praeceptorum Christi*, a triumphant prelude to the later *adventus Saxonum*, which had caused Gildas and the Britons so much heartache. Note that Gildas is speaking here not of the Augustinian mission to sub-Roman Britain in 597 but of the Christianity of a Britannia whose free inhabitants were, after the Edict of Caracalla in 212 CE, citizens of Rome's empire.[11]

Gildas labours to describe the persistence of Rome's hold on the island of Britain. This phenomenon is captured in his assertion that the Romans longed to have the island be 'non Britannia, sed Romania'. He casts this as the product of a group effort, on the part of Romans, to make the name of Roman slavery inhere in the soil ('solo nomen Romanae servitutis haerere facturos'). This is significant not simply because of what it might suggest about the malleability of, for example, conceptions of slavery, but also because it offers an instance of Gildas' eagerness to come to terms with the power that is latent in the word 'Rome'. For in a series of ways that this book will chart, it is not the 'nomen Romanae servitutis' that inhered in the soil, but rather the name of Rome itself and the vestiges of its *facta*.[12]

[11] Under Emperor Constantine, during the early fourth century, Christians across the Roman Empire were accorded freedom of worship. Under Theodosius, the Empire became officially Christian.

[12] See Alexandra Walsham, *The Reformation of the Landscape: Religion, Identity, and Memory in Early Modern Britain and Ireland* (Oxford University Press, 2011). Walsham dates to the period of Gildas a 'compound Romano-British paganism' that is 'rooted in the concept of a sacralized landscape' (23).

Living in the wake of Rome's departure from Britain, Gildas is desperate to make sense of what Rome made and left behind. He can see these remains and he knows who produced them. Scholars remark, for example, that what Gildas has to say concerning a variety of historical details and chronologies (on the construction of the northern Roman walls, for example) is both confused and confusing.[13] And yet, even in the midst of his confusions, Gildas makes us see that Rome-as-place and Rome-as-idea come together under the rubric of Rome and its *facta*. Throughout the Middle Ages many of Rome's most striking remains were still visible. They did not yet have to emerge from the soil as products of proto-archaeological labour and inquiry.[14] Like the names of Rome and Roman slavery, these things inhered in the dirt.

Gildas' attention to Rome's *facta* establishes a pattern that achieves its most elaborate forms in the Venerable Bede's *Historia ecclesiastica gentis anglorum* (completed 731). In this incalculably influential text, Bede repeatedly emphasizes that Rome's remains are conspicuous and familiar elements of the inhabited landscape of his eighth-century world.[15] Bede insists that even things fashioned during the age of Rome's first arrivals (i.e., during Julius Caesar's 55 and 54 BCE semi-abortive summer raids) have endured in a manner that leaves the present decisively pierced by the past.

[13] On this subject see Nicholas John Higham, 'Gildas, Roman Walls, and British Dykes', *Cambridge Medieval Celtic Studies* 22 (1991), 1–14. See also Hingley, *Hadrian's Wall: A Life*.

[14] On recovery projects beginning in the late sixteenth century see Hingley, *The Recovery of Roman Britain*. As a pattern for thinking about the relationship between art and archaeology during the Renaissance see especially Leonard Barkan, *Unearthing the Past: Archaeology and Aesthetics in the Making of Renaissance Culture* (New Haven: Yale University Press, 1999). On archaeology and literary criticism after the Middle Ages see Philip Schwyzer, *Archaeologies of English Renaissance Literature* (Oxford University Press, 2007). See, most recently, Andrew Hui, *The Poetics of Ruins in Renaissance Literature* (New York: Fordham University Press, 2017).

[15] I note provisionally that this particular emphasis on what is still visible seems to be a peculiarity of Bede's program in his *Historia*, even though the passage to be discussed here does mark an exception and has its own peculiarly vivid afterlife. Apart from treatments of this specific episode, the rhetoric of persistent conspicuousness does not figure anywhere near as prominently in, for example, pseudo-Nennius (although the *Historia Brittonum* does catalogue in its final sections various marvels and wonders of Britain, these are not connected to Rome) or in Geoffrey of Monmouth's *Historia Regum Britanniae*. On William of Malmesbury see William Kynan-Wilson, 'Mira Romanorum Artifitia: William of Malmesbury and the Romano-British Remains at Carlisle', *Essays in Medieval Studies* 28 (2012), 35–49. Kynan-Wilson emphasizes that during the Middle Ages, 'Roman remains survived on a scale and to an extent unmatched until the modern era of archaeology' (40). See also Kynan-Wilson's remarks on William, who distinguishes between the legibility of a Latin inscription at Carlisle and what he regarded as the incomprehensibility of the Northumbrian dialect of Old English: 'William's account attests to the reflective quality of Roman antiquities – the way in which they provoked comparison and invited self-reflection' (45). On artefacts as testaments to the persistence of the past see Michael Greenhalgh, *The Survival of Roman Antiquities in the Middle Ages* (London: Duckworth, 1989).

As Bede tells it, Caesar's progress northward from the south-east coast to the Thames, in the wake of the first pitched battles that followed the Roman landing, moved the assembled Britons to gather and fortify the river's far bank with sharpened stakes:

> quarum uestigia sudium ibidem usque hodie uisuntur, et uidetur inspectantibus quod singulae earum ad modum humani femoris grossae et circumfusae plumbo inmobiliter erant in profundum fluminis infixae.[16]
>
> [The traces of these stakes are visible even today; each of them, on inspection, is seen to be about the thickness of a man's thigh encased in lead and fixed immovably in the river bed.]

I have emphasized the utility of attending to Rome's *facta*, borrowing the term partly from Gildas and using the word to enlarge the more common, and narrower, view of Rome as place and idea. Bede's own term, as in this passage, is usually *uestigia* (traces, footprints), and he will repeatedly emphasize that they are visible 'usque hodie' (to this day). In Bede, those *uestigia* are produced not just by Rome but also by early Britons in warfaring dialogue with Caesar. Most importantly, Bede insists that Rome's arrivals on the shores of Britain produced phenomena that have endured roughly 780 years. The phenomena that interest him are open to view, subject to inspection, and reckoned in proportion to the human body, as though these defensive stakes had prompted later observers to intuit a corporate identity, a form of unity, between what might otherwise have been regarded as a subject–object relation. These vestigial stakes are at once historical survivals and visible constituents of the lived economy of space in Bede's medieval England. They are conformable to the bodies of Bede's readers and measures of the vividness with which the nearness of ancient Rome continued to be felt, understood, and lived in Anglo-Saxon Britain at large and, indeed, throughout Bede's writings.

The passage offers, in miniature, a view of the metaphors of linkage, orientation, nearness, and situatedness that will continue to characterize later negotiations and settlements with the *facta* and *uestigia* of Rome. Andrew Hui has recently treated the latter as a key word in Petrarch's work (and therefore in the forging of our traditional conceptions of periodization). Hui ties the word to what he sees as an epoch-making transition 'between the late medieval and the early humanist worlds'. But Bede's use

[16] Bede, *The Ecclesiastical History of the English People* (*HE*), ed. Bertram Colgrave and R. A. B. Mynors (Oxford University Press, 2007), 22–3.

of the same word to perform similar work predates, by many centuries, Petrarch's 'exercise of the historical imagination' upon 'sensible *vestigia*'.[17]

Through a strange and stirring transformation these stakes, measured by Bede in proportion to the human body, hover on the verge of transformation into actual body parts by the time Bede's words pass through the hands of Geoffrey of Monmouth in his twelfth-century *Historia Regum Britanniae*. Some combination of confusion, intervening tradition, and ghoulish flair for exaggeration (Geoffrey, for example, swears that these stakes killed thousands of Roman soldiers) is perhaps the best way to account for what Geoffrey does with Bede's words:

> Quod cum Cassibellaunus comperisset, urbes ubique muniuit, diruta menia renouauit, armatos milites in singulis portibus statuit. Preterea alueo Tamensis fluminis quo ad urbem Trinouantum Cesar nauigaturus erat palis ferreis atque plumbitis et ad modum humani femoris grossis subter amnem infixit ut naves Iulii superuenture illiderentur.[18]
>
> [When Cassibelaunus heard of Caesar's approach, he fortified all the cities, rebuilt the crumbling walls, and set up armed soldiers at all the gates. He also set up thick rows of stakes made of lead and human thigh bones just below the water line in the bed of the River Thames.][19]

A further variation on this theme can be found in the so-called 'First Variant Version' of Geoffrey's text, described by its most recent editor as an anonymous reworking of the *Historia* that may have been executed within Geoffrey's lifetime. In it, the anonymous redactor restores the defensive strategies of the ancient Britons to an approximation of Bede's treatment: 'Uerum Britones premuniti ita alueum fluminis palis ferreis per totum amnem fixis constipauerunt ut nulla nauis illesa et sine periculo transmeare flumen posset.'[20] Bede's emphasis on the preservation and conspicuousness to this day ('usque hodie uisuntur') of the stakes does not figure in either Geoffrey's *Historia* or in the work of the anonymous redactor of 'The First Variant'. It may be, however, that survival 'usque hodie' has become a textual phenomenon, so that the visibility of the stakes

[17] Hui, *The Poetics of Ruins*, 89, 130.

[18] Geoffrey of Monmouth, *The Historia Regum Britannie of Geoffrey of Monmouth, I: A Single-Manuscript Edition from Bern, Burgerbibliothek, MS 568*, ed. Neil Wright (Cambridge: D. S. Brewer, 1984), §59 (37–8).

[19] Geoffrey of Monmouth, *The History of the Kings of Britain*, ed. and trans. Michael A. Faletra (Peterborough: Broadview, 2008), §59 (87). I have retained Faletra's translation, but it would be considerably safer to translate Geoffrey's 'ad modum humani femoris' (his words match those of Bede quite precisely for this phrase) as 'to the measure of a man's thigh'.

[20] *The Historia Regum Britannie of Geoffrey of Monmouth, II: The First Variant Version, A Critical Edition*, ed. Neil Wright (Cambridge: D. S. Brewer, 1998), §59.

is to be understood as an epiphenomenon of the extraordinary circulation of lore concerning Rome's first incursions against the island.[21]

In any case, the detail originates in Caesar, who asserts in his *Commentarii de bello gallico* that the Britons had erected double ranks of stakes: the first projecting from the far bank, visible to the Roman invaders; the second driven deep into the river's mud, posing an invisible danger to boats.[22] The stakes re-emerge from the Thames centuries later in Bede, who is moved to emphasize their conspicuousness 'usque hodie'. From there, as if detached from the riverbed's mud, the stakes flow into the *Historia Brittonum* attributed to Nennius (where they have become 'sudes ferreos': 'iron pikes'[23]), into Geoffrey, and into the work of the redactor of the First Variant. They appear in the Anglo-Norman *Brut* (where the emphasis is, as it was in Bede, on the visibility and persistence of the stakes[24]) and also in Laȝamon's *Brut*.[25] With Caesar emphasizing the canny combination of visible and invisible stakes, their belated re-emergence in Bede's history, along with the increasingly improbable emphasis on their visibility, can be called Bede's 'invention' in the strong Latin sense of a 'finding' or 'discovery'. This is in keeping with the Latin rhetorical

[21] See Archie Green, *Wobbles, Pile Butts, and Other Heroes: Laborlore Explorations* (Urbana: University of Illinois Press, 1993), 398: 'Scholars have asserted that Bede simply made up the matter of lead-cased stakes and their visibility. We can interpret his improbable references either to Celtic tradition or to a patriotic need to enhance an act of guerrilla resistance to foreign power.' This is puzzling, since Caesar mentions the stakes.

[22] Julius Caesar, *The Gallic War*, ed. H.J. Edwards, LCL 72 (Cambridge, MA: Harvard University Press, 1917), 5.18: 'Caesar cognito consilio eorum ad flumen Tamesim in fines Cassivellauni exercitum duxit; quod flumen uno omnino loco pedibus, atque hoc aegre, transiri potest. Eo cum venisset, animum advertit ad alteram fluminis ripam magnas esse copias hostium instructas. Ripa autem erat acutis sudibus praefixis munita, eiusdemque generis sub aqua defixae sudes flumine tegebantur' ('Having obtained knowledge of their plans, Caesar led his army into the borders of Cassivellaunus as far as the river Thames, which can be crossed at one place only on foot, and that with difficulty. When he was come thither he remarked that on the other bank of the river a great force of the enemy was drawn up. The bank was fortified with a fringe of sharp projecting stakes, and stakes of the same kind fixed under water were concealed by the stream.')

[23] Nennius, [*Historia Brittonum*] *British History and The Welsh Annals*, ed. and trans. John Morris (London: Phillimore, 1980), §20.

[24] See Alexander Bell (ed.), *An Anglo-Norman Brut*, Anglo-Norman Texts Society XXI–XXII (Oxford: Blackwell, 1969), lines 485–92: 'L'ewe de Tamise fust bien palé, / Les pels tres ben asceré, / Les chefs desuis sunt ascerez, / Icels desuz tres ben plumez. / Si com dient li paisant / En cel' ewe que tant est grant / Uncore pout l'em asez trover / Ben grant trunçun de ces peus.' On Rome in Wace see Julia Marvin, *The Construction of Vernacular History in the Anglo-Norman Prose Brut Chronicle: The Manuscript Culture of Late Medieval England* (York Medieval Press, 2017), 21–56.

[25] See Laȝamon, *Brut*, ed. G. L. Brook and R. F. Leslie, Early English Text Society 250, 257 (Oxford University Press, 1963), vol. I, lines 3901–11 of BM MS. Cotton Caligula A.IX. Green writes that 'In moving from Bede and Nennius to Geoffrey, we witness a legend's growth by slow accretion and sheer exaggeration' (398). See Green, *Wobbles, Pile Butts and Other Heroes*, 393–401, for an account of the story of these stakes, their etymological history, and further references to them in the *Anglo-Saxon Chronicle*.

tradition's conviction that such *inventiones* are to be collected in the course of one's encounters with literary texts that are, like the landscape itself, known, familiar, and ready-to-hand.

When Bede turns his attention to the sack of Rome in 410, he looks back across the full sweep of Roman rule in Britain. As he does so, he is keen to remind his readers that Rome had turned the landscape of the island into the very thing with which they were familiar and in which they resided:

> Fracta est autem Roma a Gothis anno millesimo CLXIIII suae conditionis, ex quo tempore Romani in Brittania regnare cesserunt, post annos ferme quadringentos LXX ex quo Gaius Iulius Caesar eandem insulam adiit. Habitabant autem intra uallum, quod Seuerum trans insulam fecisse commemorauimus, ad plagam meridianam, quod ciuitates farus pontes et stratae ibidem factae usque hodie testantur.[26]

> [Now Rome was taken by the Goths in the eleven hundred and sixty-fourth year after its foundation; after this the Romans ceased to rule in Britain, almost 470 years after Gaius Julius Caesar had come to the island. They had occupied the whole land south of the rampart already mentioned, set up across the island by Severus, an occupation to which the cities, lighthouses, bridges, and roads which they built there testify to this day.]

This is very nearly elegiac in tone, but Bede is insisting that Rome's testaments are living, rather than dead. These testaments mark places in which the living convene: towers by which ships navigate and in response to whose signals they alter their routes; bridges and roads by which Bede and his contemporaries reach each other as they dwell in a world that is utterly familiar to them. These are elements of a broad totality of objects that make up the world of Bede's readers, and Bede associates them with the visible and conspicuous work of his island's ancient conquerors.[27] Here and elsewhere in the *Historia*, Bede's goal is to stamp the name of Rome upon the familiar.[28]

[26] *HE*, 40–1.

[27] See, for example, the essays collected in Valerie Allen and Ruth Evans (eds.), *Roadworks: Medieval Britain, Medieval Roads* (University of Manchester Press, 2016). In his contribution to the collection, Dylan Foster Evans notes that: 'The inhabitants of medieval Wales . . . were well aware that it was the Romans who were responsible for the best of the Welsh roads. It is also clear that the relationship with their Roman predecessors was an active force in constructing identity in medieval Wales' ('Conquest, Roads and Resistance in Medieval Wales', 285). Evans adds that 'Native knowledge regarding Roman roads is given its most detailed textual expression in the prose tale *Breudwyt Maxen Wledic* ('The Dream of the Emperor Maxen')', and that the story is referring to the Roman road system known as the Sarn Elen (285).

[28] The exceptionally wide and longstanding circulation of Bede's Latin text is significant, then, given that Sharon Rowley regards the much more narrowly attested anonymous Old English translation / adaptation of Bede's text as having endeavoured to 'decenter Roman authority' via abbreviation and paraphrase (Rowley, *The Old English Version*, 4).

To cities, lighthouses, bridges, and roads Bede might have added sarcophagi, carved altars, baths, vaults, splendid inscriptions in stone, arches, amphitheatres, ruined villas, city gates, huge columns, the remnants of temples, ruined forts, underground chambers, abandoned towns, defensive towers, sculptures, fine pottery, buried coins, mosaic floors, and curved walls of monumental dressed stone, were it not that he appears to be deliberately selecting structures and artefacts that do not necessarily, certainly do not automatically, fill individuals with wonder. Bede's *Historia* addresses itself to the sorts of works and *facta* that can both capture and elude conscious attention precisely because individuals are so habituated to them.

The chief issue in the *Historia* is that Rome had helped generate much, perhaps even most, of what Bede knew his readers could take for granted in their built environment: that there are such things as roads, that there are means to cross rivers and places in which people can convene, etc. Bede and his readers know that these things are Roman. These networks of made things orient and harbour individuals in a manner that is not continuously or even primarily experienced as an object of conscious thought or interpretation. It is possible to instance here certain remarkable (but nevertheless mostly invisible) legacies of Roman rule: for example, life along what has come to be known as the Fosse Way, a Roman road that stretched from the south-west of Britain to the eastern site of Lindum Colonia, stitching together several Roman sites along the way.[29] Long-distance surveying by the Romans plotted distant sites along an almost needle-straight line of some two hundred and thirty miles, sewing inhabitants into an ancient order that would have been barely perceptible to medieval and early modern men and women at sites that had once borne the names Isca Dumnoniorum (Exeter), Lindinis (Ilchester), Aquae Sulis (Bath), Corinium Dobunnorum (Cirencester), Ratae Corieltauvorum (Leicester), and Lindum Colonia (Lincoln).

In the wake of his retrospective look at the full stretch of Roman rule in Britain, Bede closes in once again on that period's final years, recurring to the words *facta* and *uestigia* in his description of the visible remnants of the Vallum Antonini, a northern turf wall built north of Hadrian's Wall at the instigation of the Emperor Antoninus Pius during the second century CE. The wall was abandoned shortly after its completion, then later

[29] On roads see Robert Witcher, 'Roman Roads: Phenomenological Perspectives on Roads in the Landscape', in Colin Forcey, John Hawthorne, and Robert Witcher (eds.), *TRAC 97: Proceedings of the Seventh Annual Theoretical Roman Archaeology Conference* (Oxford: Oxbow, 1998), 60–70.

re-garrisoned and, it seems, repaired by the Emperor Septimius Severus in the early third century. It was, in short, a limit of *imperium* from which Rome retreated, and to which it returned at least once more, before its final withdrawal from the island. Bede, like Gildas, is confused about dates and chronology in his discussions of the Vallum Antonini and the Vallum Hadriani, but he continues to emphasize their persistent conspicuousness: 'Cuius operis ibidem facti id est ualli latissimi et altissimi, usque hodie certissima uestigia cernere licet' ('The clearest traces of the work constructed there, in the form of a very wide and high wall, can be seen to this day').[30]

The wall, says Bede, was built by the Britons at the instigation of the Romans, and he asserts that its construction had marked a key moment in the history of Britain's reliance upon Rome. Having instigated the construction of the wall, Rome's soldiers (who, according to Bede, had been called in to aid the Britons against attacks) depart once again, only to have their departure summon up still more attacks against Britain. Bede says that under the fury of these renewed attacks the Britons appealed once more to Rome for aid, 'ne penitus misera patria deleretur, ne nomen Romanae prouinciae, quod apud eos tam diu claruerat, exterarum gentium inprobitate obrutum uilesceret' ('so that their wretched country might not be utterly destroyed, and the name of a Roman province, long renowned amongst them, might not be obliterated and disgraced by the barbarity of foreigners').[31] The Romans, in turn, insist that the Britons must learn to become self-sufficient in their own defence, but they do agree to build a second wall. Bede observes that this new wall, like its predecessor, is both 'famosum atque conspicuum' (famous and conspicuous) and 'usque hodie intuentibus clarum est' ('plain for all to see even to this day').[32]

Chapter 3 will have considerably more to say about the ways in which the Roman Catholic Church's mission to Britain in 597 reconfigures, even reinvents in linguistic terms, Rome's hold over the island, and thereby dramatically widens the range of *facta* that will survive to, and then beyond, Bede's day.[33] For now it can suffice simply to observe that when

[30] *HE*, 42–3. [31] *HE*, 42–3. [32] *HE*, 44–5.

[33] On these matters see especially the chapter titled 'Rome: Capital of Anglo-Saxon England', in Nicholas Howe, *Writing the Map of Anglo-Saxon England: Essays in Cultural Geography* (New Haven: Yale University Press), 101–48. It is significant in this context that centuries later, during the Avignon papacy, England supported Roman authority. See Kathy Lavezzo, *Angels on the Edge of the World: Geography, Literature, and English Community, 1000–1534* (Ithaca: Cornell University Press, 2006): 'Throughout both the Avignon papacy and the Great Schism of 1378–1409, England officially supported Rome, a move that was itself a sign of nationalism insofar as support for a Roman pope meant a rejection of England's French opponents during the Hundred Years' War. But a lingering

Bede tells the story of Augustine's earliest mission to Æthelberht and the Kingdom of Kent, Bede has Augustine announce that 'he had come from Rome bearing the best of news' ('mandauit se uenisse de Roma ac nuntium ferre optimum').[34] Rome marks the declared point of origin for the news Augustine wishes to deliver, and Rome's dominion had, of course, preceded Æthelberht's rule in these territories.[35] The *facta* and *uestigia* of Rome mark and organize the landscape that the Anglo-Saxons 'inherited, invented, and imagined'.

The latter phrase is borrowed from the title of an essay in which Nicholas Howe observes, tantalizingly, that

> no Anglo-Saxon text so much as alludes to a stone circle as prominent to the eye from afar as Stonehenge or Avebury, or a chalk image as visible as the White Horse of Uffington or the priapic giant above the monastic foundation at Cerne Abbas where Ælfric wrote his homilies and saints' lives at the turn of the last millennium, or a construction as massive as the Iron Age hillforts that still sit atop ridgeways across the southern part of the island. Nor do Anglo-Saxon texts refer specifically to anything as common as the earthworks that rise above and define the landscape in many places across the island.[36]

What inflections of the past's persistence did, or did not, drive Anglo-Saxon writers into words on the subject of their immediate surroundings? And once driven into words, what sorts of tensions between the ordinary and the wondrous do writers lay bare in their perceptions of material and imaginative frictions between different eras? From amongst the various 'uestigia' (Bronze-Age, Iron-Age, Classical, and post-Classical) that had survived 'usque hodie', Bede is perpetually moved to isolate for attention the ones to which he can grant a local habitation and a name: Rome.

The Order of the Ordinary

Gildas, Bede, and a few of their successors facilitate the project of isolating for study certain early medieval habits of regarding Rome not simply as a

investment in the idea of Rome – a lingering sense of the propriety of housing the universal church in the great classical capital – no doubt underlies that allegiance as well' (152 n.89).

34 *HE*, 72–3.

35 Rowley emphasizes that the Augustine mission to Æthelberht's kingdom would have marked 'at least the third "introduction" of Latin as a language of power and prestige to the island we now call England' (*The Old English Version*, 108).

36 See Nicholas Howe, 'The Landscape of Anglo-Saxon England: Inherited, Invented, Imagined', in John Howe and Michael Wolfe (eds.), *Inventing Medieval Landscapes: Senses of Place in Western Europe* (Gainesville, FLA: University Press of Florida, 2002), 93.

distant place and idea but as a network of local *facta* and *uestigia* that helped constitute the world in which individuals lived in medieval and Renaissance Britain. Familiarity was therefore a hallmark of Rome's remains long before the advent of early modern antiquarian projects. These *facta* and *uestigia* are part of a world of phenomena that are ready-to-hand and so intimately familiar that they can lurk beneath conscious thought and analysis. And yet, under conditions about which it is impossible to generalize (they would have to encompass everything from chance discoveries while digging to the heated, polemical atmosphere of the Reformation), these same phenomena can suddenly stand out and solicit attention, as though either longing to be regarded as marvels or demanding that individuals consciously take a stand on their relation to them. Phenomena of this kind can organize the lives of those who share space and commune with them. They situate individuals amidst entities that can, when subjected to conscious thought, either bear the name of Rome or have their origins traced back to a city that was simultaneously 'here' and 'elsewhere'. They can, in short, summon individuals into an order that is ready either to harbour or alienate them.

When Gildas and Bede attend to what has been ground into the dirt, what can still be seen by anyone, and what remains conspicuous and obvious to all, they are coming to terms with a version of Rome that is rather different from the ones that typically figure in scholarship on the Middle Ages and Renaissance. Those would necessarily include the very fruitful body of scholarship that studies, for example, Renaissance Rome's recovery of the ancient city beneath its feet, or the explicitly political stakes of medieval and Renaissance encounters with Rome, or the ways in which early modern Rome figures in emergent nationalist discourses, in discourses of religious strife, and in rhythms of reformation and counter-reformation polemic. Rome is, when regarded from British soil, commonly represented as a foreign thing or force that is distant in respect to both time and place. This is especially true of work studying relations between Rome and England in the early Middle Ages.[37] At other moments – in, for example, Edmund Spenser's sixteenth-century reworking of the French

[37] For a classic essay on traffic between Britain and Rome in the early Middle Ages see Bertram Colgrave, 'Pilgrimages to Rome in the Seventh and Eighth Centuries', in E. Bagby Atwood and Archibald Hill (eds.), *Studies in Language, Literature, and Culture of the Middle Ages and Later* (Austin: University of Texas Press, 1969), 156–72. See also Wilhelm Levison, *England and the Continent in the Eighth Century* (Oxford: Clarendon Press, 1946). For the later medieval period see Veronica Ortenberg, *The English Church and the Continent in the Tenth and Eleventh Centuries* (Oxford: Clarendon Press, 1992).

poet Joachim Du Bellay – Rome can be figured as being fundamentally at odds even with itself in its dual essence as both ancient and modern city. In any case, Rome is frequently treated by modern scholars, and even by early writers themselves, as as an inherently ideological or political or theological problem that must be embraced or solved or resisted or suborned. Rome is regularly treated, that is, as a phenomenon that is to be viewed from the outside, and whose borders can (even must) be patrolled or studied from a distance. The usually unstated assumption is that Rome's presence in Britain had decayed to such an extent as to make the city quintessentially foreign.[38]

Bede, by contrast, repeatedly emphasizes the nearness of Rome, and not simply with respect to its church. He makes his readers see that their lives are still being lived among that distant city's *facta* and *uestigia*, and his *Historia* was read and copied and re-copied across the entire span of time from the early eighth century until the sixteenth century. Bede shows, for example, that early Church authorities such as Saint Wilfrid and Benedict Biscop traveled back and forth between Britain and Rome, returning with books, relics, and architectural ambitions for holy spaces. Similarly, Bede's Life of Cuthbert shows the saint living as though he had been absorbed into the ruined backdrop of a Roman Britain that had nevertheless persisted and was still capable of nourishing him. Bede has Cuthbert take shelter in an abandoned seasonal farm building built along what appears to be the Roman road now known as Cade's Road, near the River Wear:

> Huc propter manendum ingrediens, equum in quo uenerat alligauit ad parietem, collectumque foeni fasciculum quem tecto uentus abstulerat, edendum illi apposuit, ipse orando horam ducere coepit. At subito inter psallendum uidit equum elato sursum capite, tecta casae carpentem ore iusumque trahentem atque inter cadentia foena tecti inuolutum pariter decidere linteum. Volensque dinoscere certius quid esset, finita oratione accessit, et inuenit inuolutum linteo dimidium panis calidi et carnem, quae ad unam sibi refectionem sufficere possent. Laudemque decantans benificiis coelestibus, Deo inquit gratias qui et mihi pro eius amore ieiunanti et meo comiti coenam prouidere dignatus est.

38 The most notable of several important exceptions to this is the work of Eamon Duffy, who has done much to emphasize Rome's persistence in England during the sixteenth century: see especially *The Stripping of the Altars: Traditional Religion in England, 1400–1580*, 2nd edn. rev. (New Haven: Yale University Press, 2005) and *Fires of Faith: Catholic England Under Mary Tudor* (New Haven: Yale University Press, 2010). See also Alexandra Walsham, *Catholic Reformation in Protestant Britain* (Farnham: Ashgate, 2014).

> [He entered one in order to shelter there, and fastening to the wall the horse he had been riding, he collected a bundle of straw which the wind had removed from the roof, and gave it to the horse to eat. He himself began to spend the time in prayer, when suddenly in the midst of his psalm-singing, he saw the horse lift up its head, seize the thatching of the house with its mouth and drag it down. Amid the straw falling from the roof, he saw a folded cloth fall as well; wishing to discover more certainly what it was, he drew near, when his prayer was finished, and found, wrapped in the cloth, half a loaf still warm, and some meat, sufficient for one meal for himself. Then he uttered praises for the heavenly favours. 'Thanks be to God,' he said, 'who has deigned to provide a supper for me who am fasting out of love for Him, and also for my comrade'.][39]

Cuthbert shares this miraculous gift with his horse and becomes more committed to the discipline of fasting, deriving from the experience a renewed faith that he is cared for. I propose, however, that the episode shows Cuthbert drawing sustenance not only from God's love, but also from the contiguity of the Roman past with the domestic accretions of the present, with the intersection of Roman road and modern building hosting an encounter between spiritual and physical sustenance. The remains of Rome also figure prominently at another moment in Bede's Life of Cuthbert. When the saint, in the company of the citizens of Carlisle, sees 'the walls of the city and a marvellously constructed fountain of Roman workmanship' ('moenia ciuitatis fontemque in ea miro quondam Romanorum opere extructum'), the sight appears to be in some unsettling way connected to the saint's sudden recognition that Ecgfrith will be defeated in battle by the Picts. This view of the persistence of the Roman past within the present seems to have enabled Bede's Cuthbert to glimpse the future.[40]

This is significant because the trajectory of Saint Cuthbert's life saw him trained up within the Irish monastic traditions associated with monks from Iona, and then gradually (along with his mentor Eata) committing himself

[39] Bertram Colgrave (ed. and trans.), *Two Lives of Saint Cuthbert: A Life by an Anonymous Monk of Lindisfarne and Bede's Prose Life* (Cambridge University Press, 1985), 170–1.

[40] Colgrave (ed. and trans.), *Two Lives of Saint Cuthbert*, 244–5. On this passage see Seth Lerer, '"On fagne flor": The Postcolonial *Beowulf*, From Heorot to Heaney', in Ananya Jahanara Kabir and Deanne Williams (eds.), *Postcolonial Approaches to the European Middle Ages: Translating Cultures* (Cambridge University Press, 2005), 94–5. The same episode, with its Roman walls and well, appears in an anonymous Life of St. Cuthbert. There, Cuthbert's sudden, prophetic assertion that Ecgfrith will be defeated is also timed to coincide with his view of 'the city wall and the well formerly built in a wonderful manner by the Romans' ('murum ciuitatis, et fontem in ea a Romanis mire olim constructum'). See Colgrave (ed. and trans.), *Two Lives of Saint Cuthbert*, 122–3. See also, on this topic, Joshua Davies, *Visions and Ruins: Cultural Memory and the Untimely Middle Ages* (Manchester University Press, 2018).

to Roman practices after the Synod of Whitby. This is part of a broad series of transformations that Alexandra Walsham has called 'the Romanization of Celtic Christianity in the seventh, eighth, and subsequent centuries'.[41] At this moment, Bede's *Vita Sancti Cuthberti* pivots rapidly between the ordinary and the miraculous, the Roman and the contemporary. This particular miracle can serve as a useful context for understanding what happened to Cuthbert after his death. When his remains were removed from Lindisfarne in the wake of the first Viking raids, they were resettled in a timber church purpose-built within the ruins of the ancient Roman fort of Concangis, at what is now Chester-le-Street, Durham, along Cade's Road, near the River Wear. The original timber church of St Mary and St Cuthbert (late ninth century) did not make use of the stones of Concangis, and its builders chose instead to have it take its stand in the midst of those stones. It is equally striking that the stone church that has replaced the original timber building bears conspicuous signs that it did finally repurpose the stones of Concangis. This church's earliest layers date to the eleventh century, though by this point Cuthbert's remains had, as it were, hit the road again.

To this point I have focused on the sense of familiarity fostered by the quotidian experience of living amidst visible and proximal things that alternately escape and catch the eye of writers such as Bede in the early Middle Ages. The texts and problems that dominate the rest of this chapter will move (with necessary selectiveness) through the long sweep of history that connects Bede to Sir Thomas Browne in the late seventeenth century. My goal is to establish a series of mostly broken and discontinuous conversations among writers ranging from anonymous Anglo-Saxon poets to late medieval and then Renaissance writers. Throughout, 'the fact of Rome' will continue to designate both the ancient substratum on which medieval and early modern men and women move and labour, and the complex relationship between individuals and the attainment of skills that the educated regarded as connecting them to the Roman past.

The vital concern here will be not that these need actually have been intrinsically Roman concepts, practices, or even ruins, but rather simply that they were regarded as such. Nor am I in any sense suggesting that the circumstances in which 'the fact of Rome' was encountered were identical. Even so, the encounter as such is persistent. It is staged and restaged across centuries. Across the period of time surveyed here individuals find

[41] Walsham, *The Reformation of the Landscape*, 45.

themselves living within view of ruined Roman cities.[42] They quarry the facts of Rome. They live among that city's ashes. They think and write (or at least aspire to do so) as though inhabited by its language. Facts and metaphors of this kind make it possible to see that the distant city of Rome was experienced intimately, and frequently unreflectively, as a domestic phenomenon familiar to all and yet, because of the very fact of that familiarity, almost too close to see. This thread of experience runs through the Middle Ages. We can also discern its presence in the early modern period, when we might rather have expected to see at all times a self-consciously ideological conception of what is at stake in encounters with Rome.

Whether construed simply as a name for the ancient empire that had made a province of Britain for roughly four centuries, or, as I think it must, as a name for a much broader spectrum of phenomena, Rome is never just a place or an idea at this time. Relevant supplements to that double formula would have to range, for example, from foreign city to ancient *imperium* to administrative centre of the Catholic Church, and beyond this to groups of metonymic and metaphoric clusters that will be studied in subsequent chapters of this book. These are references to different time periods and phenomena, of course, but it is significant that the name of Rome can, at any given moment, be pressed on them.

Rome had so thoroughly shaped the map of Britain, so powerfully organized the terms in which time and the calendar were experienced, so decisively entangled individual bodies in civil disciplines and practices, that to live in medieval or Renaissance England was to be absorbed into a past that had stubbornly refused to loosen its grip on the present. It was, in any case, to be absorbed into a distant and foreign thing that is nevertheless regularly experienced as something near, ordinary, and un-pierced by thought. The claim here is not that individuals lived in a fog through which they could not perceive the ideological stakes of their world, but rather that enduring, sensible, and even highly productive scholarly engagements with such ideological matters have stepped past an important aspect both of Rome's legacy and of the ways in which humans, as part of their very nature, experience the world. Probing these issues within the parameters of a new vocabulary can help us see something new about the Middle Ages and Renaissance, and something new (as I argue in Chapter 2)

[42] On the Anglo-Saxon reuse of Roman stonework see especially Tim Eaton, *Plundering the Past: Roman Stonework in Medieval Britain* (Stroud: Tempus, 2000).

about the problem of the self as it is glimpsed, as though through Roman light, in writers such as Spenser and Milton.

In its composite status as spectacle of ruination, living city, 'universal' church, maker of roads and bridges, arbiter of culture, and measure of civility, Rome is absorbed into 'the order of the ordinary'.[43] This phrase is used by the philosopher Stanley Cavell not to designate a discrete class of objects or events but rather to characterize what can be called a posture towards the world. What Cavell calls 'the ordinary' is associated with a sense of, perhaps a faith in, the world's availability to human wants and needs. More properly historical reference points for the word might be, for example, the *ordinarium missae* (i.e., the 'ordinary of the mass' – a phrase used to describe the portion of the Catholic mass that remains unchanged throughout the liturgical year) or the *glossa ordinaria* (a canonical set of influential glosses on scripture) of biblical commentary, or even a medieval professor's 'ordinary' lectures at university.[44] Cavell's understanding of the ordinary, however, provides a theoretical vocabulary with which to explore shifting medieval and early modern investments (in the etymological sense of an enwrapping) in Rome and in what that city had left behind in Britain. The ruins of Rome's dominion are at key moments regarded as marvels to be contemplated from a distance, but they are also commonly repurposed as the raw material of new structures, so that competing versions of what it means to live in Rome's wake are embedded deep in the ground of the everyday and its social practices. Part of the business of living in the wake of the Eternal City, then, involves constantly shifting into and out of the habit of regarding its marvels as ordinary features of a world that, to paraphrase Jeff Dolven's summing-up of Cavell's preoccupation, does not mean but merely is.[45]

Cavell contrasts the ordinary with philosophical skepticism, which he regards not as a product of a failure of human knowledge but rather as the epiphenomenon of a deeply felt, and indeed intrinsically human, appetite

43 See Cavell's assertion that philosophy works to 'show that what we accept as the order of the ordinary is a scene of obscurity, self-imposed as well as other-imposed, fraudulent, you might say metaphysical' ('Introductory Note to "The *Investigations*' Everyday Aesthetics of Itself"', in John Gibson and Wolfgang Huemer (eds.), *The Literary Wittgenstein* (London: Routledge, 2004), 19).

44 See, for example, Lesley Smith, *The Glossa Ordinaria: The Making of a Medieval Bible Commentary* (Leiden: Brill, 2009).

45 See Jeff Dolven, 'When to Stop Reading *The Faerie Queene*', in Jennifer Lewin (ed.), *Never Again Would Birds' Song Be the Same: Essays on Early Modern and Modern Poetry in Honor of John Hollander* (New Haven: Beinecke Library, 2002), 35–54. In a reading that engages closely with Cavell, Dolven studies tensions between Spenser's allegorical poetics and his 'representation of pleasures to do not mean but simply are' (49).

to banish the world and the other. Skepticism becomes, in Cavell's hands, an intellectual product of the speed and intensity with which humans are repelled by the ordinariness of the world. His conception of the ordinary, then, encompasses a nuanced understanding of human strength relative to the world.[46] It is a measure of our investments in the world we inhabit, and of our willingness both to accept the world itself, and to accept it as natural.[47] According to Cavell, the ordinary is a set of givens from which we continually fly and to which we continually return. It is a space or condition that at once harbours and threatens our sense that we share our humanity with those around us, and that we can be at home, authentically dwell, in the world in which we find ourselves. Cavell wants to apprehend, as he puts it, 'the fantastic in what human beings will accustom themselves to, call this the surrealism of the habitual – as if to be human is forever to be prey to turning your corner of the human race, hence perhaps all of it, into some new species of the genus of humanity, for the better or for the worst'.[48] This last formulation will return in the final sections of Chapter 4.

Efforts to attend to, and speak about, the ordinary are bedevilled by the ease with which human attention transforms what has been unreflectively accepted as ordinary into something else: say, into the Roman ruins that the Anglo-Saxons perceived along their horizon lines and, though fully familiar with their origins, characterized not as the work of men but as 'enta geweorc' (the work of giants). This formulaic phrase appears in several Anglo-Saxon texts, where it is always used to describe stone buildings and ruins.[49] In the passages I have collected from Bede, the

[46] I am borrowing the phrase from Paul Alpers' development of the idea in Chapter 2 (on 'Mode and Genre') in *What is Pastoral?* (University of Chicago Press, 1996), 44–78. Alpers, in turn, derives the phrase from Angus Fletcher, 'Utopian History and the *Anatomy of Criticism*' in Murray Krieger (ed.), *Northrop Frye in Modern Criticism* (New York: Columbia University Press, 1966), 34–5.

[47] This is one of Cavell's career-long preoccupations. See his essays, 'The Uncanniness of the Ordinary', in Stanley Cavell, *In Quest of the Ordinary: Lines of Skepticism and Romanticism* (University of Chicago Press, 1988), 153–78; 'Declining Decline', in Stanley Cavell, *This New Yet Unapproachable America: Lectures after Emerson after Wittgenstein* (Albuquerque, NM: Living Batch Press, 1989), 29–75; 'Notes and Afterthoughts on the Opening of Wittgenstein's *Investigations*', in Stanley Cavell, *Philosophical Passages: Wittgenstein, Emerson, Austin, Derrida* (Cambridge, MA.: Blackwell, 1995), 125–86. These essays show Cavell working to drive his understanding of the ordinary into conversation with work by Wittgenstein, Austin, Heidegger, Emerson, Thoreau, Freud, and others.

[48] Cavell, 'The Uncanniness of the Ordinary', 154.

[49] On the poetic formula 'enta geweorc', see Michael G. Shapland, 'Meanings of Timber and Stone in Anglo-Saxon Building Practice', in Michael D. J. Bintley and Michael G. Shapland (eds.), *Trees and Timber in the Anglo-Saxon World* (Oxford University Press, 2013): 'The phrase 'work of giants' occurs eight times in extant Old English poetry to describe ancient architecture; in all cases, stone architecture is explicitly meant, and in all cases it acts as a symbol of age and durability' (35). The formula is, therefore, a calibrated response to what Rome left behind in Britain.

ordinariness of the remains of Rome can suddenly burst into the light of thought and metamorphose into marvels that provoke awe and wonder as they fire the historical imagination.

Cavell is not generally interested in exploring the processes by which what is counted as ordinary shifts in unexpected ways across history, but in one short essay he gestures towards what he calls 'the consonance of so-called ordinary language with the visions of other intellectual quests for the ordinary'.[50] In this essay he responds to Paul Ricoeur's criticisms of the work of the *Annales* historians, whom Ricoeur regarded as having shunned their discipline's proper commitment to the event and, by extension, as having violated history's foundational connections to narrative. Cavell, by contrast, proposes that,

> The uneventful . . . is an interpretation of the everyday, the common, the low, the near; you may call it an empirical interpretation, still pre-philosophical. What is uneventful at one date and place is not the same as what is uneventful at another date and place, so that the translation of one to another may be knowable only to something we will call history.[51]

In addition to responding to Ricoeur's charges against the *Annales* school, Cavell's remarks should be regarded as taking up a pair of questions posed by Ludwig Wittgenstein in *Philosophical Investigations*:

> Macht alles, was uns nicht auffällt, den Eindruck der Unauffälligkeit? Macht uns das Gewöhnliche immer den *Eindruck* der Gewöhnlichkeit?[52]

> [Does everything that we do not find conspicuous make an impression of inconspicuousness? Does what is ordinary always make the *impression* of ordinariness?]

Responding at once to Ricoeur and Wittgenstein, Cavell insists that what counts as ordinary will change under the pressure of distinct historical and volitional forces, and even change randomly or accidentally in unprecedented ways. This helps us to see that what is commonly regarded as the rediscovery of Roman Britain is not so much a matter of recovering lost marvels as it is a series of interrelated reorientations towards a world of things, many of which had long been visible and responsive to the needs of the present, and many of which were familiar even when being dug up from the ground.

[50] Stanley Cavell, 'The Ordinary as Uneventful', in Stanley Cavell, *Themes out of School: Effects and Causes* (University of Chicago Press, 1984), 184.

[51] Cavell, 'The Ordinary as Uneventful', 193.

[52] Ludwig Wittgenstein, *Philosophical Investigations*, trans. G. E. M. Anscombe, rev. P. M. S. Hacker and Joachim Schulte, 4th edn. rev. (Chichester: Wiley-Blackwell, 2009), §600.

To this point, the chapter has prioritized early medieval accounts of, and encounters with, the remains of Roman Britain in Latin texts dating to the Anglo-Saxon period. In the remaining sections of this chapter, significant reorientations, but also significant continuities, will become conspicuous within the worlds of individual texts and also across wide stretches of time. An uneven oscillation between perceptions of ordinariness and awe marks the encounters assembled for commentary in the remaining sections of this chapter. These miniature case studies range widely, but they begin with a pair of brief explorations of well-known Anglo-Saxon poems whose implications can be unfolded in a few different historical directions. These texts see individuals being thrown back upon themselves, as though what Rome left in its wake had to be regarded as alternating between the most ordinary and the most extraordinary topic conceivable, a topic at one moment unreachable by thought and then suddenly capable of demanding that individuals settle, via Rome, the issue of their own relation to the world in which they found themselves. In these works, versions of Rome suddenly emerge as objects of thought from the familiar, the ordinary, the everyday, thereby moving from what Cavell calls the 'pre-philosophical' into the orbit of sustained, systematic attention – and then back again.

The Ordinary in History: Two Anglo-Saxon Case Studies

- Beowulf: *The Floor at Heorot*

A pair of small but stubborn phrases in *Beowulf* draw attention to an instance of the phenomenon just described. The first of these phrases lurks, as if in ambush, where the monster Grendel bursts into Heorot and, full of ire, treads across a floor to which the poet has attached the adjective 'fāgne':

Raþe æfter þon
on fāgne flōr   fēond treddode,
ēode yrremōd.[53]

The action described is straightforward enough:

Right after that,
on the *fāgne* floor   the fiend treaded,
went angrily.

[53] R. D. Fulk, Robert E. Bjork, and John D. Niles (eds.), *Klaeber's Beowulf and the Fight at Finnsburg*, 4th edn. (University of Toronto Press, 2008), lines 724–6.

Across what sort of floor is Grendel striding? Forms of the adjective that I have italicized and left untranslated have a fairly long history of close scholarly engagement. Filip Missuno is emphatic: '*Fāh* is a bewildering Old English word.'[54] In a bracing and adventurous essay on Heorot's 'fāgne flōr' and its implications, Seth Lerer observes that the word *fag* or *fah* is repeatedly used in the poem to describe patterned and ornamented objects. His composite goal is to revive, as well as reflect upon, a reading first proposed several decades ago by C. L. Wrenn.[55] Lerer proposes that,

> Grendel stands not just on a patterned floor, but a tessellated one: a mosaic relic of an older, Roman architectural past. Much like the paved road that Beowulf and his men traverse on their way to Heorot – 'stræt wæs stan-fah'[56] – this floor represents the archaeology of the Anglo-Saxon post-colonial imagination. It offers up a vision of a vernacular present set on an ancient relic. It exemplifies the status of the poem's fictive world (and, perhaps, its historical readership) as living in the afterlife of Rome.
>
> Anglo-Saxon England was acutely conscious of its life on Roman floors. In many ways, it built itself upon the ruins of the colonizers. Churches and dwellings were built on Roman foundations (though, on occasion, old villas and roads were apparently abused, or desecrated), and there is evidence throughout Anglo-Saxon literary and historical writing for a deep, cultural consciousness of the Roman past.[57]

This reading supplies a fascinating path into the plots of *Beowulf*, a poem Lerer describes as 'a narrative of elegy and loss, one conscious of a life lived on the barely maintained artistry and artifice of Roman Britain, one fearful of just what lies hidden in the wondrous arches left by leaders who have gone'.[58] Lerer's reading is potent at least partly because it catches so effectively the searching, daring, and elliptical quality of the poem's historical imagination, which frequently works through strategies of

[54] Filip Missuno, 'Glowing Paradoxes and Glimmers of Doom: A Re-evaluation of the Meaning of Old English *fāh* in Poetic Contexts', *Neophilologus* 99 (2015), 126.

[55] See C. L. Wrenn's glossary entry on 'stānfāh' in *Beowulf with the Finnesburg Fragment* (London: Allen & Unwin, 1953). See also Marijane Osborn's critique of Wrenn's proposals in 'Laying the Roman Ghost of *Beowulf* 320 and 725', *Neuphilologische Mitteilungen* 70 (1989), 246–55.

[56] Fulk, Bjork, and Niles (eds.), *Klaeber's Beowulf*, line 320.

[57] Lerer, '"On fagne flor"', 77–8.

[58] Lerer, '"On fagne flor"', 78–9. Lerer's notes are an excellent guide to the long history of the reading he is attempting to revive, though see also Missuno's more recent 'Glowing Paradoxes and Glimmers of Doom'. Eric Gerald Stanley has proposed that the phrase used to describe the wide, Roman-style pavers that lead from the coast to Heorot ('stræt wæs stanfah') is echoed in the Anglo-Saxon poem *Andreas*, where the 'stræte stanfage' are similarly impressive. He concludes that the function of the phrase in the latter is to emphasize the grandeur of stonework. See Eric Gerald Stanley, '*Beowulf*', in Eric Gerald Stanley, *A Collection of Papers with Emphasis on Old English Literature* (Toronto: Pontifical Institute of Medieval Studies, 1987), 144. Stonework was, in the eyes of Anglo-Saxons, Roman.

indirection and juxtaposition. These structural tactics enable the poem to achieve the effect of collage in its efforts to bring past and present into ceaseless dialogue.

In an introductory essay to his edition of *Beowulf*, R. M. Liuzza subtly and precisely describes this feature of the poem's historical vision:

> In many respects the poem already contains its own background and foreground, a fictionalized matrix of past and present within the text; our modern efforts to explain Beowulf's origins or contexts or even to place the hero's actions into some perspective can only mimic or mirror the poem's own contextualizing impulses.[59]

In short, it is no strike against Lerer's reading that the text of *Beowulf* is not more explicit about the nature of the floor across which Grendel strides, and that this lone and enigmatic adjective might be regarded as capable of opening up worlds of unexpected implications. Lerer proposes that readers ought to regard Heorot's 'fāgne flōr' as a mosaic floor of the kind that Anglo-Saxons could have seen in the remnants and ruins of Roman villas in Britain. He emphasizes that roughly four hundred of these mosaic floors survive in various states of integrity and ruination. The chief implication of this, according to Lerer, is that Heorot may be 'something like a Saxon hall built on the tessellated floor of an abandoned mansion'.[60]

Lerer proposes that 'The *fagne flor* of Heorot' is 'a memory of magnificence, an allusion to something old, rich, artistic, and alien.'[61] I would counter, however, that it is the familiarity that strikes, as the adjective slides past without commentary by the poet. Other passages in the poem call attention, even obsessively, to interrelations between discrete historical strata and phenomena. The poem's tangled, non-chronological treatment of wars between the Geats and Swedes is arguably the most notable example of this tendency. Though the floor may be, in objective terms, 'old, rich, artistic, and alien', both Grendel and the *Beowulf* poet take it in stride, leaving the bewildering adjective to solicit interpretation as best it can. The phrase is terse enough to suggest that Rome and its underfoot *facta* were much too familiar for the poet to regard them as alien. Indeed, familiarity is an essential component of the floor's role in the historical economy of *Beowulf*. Lerer is more closely attuned to this dynamic later in the essay, where he describes the Anglo-Saxons as

59 R. M. Liuzza, 'Introduction', in R. M. Liuzza (ed. and trans.), *Beowulf*, 2nd edn. (Peterborough: Broadview Press, 2013), 16.

60 Lerer, '"On fagne flor"', 83. 61 Lerer, '"On fagne flor"', 84.

> a people who would build hearths on mosaics; who would turn bath-houses into granaries; who would pull out the cobble of a massive past and mortar it into a local present – these are a people who are constantly *domesticating* (in the root sense of that word) the ancient other.[62]

This is, once again, useful, but it is not entirely clear that stones treated in the ways described by Lerer would need to have been first experienced either as ancient or as 'other'. As this chapter's citations from Bede have already shown, and as I will continue to emphasize across the remainder of this chapter, ruins of the kind described by Lerer were conspicuous and widely distributed in medieval Britain. They were, in short, already 'domestic' enough to provide a setting fit to host, in their own midst, the construction of Cuthbert's shrine at the original timber church of St Mary and St Cuthbert.

For a slightly different, and potentially more illuminating, depiction of the shaping role played by other familiar and ordinary Roman *facta* and *uestigia*, consider Lerer's gloss on the *Beowulf* poet's suggestion that the haunted mere of the Grendel-kin is not far from Heorot, were that distance to be marked or measured in miles: 'Nis þæt feor heonon / mīlġemearces / þæt se mere standeð.'[63] Lerer asks, 'What else is that measurement in miles than an allusion to the Roman milestones that still dotted the Anglo-Saxon (and, indeed, the entire Northern European) landscape?'[64] It is a nice gauge of the *Beowulf* poet's historical and geographic distance from the story he is telling that these milestones do not *actually* dot the path from Heorot to the mere. Instead, the poem's narrative voice imagines them into place for an instant, granting audiences a temporary purchase on the poem's haunted conviction that the mere is at once measurably proximate to, and worlds away from, the battle hall built by Hrothgar.

To put this another way, although Heorot's 'fāgne flōr' is said to belong to the inner world of the poem's plots (that is, to be a material surface across which the poem's Danes and monsters actually stride), those milestones are figments of the Christian poet-narrator's historical imagination. They are tools to think with as the poet orients himself and his audience to the landscapes of their culture's past. This Anglo-Saxon view of the pre-emigration Continental past is seen through the eyes of one deeply habituated to the ways in which the Romans had measured and apportioned the territories of Britain. Addressing an Anglo-Saxon audience and

62 Lerer, '"On fagne flor"', 94.
63 Fulk, Bjork, and Niles (eds.), *Klaeber's Beowulf*, lines 1361–2.
64 Lerer, '"On fagne flor"', 88.

reckoning for their benefit miles traversed in a distant Scandinavian landscape, he instinctively appeals to their experience of how Roman milestones operate in the land that had once been Britannia.

It must be emphasized, then, that the *Beowulf* poet is driving this 'fāgne flōr', this vestigial layer of Roman civility, not into the soil of the island that really had been colonized by both Romans and Anglo-Saxons, but into the soil of a Scandinavian landscape inhabited and ruled by Spear-Danes, but never by Romans, in the 'ġeārdagum' (bygone days) of the poem's opening line. These 'ġeārdagum' are characterized chiefly by their temporal as well as geographic distance from the poet's present. What is most striking about this is that the *Beowulf* poet appears to have so habituated himself to these Roman survivals (mosaic floors, milestones), so thoroughly accustomed himself to the ordinariness of his encounters with Rome's *facta* and *uestigia*, that he imagines them not only as features of the landscape of the former Roman province in which he lives, but as underwriting a Scandinavian landscape never ruled and administered by Rome. There had been trade contacts between, for example, Jutland and Rome, but southern Scandinavia was not laced into order by arrow-straight Roman roads or dotted with *coloniae* and villas.[65]

The dirt-deep Roman 'ordinary' of Anglo-Saxon Britain could hardly have counted as ordinary for Anglo-Saxons' Continental ancestors, who had not built their battle halls on the remnants of Roman villas in the way that the *Beowulf* poet seems to imagine them to have done. Finding himself entangled within his poem's historical layers, the poet has awakened to the possibility, perhaps instinctively assumed, that it was in the very nature of dirt to be supported from below by what even shallow digging can sometimes lay bare in Britain.[66] This goes hand-in-hand with the poet's absorption into a landscape dotted with the milestones that he can imagine as measuring the distance from Heorot to the underwater lair of the Grendel-kin.

More spectacularly, these milestones measure the distance separating the poet's present from a geographic and temporal past that he is either unwilling or unable to imagine as having been anything other than fully

[65] See Thomas Grane, 'Did the Romans Really Know (or Care) About Southern Scandinavia? An Archaeological Perspective', in Thomas Grane (ed.), *Beyond the Roman Frontier: Roman Influences on the Northern Barbaricum* (Rome: Edizioni Quasar, 2007), 7–29 (esp. 20).

[66] Impressive finds continue to this day. In 2015, for instance, workers attempting to bury an electric cord so that a family's children might have lights by which to play table tennis in a barn on their property unearthed, beneath 18 inches of soil, a massive Roman mosaic floor near Tisbury in Wiltshire – the remains of a huge and impressive villa that seems to have been occupied during both the Roman sub-Roman periods. The site has come to be known as the Deverill Villa.

continuous with his own culture. All this gives form to the poem's fantasy that Rome is going to be visible when you clear ground or brush dirt from a floor – any floor in any territory or realm or nation.[67] At this moment, the poem appears to be willing to regard as ordinary layers of history that can only have been regarded as fantastic by the cultures taken in hand by the *Beowulf* poet. This is, once again, an image of the ordinary as it sits in restive tension with the wondrous. In a pair of assertions that have been foundational for Western traditions, Plato's Socrates and Aristotle insisted that wonder is the foundation of philosophy.[68] Cavell (writing against the background of Wittgenstein, Heidegger, and others) urges us to regard the ordinary in the same light. *Beowulf* helps us to see the explanatory force of Cavell's view.

In a now-classic essay J. C. Higgitt set out decades ago to describe what he called 'the Roman background to Medieval England'. And 'background', at least when driven towards one of its modern philosophical inflections, really is the ideal term for the phenomenon sketched by Higgitt.[69] Higgitt describes at length just how much of Ancient Rome's work in Britain had remained visible throughout the Middle Ages. The stakes and explanatory power of this 'background' – that is, the question of

[67] A compelling sixteenth-century analogue to this moment in *Beowulf* is a notorious anachronism in William Shakespeare's *Titus Andronicus*. In Act 5, scene 1, a Goth poised to enter the ancient city of Rome reports a discovery: 'from our troops I stray'd / To gaze upon a ruinous monastery, / And as I earnestly did fix mine eye / Upon the wasted building, suddenly / I heard a child cry underneath a wall' (5.1.20–4). Aaron, in this same scene, associates the workings of conscience with 'twenty popish tricks and ceremonies' (5.1.76). The sight of a ruined monastery and the perceived danger of 'popish' impostures were common enough in 1590s England, but not in ancient Rome. It is tempting to read this passage as a curious piece of Reformation polemic. I regard it, however, as a moment in which Shakespeare's sense of the ordinariness of such sights has moved him to treat them as a part of the world's essential texture – here, there, perhaps everywhere to be imagined as an object of earnest gazes. On Renaissance England's 'new' ruins see Margaret Aston, 'English Ruins and English History: The Dissolution and the Sense of the Past', *Journal of the Warburg and Courtauld Institutes* 36 (1973), 231–55. The great printed testament to these institutions is William Dugdale's three-volume *Monasticon anglicanum* (1655–1673), in Latin. An abridged treatment, in English translation, was printed in 1693. On post-Reformation Catholics and Britain's monastic ruins see Walsham, *The Reformation of the Landscape*, 153–232.

[68] See Plato: 'μάλα γὰρ φιλοσόφου τοῦτο τὸ πάθος, τὸ θαυμάζειν· οὐ γὰρ ἄλλη ἀρχὴ φιλοσοφίας ἢ αὕτη' ('For this feeling of wonder shows that you are a philosopher, since wonder is the only beginning of philosophy'; *Theaetetus*, in *Theaetetus, Sophist*, ed. and trans. Harold North Fowler, LCL 123 (Cambridge, MA: Harvard University Press, 1921), 54–5 (155D)). See Aristotle: 'διὰ γὰρ τὸ θαυμάζειν οἱ ἄνθρωποι καὶ νῦν καὶ τὸ πρῶτον ἤρξαντο φιλοσοφεῖν' ('It is through wonder that men now begin and originally began to philosophize'; *Metaphysics*, ed. and trans. Hugh Tredennick, 2 vols. LCL 271, 287 (Cambridge, MA: Harvard University Press, 1933, 1935), vol. I, 12–13 (book I. ii.982b12-13)).

[69] J .C. Higgitt, 'The Roman Background to Medieval England', *Journal of the British Archaeological Association*, 3rd ser., 36 (1973), 1–15. Higgitt, too, pauses over the passage that interests Lerer and observes that Heorot's 'fāgne flōr' has been 'transposed from Britain to Denmark' (2).

what the very notion of a background permits and enables us to make sense of – are considerably larger than Higgitt's modest, but still important, conclusion that 'Bede and related accounts helped medieval readers to see Britain as part of that Roman world.'[70] The matter turns, roughly speaking, on the question of what sorts of significance can be attributed to the 'background', and on the relationship between human behaviour and the spaces in which we act and strive to make sense of the world.

This can be clarified by looking at the role of the background (i.e., the *Hintergrund*) in late Wittgenstein. As Wittgenstein establishes in one of the remarks collected in *Zettel*,

> Wie könnte man die menschliche Handlungsweise beschreiben? Doch nur, insofern man die Handlungen der verschiedenen Menschen, wie sie durcheinanderwimmeln, schilderte. Nicht, was *einer jetzt* tut, eine einzelne Handlung, sondern das ganze Gewimmel der menschlichen Handlungen, der Hintergrund, worauf wir jede Handlung sehen, bestimmt unser Urteil, unsere Begriffe und Reaktionen.[71]

> [How could human behaviour be described? Surely only by sketching the action of a variety of humans, as they are all mixed up together. What determines our judgment, our concepts and reactions, is not what *one* man is doing *now*, an individual action, but the whole hurly-burly of human actions, the background against which we see any action.]

The remarks collected in *Zettel* are drawn from a pair of typescripts known as TS 229 and TS 232. The remark cited above is further unfolded elsewhere in TS 232: 'Der Hintergrund ist das Getriebe des Lebens. Und unser Begriff bezeichnet etwas in *diesem* Getriebe' [The background is the bustle of life. And our concept points to something within *this* bustle].[72] In the remarks published under the title *Culture and Value*, Wittgenstein returns once again to this view of the *Hintergrund* not simply as some sort of neutral frame of reference for human activity, but rather as the totality of experiences and conditions that enable us to regard the world as intelligible:

70 Higgitt, 'The Roman Background', 8.

71 Wittgenstein, *Zettel*, ed. G. E. M. Anscombe and G. H. von Wright, trans. G. E. M. Anscombe (Oxford: Basil Blackwell, 1967), § 567. My understanding of the connection between Heidegger and Wittgenstein on the topic of the 'background' is derived from Hubert Dreyfus' reading of *Being and Time*. On this topic see Denis McManus, 'Rules, Regression and the "Background": Dreyfus, Heidegger and McDowell', *European Journal of Philosophy* 16 (2007), 432–58. See also Lee Braver, *Groundless Grounds: A Study of Wittgenstein and Heidegger* (Cambridge, MA: MIT Press, 2012).

72 Ludwig Wittgenstein, *Remarks on the Philosophy of Psychology*, ed. G. H. von Wright and Heikki Nyman, trans. C. G. Luckhardt and M. A. E. Aue, 2 vols. (Oxford: Basil Blackwell, 1980), vol. II, §625.

> Das Unaussprechbare (das, was mir geheimnisvoll erscheint und ich nicht auszusprechen vermag) gibt vielleicht den Hintergrund, auf dem das, was ich aussprechen konnte, Bedeutung bekommt.
>
> [Perhaps what is inexpressible (what I find mysterious and am not able to express) is the background against which whatever I could express has its meaning.][73]

Such a *Hintergrund* or 'background' makes it possible for us to see what we claim to see, to understand what we manifestly understand, to dwell in the world in which we find ourselves.

Having thrown himself into the depths of his poem – which is to say, into one of the pasts of his culture – the *Beowulf* poet surfaces with stray phrases that show us that his world stands upon a visible Roman substratum, and that this substratum helps make intelligible the poem's complex historical vision. The poem thereby takes in a vision of a past that does more than simply pierce the present in the way that unexpected flashes of memory, or even systematic historical inquiry, might do. Rather, the poet's vision entangles, structures, and supports past, present, and self all at once. We are not dealing here with folk memory or oral tradition, but rather with quotidian encounters with *facta* and *uestigia* that Rome had left in and on the soil. The monastic world in which the *Beowulf* manuscript was produced knew perfectly well that pagan Rome had built Britain's floors and foundations. This was, after all, the main locus in which Bede's *Historia* circulated and first achieved its fame. All this amounts to a vital precedent for Bodel's insistence that 'the matter of Rome' is 'de san aprenant', for quotidian encounters with Rome had enabled those who lived among its vestiges to perceive something like the roots of meaning itself, as the intellectual stakes of familiarity flash out in unexpected ways against a background to which we ourselves belong. The Anglo-Saxon present was encrusted with Rome's.

• *'The Ruin' and Its Ruins*

The fragmentary text of an Anglo-Saxon poem known to modern readers as 'The Ruin' offers further testimony to the power, durability, and scope of these considerations. It survives in a single manuscript – the so-called Exeter Book – that is roughly contemporaneous with the *Beowulf*

[73] Ludwig Wittgenstein, *Culture and Value*, ed. G. H. von Wright with Heikki Nyman, trans. Peter Winch, rev. 2nd edn. (Oxford: Basil Blackwell, 1980), 16-16e.

manuscript (*circa* 1000). The effort to recover something of the force and intellectual energy of this poem depends on properly grasping the circumstances under which Anglo-Saxons came to settle and rule most of what had been Britannia. Tim Eaton is an excellent guide to the nature and breadth of Anglo-Saxon encounters with the Roman past:

> When Roman troops were withdrawn from Britain at the beginning of the fifth century in response to insecurity at the heart of the empire, they left behind a landscape littered with settlements: small military outposts and large walled forts, humble farmsteads and sumptuous villas; unpretentious towns and monumental capitals. The native population of this period was inclined to inhabit timber-framed and sunken-floored buildings – indeed, the erection of secular buildings in stone did not recommence until the early eleventh century – so stone-built structures of the classical period were left to decay. However, from the late sixth century onwards some of the more important ecclesiastical buildings erected in England were manufactured from stone and/or brick. Until the late tenth century, the source of that building material was exclusively *spolia* from Roman ruins.

Eaton emphasizes that Anglo-Saxon builders energetically re-used what they found:

> Over the past 400 years or so more than 200 inscriptions and carvings have been identified in medieval contexts. Many of these were presumably recycled inadvertently, evocative remnants of a Roman civilisation that went unidentified when medieval labourers scoured ancient settlements for building stone. However, other pieces appear to have been selected intentionally and then been placed on display: Roman altars were adapted into medieval cross bases, fonts and other church furnishings; Roman milestones were reinvented as early British memorials; a variety of monument-types were embedded conspicuously in walls as plaques; and Roman coffins and tombstones were exhibited over post-Roman burials. There is no question that these carvings and inscriptions were meant to be seen, to be recognised as something alien to their medieval context.[74]

Scholars such as Michael G. Shapland emphasize that the Anglo-Saxons were timber-builders who had come to inhabit an island formerly ruled and administered by an empire committed to building its monumental architecture, as well as its public and private buildings, in stone.[75] We must

[74] Eaton, *Plundering the Past*, 133–4. On the wider context in which re-use was practiced see Michael Greenhalgh's *Marble Past, Monumental Present: Building with Antiquities in the Mediaeval Mediterranean* (Leiden: Brill, 2009).

[75] See Shapland, 'Meanings of Timber and Stone', 21–44.

work to imagine the drama of that cultural encounter if we are to come to terms with what is at stake in a poem such as 'The Ruin'.

The poem entangles poet and present, self and other, seer and seen, in a lone speaker's effort to describe a feature of the landscape that must have seemed alternately ordinary and wondrous to the poet and his audience.[76] The poem is commonly regarded as providing an image of the Aquae Sulis at Bath, but scholars nevertheless recognize that there is no way to determine which (or even whether any specific) site is intended. I cite the poem, or as much of it as is legible and susceptible to reconstruction, in full:

Wrætlic is þes wealstan – wyrde gebræcon,
burgstede burston; brosnað enta geweorc.
Hrofas sind gehrorene, hreorge torras,
hrungeat berofen, hrim on lime,
scearde scurbeorge scorene, gedrorene,
ældo undereotone. Eorðgrap hafað
waldendwyrhtan forweorone, geleorene,
heardgripe hrusan, oþ hund cnea
werþeoda gewitan. Oft þæs wag gebad
ræghar ond readfah rice æfter oþrum,
ofstonden under stormum; steap geap gedreas.
Worað giet se[. . . . .]num geheawen
felon [. . . . .]
grimme gegrunden [. . . . .
. . . . . .] scan heo [. . . . .
. . . . . .]g orþonc ærsceaft [. . . .
. . . .]g[.]. lamrindum beag
mod mo[nade m]yne swiftne gebrægd
hwætred in hringas, hygerof gebond
weallwalan wirum wundrum togædre.
Beorht wæron burgræced, burnsele monige,
heah horngestreon, heresweg micel,
meodoheall monig mondreama full,
oþþæt þæt onwende wyrd seo swiþe.
Crungon walo wide cwoman woldagas,
swylt eall fornom secgrofra wera;
wurdon hyra wigsteal westen staþolas,
brosnade burgsteall. Betend crungon
hergas to hrusan. Forþon þas hofu dreorgiað,
ond þæs teaforgeapa tigelum sceadeð
hrostbeages rof. Hryre wong gecrong

[76] See, once again, Higgitt's emphasis on just how much of Ancient Rome's work in Britain was still visible during the Middle Ages (*The Roman Background*, 1–4).

gebrocon to beorgum, þær iu beorn monig
glædmod ond goldbeorht gleoma gefrætwed,
wlonc ond wingal wighyrstum scan;
seah on sinc, on sylfor, on searogimmas,
on ead, on æt, on eorcanstan,
on þas beorhtan burg bradan rices.
Stanhofu stodan, stream hate wearp
widan wylme; weal eall befeng
beorhtan bosme, þær þa baþu wæron,
hat on hreþre. Þæt wæs hyðelic [þing].
Leton þonne geotan [. . . . .]
ofer harne stan hate streamas
un[. . . . .]
[o]þ þæt hringmere hate [. . . . . . .
. . . .] þær þa baþu wæron.
Þonne is [. . . . .
. . . . . .]re. Þæt is cynelic þing –
hu s[e. . . . .] burg [. .].[77]

[Wondrous is this wall's foundation – *wyrd* has broken
and shattered this city; the work of giants crumbles.
The roofs are ruined, the towers toppled,
frost in the mortar has broken the gate,
torn and worn and shorn by the storm,
eaten through with age. The earth's grasp
holds the builders, rotten, forgotten,
the hard grip of the ground, until a hundred
generations of men are gone.
This wall, rust-stained
and covered with moss, has seen one kingdom after another,
stood in the storm, steep and tall, then tumbled.
The foundation remains, felled by the weather,
it fell . . .
grimly ground up . . . .
. . . . . . cleverly created . . . .
. . . . . . a crust of mud surrounded . . .
. . . . ..put together a swift
and subtle system of rings; one of great wisdom
wondrously bound the braces together with wires.
Bright were the buildings, with many bath-houses,
high noble gables and a great noise of armies,

[77] I follow the text as it is reconstructed in Bernard Muir (ed.), *The Exeter Anthology of Old English Poetry: An Edition of Exeter Dean and Chapter MS 3501*, 2 vols., rev. 2nd edn. (University of Exeter Press, 2000), vol. I, 357–8.

many a meadhall filled with men's joys,
until mighty *wyrd* made an end to all that.
The slain fell on all sides, plague-days came,
and death destroyed all the brave swordsmen;
the seats of their idols became empty wasteland,
the city crumbled, its re-builders collapsed
beside their shrines. So now these courts are empty,
and the rich vaults of the vermilion roofs
shed their tiles. The ruins toppled to the ground,
broken into rubble, where once many a man
glad-minded, gold-bright, bedecked in splendor,
proud, full of wine, shone in his war-gear,
gazed on treasure, on silver, on sparkling gems,
on wealth, on possessions, on the precious stone,
on this bright capital of a broad kingdom.
  Stone buildings stood, the wide-flowing stream
threw off its heat; a wall held it all
in its bright bosom where the baths were,
hot in its core, a great convenience.
They let them gush forth . . . .
the hot streams over the great stones,
under . . .
  until the circular pool . . . hot . . .
  . . . .where the baths were.
Then . . .
. . . . . . .that is a noble thing,
how . . . .the city . . . .][78]

Nicholas Howe captures the poem's central dynamic when he characterizes it as being 'haunted with a meaning that can be articulated only through precise description'.[79] The poem appears to insist that such description would have to attend to the ongoing process by which a remarkable ('wrætlic') creation is being absorbed by the earth into an elemental order and made ordinary. The poem provides modern readers with a still-life, as it were, drawn from an otherwise dynamic and continuous process of absorption. If this process is in obvious ways destructive, it is also, in perhaps less obvious a way, susceptible to being read as a form of domestication to the world.[80] These ruins can therefore be described as emerging

[78] I cite R. M. Liuzza's translation of the text established by Bernard Muir: R. M. Liuzza (ed. and trans.) *Old English Poetry: An Anthology* (Peterborough: Broadview Press, 2014), 43–4.

[79] Howe, 'Inherited', 95. This proposition sets us down unexpectedly close to what Wittgenstein regards as the proper ambition of philosophy.

[80] For medieval perspectives see Patricia Dailey, 'Questions of Dwelling in Anglo-Saxon Poetry and Medieval Mysticism: Inhabiting Landscape, Body, and Mind', *New Medieval Literatures* 8 (2006),

into new forms of significance and intelligibility even as they retreat from view and utility. Frost and lichen have insinuated themselves into stone and mortar, and the earth has seized the ruined city's dead builders in its 'Eorðgrap'. There is a sharing-across of material and process, an obliteration of spaces that might enclose and separate, and an openness to the experience of the world and time. The ruins have become uninhabitable in the very process of having come more explicitly to dwell in the world.

As the disintegrating structure is altered in and by time, it prepares the ground for elegy. Time's passage, its work upon the world, is the poem's rhetorical occasion, but the fragment is most striking because of its poise and reticence. It is clearly working in dialogue with the *ubi sunt* topos, in which the absence of people and things is mourned, but the explicit ethical reflection we commonly expect to flow from such mourning remains unvoiced in the surviving fragment.[81] The poem, at least in the fragmentary form in which it survives, resists the temptation to moralize. This poetic fragment is remarkable chiefly because of its discipline in the face of matters that, to cite Dolven once again, do not mean but simply are. It is organized in such a way as to establish a delicate equilibrium. The wall, for example, has remained 'wrætlic' even in its current state as something broken by fatidic power ('wyrde gebræcon'). Characterized as the work of giants ('enta geweorc') rather than of master builders, the walls described in the poem are not merely stone but curved ('hwætred in hringas'). They have, in short, been granted all the monumental extravagance a stone-building culture could muster.

This ruined poem preserves, as its lyric moment, the poet's being startled into verse and reflection by the quotidian. Ruined Roman cities such as the one described here (again, it need not be Bath) dotted those sections of Britain that had been ruled by Rome. Later Anglo-Saxon and Norman builders quarried them to make some of their churches, but

175–214. My own analogue here is to a text that sits a long way from the scene of Anglo-Saxon England, but close to the heart of Cavell's conception of the ordinary. In *Walden* Henry David Thoreau describes his cabin as, in effect, 'a picture in outlines', with 'wide chinks' between the boards that make up its walls and leave it open to the air. He contrasts this new cabin, even in its unfinished state, with the tent he had previously inhabited: 'With this more substantial shelter about me, I had made some progress toward settling in the world' (*Walden*, in *A Week, Walden, The Maine Woods, Cape Cod*, ed. Robert F. Sayre (New York: Library of America, 1985), 389–90. What I want here is the view of a settlement in the world that is also a settlement or coming to terms with the world, and a view of openness to the air as a participation in the world.

[81] On the poem see Renée R. Trilling, 'Ruins in the Realms of Thoughts: Reading as Constellation in Anglo-Saxon Poetry', *Journal of English and Germanic Philology* 108 (2009), 141–67; Andy Orchard, 'Reconstructing "The Ruin"', in Virginia Blanton and Helene Scheck (eds.), *Intertexts: Studies in Anglo-Saxon Culture Presented to Paul E. Szarmach*, ed. (Tempe, ACMRS, 2008), 45–68.

even where they stood touched only by the work of the elements they remained, in a clear and almost intimate sense, familiar. Such phenomena are, to borrow a distinction from Heidegger, objects of concern rather than interpretation when they make up ordinary features of our surroundings.[82] These Roman ruins were present to the Anglo-Saxon imagination not as surface ornaments or embellishments, but rather as the world's exoskeleton. One of the labours of this fragmentary poem is to forge a language capable of confronting these ruins and easing them into the domain of thinking before finally returning them to their nest in the quotidian. This is the peekaboo of the ordinary: a game in which one alternately sees and does not see the ordinariness of the world as the mind transforms it into something both new and newly provocative. It is a game played across the centuries during which medieval writers encountered Rome's *facta* and *uestigia* as parts of their world.

Stones and Eggshells

This, then, is just some of what survives: coins, wooden writing tablets, glass shards, roads, mosaic floors, sword hilts, curses inscribed in lead and pewter (*defixiones*, as they are called), mile markers, carved stone, bells, ruined baths, altars, walls, amphitheatres, dykes, forts, combs, hairpins, urns, statues, and iron window grilles. Much of this teeming variety remains, as it must, *in situ*.[83] Much of it has scattered to museums, libraries, and private homes, where it has been preserved, displayed, or hidden under conditions ranging from temperature-controlled showcases to, presumably, unlabeled bags, cardboard boxes, and sock drawers in which unreported finds by searchers who are sometimes called 'nighthawks' have been squirreled away. None of it speaks, and the drama of its survival

[82] Heidegger asserts that, 'Die Gewinnung des phäenomenologischen Zugangs zu dem so begegnenden Seienden besteht vielmehr in der Abdrängung der sich andrängenden und mitlaufenden Auslegungstendenzen, die das Phänomen eines solchen "Besorgens" überhaupt verdecken und in eins damit erst recht das Seiende, *wie* es von ihm selbst her *im* Besorgen für es begegnet' (*SZ*, 67). ['The achieving of phenomenological access to the entities which we encounter, consists rather in thrusting aside our interpretative tendencies, which keep thrusting themselves upon us and running along with us, and which conceal not only the phenomenon of such "concern", but even more those entities themselves *as* encountered of their own accord *in* our concern with them'] (*BT*, 96). Our interpretative tendencies generate what Heidegger calls 'entangling errors' ('verfänglichen Mißgriffe') (*BT*, 96; *SZ*, 97).

[83] For an archaeological study that examines the material remains of Roman Britain in relation to patterns of quotidian use see Lindsay Allason-Jones (ed.), *Artefacts in Roman Britain: Their Purpose and Use* (Cambridge University Press, 2011).

involves fitful patterns of inquiry, re-use, accident, and bustle across many centuries.[84]

The conditions gathered here under the quadruple rubric of inquiry, re-use, accident, and bustle are commonly described otherwise: that is, as part of methodical programs (chiefly Renaissance humanism and antiquarian inquiry) whose genesis can be dated with considerable precision, and whose methods are usually treated as marking decisive departures from those of preceding ages. But Bede's subtle and deliberate engagements with the historical foundations of Rome's footprint in Britain have shown that these basic instincts, methods, and vocabularies are in place far earlier than is usually acknowledged.[85]

Still more importantly, the texts assembled here also show that an interplay between self-conscious wonder, on the one hand, and a sense of the ordinariness of the fact of Rome, on the other, can occur not just across wide stretches of time but even within individual texts. Rome's *facta* and *uestigia* are therefore quite precisely 'familiar' in the way that word can conjure up both everydayness and magical accompaniment. Because of this, I propose that a more nuanced understanding of what is at stake, or in play, in the reception of the fact of Rome can be achieved by ranging over a wide period of time and emphasizing the simultaneous interplay of certain forms of continuity and oscillation, rather than by narrowing the investigative focus in a hunt for texts, or even decades, that might be treated as inaugurating decisive change. Most importantly, however, the material surveyed in this chapter supplies a prehistory for strains that continue to lurk within Renaissance encounters with the fact of Rome.

To proceed in this manner is to retell the story of the reception of Rome across the Middle Ages and Renaissance as a sequence of shifting – sometimes radical, sometimes subtle, but in any case ceaselessly repeatable and reversible – reorientations towards the ordinary. To this end, this chapter has tried to show that many aspects of the basic interests and casts of mind associated with Renaissance humanism's historical imagination

[84] The view that these discoveries entail dialogues between present and past is the central argument in Schwyzer, *Archaeologies of English Renaissance Literature*.

[85] Paul Avis has argued, for example, that Renaissance humanism emerges from the methodical cultivation of a 'basic feeling for the pastness of the past' (*Foundations of Modern Historical Thought: From Machiavelli to Vico* (New York: Routledge, 2016), 10). There can be no denying that this same 'basic feeling' is laboriously cultivated in Bede, whose *Historia* helped establish standards of historicist rigour that were admired during the Middle Ages, Renaissance, and beyond. Avis' phrasing has its roots in T. S. Eliot's assertion, in 'Tradition and the Individual Talent', that 'the historical sense involves a perception, not only of the pastness of the past, but of its presence' (*Selected Essays* (London: Faber and Faber, 1999), 14).

weave their way through Gildas and Bede, through Lerer's arguments about the significance of the 'fāgne flōr' in *Beowulf*, through 'The Ruin', and into the sorts of architectural practises of re-use catalogued by Tim Eaton and others.

With this backdrop in place, the remainder of this chapter will move towards, and then finally beyond, the late sixteenth century – in effect, encircling the period flagged by Richard Hingley as marking the dawn of 'a self-critical and conscious appreciation of the classical writings that addressed Britain', and of a new recognition of 'the value of past objects and sites'.[86] The goal of this move is not to establish breaks but rather rhythms of continuity, and to show that attitudes towards what gets dug up are equally complex on either side of those decades. My dual contention is that the forms of 'self-conscious and critical' engagement Hingley sees as having been inaugurated by late sixteenth-century humanism and antiquarianism are already flourishing centuries earlier in medieval responses to Rome, and that they move hand-in-hand with an acceptance of the ordinariness of Rome's *facta* and *uestigia*. These oscillations, in turn, continue well into the seventeenth century, when the reception of Roman Britain is still frequently, perhaps almost inescapably, a method of encountering and constituting the self (rather than an objective and methodical process of reconstituting the past), and a spur to thinking about the terms in which we allow the world to disclose itself to us.

An example of these reorientations can be detected in finds of ancient coins. Old Roman coins had been found throughout the Middle Ages in Britain.[87] What changes, though, during the sixteenth century, is in some sense the collection of attitudes towards the quotidian nature of those finds – which is to say, attitudes towards what commonly gets dug up – as discoverers of coins begin either cataloguing their finds or passing them along to men who would catalogue them.[88] What was new behaviour in the world of numismatics, however, was not at all new to other modes of

86 Hingley, *The Recovery of Roman Britain*, 2.

87 See Richard Kelleher, 'The Re-use of Coins in Medieval England and Wales c.1050–1550: An Introductory Survey', *Yorkshire Numismatist* 4 (2012), 183–200.

88 On the early modern 'archaeological economy' see especially D. R. Woolf, *The Social Circulation of the Past: English Historical Culture, 1500–1730* (Oxford University Press, 2003), 221–56. With respect to coins Woolf hovers between two possibilities: 'in the sixteenth century such discoveries either became more commonplace or were at least much more frequently recorded' (232). He asserts that 'In many cases there were middlemen, as someone other than the initial discoverer was responsible for saving the item and eventually bringing it to an antiquarian's attention' (224). Woolf notes, further, that the so-called discoveries of sixteenth- and seventeenth-century antiquaries were often wholly reliant on what was already 'common knowledge' among locals (223–4).

relation and response to the past. Similar patterns of reorientation, for example, have been catalogued by Eaton with respect to the re-use by Anglo-Saxon builders of stone quarried from Roman buildings. First, Eaton (as in the passages already cited from his work) shows that Anglo-Saxon re-use of Roman stonework from the seventh to the eleventh centuries frequently looks very much like the sorts of 'self-critical and conscious' engagements that Hingley sees as beginning during the later sixteenth century. Second, Eaton demonstrates that Anglo-Saxon builders were sometimes moved to distant sites to secure particular Roman stones when other sources of Roman stonework were unquestionably closer and more near-to-hand. Each of these reveals a self-critical and conscious engagement with the Roman past many centuries earlier than conventional wisdom would have it.

Eaton persuasively argues that Anglo-Saxon builders were making deliberate selections among various sources of Roman stone.[89] Though it would be impossible to give more than the most narrow view of the enormous number of examples of significant re-use discussed by Eaton, structural and decorative stone is redeployed prominently and to obvious decorative effect at St Mary's Church, Reculver, at St Martin's, Canterbury, at St Pancras', London, in the keep at Chepstow castle, and at numerous other sites whose remains can be confidently dated to the Anglo-Saxon and Norman periods. Eaton notes many instances where Roman inscriptions have been pointedly and visibly integrated into the walls of medieval churches. He spends considerable time cataloguing and discussing the conversion of ancient Roman altars into church fonts, stoups, and piscinas. He takes pains to show that Christian altars (for example) were sometimes reworked so as to preserve, and leave conspicuous, their original pagan dedicatory inscriptions. He notes fascinating cases of the conversion of ancient pagan altars into monumental cross bases at Corbridge and at St Oswald-in-Lee.[90]

[89] Eaton, *Plundering the Past*, *passim*. Eaton speaks of the 'iconic use' of Roman materials by Anglo-Saxon builders, borrowing the term from D. Stocker and P. Everson, 'Rubbish Recycled: A Study of the Re-use of Stone in Lincolnshire', in D. Parsons (ed.), *Stone Quarrying and Building in England, A.D. 43–1525* (Chichester: Phillimore & Co.), 83–101. A foundational case for deliberate, ideologically motivated re-use of Roman stone is Higgitt, 'Roman Background'. See also R. Cramp, 'The Anglo-Saxons and Rome', *Transactions of the Architectural and Archaeological Society of Durham and Northumberland*, n.s. 3 (1974), 27–37.

[90] An important early essay on these topics is R. K. Morris and Julia Roxan, 'Churches on Roman Buildings', in W. Rodwell (ed.), *Temples, Churches and Religion: Recent Research in Roman Britain*, BAR British Series 77 (1980), 175–209. See also John F. Potter, 'The Occurrence of Roman Brick and Tile in Churches of the London Basin', *Britannia* 32 (2001), 119–42; Tyler Bell, 'Churches on Roman Buildings: Christian Associations and Roman Masonry in Anglo-Saxon England', *Medieval Archaeology* 42 (1998), 1–18.

Most remarkable is the well-known site of the Anglo-Saxon crypt at Hexham, constructed at the instigation of Wilfrid, who figures prominently in Bede's *Historia* as a respected authority (and as a traveler to Rome). Seven Roman altars, two dedication stones, a gigantic tombstone, and large amounts of both structural and decorative Roman stonework were redeployed in the construction of the crypt. Eaton observes that 'the re-use of Roman inscriptions and carvings in Hexham Abbey is on a scale that is unprecedented elsewhere in Britain'.[91] This was not, he insists, slapdash or accidental work. He proposes that Wilfrid's 'abbey builders must have targeted the monumental structures that lay at the heart' of the nearby Roman fort of Coria. This would mean that 'a conscious decision had been made to ignore the humble structures on the periphery in favour of the monumental ruins of public buildings at the centre'.[92] Hexham is only the most remarkable instance of a tendency visible across the full range of early Christian churches and minsters in what had been Roman Britannia.[93] As David Stocker has emphasized, only a particular brand of hyperbolic rigour could regard these forms of re-use as anything other than self-critical and conscious: 'It would be naively patronising to think that the medieval mind would not have perceived the symbolic significance' of this kind of 'transportation and "conversion"' of material from a pagan to a Christian context.[94]

Selecting among and dismantling (rather than cataloguing) the remains of the past, and then displaying those remains, cannot simply be regarded as uncritical and unconscious – or, for that matter, purely destructive – work. Nor can it be regarded as work that fails to take into account the potential value (for value can be conceived of in multiple ways) of those remains. It is far from clear that it was ignorant, naïve, or uncritical to dismantle a Roman building in order to build a church or granary. My own suggestion will be that we ought not to look for a watershed moment (whether that be, as in Hingley, the later sixteenth century, or at any other discrete historical moment) at which a suddenly 'self-critical and conscious appreciation', or properly calibrated valuation of objects, defines forever the afterlife of Roman Britain. Nor should we

[91] Eaton, *Plundering the Past*, 116. [92] Eaton, *Plundering the Past*, 121, 122.

[93] See, on this topic, Paul Bidwell, 'A Survey of the Anglo-Saxon Crypt at Hexham and its Reused Roman Stonework', *Archaeologia Aeliana: Miscellaneous Tracts Relating to Antiquity*, 5th ser., 39 (2010), 53–145; Robert Coates-Stephens, 'Epigraphy as Spolia: The Reuse of Inscriptions in Early Medieval Buildings', *Papers of the British School at Rome* 70 (2002), 275–96.

[94] See David Stocker, '*Fons et Origo*: The Symbolic Death, Burial and Resurrection of English Font Stones', *Church Archaeology*, 1 (1997), 17–25, cited in Eaton, *Plundering the Past*, 67.

accept that such a moment could have come so late as the final decades of the sixteenth century. We ought rather to speak of a long stretch of many centuries during which the forms of life, practices, and postures adopted towards the ordinary and familiar were fitfully reoriented and re-calibrated as individuals found themselves alternately accepting the ordinariness of what they saw, and feeling goaded into thought, systematic classification, re-use, and reinvention. Each of these reactions occurs early. Each occurs late.

This is something different from the complex relationships to the Roman past brilliantly charted by Leonard Barkan in his *Unearthing the Past*. There, Barkan argues persuasively that sixteenth-century discoverers lovingly preserved the notion of the marvellous nature of the things that they had found – strategically protecting themselves, he suggests, from the knowledge that ancient Rome lay beneath Renaissance Rome.[95] In Britain, by contrast, there is a more energetic disowning of what had long been the perennial ordinariness of the objects being found. Long lived with as aspects of the inhabited world, the world that lay out in the open, these objects are programmatically estranged and made paradoxically unavailable by the process of finding and cataloguing them. But standing over and against such an approach, many medieval and Renaissance texts alike persuasively adumbrate the ways in which the fact of Rome – its past, its present, its residual traces – insinuates itself into the individual's relationship to the ordinary.

Though the chronological leap is gigantic I want to turn to a 1658 meditation by Sir Thomas Browne, titled *Hydriotaphia*. In this treatise, Browne is driven into his gorgeous, searching prose by the unearthing of a group of sepulchral urns at Norfolk. Historical error fuels Browne's project as he writes *sub specie Romae*:

> In a Field of old *Walsingham*, not many moneths past, were digged up between fourty and fifty Urnes, deposited in a dry and sandy soile, not a yard deep, nor farre from one another: Not all strictly of one figure, but most answering these described: Some containing two pounds of bones, distinguishable in skulls, ribs, jawes, thigh-bones, and teeth, with fresh impressions of their combustion. Besides the extraneous substances like peeces of small boxes, or combes handsomely wrought, handles of small brasse instruments, brazen nippers, and in one some kinde of *Opale*.[96]

[95] See Barkan's first chapter, 'Discoveries', for the story of 'the conditions that made discovery possible and gave it meanings' (Barkan, *Unearthing the Past*, 17).
[96] Browne, *Hydriotaphia*, 274.

The treatise, like the urns themselves, is full of quotidian objects. Browne will return more than once to that alluring opal, but he is for the most part less interested in jewels and luxury urn-goods than he is in combs, small boxes, 'Iron pins', remains of the 'necks or Bridges of Musicall Instruments', 'long brasse plates overwrought like the handles of neat implements', and those 'brazen nippers to pull away hair'.[97] These are, as far as Browne is concerned, the residual traces of ancient Rome's footprint in Britain: the ashes and urns, he says, of '*Romanes*, or *Brittains Romanized*'. Browne's text is, among other things, a meditation on the personal and intellectual stakes of having spent a lifetime internalizing Roman ingenuity: of having had Rome's words and stories in his mouth forever, and of having lived with the ashes of its men and women beneath his feet.[98]

Browne is, by the way, wrong about the attribution. The urns have long been securely identified as Saxon, rather than Roman, work. But the error is, for Browne as well as for his latter-day readers, a fortuitous one, since it supplies him with a meditative opportunity for which he has been perfectly trained by both education and inclination.[99] Indeed, Browne makes precisely the kind of error that the humanistic pedagogical dispensation could generate. After all, Polydore Vergil, Bishop John Jewel, and Inigo Jones had all concluded that Stonehenge was a Roman ruin.[100] Browne's mistaken sense that the urns are Roman acts as a valve that opens up, and determines the content and direction of, a flow of words and meditations on Rome, Britain, mortality, and the nature of the self. Above all, his conviction that they are Roman provides him with a keen sense of the place of the Roman past and present within fantasies of self-constitution

[97] Browne, *Hydriotaphia*, 280. [98] Browne, *Hydriotaphia*, 283.

[99] See Graham Parry, 'Thomas Browne and the Uses of Antiquity' in Reid Barbour and Claire Preston (eds.), *Sir Thomas Browne: The World Proposed* (Oxford University Press, 2008), 63–79.

[100] See Walsham, *Reformation of the Landscape*, 297–300. Polydore Vergil regarded Stonehenge as a monument commemorating the death of Ambrosius Aurelianus, who figures as an aristocratic Roman survival and military leader in Gildas. Jewel believed that the Romans had arranged the monumental stones in the form of yokes. Jones' theory, preserved in Inigo Jones, *The most notable antiquity of Great Britain, vulgarly called Stone-Heng on Salisbury plain. Restored by Inigo Jones Esquire, architect generall to the late King* (London, 1655) [Wing J954], is particularly relevant to Browne's error, arising as it does from what Jones calls 'the intricate, and obscure study of *Antiquity*' (B1^{v}). Jones describes Stonehenge as the vestiges of a Roman temple whose refinement and precision he attempts to reconstruct in a striking series of images. 'Order' is a kind of watchword in the treatise (its various forms appear more than seventy times), and Jones insists that Stonehenge could only be the product of the labours of 'grand masters in the Art of building, and liberall sciences' (B4^{v}). In Jones' eyes the very existence of the monument presupposes the magnificent totality of the Roman socio-intellectual world. For a recent assessment of Jones' work see Ryan Roark, '"Stonehenge in the Mind" and "Stonehenge on the Ground": Reader, Viewer, and Object in Inigo Jones' *Stone-Heng Restored* (1655)', *Journal of the Society of Architectural Historians* 77 (2018), 285–99.

and self-discipline: 'we', says Browne, as though still in the grips of his own schooldays, 'have enough to do to make up our selves from present and passed times, and the whole stage of things scarce serveth for our instruction'.[101]

The world that Browne conjures up in this endlessly alluring and hymn-like text is filled with inquiries into religion, mortality, and physical laws, but it really is vital to him that those urns be Roman. I take this to be the case not because, as Philip Schwyzer has argued, Browne is reluctant to intervene in highly charged contemporary debates about Germanic settlement in Britain, but because he wants the urns to be relics of a Roman past that still exerts, against all odds, an enduring influence on any individual's situatedness in the world: 'Unto these of our Urnes none here can pretend relation . . . But remembring the early civility they brought upon these Countreys, and forgetting long passed mischiefs: We mercifully preserve their bones, and pisse not upon their ashes.'[102] He wants them to be Roman – or in any case instinctively accepts that they are – because he is hungry to speak on behalf of a past that still exerts an enduring shape on his understanding of his relationship to his own body, to the words that flow from it, to the created world into which those words flow, and to time itself. Browne's remarks here can stand as a final record of the energy with which Rome insinuates itself not just into arts of rhetoric, rules of reason, and conceptions of nationhood, but into the thinking individual's effort to grasp the problem of the self, and into the processes by which individuals care for their bodies and make themselves at home in the world, surrounded by pins, combs, boxes, and 'brazen nippers to pull away hair'.

It is at once striking and natural that so many of medieval and Renaissance England's texts, spaces, and institutions understood themselves as being haunted by the spectre of Rome, from the seventh-century Anglo-Saxon crypt at Hexham Abbey in the north-east of England, where decorative Roman stones, ancient dedicatory inscriptions, and pagan altars have been conspicuously redeployed, to 'the bare ruined choirs' that stand as records of another, equally vivid encounter with a rather different version of Rome in Shakespeare's 'Sonnet 73'. It is still more striking that for writers as different as the anonymous maker of the Anglo-Saxon poem now known as 'The Ruin' and the seventeenth-century doctor Sir Thomas Browne, Rome constitutes, in the broadest possible sense of that verb, the self and its place in the world. Because of this, to strive to view Rome at or from a distance is less an act of supposedly modern, disinterested intellectual rigour than it is a form of attenuated introspection and scrutiny

[101] Browne, *Hydriotaphia*, 265. [102] Browne, *Hydriotaphia*, 265.

in which the self hunts for the foundations of its phenomenological entanglement in the world. This hunt is, moreover, a form of life that stretched back many centuries earlier than is commonly accepted by scholars of the Renaissance and later periods. To strive to escape from such a Rome would be to escape, or yearn to escape, from the self. That yearning is one of the subjects of Chapter 2.

In an important essay on the subject of burial practices, Howard Williams emphasizes that Anglo-Saxons encountered ancient monuments 'during the routines of everyday life, and that these associations were not static but altered over time'.[103] Williams thus emphasizes the openness and regularity of these encounters in ways to which Bede himself testifies repeatedly. Williams goes still further in tentatively suggesting that the Anglo-Saxon dead 'were deliberately placed in the landscape in order to symbolize and maintain relationships with ancient monuments'.[104] To cast this as a relationship, and therefore as something that can be nurtured and maintained, is to emphasize the importance of the everydayness of these encounters as well as their importance to the individual's efforts to make a home of the world.

The story of the *facta* and *uestigia* of Rome, then, is perpetually a story of re-use: one that figures re-use as a deeply significant and perhaps quintessentially human form of life. The category of the human, then, might be described not only, as Kenneth Burke (answering and extending Aristotle's image of the human as the animal that reasons) puts it in a classic study, 'the symbol using animal', but also as the animal that re-uses or, more accurately, understands itself as re-using in a significant manner.[105] The instinct to re-use, and the ability to conceptualize certain forms of life as re-use, is meaningfully human, and it enables us to see that the terms in which the Renaissance is still commonly described might actually be regarded as helping to constitute our shared humanity – so long as the Renaissance not be seen as the cradle of these practices and casts of mind. Those practices and casts of mind were, as Tyler Bell has shown, already deeply constitutive of the Anglo-Saxon culture's understanding of itself as living within the fact of Rome.[106]

103 Howard Williams, 'Ancient Landscapes and the Dead: The Reuse of Prehistoric and Roman Monuments as Early Anglo-Saxon Burial Sites', *Medieval Archaeology* 41 (1997), 25.

104 Williams, 'Ancient Landscapes', 25.

105 Kenneth Burke, *Language as Symbolic Action: Essays on Life, Language, and Method* (Berkeley: University of California Press, 1968), 3.

106 Tyler Bell, *The Religious Reuse of Roman Structures in Early Medieval England* (Oxford: Archaeopress, 2005).

Having moved from Gildas to Browne, this chapter will conclude by stepping backwards once again to material in Bede's *Historia*. For when Bede speaks of the construction of stone churches in Britain, he describes them as having been built 'morem Romanorum' (that is, 'in the manner of the Romans'):

> Sed et architectos sibi mitti petiit, qui iuxta morem Romanorum ecclesiam de lapide in gente ipsius facerent, promittens hanc in honorem beati apostolorum principis dedicandam; se quoque ipsum cum suis omnibus morem sanctae Romanae et apostolicae ecclesiae semper imitaturum, in quantum dumtaxat tam longe a Romanorum loquella et natione segregati hunc ediscere potuissent.[107]
>
> [He [i.e., Nechtan, King of the Picts] also asked for builders to be sent to build a church of stone in their country after the Roman fashion, promising that it should be dedicated in honour of the blessed chief of the apostles. He also said that he and all his people would always follow the customs of the holy Roman and apostolic Church, so far as they could learn them, remote though they were from the Roman people and from their language.]

The story told here by Bede attests to the durable fantasy that past and future, distant and domestic, self and world, could be made coterminous under the name Rome.[108] Michael Shapland puts the matter quite plainly: 'the Christian Church *was* Roman; therefore a masonry church *was* a Roman building, especially if it was made with Roman stone, regardless of its objective age'. Calculations of this kind, he emphasizes, 'placed the very concept of stone at the heart of Roman Christendom'.[109]

The fact of Rome was appropriated and transformed not simply for ideological or political ends, but for the purpose of making a home for the body in the world. This is true both in life and in death, as Bede's account of the search for a means of properly burying St Æthelthryth makes clear. Bede's narrative of her life and death was extremely influential. His depiction of her as a vital figure in the development of the Anglo-Saxon Church

107 *HE*, 532–3. Singing, too, is performed 'iuxta morem Romanorum' in *HE*, 206–7. Colgrave's note on this phrase and the type of singing it describes is instructive: 'What the system of church music was that he taught, and how it differed from the earlier (perhaps Irish) system, is a matter of conjecture' (207 n.1). The phrase 'morem Romanorum' is also used by Bede in the *Historia Abbatum*.

108 On the ideological work of architecture in establishing these connections see Eric Cambridge, 'The Architecture of the Augustinian Mission', in Richard Gameson (ed.), *St Augustine and the Conversion of England* (Stroud: Sutton, 1999), 202–36. Nechtan's ambitions here return him, metaphorically, to the origins of his people. T. M. Charles-Edwards regards the very existence of the Picts (in their status as a federation of peoples beyond the northern walls) as a 'political effect of the Roman frontier' (*Wales and the Britons*, 35).

109 Shapland, 'Meanings of Timber and Stone', 30.

contributed directly to both the popularity and longevity of her cult.[110] Æthelthryth had entered a monastery after the death of her husband, King Ecgfrith. She lived on for some dozen years, and then, another sixteen years after her death, the Abbess Æbbe determined that the virtuous woman's corpse deserved a more dignified and enduring home than the one it had received at the time of her death:

> Qui ascensa naui (ipsa enim regio Elge undique est aquis ac paludibus circumdata, neque lapides maiores habet) uenerunt ad ciuitatulam quan/dam desolatam non procul inde sitam, quae lingua Anglorum Grantacaestir uocatur, et mox inuenerunt iuxta muros ciuitatis locellum de marmore albo pulcherrime factum, operculo quoque similis lapidis aptissime tectum. Vnde intellegentes a Domino suum iter esse prosperatum, gratias agentes rettulerunt ad monasterium.[111]

> [So they got into a boat (for the district of Ely is surrounded on all sides by waters and marshes and has no large stones) and came to a small deserted fortress not far away which is called *Grantacæstir* (Cambridge) in English, and near the walls of the fortress they soon found a coffin beautifully made of white marble, with a close-fitting lid of the same stone. Realizing that the Lord had prospered their journey, they brought it back to the monastery.]

The corpse of the now-sainted Æthelthryth has not mouldered in death but rather flowered back into health and beauty. Her original grave clothes, and even the original coffin, perform miraculous acts of healing, so that the bringing to light once again of Æthelthryth's body is seen as an act of extraordinary auspiciousness. Another miracle occurs: when she is newly laid to rest, the repurposed Roman sarcophagus makes room for her:

> Lauerunt igitur uirgines corpus, et nouis indutum uestibus intulerunt in ecclesiam, atque in eo quod adlatum erat sarcofago posuerunt, ubi usque hodie in magna ueneratione habetur. Mirum uero in modum ita aptum corpori uirginis sarcofagum inuentum est, ac si ei specialiter praeparatum fuisset, et locus quoque capitis seorsum fabrefactus ad mensuram capitis illius aptissime figuratus apparuit.[112]

> [So the maidens washed her body, wrapped it in new robes, carried it into the church, and placed it in the sarcophagus which they had brought, where it is held in great veneration to this day. This sarcophagus was found to fit the virgin's body in a wonderful way, as if it had been specially prepared for

[110] The best guide is Virginia Blanton, *Signs of Devotion: The Cult of St. Æthelthryth in Medieval England, 695–1615* (University Park, PA: Penn State University Press, 2007).
[111] *HE*, 394–5. [112] *HE*, 396–7.

> her; and the place for the head, which was cut out separately, seemed to be exactly shaped to its size.]

Two main points can be emphasized here. First, Bede is once again keen to underscore that Rome's *facta* and *uestigia* had remained in view to his own day ('usque hodie in magna ueneratione habetur'). As in so many other instances, therefore, the reception of Bede's highly influential text involves the reception of the view that Rome is persistent and conspicuous. Second, Bede is unfolding a providential plot in which what Rome has left behind in Britain seems to have been fitted exactly, as though before the fact and by design, to the needs of those who, in the present, long to make a home for themselves in life and in death.[113] Virginia Blanton's remarks on this passage are apt: 'Bede says "it" is held in great veneration, presumably referring to the body. But by now the body is associated with the sarcophagus and its perfect fit. The sarcophagus becomes an extension of the body worthy of veneration.'[114]

The most suitable gloss on these activities may be the reflection by Browne cited earlier, where he observed that 'we have enough to do to make up our selves from present and passed times, and the whole stage of things scarce serveth for our instruction'. To 'make up our selves from present and passed times' is not a matter of systematically conceptualizing the self, but rather of making a home for it in the world and making a fact of its situatedness – even, in a sense, a matter of accepting the world *as though* it had been made to accommodate us. To regard oneself as being entangled among, and absorbed into, the facts and vestiges of Rome, extending those terms to everything from ruined buildings to the Latin language (that is, to all that plural Romes had left in their wake in Britain) is one of the means by which individuals acknowledge the world and make a home there. One of the early injunctions against the Germanic pagans (whom Bede derides as worshippers of carved sticks and stones) is the Northumbrian King Oswiu's attempt to make the East Saxon King Sigeberht realize that 'deos esse non posse, qui hominum manibus facti essent' ('objects made by the hands of men could not be gods').[115] And yet, those *facti*, as Bede calls them – those objects made by hand, false gods though they may be – grant us an important part of our hold on the world.

[113] For another miraculous fit between a dead Anglo-Saxon body and a stone sarcophagus see *HE*, 366–9. Colgrave proposes that Roman sarcophagi served as models for house-shaped Christian shrines during the early Middle Ages (346 n. 1).

[114] Blanton, *Signs of Devotion*, 52 n. 84.

[115] *HE*, 280–1, echoing Acts 19:26. See Chapter 3 for a discussion of the importance of the biblical Book of the Acts of the Apostles in establishing an orientation towards Rome.

Over and over, Bede surveys the remains of Rome and tells his readers about the disparate Roman objects and efforts that have survived to be seen 'usque hodie'. This is one of two important categories of objects whose persistent visibility is an important matter for Bede. The other is, not surprisingly, made up of the specific edifices of the Roman Church in Britain. These have, like the first version of Rome to arrive on the shores of Britain, survived to become significant features of the inhabited world. A single example can stand here for a large number of sites and objects described in the *Historia*:

> Ostenditur autem usque hodie et in magna ueneratione habetur locus ille, ubi uenturus ad hanc pugnam Osuald signum sanctae crucis erexit, ac flexis genibus Deum deprecatus est, ut in tanta rerum necessitate suis cultoribus caelesti succurreret auxilio. Denique / fertur quia facta citato opere cruce, ac fouea praeparata in qua statui deberet, ipse fide feruens hanc arripuerit ac foueae inposuerit atque utraque manu erectam tenuerit, donec adgesto a militibus puluere terrae figeretur.[116]
>
> [The place is still shown today and is held in great veneration where Oswald, when he was about to engage in battle, set up the sign of the holy cross and, on bended knees, prayed God to send heavenly aid to His worshippers in their dire need. In fact it is related that when a cross had been hastily made and the hole dug in which it was to stand, he seized the cross himself in the ardour of his faith, placed it in the hole, and held it upright with both hands until the soldiers had heaped up the earth and fixed it in position.]

This wooden cross marks a commitment to God by memorializing the significance of a particular intersection of time, space, and human effort. To the extent that ruined stone buildings, roads, lighthouses, and monumental crosses are facets of the fact of Rome, Rome itself can stand provisionally as a name for the world in which inhabitants of the island of Britain, from Gildas and Bede to Sir Thomas Browne and beyond, understood themselves to be living out their lives and making up their selves.

[116] *HE*, 214–15. Colgrave proposes that this early conversion-era cross may have served as a model for the standing stone crosses of the later Anglo-Saxon period. Shapland asserts that by means of these later crosses, 'The idea of Rome was broadcast in the landscape, with stone crosses copying Roman sculptural forms and commonly erected at sites of Roman occupation' (Colgrave, 'Meanings of Timber and Stone', 28–9). See on this topic Jane Hawkes, '*Iuxta Morem Romanorum*: Stone and Sculpture in Anglo-Saxon England', in C. E. Karkov and G. H. Brown (eds.), *Anglo-Saxon Styles* (Albany: State University of New York Press, 2003), 69–99. Hawkes emphasizes that 'By setting these monuments firmly within definable centers of Roman activity, those responsible for their production would seem to have been deliberately reclaiming and appropriating that which was Rome in order to establish it as part of the new Rome of Christ' (82).

CHVRCH OF ENGLAND. The firſt booke. 31

The firſt face, ſhewe, and maner of preaching the ghoſpel to vs Engliſhmen, by S. Auguſtin our Apoſtle, in the preſence of Elbert then kinge of kent &c, An. 596.

H 3 all thin-

Figure 1.1 From *The history of the Church of Englande. Compiled by Venerable Bede, Englishman. Translated out of Latin in to English by Thomas Stapleton student in diuinite* (Antwerp, 1565), H3^{r} [STC 1778]. Image courtesy of the British Library.

Bede's Latin was first translated into early modern English by an exiled Catholic theologian named Thomas Stapleton, a little more than thirty years after the Henrician break with Rome.[117] Stapleton's translation, printed in 1565 at Antwerp and dedicated to Queen Elizabeth, was accompanied by a handful of images, one of which depicts the decisive moment of Augustine's mission to Æthelberht's kingdom. (See Figure 1.1.) A cross with pendant standard reaches diagonally across the image's two planes, which are otherwise sharply divided by a horizontal line. Dressed in finery that is a long way from what we would expect of late sixth-century Kent, Æthelberht and his court fill the upper half of the frame. Almost every bit of this upper half of the image is stuffed with detail and cross-hatching. By way of contrast, Augustine and the co-partners in his mission dominate, but do not fill, the bottom half of the image. This section is notable for its strikingly sculptural handling of the Roman missionaries, and for the way their figures are distributed within the white space of the bottom half of the image.

The image, emerging as it does from the Counter-Reformation world of the 1560s Low Countries, is reasserting precisely the story that Bede's *Historia* had been telling since 731: namely, that Augustine's mission was a kind of emanation from the Roman substratum that was always-already beneath Æthelberht's feet. In this image, two groups of men of the late sixth century have come face-to-face. The compositional logic of the image, however, suggests that one of these groups possesses an authority that is at once divine and chthonic, and that the white space inhabited by Augustine and his men had somehow always been beneath the floorboards of Æthelberht's world.

117 See Marvin R. O'Connell, *Thomas Stapleton and the Counter Reformation* (New Haven: Yale University Press, 1964); Paul J. Stapleton, 'Pope Gregory and the *Gens Anglorum*: Thomas Stapleton's Translation of Bede', *Renaissance Papers* (2008), 15–34.

CHAPTER 2

The Self

Ranging widely across medieval and, to a much lesser extent, early modern texts, Chapter 1 promulgated a view of Rome as perpetually familiar and available rather than mysterious and decisively alien. I argued that the persistence in Britain of the Roman Empire's material remains influenced by the terms in which writers as different as Gildas, Bede, and Sir Thomas Browne experienced and expressed their situatedness in the world. The chapter's lines of inquiry thereby began to connect, even if only in a preliminary fashion, the fact of Rome to the problem of the self.

Chapter 2 turns explicitly to that topic, but now with a consistent emphasis on sixteenth- and seventeenth-century writers and texts. My principal focus is on English writers ranging from Edmund Spenser to John Milton, but English perspectives on Rome were mediated to a significant extent by Continental writers such as Petrarch, Joachim Du Bellay, and Michel Eyquem de Montaigne. Writers trained within (and in Petrarch's case, actively forging) the traditions of humanist inquiry celebrated their commitment to returning *ad fontes*. In practice, however, their engagements with a 'text' as complex and ramified as Rome risked leaving them endlessly navigating tributary brooks, creeks, streams, and rivers rather than reposing comfortably at the source.

This chapter's understanding of the problem of the self is influenced by Søren Kierkegaard's riddling assertion that 'The self is a relation that relates itself to itself' ('Selvet er et Forhold, der forholder sig til sig selv').[1] This

[1] Establishing this view of the self is Kierkegaard's opening move in *The Sickness Unto Death: A Christian Psychological Exposition for Upbuilding and Awakening*, ed. and trans. Howard V. Hong and Edna H. Hong, Kierkegaard's Writings 19 (Princeton University Press, 1983): 'The self is a relation that relates itself to itself or is the relation's relating itself to itself in the relation; the self is not the relation but is the relation's relating itself to itself' (13); 'Selvet er et Forhold, der forholder sig til sig selv, eller er det i Forholdet, at Forholdet forholder sig til sig selv; Selvet er ikke Forholdet, men at Forholdet forholder sig til sig selv') (*Sygdommen til Døden*, in *Søren Kierkegaards Skrifter* (*SKS*), ed. Niels Jørgen Cappelørn, Joakim Garff, Jette Knudsen, Johnny Kondrup, Alastair McKinnon, and Finn Hauberg Mortensen (Copenhagen: Gads Forlag, 1997–), vol. 11.129).

relation entangles what Cavell calls the 'metaphysical finitude' of the embodied self (that I am not you, as Cavell puts it) within the networks of material and social practices that we make our own over the courses of our lives.[2] Kierkegaard's and Cavell's formulations let us catch glimpses of the self as it swings in and out of view under a wide range of conditions. This version of selfhood is experienced as something perfectly evident and unproblematic at one moment, only to emerge suddenly into view as an entity whose nature, contours, and limits are enigmatic, and whose elusiveness as an object of analysis hopelessly blurs lines between inner and outer worlds.

Rome is critical here because it brings the embodied self face-to-face with networks of skills and attainments that individuals were expected to internalize via years of effort (study, reading, travel, etc.). The chapter's temporal focus is mostly devoted to the period after Reformation polemics had significantly adjusted English attitudes towards Rome. Rome was ostentatiously 'problematic' throughout this time, but the city's name nevertheless continued to stand metonymically for entangled skills and attainments (eloquence, the capacity to reason, etc.).[3] Because of this, encounters with Rome are interpretable as encounters with the self made 'strange' – with that adjective being offered in the etymological sense of something that is positioned 'outside'. What Gildas called the *nomen Romae*, then, connects individuals to phenomena that can be understood as entering the body (or, alternately, as seeming to emerge from it) under the force of Rome.

Early modern pedagogy was one of the great staging grounds for this encounter.[4] The scene of instruction positioned schoolboys within a dynamic network of relations with authorities of several kinds: schoolmasters, ancient writers, parents, humanist educational theorists, the state, schoolbooks, booksellers, and more. It also dragged them into waves of encounters with the self: that is, with their own shifting capacities and limitations, their mutating self-understandings. I argue that English

[2] See Stanley Cavell, 'Knowing and Acknowledging', in Stanley Cavell, *Must We Mean What We Say?*, rev. edn. (Cambridge University Press, 2002). Cavell wields this phrase in the course of arguing that skepticism emerges from the philosophical problem of privacy: 'I am filled with this feeling – of our separateness, let us say – and I want you to have it too. So I give voice to it. And then my powerlessness presents itself as ignorance – a metaphysical finitude as an intellectual lack' (263).

[3] This metonymy remains on view in the title of W. Martin Bloomer's *The School of Rome: Latin Studies and the Origins of Liberal Education* (Berkeley: University of California Press, 2011).

[4] On early modern grammar-school pedagogy see, among other recent studies, Jeff Dolven, *Scenes of Instruction in Renaissance Romance* (University of Chicago Press, 2007); Lynn Enterline, *Shakespeare's Schoolroom: Rhetoric, Discipline, Emotion* (Philadelphia: University of Pennsylvania Press, 2011); Andrew Wallace, *Virgil's Schoolboys: The Poetics of Pedagogy in Renaissance England* (Oxford University Press, 2010).

schoolboys were Rome's spectators, and that the decorum of spectatorship brought them face-to-face with something that they had been taught to recognize as images of themselves: perhaps at their best, perhaps at their worst. Even in the midst of life-and-death Reformation controversies, writers from Spenser to Milton were repeatedly compelled to acknowledge the resemblance and, by extension, the stakes of that acknowledgement.

Because grammar schools and private education served as rather different kinds of primal scenes for the discovery that the self is entangled in Rome, the first half of the chapter studies material from the educational careers and mature writings of Edmund Spenser and John Donne. In spite of Spenser's and Donne's quite different backgrounds, educations, temperaments, and achievements, Rome organized each of their efforts to reflect upon the self's relation to language, space, time, instruction, and experience. To put matters in this way is to propose that the word 'Rome' can stand not simply as the name of a dangerously seductive city in distant Italy, but as shorthand for a metaphysical condition of the educated self. In and around the works of Spenser and Donne (and eventually, as the chapter proceeds through its second half, in actual flights from the Eternal City by Sir Thomas Wilson and Milton), Rome is the name not simply for things that are 'out there' in the open (vestiges of ancient monuments, Popish impostures, crypto-Catholic ceremonies), but for the work of inner drives and faculties, and for the development of capabilities that are either native to, or trained into, bodies and minds.

Looking at Rome

Poems that command their readers to look at Rome constitute a miniature literary tradition in sixteenth-century poetry. This tradition, such as it is, runs from neo-Latin into a range of continental vernaculars, establishing along the way a set of nuanced reflections on humanist convictions concerning origins and imitations.[5]

Two Latin poems by the sixteenth-century poet Janus Vitalis cast long shadows across this tradition, helping to formalize the view of Rome's doubleness as an entity that is simultaneously ruined and reborn.[6] The first is titled 'Roma Prisca':

5 The bibliography on this subject is enormous, but the classic treatment of *imitatio* in humanist poetics remains Thomas M. Greene, *The Light in Troy: Imitation and Discovery in Renaissance Poetry* (New Haven: Yale University Press, 1982).

6 On the afterlife of Vitalis see Margaret M. McGowan, *The Vision of Rome in Late Renaissance France* (New Haven: Yale University Press, 2000), 226–7. See also G. H. Tucker, '*Roma Rediviva*: André de Resende, Joachim Du Bellay, and the Continuing Legacy of Janus Vitalis's Roman Diptych',

Qui Romam in media quæris novus advena Roma,
  Et Romam in Roma vix reperis media,
Aspice murorum moles, praeruptáque saxa,
  Obrutáque horrenti vasta Theatra situ,
Haec sunt Roma: viden velut ipsa cadavera tantae
  Vrbis, adhuc spirent imperiosa minas?
Vicit ut haec mundum, nisa est se vincere, vicit,
  A se non victum ne quid in orbe foret,
Nunc victa in Roma Roma illa invicta sepulta est,
  Atque eadem victrix, Victácque Roma fuit,
Albula Romani restabat nominis index,
  Quin fugit ille citis non rediturus aquis;
Disce hinc quíd possit Fortuna, immota labascunt
  Et quae perpetuo sunt agitata, manent.[7]

[You who in the midst of Rome, a newcomer, seek Rome, and barely find Rome in Rome's midst, look upon the shapeless mass of walls and rugged stones, and vast Theatres overcome by bristling decay. These are Rome. Do you see how this same corpse of so great a city is still imperiously breathing threats? Having conquered the world she set about conquering herself; she conquered, so that nothing in the world might remain unconquered by her, so that now, conquered, in Rome that unconquered Rome lies buried. And yet, the same Rome was conqueror and conquest. Albula remained as an index of the Roman name. But indeed there it is driven away with swift waters, not ever to return. Learn to know from this what Fortune can do: immovable things waver, and what is perpetually agitated remains.]

Vitalis' readers were predominantly learned humanists, but the poem makes a show of addressing itself to a reader who barely belongs to that world. This newcomer might as well be a schoolboy on the verge of being initiated into the procedural mysteries of humanist pedagogy and inquiry. He is promptly commanded to look ('Aspice') and then, just as promptly, asked whether he can see ('viden') rather than whether he understands.[8] He

Bibliothèque d'Humanisme et Renaissance 54 (1992), 731–6; G. H. Tucker, 'A Roman Dialogue with Virgil and Homer: Capilupi, the *Cento* and Rome', in Carlo Caruso and Andrew Laird (eds.), *Italy and the Classical Tradition: Language, Thought and Poetry 1300–1600* (London: Duckworth, 2009), 204–38. On the fifteenth-century humanist poet Janus Pannonius, whose work influenced Vitalis, see Raymond Skyrme, '"Buscas en Roma a Roma": Quevedo, Vitalis, and Janus Pannonius', *Bibliothèque d'Humanisme et Renaissance* 44 (1982), 363–7.

7 I cite Vitalis' poems as they are given by G. H. Tucker in '*Roma Instaurata* en Dialogue Avec *Roma Prisca*: La Représentation néo-Latine de Rome Sous Jules III, 1553–55, chez Janus Vitalis, Joachim du Bellay et Lelio Capilupi (de l'Ekphrase à la Prosopopée)', *Camenae* 2 (2007). Tucker is citing Janus Vitalis, *Iani Vitalis Panormitani Sacrosanctae Romanae Ecclesiae Elogia* (Rome: 1553), 8 ('Roma Prisca'), 9 ('Roma Instaurata').

8 Wittgenstein's mistrust of narratives of cognition is relevant here: 'denk nicht, sondern schau!'; 'don't think, but look!' (*Philosophical Investigations*, §66).

is expected to pivot, over the course of the poem's fourteen lines, from looking at what is self-evidently constellated before his eyes (the ancient city's ruined material remains) to seeing something altogether less obvious (that 'this same corpse of so great a city is still imperiously breathing threats'). The order to shift from looking at the world as it is to seeing it otherwise culminates in yet another schoolroom imperative verb ('disce'), whereby the newcomer is commanded to learn how to derive from this decayed spectacle a series of lessons about Fortune, mutability, and endurance. 'Roma Prisca' is, in effect, a pedagogical *cursus* in which an invitation to attest to the world's availability to the eye culminates in a command to learn to see what cannot be seen.[9]

Vitalis paired 'Roma Prisca' with 'Roma Instaurata', a companion piece in which the poet celebrates, without quite managing to depict, Rome's rebirth:

> Quicunque immensi septem miracula mundi
> Fortunae arbitrio praecipitata stupes,
> En quae Roma suo mundum comprehendit in orbe
> Quantum sit spoliis facta decora novis,
> Quàm veré est mundi Roma una unius imago,
> Quam ve unam Romam non nisi Roma refert,
> En velut expurgata repullulat ardua Quercus,
> Grandior è cinere est Roma renata suo,
> En velut hi montes, saxa haec immania passim
> Excutiant Iulos, Scipiadas'que novos,
> Virtutem'que animis, maiestatem'que superbam
> Infundant Genii bellipotentis ope,
> Ergo qui Romam hanc, mundum'que tueris in illa
> Nil debes oculis grandius inde tuis.

[Whoever you are, captivated by the seven wonders of the world cast down by a whim of Fortune, see there how Rome, which contains the entire world within her circumference, is made elegant with new spoils. How true it is that Rome alone is the one image of the world, or if you will, that nothing but Rome concerns the one Rome. See there: just as a tall oak sprouts again when cut, a greater Rome is reborn from her ash. See there, just as these mountains, these immense stones would rumble out everywhere new Iuluses

[9] I am invoking Maurice Merleau-Ponty's account of the child's experience of the world. See his *Phénoménologie de la Perception* (1945; Paris: Gallimard, 2011): 'L'enfant vit dans un monde qu'il croit d'emblée accessible à tous ceux qui l'entourent, il n'a aucune conscience de lui-même, ni d'ailleurs des autres, comme subjectivités privées, il ne soupçonne pas que nous soyons tous et qu'il soit lui-même limité à un certain point de vue sur le monde. C'est pourquoi il ne soumet à la critique ni ses pensées, auxquelles il croit à mesure qu'elles se présentent, et sans chercher à les lier, ni nos paroles. Il n'a pas la science des points de vue. Les hommes sont pour lui des têtes vides braquées sur un seul monde évident où tout se passe' (412).

> and Scipios, just so would they pour into spirits courage and superior majesty by means of their Genius, mighty in war. Therefore, you who see this Rome, and in her the world, you are to render to your eyes nothing greater than this.]

The two poems parcel out, in the form of a diptych, phenomena that could be experienced all at once by a traveler or viewer of the kind these poems imagine. That ancient and modern Rome occupy the same space, and that glimpses of the former flash within the latter, make it difficult – possibly even pointless – to imagine them as an historical sequence. This effort to collapse ancient and modern Rome into a single node feeds directly into the metonymies by which the city is said to contain the world, and by which the name 'Rome' can seem to sum up the world's possibilities.

One influential mid-century vernacular enlargement of Vitalis' project is to be found in the work of the French Catholic poet Joachim Du Bellay, whose poems form a vital prehistory for sixteenth-century English poetic encounters with Rome and, indeed, for Spenser's career specifically. Du Bellay was by no means the only model available, but even as a Catholic writer he was, in a basic way, closer to the interests and temperaments of sixteenth-century English poets than were texts such as the *Topographia antiquae Romae* of Bartolomeo Marliani (1534), or older medieval collections such as the twelfth-century *Mirabilia urbis Romae*.[10] That a French poet's view of Rome should prove to be decisive for English poets is fitting, given that ancient Rome had come to Britannia via Gaul when Caesar invaded the island on the relatively slim pretext that Britons had been reinforcing Gallic tribes in their resistance to Rome. Here and elsewhere, France is frequently a crucial mediator between English writers and Roman antiquity.[11] Montaigne is another important example of this phenomenon; he will figure later in this chapter.

[10] Rome was a significant point of reference even in considerably more local antiquarian work. The opening sentence of John Stow's *Survey of London* establishes a foundational link between Rome and London via Troy: 'As the Roman writers to glorify the city of *Rome*, derive the originall thereof from gods and demie Gods, by the Troian progenie, so *Giffrey* of *Monmouth* the Welsh historian, deduceth the foundation of this famous Citie of London, for the greater glorie therof, and emulation of *Rome*, from the very same originall' (*A Survey of London*, 2 vols. (Oxford: Clarendon Press, 1908), vol. I.1). On the early period see Gordon Home, *Roman London, A.D. 43–457*, rev. edn. (London: Eyre and Spottiswoode, 1948). On Rome and the English historical tradition see John E. Curran, *Roman Invasions: The British History, Protestant Anti-Romanism, and the Historical Imagination in England, 1530–1660* (Newark: University of Delaware Press, 2002). The classic English antiquarian engagement with Rome and Britain is Camden's *Britannia*, first published in Latin in 1586 and then in enlarged editions thereafter. Philemon Holland's English translation was printed in 1610.

[11] On the cult of ancient Rome in sixteenth-century France see Richard Cooper, *Roman Antiquities in Renaissance France, 1515–65* (Farnham: Ashgate, 2013). A classic study is Dorothy Gabe Coleman, *The Gallo-Roman Muse: Aspects of Roman Literary Tradition in Sixteenth-Century France* (Cambridge University Press, 1979).

Du Bellay had traveled from France to Rome in 1553 to perform secretarial duties within the household of his older cousin, the Cardinal Jean Du Bellay.[12] He remained there until the final months of 1557, by which time the Cardinal had fallen from favour with both the French King Henry II and Pope Paul IV in the course of a series of ongoing conflicts among the French throne, the Papacy, and the Holy Roman Emperor Charles V. By any measure, Rome occupies the very centre of Du Bellay's poetic imagination throughout this period, with four sequences wholly dominated by the spectacle of the city, its ghosts, and its living inhabitants: *Les Antiquitez de Rome*, *Le Songe*, *Les Regrets* (sonnet sequences written in French and printed in 1558), and the Latin *Poemata* (a group of elegies, also printed in 1558).[13] As Daniel Aris and Françoise Joukovsky have emphasized, Du Bellay encountered at Rome not a legible image of an Eternal City, but rather something considerably more recalcitrant. This Rome was fractured to such an extent that the city's ruins barely find their way into words in *Les Antiquitez de Rome*. For as Aris and Joukovsky remind us, 'l'apparence matérielle des ruines n'est evoquée que de la façon la plus vague. Il est vrai que cette apparence était confuse, les monuments n'étant exhumés que partiellement, et ce chaos étant envahi par la végétation'.[14] Du Bellay's poems are not, for the most part, archaeological or reconstructive projects, but rather moralizing reflections on a Rome that is simultaneously absent and present. Peeking out, here and there, from amidst vegetation, it is at best only ever partly visible to Du Bellay. Even so, the poems ceaselessly foreground a single, basic activity: looking at Rome.

The chaotic interpenetration of vestige and vegetation described by Aris and Joukovsky feeds directly into Du Bellay's emphasis on the self's entanglement in the world defined by Rome. This dynamic comes into view in the third sonnet of *Les Antiquitez*. This poem is a direct translation of Vitalis' 'Roma Prisca'. In it, once again, the poet addresses a newcomer who has traveled to Rome in search of Rome. But where the novice in Vitalis' poem had been addressed from within the linguistic boundaries of neo-Latin humanist poetics, Du Bellay's French creates new possibilities and new sounds:

[12] See Tucker, *The Poet's Odyssey: Joachim Du Bellay and the 'Antiquitez de Rome'* (Oxford: Clarendon Press, 1990).

[13] For a study of this portion of Du Bellay's career see McGowan, *The Vision of Rome*, 187–227.

[14] Joachim Du Bellay, *Œuvres Poétiques*, ed. D. Aris and F. Joukovsky, 2 vols. (Paris: Classiques Garnier, 1993), vol. II.xiv.

Nouveau venu qui cherches Rome en Rome,
Et rien de Rome en Rome n'apperçois,
Ces vieux palais, ces vieux arcz que tu vois,
Et ces vieux murs, c'est ce que Rome on nomme.

Voy quel orgueil, quelle ruine: et comme
Celle qui mist le monde sous ses loix
Pour donter tout, se donta quelquefois,
Et devint proye au temps, qui tout consomme.

Rome de Rome est le seul monument,
Et Rome Rome a vaincu seulement,
Le Tybre seul, qui vers la mer s'enfuit,

Reste de Rome. O mondaine inconstance!
Ce qui est ferme, est par le temps destruit,
Et ce qui fuit, au temps fait resistence.[15]

Rome is a spectacle of ruination, and even in its wreckage it urgently presses itself upon visitor and reader. The sonnet's terse pronouncements call attention to the poet's struggle to determine just what *will* finally deserve to bear the name of Rome.

Though the poem continues to emphasize the central predicament of looking at the ruined city, a struggle over the sound of the word 'Rome' organizes its diction. The name wields talismanic power within the poem, and cascading doublets insist on the city's essentially plural nature: 'Rome en Rome' (invoked twice), 'Rome de Rome', 'Rome Rome'. A half rhyme in the phrase 'ce que Rome on nomme' bolsters Du Bellay's extended effort to make Vitalis' echo chamber resonate. The two-stanza rhyme on 'Rome', 'nomme', 'comme', and 'consomme' adds to this effect by producing a series of deft variations on the word and its related sounds, lovingly preserving the city's name, even reproducing it, in the act of reflecting on the city's destruction, its consumption by predatory time, and its victimization at the hands of 'mondaine inconstance'. The sound of the city's name is already at the mercy of mutability.

Under the pressure of these repetitions the city's name strains against its own limits, as though telling the story of Latin's metamorphoses into the Romance languages. As part of this process, new sounds are generated in a kind of colonial expansion of semantic boundaries. This is characteristic

[15] Du Bellay, *Œuvres Poétiques*, vol. II, Sonnet 3. Subsequent references to Du Bellay's poems refer to sonnet and line numbers in volume two of this edition. Spenser's translation of this sonnet follows, below.

of the sequence as a whole. Throughout the *Antiquitez*, punning lends verbal form to Rome's composite nature. In *Antiquitez* 18, for example, Du Bellay connects the 'monceaux pierreux' of the city's ruins to its new status as a holding of the 'successeur de Pierre', so that the sonnet orbits around stones and Sanctus Petrus, the rock. Scholars are right to call attention to the fact that Rome's *provinciae* do not figure in the imagined landscapes of *Les Antiquitez*.[16] Even so, the name of the city itself thrashes to life over the course of the sequence. In Du Bellay, plural Romes are Rome's inhabitants.

A further relevant point here may be that doubleness, if not multiplicity, is woven directly into the formal structures of *Antiquitez* and *Songe*, given that in these sequences decasyllabic and alexandrine sonnets alternate. This is, at the level of poetic form, an effort to capture the commonplace that multiple Romes coexist. The echoes and repetitions of the city's name in *Antiquitez* 3 (and, by extension, the ancient city's hold on both Du Bellay and on the disappointments of the 'Nouveau venu') contribute to the impression that the poem is a riddle, provided that riddle is the right way to characterize Du Bellay's unsettling questions about the ethical and spiritual wisdom of contemplating at length the wrecked images and sites of Rome. For to look at this particular wreckage is to court injury.

Les Antiquitez and *Le Songe* are companion pieces whose aims and methods are nevertheless distinct. The former is a meditative project occasioned by the self's situation amidst ruins it barely describes; the latter offers up a series of dream visions in which iconographic representations of Rome are destroyed. These paired sequences give us, as Du Bellay's editors observe, 'D'une part la réalité réduite à néant, de l'autre la prolifération fulgurant de l'imaginaire.'[17] In the sonnets of *Le Songe*, in particular, the bare act of seeing is obsessively described. Just two of the sequence's fifteen sonnets (Sonnets 10 and 11) withhold some explicit reference or call to seeing, but even those sonnets are structured around a dreamer's recounting of a vision. Sonnet 1 repeats the imperative 'Voy'.[18] Thereafter, forms of 'Je vy' or 'Je vis' appear in all but two of the sonnets until the poet awakens ('je m'esveille') in the final two words of *Songe* 15. In every case the dreamer witnesses the fall and ruination of a structure or living thing by the sudden imposition of environmental, human, or supernatural forces. Although the name of Rome clatters along noisily in the sonnets of *Les Antiquitez*, the emphasis of *Le Songe* is on witnessing the destruction of things upon which the name of Rome is never formally

[16] Du Bellay, *Antiquitez*, 18.1, 12. [17] Du Bellay, *Œuvres Poétiques*, vol. II.xxxiii.
[18] Du Bellay, *Songe*, 1.9, 11.

bestowed. Not that there is any possibility of uncertainty: hills counted by sevens, named emperors, northern invaders, and lactating she-wolves ensure that the application to Rome is always foregrounded.

Throughout these companion sequences, Du Bellay shows that the encounter with Rome compels the viewer to consider what spaces and things might pertinently carry the name of Rome. His language frequently, as in *Antiquitez* 3, betrays a suspicion that naming is merely, and disappointingly, a matter of convention, as though Du Bellay found himself embarrassed to admit that there really is nothing better, newer, or more whole to which the august name might be applied: 'Ces vieus palais, ces vieux arcz que tu vois, / Et ces vieux murs, c'est ce que Rome on nomme.'[19] As I will have occasion to note in the final sections of this chapter, Du Bellay's move from 'palais' to 'arcz' in relation to visions of Rome is one that Milton later reprises in the prospect of Rome that is granted to the Saviour in *Paradise Regained*. For the moment I want to emphasize that if there are hints of embarrassment and insufficiency in the face of conventions of naming, and with respect to the meagreness of the truth such conventions are capable of revealing, Du Bellay is nevertheless uncompromising in his insistence that Rome makes the world intelligible: 'Ainsi le monde on peult sur Rome compasser, / Puis que le plan de Rome est la carte du monde.'[20] The double movement of this cartographic metaphor insists that the world can be folded into Rome, and that Rome folds out across the entire world. Like a trusty map, Rome helps individuals find their way – even the Britons whom Virgil's Meliboeus had regarded as living lives 'wholly sundered from all the world'.

The corollary to the unsettling possibility that a newcomer to Rome might believe that the city in which he finds himself is somehow, impossibly, elsewhere, is the notion that it is possible to live far from Rome and yet burn with the knowledge that one is already living in its grip, inhabited by it, folded into its complex logic. Du Bellay bears one kind of witness to the force of this intuition in his Roman poems. Edmund Spenser, who never found himself at Rome, bears another.

English schoolboys of the sixteenth and early seventeenth centuries were continually facing and outfacing versions of Rome. To confront serial versions of Rome was not simply a matter of coming to terms with pagan texts in a Christian era, or of negotiating the threats posed by Catholic Rome from within the boundaries of a reformed grammar school, or even

[19] Du Bellay, *Antiquitez*, 3.3–4. [20] Du Bellay, *Antiquitez*, 26.13–4.

of finessing cross-confessional literary influences.[21] It involved learning to understand that metaphorical and literal encounters with Rome helped organize the methods by which the educated confronted, broke down, rebuilt, and made themselves at home in the world. One precondition for this understanding is the need to acknowledge the elusive nature of the relationship between the self and its attainments.

As Barkan puts it, Du Bellay is 'the poet who brought Rome to Spenser'.[22] Du Bellay granted Spenser a topic (the obsessive staring, from afar, at Rome), affirmed the international reach of the English poet's apprenticeship, and afforded Spenser several of the constituent parts of the poetic voice that would become his own. Anne Coldiron, Ann Lake Prescott, and Margaret Ferguson have all shown that Du Bellay's influence on Spenser is pervasive, stretching as it does from the near-juvenilia of Spenser's earliest, anonymously published poems, to the 1596 *Faerie Queene* and to the posthumous 1609 printing of *Two Cantos of Mutabilitie.*[23]

Good pupil that he was, Spenser first put his hand to Du Bellay's work as the anonymous translator of eleven sonnets drawn from Du Bellay's *Songe* in the Dutch poet Jan van der Noot's *A theatre wherein be represented as wel the miseries & calamities that follow the voluptuous worldlings as also the greate ioyes and plesures which the faithfull do enioy* (1569).[24] Spenser's translations of Du Bellay appear alongside a group of epigrams translated into English by Spenser from Clément Marot's French translations of Petrarch's *Rime sparse* 323. The volume also contains four apocalyptic sonnets based on biblical texts, along with a lengthy prose commentary

21 A helpful account of English grammar schools during the Reformation can be found in Joan Simon, *Education and Society in Tudor England* (Cambridge University Press, 1966). See especially 165–287.

22 Leonard Barkan, 'Ruins and Visions: Spenser, Pictures, Rome', in Jennifer Klein Morrison and Matthew Greenfield (eds.), *Edmund Spenser: Essays on Culture and Allegory* (Aldershot: Ashgate, 2000), 12.

23 See A. E. B. Coldiron, 'How Spenser Excavates Du Bellay's *Antiquitez*; or, The Role of the Poet, Lyric Historiography, and the English Sonnet', *Journal of English and Germanic Philology* 101 (2002), 41–67; Anne Lake Prescott, 'Spenser (Re)Reading Du Bellay: Chronology and Literary Response', in Judith H. Anderson, Donald Cheney, and David A. Richardson (eds.), *Spenser's Life and the Subject of Biography* (Amherst: University of Massachusetts Press, 1996), 131–45. Ferguson proposes that Spenser's return, in the *Complaints* volume, to his earlier translations of Du Bellay can be read as a species of idolatry. See Ferguson, 'The Afflatus of Ruin": Meditations on Rome by Du Bellay, Spenser, and Stevens', in Annabel Patterson (ed.), *Roman Images: Selected Papers from the English Institute* (Baltimore: Johns Hopkins University Press, 1984), 23–50.

24 *A Theatre* had already been published in Dutch and French editions in 1568. The poems in these editions were accompanied by striking engravings based on images by Lucas de Heere of Ghent. The English edition in which Spenser's work appeared featured instead woodcuts based on the earlier engravings. For an excellent overview of van der Noot's career, Spenser's contributions to the 1569 volume, and the theological contexts in which the volume intervenes, see Andrew Hadfield, *Edmund Spenser: A Life* (Oxford University Press, 2012), 38–47.

that is advertised as having been 'translated out of French into Englishe by Theodore Roest'.

Spenser's 1591 *Complaints* volume contains translations of Du Bellay's *Antiquitez de Rome* under the new title *Ruines of Rome: by Bellay*, new versions of all fifteen sonnets of Du Bellay's *Songe* (under the title *The Visions of Bellay*), along with the 'epigrams' based on Petrarch (designated here as *The Visions of Petrarch. formerly translated*). It is by virtue of the 1591 volume that we know that the anonymous translations that had appeared in *A Theatre* were Spenser's. In this 1591 collection the sonnets of Du Bellay are driven out of blank verse and into rhyme, decisively altering *A Theatre*'s curious combination of workmanlike and experimental effects.

It is striking that Spenser should have been in a position to contribute to a venture of this kind in 1569. At the time Spenser was almost certainly still a schoolboy at Merchant Taylors' School in London. His schoolmaster, Richard Mulcaster, would presumably have played a major role in facilitating his involvement in the project. The protestant convert van der Noot (who would reconvert to Catholicism in 1578) was in exile in England and living at St Botolph Ward in London. Andrew Hadfield establishes that this put him in the immediate vicinity of Mulcaster's school, and that Mulcaster was directly connected to the Dutch emigré community in London.[25] Hadfield emphasizes, too, that Mulcaster was 'the principal source of Du Bellay's influence in England'.[26] Spenser's engagements with Du Bellay, therefore, were inextricably tied to an entire network of pedagogical and careerist negotiations in which the world of Elizabethan grammar-school pedagogy generally, along with the specific contours of the poet's early career, converge on the spectacle of Rome.

Deaths and origins are hopelessly intermixed here. Du Bellay's meditations on Rome's destruction are an unexpected analogue to English grammar-school pedagogy's complex investment in Rome as a civilization that was to be both resisted and imitated. The *memoriae Romae* are a sub-genre of the *memento mori*, but these memories are also rhetorical scenes of genesis and possibility at which the schoolboy Spenser begins to assert his public voice. Spenser's 1591 translation of the third sonnet of Du Bellay's *Antiquitez* is therefore the natural place to begin:

> Thou stranger, which for *Rome* in *Rome* here seekest,
> And nought of *Rome* in *Rome* perceiu'st at all,

[25] Hadfield, *Edmund Spenser*, 39. [26] Hadfield, *Edmund Spenser*, 38.

These same olde walls, old arches, which thou seest,
Old Palaces, is that which *Rome* men call.
Behold what wreake, what ruine, and what wast,
And how that she, which with her mightie powre
Tam'd all the world, hath tam'd herselfe at last,
The pray of time, which all things doth deuowre.
Rome now of *Rome* is th'onely funerall,
And onely *Rome* of *Rome* hath victorie;
Ne ought saue *Tyber* hastning to his fall
Remaines of all: O worlds inconstancie.
That which is firme doth flit and fall away,
And that is flitting, doth abide and stay.[27]

Spenser has preserved Du Bellay's implied sense that an unsatisfying convention of naming, rather than a continuous or stable essence, connects the present city to its past. These ratty old things ('olde walls, old arches, . . . / Old Palaces') are nothing more than 'that which *Rome* men call', and they convey ineluctable confusion rather than sense, stability, and continuity. Only the flowing Tiber, conceived of as an emblem of inconstancy, 'Remaines of all'. That verb is haunted by the 'Romans' themselves, who do not appear in the poem.

The stranger, having come to Rome in search of Rome, finds only a space in which all expectations have been reversed: 'That which is firme doth flit and fall away, / And that is flitting, doth abide and stay.' This is Rome as Wittgenstein's 'das ganze Gewimmel der menschlichen Handlungen' (i.e., 'the whole hurly-burly of human actions'). In Spenser, however, the hurly-burly can only confuse, rather than explain. Similarly, in Spenser's translation of *Antiquitez* 19, Rome is a chaos in which 'all good and euill' are 'turmoyling'.[28] It is as though Rome, in its perpetual state of confusion between past and present, had come to stand not as a confirmation of, but rather a challenge to, the poetics and pedagogy of order and method that humanism, taking its models from Cicero and others, had helped spawn. We are considerably closer here to Ovid's poetics of flux than we are to the inexorable, divinely ordained teleology of Virgil's *Aeneid*. Du Bellay, Spenser, and their shared poem are left twisting in the winds of schoolroom engagements with Rome.

[27] Edmund Spenser, *Ruines of Rome: by Bellay*, in *Edmund Spenser: The Shorter Poems*, ed. Richard A. McCabe (Harmondsworth: Penguin, 1999). All citations from Spenserian poems other than *The Faerie Queene* are from this edition, though I give sequence or poem name along with sonnet and line numbers rather than the continuous volume-lineation provided by McCabe.

[28] Spenser, *Ruines of Rome*, 19.9–10.

Tom Muir has argued persuasively that Du Bellay's *Antiquitez de Rome* and Spenser's *Ruines of Rome* share a deep 'anxiety towards – or recoil from – the humanist project'.[29] Muir proceeds to note, first, that for a writer such as Spenser, 'Rome is dead, foreign, alien, pagan, bewildering and remote', and second, that 'the study of its "braue writings", the absorption of its culture and history, the rapt fascination at its ruins – these are things that bring that foreignness within, and invite it to gestate'.[30] The sequence does indeed press its readers to see that the crises it observes are 'within'. This is so, however, at least partly because Muir's first premise does not quite capture what is most essential to Spenser's representation of Rome. The gestation to which Muir adverts occurs not because Rome is 'dead, foreign, alien, pagan, bewildering and remote', but specifically because it is always-already living, domestic, ordinary, and ready-to-hand. Seen in this light, familiar parts of the sequence can be read in terms of the sheer urgency with which Spenser calls out to the city.

An example of this urgency can be discerned in Spenser's handling of the necromantic fantasy of *Antiquitez* 5:

> Rome is no more: but if the shade of Rome
> May of the bodie yeeld a seeming sight,
> It's like a corse drawne forth out of the tombe
> By Magicke skill out of eternall night.[31]

These lines stage an encounter not with a 'dead, foreign, alien, pagan, bewildering and remote' thing, but rather with the life and persistent explanatory power of phenomena that organized the ordinary, the domestic, and the ready-to-hand of Spenser's world. That world is troped here as a walking corpse moving 'By Magicke skill' of the poet-as-maker. Spenser knows well that Rome is still lurching under its own living, thrilling, and enervating power.

The poem's most disorientating effects are rooted in the protasis of Spenser's conditional sentence ('if the shade of *Rome* / May of the bodie yeeld a seeming sight'). One form of the embedded question can be articulated clearly enough: can 'the shade of *Rome*' (i.e., the conspicuously ruined remains of the ancient city) grant us a sufficiently accurate image of its 'bodie' (i.e., the ancient city's former grandeur)? This same clause, however, can also be regarded as expressing a considerably more intimate and unsettling connection between self and city. Indeed, 'the bodie' in play

29 Tom Muir, 'Specters of Spenser: Translating the *Antiquitez*', *Spenser Studies* 25 (2010), 331.
30 Muir, 'Specters of Spenser', 341–2. 31 Spenser, *Ruines of Rome*, 5.5–8.

here can be read not simply as the wrecked body of Rome, but also as the body of the living traveler who stands now in the company of 'the shade of *Rome*'.[32] (This reading hangs on the possibility of a double movement of the kind that Du Bellay also explores, as noted above, in *Antiquitez* 26: 'Ainsi le monde on peult sur Rome compasser, / Puis que le plan de Rome est la carte du monde'.)[33] On this reading, the creature 'drawn forth out of the tombe / By Magicke skille out of eternall night' is not the modern city but rather the newcomer who has been compelled to recognize that he is inhabited by 'the shade of *Rome*'.

This translation of *Antiquitez* 5 explains what might otherwise be a merely puzzling image of Rome's persistence in Spenser's mature poetry, where a glimpse of the city is regarded as having the power to convey to individuals the perilous secret of their condition. The episodes in question occur in Book One of *The Faerie Queene*, where the Dwarf sees 'The Antique ruines of the *Romanes* fall' trapped (somehow) in the dungeon of the House of Pride, and immediately intuits that the presence of these ruins constitutes a mortal threat to Redcrosse.[34] To sequester the ruins of a fallen city and its people (in this case, 'Antique ruines' may be standing metonymically for Romulus, Tarquin, etc., who are named later in the stanza), as Spenser does here, is to insist that the spectacle of these living ruins needs still to be disciplined and contained. Even simply *as* a spectacle those ruins are dangerous. And what, in any case, does Spenser want us to see (i.e., visualize) in this reference to 'The Antique ruines of the *Romanes* fall'?[35] We hover, disturbingly, between collapsed walls and human carcasses, so that the moralized spectacle of Rome's ruination grades into a harrowing identification of seer with seen.

Equivalencies of this kind structure the allegorical calculus of Book One of *The Faerie Queene*. They are especially prominent when Spenser's narrative appears to pause for the purpose of studying the delicate interplay between scripture and marginal glosses in the Geneva Bible's Book of Revelation. When, in Canto Eight, Duessa enters battle 'High mounted

[32] This syntax brings the poem's readers, unexpectedly, within striking distance of a famous pronouncement in Paul's Epistle to the Romans: 'And if Christ be in you, the body is dead because of sin' (Romans 8:10).

[33] Du Bellay, *Antiquitez*, 26.13–4.

[34] Edmund Spenser, *The Faerie Queene*, ed. A. C. Hamilton with text by Hiroshi Yamashita and Toshiyuki Suzuki, rev. 2nd edn. (Harlow: Longman, 2007), I.v.49.4. References to *The Faerie Queene* give book, canto, stanza, and line numbers.

[35] For the view that ruins constitute 'a master metaphor of sorts in the Renaissance for disinterring the past for the present' see Rebecca Helfer, *Spenser's Ruins and the Art of Recollection* (University of Toronto Press, 2012), 9.

on her many headed beast',[36] she is (among other things) a representation of Rome atop a representation of Rome, for Spenser's composite intertext in that scene is Revelation 17 and its Geneva glosses. According to those glosses, the chapter's beast 'signifieth ye ancient Rome: ye woman that sitteth thereon, the newe Rome which is the Papistrie, whose crueltie and blood sheding is declared by skarlat'.[37] When Duessa is defeated by Arthur and stripped bare at the command of Una, her monstrous and superannuated deformities offer a kind of belated gloss on what we saw of Redcrosse's own decrepitude when he was lifted from the dungeon of Orgoglio a handful of stanzas earlier. Redcrosse may be St George, and therefore an allegorical expression of England's rebirth in the Truth, but he is also one of 'The Antique ruines of the *Romanes* fall'. These heady substitutions are records of Spenser's apprenticeship under Du Bellay.

Du Bellay's Roman sequences are, at least in part, lessons concerning what Spenser, in his translation of *Antiquitez* 3, calls the 'worlds inconstancie'. This, of course, feeds directly into Spenser's rapt, career-long fascination with the phenomenon of mutability. But Du Bellay's sequences, especially when Spenser gets his hands on them, also look like serial attempts to come to terms with, even to contain or kill, a living thing whose ties to the self are too robust and comprehensive to be undone or forgotten. Though Du Bellay and Spenser work from different sides of the period's confessional divide (and therefore from within what might be expected to have been different instinctive understandings of their relations to Rome), they are united by the intensity of their 'hyperbolic, unprecedented attention' to Rome's ruins. This phrase is used by Cavell to characterize the ways in which certain kinds of objects or phenomena are singled out for attention in the arguments of philosophers: 'It is not just careful description, or practical investigation, under way here. The philosopher is as it were looking for a *response* from the object, perhaps a shining'.[38]

Though specific scenes of ruination are mostly absent from Du Bellay's *Antiquitez*, the business of staring over and over at the decisive moment of Rome's destruction is the dominant concern of the French poet's *Songe*,

[36] Spenser, *The Faerie Queene*, I.viii.6.2.

[37] Gloss on Revelation 17:3 in *The Geneva Bible: A Facsimile of the 1560 Edition* (Madison: University of Wisconsin Press, 1969), GGG.iiii.[r].

[38] See Stanley Cavell, *Disowning Knowledge in Six Plays of Shakespeare* (Cambridge University Press, 1987). Cavell associates 'hyperbolic, unprecedented attention' with philosophy's flights from our ordinary relations to the world. He offers the following examples: melting beeswax (Descartes), a 'tomato with nothing but its visual front aspect remaining' (H. H. Price), 'raised moving hands' (G. E. Moore), a tree in bloom (Heidegger) (8).

and, therefore, of Spenser's protracted, serial engagements with that sequence (in 1569's *A Theatre* and in 1591's *Visions of Bellay*). As the lyric speaker stares and dreams (for with Du Bellay situated at Rome, each of these verbs seems to trope the other), iconographic representations of Rome are cast down by earthquakes, storms, and invaders. Throughout, the central drama of Du Bellay's *Songe* sees external agents and elemental forces acting decisively upon surfaces of ivory, pillars of diamond, trunks of trees, and bodies of she-wolves. The sequence's obsessive variations on the same repeated scenario, in which an object is carefully built up via description and then violently unmade in the space of two or three lines, are amplified by Spenser's own effort to come to terms with his relation to Du Bellay's achievement.

Spenser's 1569 translation of *Songe* 2, and its accompanying woodcut, emphasize Rome's power to dominate space:

On hill, a frame an hundred cubites hie
I sawe, an hundred pillers eke about,
All of fine Diamant decking the front,
And fashiond were they all in Dorike wise.
Of bricke, ne yet of marble was the wall,
But shining Christall, which from top to base
Out of deepe vaute threw forth a thousand rayes
Vpon an hundred steps of purest golde.
Golde was the parget: and the sielyng eke
Did shine all scaly with fine golden plates.
The floore was Iaspis, and of Emeraude.
O worldes vainenesse. A sodein earthquake loe,
Shaking the hill euen from the bottome deepe,
Threwe downe this building to the lowest stone.

The pattern on view here remains in place for the full sequence: eleven or more lines of description dominate the surface area of each sonnet, and the splendour of what has been described in those lines is ultimately destroyed in a cataclysm that is described tersely, and usually without moralizing. What there is in the way of moralizing comes mostly as a silent aftereffect of the obsessive accumulation of these catastrophes.

The accompanying woodcut amplifies this effect. (See Figure 2.1.) In it, a raised temple bearing the famous acronym 'S.P.Q.R.' fully dominates the frame, touching three edges and nearly touching the fourth. It is, in effect, as imposing a structure as one can imagine, angled so as to lure the viewer into its world as the eye follows perspective lines that move inward, from left to right. The temple is wholly intact at the

Figure 2.1 From Jan van der Noot, *A theatre wherein be represented as wel the miseries & calamities that follow the voluptuous worldlings as also the greate ioyes and plesures which the faithfull do enioy. An argument both profitable and delectable, to all that sincerely loue the word of God. Deuised by S. Iohn vander Noodt. Seene and allowed according to the order appointed* (London, 1569), Ci[r] [STC 18602]. Image courtesy of the British Library.

woodcut's left edge, but its deepest corner, towards its right edge, is in the process of shattering. The little we can see of a distant background is, in turn, wholly taken up by another columned temple. Making an emblem of the woodcut's apocalyptic moment, broken columns are not simply lying on the ground but somehow hovering above the temple. In what looks like a clever response to the original dance of word and image, the revised translation published in 1591 appears to have been guided by this striking feature of the woodcut. The 1569 version asserts that an earthquake 'Threwe downe this building'; in the 1591 *Visions of Bellay* Spenser writes instead that the earthquake 'ouerthrew this frame', thereby driving into his new translation (which was no longer accompanied into print by a woodcut) the sense of an order not simply ruined but explosively airborne.

The desolate scenes of Spenser's 1569 translation of *Songe* 3, along with its accompanying woodcut (see Figure 2.2), are similarly instructive:

> Then did appeare to me a sharped spire
> Of diamant, ten feete eche way in square,
> Iustly proportionde up into his height,
> So hie as mought an Archer reache with sight.
> Vpon the top therof was set a pot
> Made of the mettall that we honour most.
> And in this golden vessell couched were
> The ashes of a mightie Emperour.
> Vpon foure corners of the base there lay
> To beare the frame, foure great Lions of golde.
> A worthie tombe for such a worthie corps.
> Alas, nought in this worlde but griefe endures.
> A sodaine tempest from the heauen, I saw,
> With flushe stroke downe this noble monument.

The 1591 version of the sonnet takes no substantial liberties with this, and even manages to locate some of its rhymes within the earlier version's diction. Standing and ruined versions of the sonnet's 'sharped spire / Of diamant' coexist. Another obelisk and city lurk amidst the folds of distant hills, serving as expressions of Rome's ability to get itself reproduced in the world. As elsewhere in Du Bellay's *Songe*, the emphasis is on the suddenness with which the monument is struck down. The sonnets of *Songe* study a single, basic scenario in which a dreamer's eyes are forever trained (as though watching were the only form of life available to him) upon scenes of loss and destruction. As the sequence proceeds, the disasters are visited upon increasingly attenuated expressions of Rome.

Figure 2.2 From Jan van der Noot, *A theatre wherein be represented as wel the miseries & calamities that follow the voluptuous worldlings as also the greate ioyes and plesures which the faithfull do enioy. An argument both profitable and delectable, to all that sincerely loue the word of God. Deuised by S. Iohn vander Noodt. Seene and allowed according to the order appointed* (London, 1569), Cii^{r} [STC 18602]. Image courtesy of the British Library.

What happens when someone stares forever at these particular scenes of destruction? What happens to someone who contemplates them at length, bearing the full weight of what they might be taken to mean not, say, as geopolitical predicaments, but as methods of shedding light on the problem of the self at a moment where it seems possible that 'the shade of *Rome* / May of the body yeeld a seeming sight'? These questions cut to the heart of Du Bellay's project in *Antiquitez*, in its enigmatic companion piece *Songe* and, by extension, in Spenser's career generally. Significantly, Du Bellay's influence upon Spenser slips the limits of his translations of *Antiquitez* and *Songe*. His highly self-conscious response to the stakes of seeing in Du Bellay's *Songe* generates, in a process that is equal parts imitative and diagnostic, the 1591 sequence *Visions of the Worlds Vanitie*. Whereas the *Visions of Bellay* obsessively depict Rome as an entity that can be observed from a distance, Spenser's *Visions of the Worlds Vanitie* see the world destructively, painfully, working its way into the beings who inhabit it.

In the *Visions of Bellay*, versions of Rome and its vestiges are repeatedly destroyed by decisive forces that crush or smash or shake the earth from beneath foundations: all this as the dreamer stares on safely from a distance. In Spenser's *Visions of the Worlds Vanitie*, however, the bodies of living beings are infiltrated by enemies and destroyers. These new visions are described as emerging from 'meditation deepe / Of things exceeding reach of common reason'.[39] They ought, therefore, to be viewed as studies of the stakes of acknowledging the extent to which vision and meditation entangle us in the world and thereby help constitute us – or at least alter us forever. The sequence, that is, proposes that the self is a condition of ontological entanglement in the world. It can therefore be understood as Spenser's effort to come to terms with what he has learned from Du Bellay's visions of Rome.

In the sequence's second sonnet a bull stands in a 'fresh flowring meadow'.[40] He is, to put this another way, immersed in his world: 'Vp to his eares' in the grass and wallowing 'in the weedes downe beaten', when a 'Brize' (i.e., a gnat), 'a scorned litle creature', drives its sting 'Through his faire hide'.[41] The core dynamic (it shapes every aspect of the sequence) is that the great are repeatedly brought low by the small. Du Bellay's *Antiquitez* and *Songe* had both pressed this same lesson upon their readers. And yet, the

[39] Spenser, *Visions of the Worlds Vanitie*, 1.3–4, in Spenser, *Edmund Spenser, Shorter Poems*.
[40] Spenser, *Visions of the Worlds Vanitie*, 2.4.
[41] Spenser, *Visions of the Worlds Vanitie*, 2.5, 8, 10–11.

central figure in almost every one of Spenser's twelve *Visions of the Worlds Vanitie* is pierced or penetrated and then brought low by something in its environment. On the whole, then, the sequence's efforts to moralize relations of scale are perhaps less significant than are its studies of the metaphysics of proximity, connection, and invasion. Spenser's labours upon the texts of Du Bellay's sequences taught him that something capable of bearing the name Rome can threaten to enter bodies by secret avenues, and his *Visions of the Worlds Vanitie* proffer a string of miniature fables of the means by which the world worms its way into the embodied self.

In the sequence's third sonnet a crocodile's appetite leaves him 'cram'd with guiltles blood, and greedie pray'.[42] This is a measure of the crocodile's predatory mastery of its world, but the creature is immediately subjected to the power of 'a little Bird' that 'forst this hideous beast to open wide / The griesly gates of his devouring hell, / And let him feede' from his open mouth.[43] In Sonnet 4 a scarab sets about 'kindling fire within the hollow tree' to burn it up from the inside and thereby unhouse an eagle.[44] In Sonnet 5 a swordfish pierces the body of a leviathan and the infiltration inaugurates a double movement: the leviathan suffers violence and his draining gut leaves the ocean 'stain'd with filthie hewe'.[45] In Sonnet 6 a dragon is invaded by a spider:

> The subtill vermin creeping closely neare,
> Did in his drinke shed poyson priuilie,
>   Which through his entrailes spredding diuersly,
> Made him to swell, that nigh his bowells brust.[46]

Sonnet 7 describes the growth and decay of a cedar:

> Shortly within her inmost pith there bred
> A litle wicked worme, perceiu'd of none,
> That on her sap and vitall moysture fed.[47]

In Sonnet 8 an elephant scorns everything it encounters,

> Till that a little Ant, a silly worme,
> Into his nosthrils creeping, so him pained,
> That casting downe his towres, he did deforme
> Both borrowed pride, and natiue beautie stained.[48]

[42] Spenser, *Visions of the Worlds Vanitie*, 3.4.
[43] Spenser, *Visions of the Worlds Vanitie*, 3.7, 9–11. [44] Spenser, *Visions of the Worlds Vanitie*, 4.7.
[45] Spenser, *Visions of the Worlds Vanitie*, 5.12. [46] Spenser, *Visions of the Worlds Vanitie*, 6.7–10.
[47] Spenser, *Visions of the Worlds Vanitie*, 7.6–8.
[48] Spenser, *Visions of the Worlds Vanitie*, 8.9–12.

In Sonnet 9 a ship's progress is stopped when 'A little fish, that men call *Remora*' cleaves to its keel.[49] In Sonnet 10 a lion is stung by a wasp and 'fild with fretting ire'.[50] In Sonnet 11, where Spenser fuses a pair of stories from Livy, the matter of Rome is foregrounded but the dynamic is somewhat different. Sonnet 12, however, returns to the established pattern, so that the sequence concludes with an emphasis on the external origins of 'inward ruth'.[51] It is easy to imagine a pun lurking in Spenser's characterization of his 'engreiued brest',[52] as though that breast has been scored or engraved – which is to say, visibly and materially altered – by the sights to which it has been subjected in the course of these visions.

These poems repeatedly deny that creatures are self-sufficient and separate from their surroundings, insisting instead that these same creatures are pierced, invaded, and inhabited by their surroundings. Over and over a creature's fantasy of autonomy is brought low when the fact of its entanglement in the world is forced upon it. This lesson flows directly from the imitative logic of Spenser's own entanglement in Du Bellay's Roman project. The passages collected here show that although the sequence's declared emphasis is on seeing vanity and grandeur destroyed by the unexpected and insignificant, that preoccupation is subtended by a poetics of secret infiltration, whereby various beings or entities are invaded and forever altered by some aspect of their environment. The contents of Spenser's *Complaints* volume see the *Visions of the Worlds Vanitie* leading directly into *Visions of Bellay* and *Visions of Petrarch* (reworkings, via Marot's French translation, of Petrarch's *Rime sparse* 323 – a poem on the death of Laura). The *Visions of Bellay* and *Visions of Petrarch* depict the self in ways that suggest that it can be regarded as an observing subject standing over and against a world that is radically separate from it. In *Visions of the Worlds Vanitie*, however, where Spenser is working not as Du Bellay's translator but rather as his pupil, we are given a series of fables that show how agents are pierced and altered and inhabited by what they see and by what they absorb.

The sequence, therefore, is to be understood as an effort to come to terms with the elusive processes by which individuals are altered by spectacles and visions of the kind set forth in *Antiquitez* and *Songe*. This is related, of course, to the particular forms of Du Bellay's decisive influence on Spenser and, for that matter, to Rome's decisive influence on each of them. Spenser knows that there is no escaping the self, and that what

[49] Spenser, *Visions of the Worlds Vanitie*, 9.10.
[50] Spenser, *Visions of the Worlds Vanitie*, 10.10.
[51] Spenser, *Visions of the Worlds Vanitie*, 12.3.
[52] Spenser, *Visions of the Worlds Vanitie*, 12.5.

modern phenomenology calls the structures of consciousness and experience are radically entangled in the world in which humans are situated. To the extent that, as Du Bellay puts the matter, 'Le plan de Rome est la carte du monde', Rome is also a map of the self and its possibilities. This is a lesson pressed upon modernity by Freud, who proposed an extended analogy between Rome's historical strata and the human psyche, but its basic contours and implications have been explored for many centuries.[53]

'At *Rome* in their hearts'

Spenser's earliest encounters with Du Bellay's Roman project, occurring as they did in or around his schooldays under Mulcaster at Merchant Taylors' School, provide one view of the pedagogical (and almost immediately poetic) stakes of the encounter with Rome. The education and career of John Donne rest on a rather different configuration of the relationship between Rome, schooling, and self. Spenser's imaginative encounters, negotiated partly via readings of Du Bellay's poetry, produce permanent traces that can be studied with the aid, for example, of the critical vocabularies that have been developed to study literary influence. Donne, however, lets us see that Rome can hide, rather than produce, evidence. Indeed, it is owing to Rome that we know as little as we do about the earliest and most formal stages of Donne's education.

Born in 1572, he was privately educated by teachers whose names will not be recovered with anything approaching certainty. He was matriculated at Hart Hall, Oxford, in Michaelmas term 1584. He left Oxford, we do not know when, without taking a degree. In May 1592 he was admitted to Lincoln's Inn, one of the law schools that made up the sprawling network of London's Inns of Court. His admission documents constitute our evidence that the entry to Lincoln's had been preceded by a period of study, presumably a year, at Thavie's Inn, an Inn of Chancery designed to

[53] See Freud: 'Nun machen wir die phantastische Annahme, Rom sei nicht eine menschliche Wohnstätte, sondern ein psychisches Wesen von ähnlich langer und reichhaltiger Vergangenheit, in dem also nichts, was einmal zustande gekommen war, untergegangen ist, in dem neben der letzten Entwicklungsphase auch alle früheren noch fortbestehen' (*Das Unbehagen in der Kultur*, in *Sigmund Freud Studienausgabe*, 10 vols. (Frankfurt: S. Fischer Verlag, 1969–1975), vol. IX.202); 'Now let us, by a flight of imagination, suppose that Rome is not a human habitation but a psychical entity with a similarly long and copious past – an entity, that is to say, in which nothing that has once come into existence will have passed away and all the earlier phases of development continue to exist alongside the latest one' (Sigmund Freud, *Civilization and Its Discontents*, trans. Joan Riviere, rev. James Strachey (London: Hogarth Press, 1969), 7). On the role of Classical culture in Freud's development of psychoanalysis see Richard H. Armstrong, *A Compulsion for Antiquity: Freud and the Ancient World* (Ithaca: Cornell University Press, 2005).

prepare students for the transition to the Inns of Court. Donne drifts from the records of Lincoln's Inn in 1594. He never formally practiced the law.

This educational *cursus* is worth exploring in detail because it was silently organized by what I have been calling the fact of Rome. Donne's Catholicism would have played the decisive role in determining the trajectory of his private education. Among other (considerably greater) threats to a young boy and his recusant family, private education would have kept Donne beyond the reach of the casual but energetic anti-Catholicism that permeated standard curriculum texts in the grammar schools of the late sixteenth century.[54] Private education in a family like Donne's would have immersed the boy, all at once, in versions of Rome that Reformation grammar-school pedagogy in England had worked strenuously, and ultimately in vain, to separate. For the process of reforming grammar-school texts and curricula involved striving to distinguish among versions of pagan Rome that could be accommodated to Christian education, versions of Rome that could be accommodated to Protestantism, and versions of Rome that could be accommodated to neither.

Donne had close and deep family ties to Rome via the Jesuits. His maternal uncles, Ellis and Jasper Heywood, had been received into the *Societas Iesu* in 1566 and 1562 respectively. Jasper Heywood returned to England from exile in 1581 and remained there (with time spent incarcerated in the Tower of London) until his deportation in January 1585. Whether or not Donne was educated by Roman Catholic missionary priests specifically, as Dennis Flynn has argued, it is reasonable to suppose that the elite private education his uncles had received as boys at the court of Henry VIII, along with Jasper Heywood's own long immersion in the world of Jesuit schooling, would have informed family attitudes and provisions for their nephew's early education.[55] In any case, Jesuit pedagogical rhetoric echoes much of the practice of advanced humanist pedagogical theorists in placing ancient Latin (and to a more limited extent Greek)

[54] On grammar schools and the Reformation see Ian Green, *Humanism and Protestantism in Early Modern English Education* (Farnham: Ashgate, 2009), 267–306.

[55] Dennis Flynn, 'Donne's Education', in Jeanne Shami, Dennis Flynn, and M. Thomas Hester (eds.), *The Oxford Handbook of John Donne* (Oxford University Press, 2011), 408–23. The central claim of Flynn's essay is that Donne did not return to Oxford after the 1584 Michaelmas term, and that with the aid of Jasper Heywood he departed for Europe, returning to England at some unknown point before his undertaking studies at Thavie's Inn in 1591. I am not persuaded by Flynn's argument that Donne was present at the siege of Antwerp in 1585, but the more basic possibility that anxieties about the dangers to which his presence at Oxford would expose him led his family to send him abroad as early as 1584 merits further investigation.

texts at the heart of the reading programs of schoolboys.[56] All this serves as a reminder that the matter of Rome was one of the great fault lines running through grammar-school education during the period.

Henry VIII's 1540 proclamation that the two parts of 'Lily's Grammar' would be the sole authorized Latin grammar in England had brought earlier versions of that text's composite image of Rome (its ancient Latin authors, its Roman Church, and Catholic prayers) under the power of the monarchy's efforts to secure educational as well as religious conformity. For since the time of the earliest layers of the work that would come to circulate under William Lily's name (in this particular case work initiated many years before the Reformation by John Colet in his Latin accidence, the *Aeditio*, and by Lily himself in his syntax, the *Rudimenta grammatices*), the goal of grammar-school education had been to offer instruction in Christian principles and in the linguistic skills necessary to digest ancient Roman authors.[57]

Private education would have aimed to ensure that Donne's schooldays could unroll, by design, away from prying eyes, even if these circumstances still posed a danger to the boy and his family. This is one of the inevitable complications spawned by the fact of Rome in the decades following the Reformation. At a time when even ambivalent ceremonies, wavering sympathies, and possibly 'innocent' material practices were susceptible to being identified as visibly and quintessentially Roman, a genuine attachment to Rome was to be worn like a cloak of invisibility – perceptible only as a kind of absent presence.[58]

Donne's early matriculation at Oxford, for example, was probably a strategic response to several pressing considerations stemming once again from the problem of Rome. Under ordinary circumstances, matriculation at an Oxford Hall or College at the age of twelve would have ensured that a young Catholic scholar could pursue a full course of study

56 On early Jesuit educational theory and practice see A. C. F. Beales, *Education Under Penalty: English Catholic Education from the Reformation to the Fall of James II* (London: Athlone Press, 1963), 3–16; Maurice Whitehead, *English Jesuit Education: Expulsion, Suppression, Survival and Restoration, 1762–1803* (Farnham: Ashgate, 2013), 9–22.

57 A 1527 edition of the Colet accidence (the oldest surviving version) is preceded by Colet's catechism, the articles of faith, an account of the seven sacraments, a discussion of penance, the Apostle's Creed, the Lord's Prayer, the Hail Mary, and two more Latin prayers. See V. J. Flynn, 'The Grammatical Writings of William Lily, ?1468–?1523', *Papers of the Bibliographical Society of America* 37 (1943), 86–9. On the fortunes of the grammar before and after the Reformation see especially the Introduction to Hedwig Gwosdek (ed.), *Lily's Grammar of Latin in English: An Introduction of the Eyght Partes of Speche, and the Construction of the Same* (Oxford University Press, 2013).

58 Dennis Flynn, for example, connects Donne's skilful internalization of the syntax of epigrammatic wit to Jesuit pedagogical procedures (Flynn, 'Donne's Education', 419).

without having to subscribe to the Thirty-Nine Articles and the Oath of Supremacy. This subscription was required of all Oxford scholars at the age of sixteen, but Dennis Flynn emphasizes that in the early 1580s twelve-year-old Oxford scholars were newly at risk of being called upon to subscribe to the terms of the Elizabethan settlement.[59] Accordingly, the family played fast and loose with the ages of Donne and his younger brother Henry when they joined Hart Hall, which appears to have been regarded as a point of relative safety for boys from recusant families during the second half of the sixteenth century. Donne was already twelve at the time but was listed as eleven; Henry was eleven but listed as ten. Once again, it is not known when the boys left Oxford, but their Catholicism would leave them vulnerable, even at the scene of instruction, for years to come. The fate of Henry Donne makes that clear enough. In 1593 he was caught sheltering a Catholic priest in his rooms at Thavie's Inn. He died under horrific conditions at Newgate prison a month later.

To step beyond the reach of the few facts that can be documented is to become almost wholly dependent upon Izaak Walton, who depicts Donne's life as a sequence of scenes in which education becomes a condition of existence for the young man. Walton's 'Life of Dr. John Donne' is our authority for the possibility that Donne's time at Oxford was curtailed 'About the fourteenth year of his age', by a period of study at Cambridge whose duration Walton does not set.[60] Cambridge records are silent on this point. There was no matriculation statue there to vex young Catholics, and Donne and his brother need not have matriculated or joined a college at all in order to study at Cambridge.

Jeff Dolven has shown that writers such as Spenser, Sir Philip Sidney, and John Lyly were 'haunted by the scene of their own instruction'.[61] In each case the mature works of these authors can be read against the backdrop of what we know concerning the nuts and bolts of humanist pedagogical practices at Merchant Taylors' School, Shrewsbury School, and King's School, thereby enabling scholars to reconstruct with considerable confidence the methods by which they were instructed as boys. We have no such backdrop against which we can read Donne.

This is a great loss since Donne, the great poet and preacher of immoderate desire, spoke more explicitly than any of these authors about the

[59] Flynn, 'Donne's Education', 411.

[60] Izaak Walton, *The Lives of John Donne, Sir Henry Wotton, Richard Hooker, George Herbert and Robert Sanderson* (Oxford University Press, 1936), 24. This edition reprints the 1675 fourth edition of Walton's 'Life of Dr. John Donne'.

[61] Dolven, *Scenes of Instruction*, 57.

kind of haunting described by Dolven. Donne would, in his later years, describe himself as having spent his youth '*imbracing the worst voluptuousness*, an hydroptique immoderate desire of humane learning and language'.[62] Remarks of this kind cast the hunger for learning as an appetite that sickens and weakens. It threatens the health even as it demands to be satisfied, and enthrals the schoolboy instead of liberating him.[63] It is striking that Donne ascribes to his studies a 'voluptuousness' and 'immoderate desire' that readers are more likely to associate with the scenes on view in his love poems. Donne offers this account of himself in a letter recalling his turn away from the study of the law. In its original context (the letter was printed in Walton's biography) the statement is part of Donne's attempt to depict his immoderate desire for learning as an extended process by which he unmade himself: '*and there I stumbled, and fell too: and now I am become so little, or such a nothing, that I am not a subject good enough for one of my own letter*'.[64] These remarks bring us, as though through a back door, to a negative image of Thomas Browne's efforts to place Rome within the economy of the call to 'make up our selves' from 'past and present days'.

We learn, via Walton, that Donne's tutors had been retained by his mother 'to instil into him particular Principles of the *Romish Church*; of which those Tutors profest (though secretly) themselves to be members', and that Donne would later undertake a protracted study of 'the Body of Divinity, as it was then controverted betwixt the *Reformed* and the *Roman Church*'. This new program of study is said by Walton to have been carried out via a close engagement with the works of Cardinal Bellarmine.[65] Walton further claims that these books were soon 'marked with many weighty observations under his own hand', as though preparing for the possibility that the books themselves might one day have to stand as evidence of the critical intelligence with which Donne had disentangled himself from Rome.

62 Walton, 'The Life of Dr. John Donne', 37. Italics in original.

63 On the interplay of self-assertion and self-annihilation in grammar-school pedagogy see Andrew Wallace, 'Pedagogy, Education, and Early Career', in *Edmund Spenser in Context*, ed. Andrew Escobedo (Cambridge University Press, 2016), 7–13.

64 Walton, 'The Life of Dr. John Donne', 37. Italics in original.

65 On this topic see R. V. Young, 'Donne and Bellarmine', *John Donne Journal: Studies in the Age of Donne* 19 (2000), 223–34. Young notes that 'Walton's dating is typically improbable, since the complete set of Bellarmine's *Controversies* did not see publication until 1593, the twenty-first year of Donne's life. Still, the main point is correct: occasional efforts in his sermons to refute or discredit Bellarmine's arguments provide evidence that Donne knew the *Controversies* and studied them throughout his clerical career' (223).

Donne's 'Learning, Languages, and other Abilities', says Walton, led to his employment by Thomas Egerton. The disappointments that follow these years and Donne's quest for a career are followed by further self-study, now in 'the *Civil* and *Canon Laws*', a prelude to 'a constant study of some points of Controversie betwixt the *English* and *Roman Church*; and especially those of *Supremacy* and *Allegiance*'. Walton says that Donne's decision to enter sacred orders was formalized by means of application 'to an incessant study of Textual Divinity, and to the attainment of a greater perfection in the learned Languages, *Greek* and *Hebrew*'.[66] Walton is clearly committed to depicting Donne's life as a continuous series of educations and reformations, both when the young Donne is under the thumb of family-appointed tutors and also when, as an adult, he is working to make himself fit first to speak publicly on matters of faith and obedience in *Pseudo-Martyr* and, later, from the pulpit.[67] Walton is, in effect, producing a carefully constructed narrative of Donne's turn away from Rome in the course of protracted studies. Studies of matters related to Rome are, for Donne, studies of his own self-division.

The matter of Rome sits at the centre of Donne's entire educational trajectory. This is so because the relation to Rome governed both the particular rhythms of Donne's educational career and also his negotiations with the discourses, and even the possibility, of education itself. Clear testimony to this dynamic comes in the 'Advertisement to the Reader' that opens *Pseudo-Martyr* (1610), where Donne gathers his entire family and its history into a scene of instruction and suffering. The sequence of reflections on view here begins by acknowledging with some irritation what Donne regards as overly hasty expressions of disappointment among Catholics. It then moves, as though inexorably, to an effort to describe, for the benefit of readers, the conditions under which Donne and his family were educated:

> And for my selfe, (because I have already received some light, that some of the Romane profession, having onely seene the Heads and Grounds handled in this Booke, have traduced me, as an impious and profane under-valuer of Martyrdome,) I most humbly beseech him, (till the reading of the Booke, may guide his Reason) to beleeve, that I have a just and Christianly estimation, and reverence, of that devout and acceptable Sacrifice of our lifes, for the glory of our blessed Saviour. For, as my fortune hath never been so flattering nor abundant, as should make this present life sweet and

[66] Walton, 'The Life of Dr. John Donne', 23–46.

[67] For an account of Donne's conversion in relation to grammatical culture see Brian Cummings, *The Literary Culture of the Reformation: Grammar and Grace* (Oxford University Press, 2002), 365–77.

> precious to me, as I am a Moral man: so, as I am a Christian, I have beene ever kept awake in a meditation of Martyrdome, by being derived from such a stocke and race, as, I beleeve, no family, (which is not of farre larger extent, and greater branches,) hath endured and suffered more in their persons and fortunes, for obeying the Teachers of Romane Doctrine, then it hath done. I did not therefore enter into this, as a carnall or over-indulgent favourer of this life, but out of such reasons, as may arise to his knowledge, who shall be pleased to read the whole worke.[68]

Donne takes pains throughout this passage to emphasize that he was no recalcitrant student of the men who had taught him as a child, no 'under-valuer' of the harrowing visions of martyrdom that must have been held before his eyes for emulation during the course of his early education. After all, the spectacle of martyrdom was, for this descendant of Sir Thomas More, the spectacle of his own family tree rather than of the stories preserved in John Foxe's *Actes and Monuments*.

The secret necessity of 'obeying Teachers of Romane Doctrine' would have been pressed upon him throughout his early educational experience. Donne is shoring up his reputation as a student in the first half of this passage, emphasizing that he did not instinctively scorn any of the lessons set before his eyes as a boy under conditions that had necessarily kept him cloistered. Even his response to early word of Catholic disappointments with his work comes wrapped in a conventional educational trope, as he asserts that he has 'received some light' concerning the reactions of the unborn book's critics. It is important to note in this context that *Pseudo-Martyr* returns almost ceaselessly to the language of teaching, with matters of doctrine (appropriately enough given that word's etymology) treated as matters of teaching. These passages see Donne depicting his entire life (much as Walton would do on his behalf) as a series of scenes of teaching that pitted him against himself just as frequently as they pitted him against the Protestant order of Tudor and Stuart England. For this reason and others, Donne's age could hardly resist the temptation to understand education as inevitably orienting students both towards and against Rome.

The possibility that an educational *cursus* pursued to a significant extent under the name of Rome could be less potent as a public handicap than as

[68] John Donne, *Pseudo-Martyr*, ed. Anthony Raspa (Montreal and Kingston: McGill-Queen's University Press, 1993), 8. It must be emphasized here that Donne's statements about learning are fitted to rhetorical occasions. For though the letter cited by Walton describes an immoderate attraction to learning, Donne speaks otherwise in the Preface to *Pesudo-Martyr*. He notes there that if priests and Jesuits wish to impute to him 'all humane infirmities, they shall neede to faine nothing: I am, I confesse, obnoxious enough'. Donne continues by speaking of his 'naturall impatience not to digge painefully in deepe, and stony, and sullen learnings' (12).

a condition of self-division is legible throughout Donne's career. At a climactic moment in a 1622 sermon he speaks of the irresistible duty of preaching, insisting that many members of his audience will be deeply, even inescapably, at odds with themselves:

> preaching is in season to them who are willing to hear; but though they be not, though they had rather the Laws would permit them to be absent, or that preaching were given over; yet I must preach. And in that sense, I may use the words of the Apostle, *As much as in me is, I am ready to preach the Gospel to them also that are at Rome:* at *Rome* in their hearts; at *Rome*, that is, of *Rome*, reconciled to *Rome*.[69]

Donne is citing and glossing material from the opening chapter of Paul's Epistle to the Romans, a text whose importance is taken up in Chapter 3. Here, it is only necessary to observe that Paul's straightforward and literal assertion that he intends to preach 'at Rome' (Romans 2:15) generates, in Donne, a squall of metaphorical relations and tentative glosses via new prepositions (in, of, to). Donne's 'at *Rome* in their hearts' is something more than a means of asserting that his remarks are directed at crypto-Catholics, since the rest of the passage goes on to generalize the lesson by emphasizing that God 'can make a Moral Man, a Christian; and a Superstitious Christian, a sincere Christian; a Papist, a Protestant; and a dissolute Protestant, a holy man, by thy preaching'.[70]

In this sermon Rome is hardly to be understood as a city whose coordinates can be plotted on a map, since to be 'at *Rome*' is to be 'of *Rome*', and to be 'of *Rome*' is to be 'reconciled to *Rome*' – all this in London. Donne's Rome is a condition in which one finds oneself, or, perhaps, the occasion of a discovery of self-division. Donne's conviction that his audience will include many who are 'at *Rome* in their hearts' must mean that he worries that their hearts are organized by the world, by its preoccupations and teachings, rather than by the Word. Each of them, he seems to fear, may secretly be the thing he had sworn that he was not in *Pseudo-Martyr* – namely, 'a carnall or over-indulgent favourer of this life'. The point is further developed later in the sermon, where Donne proposes that when Christians are gathered to God,

> Then and there, we shall have an abundant satisfaction and accomplishment, of all St. *Augustines* three Wishes: He wish'd to have seen *Rome* in her

[69] John Donne, 'A Sermon Preached at the Spittle, Upon Easter-Munday, 1622', in *Sermons of John Donne*, ed. Evelyn M. Simpson and George R. Potter, 10 vols. (Berkeley: University of California Press, 1953–1962), vol. IV.109–10. I owe thanks to Jeanne Shami for this reference.

[70] Donne, *Sermons*, vol. IV.110.

> glory, to have heard St. *Paul* preach, and to have seen Christ in the flesh. We shall have all: we shall see such a *Jerusalem*, as that *Rome*, if that were literally true, which is hyperbolically said of *Rome*, *In Urbe, in Orbe*, that City is the whole world, yet *Rome*, that *Rome*, were but a Village to this *Jerusalem*.[71]

Rome – the name itself, that is – provides a lesson in the powers of synecdoche and substitution, and a means of establishing (as Augustine himself does in *De civitate dei*) that everything from carnal passions to intellectual pursuits and spiritual ambitions is organized in terms set by that name. The passage also returns us to Virgil's First Eclogue's image of Rome as the teacher of secrets concerning ratios of size and power.

Rome's entanglements in discourses of education and identity construction help explain why the language of teaching is so closely tied to scenes of self-division in Donne's prose and poetry. Consider, as a solitary but conclusive example, the famous penultimate line of Donne's 'To his Mistress Going to Bed' ('To teach thee I am naked first'), where it is hardly possible to determine whether recourse to pedagogical diction is to be regarded as having empowered or disabled the speaker.[72] Away from the eyes of an educational culture bent on simultaneously fostering and ferreting-out different forms of devotion to Rome, Donne was systematically educated out of the possibility of comfortably regarding his training-up as a process of coming into his own. I have already referred to Freud's proposition that a trans-historical map of Rome, in which the city's various historical layers could somehow be perceived all at once, can make visible the otherwise ineffable structures of the human psyche. But Rome is also, as Donne's case shows, an enforcer of secrets.

I have, to this point, focused primarily on how Rome shaped Donne's life and education, but the city's fingerprints are, of course, all over his poems. Catholic thematics organize aspects of Donne's erotic poetry, and they supply the religious poems with much of the subtlety of their architecture. 'How are we to read a poem', asks David Marno, 'that begins by performing Catholic spiritual exercises but ends with a Protestant prayer?'[73] Marno's point of reference here is the first of Donne's *Holy Sonnets*, but (setting aside Marno's emphasis on a teleological trajectory within a single poem) the lesson could be generalized across a wide range of

71 Donne, *Sermons*, vol. IV.129.

72 John Donne, '*To his Mistress Going to Bed*', in *The Complete Poems*, ed. Robin Robbins (Harlow: Pearson, 2010), line 41.

73 David Marno, 'Divine Poems', in Michael Schoenfeldt (ed.), *John Donne in Context* (Cambridge University Press, 2019), 89. See, on these topics, Arthur F. Marotti, 'John Donne's Conflicted Anti-Catholicism', *Journal of English and Germanic Philology* 101 (2002), 358–79.

other works. Hovering behind the seven interlinked sonnets of *La Corona* is the rosary of St Bridget and its materialization of Marian devotion. *A Litany* recuperates and reimagines, but now in a personal mode, a form of recited communal prayer whose status was hotly debated along confessional lines during the sixteenth and seventeenth centuries. In all these poems Donne patrols fault lines as though bent on showing that it is possible to do so. These poems repeatedly take in hand Catholic forms and titles only, as it were, to strive to buff out the maker's mark. This view of the power of Marian prayer as one of Rome's exports will return, in a different historical context, in Chapter 4. For the moment, I will simply propose that the structures of Catholic devotional exercises and spiritual disciplines served as the dematerialized memory palaces in which Donne constructed his religious poems. Wandering the corridors of these memory palaces, he populated them with words and spiritual convictions selected in order to maximize tensions between the memory *loci* themselves and the utterances they were compelled to shelter.

The Escape from Rome

Spenser's and Donne's rather different entanglements in Rome are nevertheless linked by their repeated efforts to account for the thoroughness with which the city and its legacies had come to inhabit them. In the course of these efforts, the embodied self learns to accept – as a part of itself – the versions of Rome that it has encountered in, for example, the structure of schooldays, genealogies of poetic imitation, and the activity of sermonizing on texts such as Paul's Letter to the Romans. All this has been explored, to this point, from English (or in Spenser's case, English as well as Irish) soil. Further complexities emerge when literal voyages to, and departures from, the city are in play.

Some important stakes of sixteenth- and seventeenth-century voyages of this kind were identified years ago by Diana Treviño Benet.[74] Benet argues that 'the escape from Rome' became a significant literary topos during the period. She sees this topos as having facilitated explicitly polemical work for militant (or, in some cases, defensive) English writers. She cites examples from texts by authors ranging from Anthony Munday and a sailor named Edward Webbe to George Sandys, Fynes Moryson,

74 Diana Treviño Benet, 'The Escape From Rome: Milton's *Second Defense* and a Renaissance Genre', in Maria Di Cesare (ed.), *Milton in Italy: Contexts, Images, Contradictions* (Binghamton, NY: Medieval and Renaissance Texts and Studies, 1991), 29–49.

William Lithgow, and Edward Herbert, but she proposes that Munday, whose book titled *The English Romayne Lyfe* was printed in 1582, 'was probably the first to publish an "Escape from Rome" narrative'.[75] The text in question was Munday's self-defence in the wake of having publicly acknowledged that he had lived as a member of the English College in Rome in 1578. Though my goal is not simply to identify an earlier iteration of the topos identified by Benet, the second edition of Thomas Wilson's *Arte of Rhetorique* predates Munday's text by a little more than twenty years.[76] First printed in 1553, the book's 1560 edition features a new Prologue in which Wilson shows the extent to which Rome sets conditions for the individual's immersion in the world. That world of quotidian exchanges and interactions with the ordinary was constantly making and unmaking itself in relation to Rome and its language, its Caesars, its Virgil, its Ovid, its Church, its ruins, and its dead.

As I showed in relation to Spenser and Donne, boys trained up in these circumstances learned to recognize that they were *inhabited* by Rome. Because of this, an actual trip to Rome of the kind described by Wilson was susceptible to being understood as an especially vexatious encounter not with the unknowable other, but with a self bent into forms at once troubling, familiar, and somehow unhinged from the body. In his 1560 Preface Wilson declares that he wants nothing to do with the book that he is nevertheless sending back into the world in a jauntily updated new edition. He claims that *The Arte of Rhetorique*, along with his treatise on logic, titled *The Rule of Reason* (1551, rev. 1552 and 1553), almost cost him his life in the course of a visit to what he calls 'Roome toune'.[77] He asserts that he was charged with heresy in spite of an amnesty declared by Pope Paul IV, and he insists that his life was ultimately in mortal danger. The story is complicated. Wilson had ignored a summons back to England in 1558, and he is said to have been brought to the attention of the Inquisition by Cardinal Pole. Wilson was tortured and incarcerated at the Inquisitorial prison for roughly nine months. He escaped in August 1559 when a Roman

[75] Benet, 'The Escape From Rome', 38.

[76] Thomas Wilson, *The arte of rhetorique, for the vse of all soche as are studious of eloquence, set forthe in Englishe* (London, 1560) [STC 25800]. It is worth noting that Spenser could well have known Wilson's extremely influential text firsthand, since his friend Gabriel Harvey owned, and carefully annotated, a 1567 edition of the book. This later edition also contained the Prologue from which I cite here. It is possible, then, to see Spenser as wholly familiar with the 'escape from Rome' motif at a formative stage in his long engagements with Du Bellay. On Harvey's annotations see the Introduction to Wilson, *Arte of Rhetorique*, ed. Thomas J. Derrick (New York: Garland, 1982), lxxxviii–xci.

[77] Wilson, *The arte of rhetorique*, Aiiii^{v}.

crowd, supposed to have been angered by the Inquisition's excesses, burned down the prison on the day of Pope Paul IV's death. Following his return to England, Wilson would pay back the favour as an interrogator of Catholic prisoners under Elizabeth.[78]

Wilson's reflections on this nightmare press upon his book's readers a singular testament to Rome's ability to destabilize time and space: all this, he says, to what he called his 'greate daunger and utter undoyng'.[79] The city's famous name plays a key role in the process by which, as Wilson puts it, his antagonists had laboured 'to burden me with those backe reckoninges'.[80] 'A straunge matter', he observes as though still perplexed by the Eternal City's disorienting power, 'that thinges doen in Englande seuen yeres before, and the same uniuersallie forgiuen, should afterwardes be laide to a mannes charge in Roome'. Though Wilson asserts that Rome itself, and his books on rhetoric and logic (two arts with shared Greek and Roman histories), had conspired to endanger his life, he proposes that even in the midst of being fiercely questioned by his inquisitors he managed to impress them with his courage and boldness. These are, of course, values of the stamp that Wilson associates with countless figures from ancient Rome.[81] To offer just one example, the 'Epistle Dedicatorie' to the 1553 edition of Wilson's text, reprinted again in 1560, opens with an account of the force of eloquence in the conflicts between Pyrrhus and Rome. Wilson also asserts that his jailbreak was secured both 'by Gods grace' and 'through plain force of the worthie Romaines'. He concludes his little performance by disavowing any interest in the fortunes of this new edition of his book:

> And now that I am come home, this boke is shewed me, and I desired to loke upon it, to amende it, where I thought meete. Amende it quoth I? Naie, let the booke firste amende it self, and make me amendes. For surely I have no cause, to acknowlege it for my boke, bicause I have so smarted for it ... Nowe therefore, I will none of this booke from henceforthe, I will none of him I saie: take him that liste, and weare him that will.[82]

Wilson insists that 'Roome toune' and its cruelties have forever changed the nature of his connection to his own words: 'If the soonne were the

[78] See Susan Doran and Jonathan Woolfson, 'Wilson, Thomas (1523/4–1581), Humanist and Administrator', in *Oxford Dictionary of National Biography*, 23 Sep. 2004, accessed 22 Mar. 2020, www-oxforddnb-com.

[79] Wilson, *The arte of rhetorique*, Aiiii^{v}. [80] Wilson, *The arte of rhetorique*, Av^{r}.

[81] For a view of some of the cultural and personal values that sixteenth- and seventeenth-century writers associated with Rome see Warren Chernaik, *The Myth of Rome in Shakespeare and His Contemporaries* (Cambridge University Press, 2011).

[82] *The arte of rhetorique*, Aiv^{v}–Av^{r}.

occasion, of the fathers imprisonmente, would not the Father be offended with him thinke you? Or at the leaste, would he not take heede, how hereafter he had to dooe with him?'[83] Writer and book may be father and son, but *Roma nutrix* is their shared mother, and *The Arte of Eloquence* is every bit as much an image of Rome as it is of Wilson. Though Wilson is finally incapable of abandoning his book, he urges his readers to do so:

> Who that toucheth pitch shall be filed with it, and he that goeth in the Sonne, shalbe Sonne burnt, although he thinke not of it. So thei that wil reade this, or soche like Bookes, shall in the ende, bee as the Bookes are . . . And therefore to auoide the worste for all partes, the beste were neuer ones to looke on it: for then I am assured, no manne shall take harme by it.[84]

These passages capture with considerable force what is most disquieting about Rome's ceaseless oscillations between negative and positive. Wilson is every bit as confused about the nature of Rome's hold over him (especially with respect to its hold over what he loves and fears most) as Gildas and Bede were about the timing of construction on Britain's northern walls. The crux of the matter, however, is that Wilson's escape from Rome has thrown into vexatious question the nature of the relationship between the trained self and its capabilities.

As Wilson struggles to describe Rome's ability to destabilize time and space, he is poring over lessons drafted by Italian humanists. The notion that Rome was a palimpsest in which sequential events could be reconceived as simultaneously perceptible had found one of its most elaborate expressions in Petrarch's letter to Giovanni Colonna. In it, Petrarch reminds his friend of their shared walks among the ruins of Rome's ancient core. The letter is an explosion of literary and historical memory for which the city itself had served as detonator. Petrarch, like Wilson, was a visitor to the city that loomed so large in his imagination:

> Vagabamur pariter in illa urbe tam magna, que cum propter spatium vacua videatur, populum habet immensum; nec in urbe tantum sed circa urbem vagabamur, aderatque per singulos passus quod linguam atque animum excitaret: hic Evandri regia, hic Carmentis edes, hic Caci spelunca, hic lupa nutrix et ruminalis ficus, veriori cognomine romularis, hic Remi transitus, hic ludi circenses et Sabinarum raptus, hic Capree palus et Romulus evanescens, hic Nume cum Egeria colloquium, hic tergeminorum acies. Hic fulmine victus victor hostium artifexque militie Tullus Hostilius, hic rex architector Ancus Martius, hic discretor ordinum Priscus Tarquinius habitavit; hic Servio caput arsit, hic carpento insidens atrox Tullia transivit

83 *The arte of rhetorique*, Av^{r}. 84 *The arte of rhetorique*, Av^{v}.

et scelere suo vicum fecit infamem. Hec autem Sacra Via est, he sunt Esquilie, hic Viminalis, hic Quirinalis collis, hic Celius, hic Martius Campus et Superbi manibus decussa papavera. Hic miserabilis Lucretia ferro incumbens, et in mortem fugiens adulter, et lese pudicitie vindex Brutus.

[We wandered together in that mighty city, which seemed empty because of its expanse, but which has a huge population, and we wandered not just inside the city but all round it, and at every step there was something to provoke our speech and thought. Here was the palace of Evander, here Carmenta's home, here the cave of Cacus, here the suckling wolf and the ruminal fig tree, better named from Romulus, here Remus' leap, here the chariot games and the rape of the Sabines. Here was the Goat's marsh and Romulus' disappearance, here Numa's conversation with Egeria, here the combat of the two families of triplets. This is where victorious Tullus Hostilius, creator of the army, was victim of the thunderbolt, where King Ancus the builder lived, and where Tarquinius Priscus lived, who divided the classes. Here King Servius' head burned with a magic flame, here the savage Tullia, riding in her wagon, passed through and made the street shameful with her crime. Now here is the Sacred Way, here the Esquiline, here the Quirinal and Viminal hills, here the Caelian hill, here the Field of Mars and the poppies chopped off by the hands of Tarquin. Here the pitiable Lucretia fell on her sword, here the adulterer fled to his death and Brutus came as avenger of her wounded chastity.][85]

Petrarch continues at considerable length, with further gestures to great names, events, and spaces. The sense – or at least the grammar and diction – of the past's persistence is rather different here than it was in Bede. Bede, far from the banks of the Tiber, was moved to emphasize the work of the eyes in his efforts to document the survival 'usque hodie' of all that was conspicuous and visible of Rome in what was once Britannia, even though Bede and his monastic community were physically distant from the sites in question. Petrarch, by contrast, who has been moving amidst the ruins of the ancient city itself, emphasises nearness ('hic') and experiences every step as an enticement to tongue and mind rather than eye: 'aderatque per singulos passus quod linguam atque animum excitaret'. This is a view of the city as rhetorical occasion, and present participles ('evanescens', 'incumbens', 'fugiens', etc.) do much of the work of establishing both the immediacy and the subsistence of phenomena that Petrarch and

[85] See 'Ad Iohannem de Columna ordinis predicatorum, non sectas amandas esse sed verum, et de locis insignibus urbis Rome', in Francesco Petrarca, *Selected Letters*, trans. Elaine Fantham, 2 vols. (Cambridge, MA: Harvard University Press, 2017), vol. I.64–7.

Giovanni could not, for the most part, actually see as they wandered. For the ancient core of Rome was already, in Petrarch's time, the confusion that it would later be for Du Bellay. All of this energizes what is, for Petrarch, a decisive turn towards the self – and, by extension, Rome's self – as he works towards what might seem like a triumphant question: 'Indeed who can doubt that Rome will rise up again once she begins to recognize herself?' ('Quis enim dubitare potest quin illico surrectura sit, si ceperit se Roma cognoscere?').[86] That question, however, is preceded by a detailed record of the grounds of Petrarch's pessimism:

> Sed quo pergo? possum ne tibi in hac parva papiro Romam designare? profecto, si possim, non oportet; nosti omnia, non quia romanus civis, sed quia talium in primis rerum curiosissimus ab adolescentia fuisti? Qui enim hodie magis ignari rerum romanarum sunt, quam romani cives? invitus dico: nusquam minus Roma cognoscitur quam Rome. Qua in re non ignorantiam solam fleo – quanquam quid ignorantia peius est? – sed virtutum fugam exiliumque multarum.
>
> [But where do I think I am going? Can I sketch out Rome on this small roll of paper? Indeed even if I can, I should not: for you know it all, not because you are a Roman citizen, but because you have been most keen in investigating such things since your youth. Today in fact who are more ignorant of Roman history than Rome's citizens? I hate to say this, but nowhere is Rome less known than at Rome itself. In this I am not weeping just for their ignorance – though what is worse than ignorance? – but for the flight and exile of many virtues.][87]

To be distant from Rome – or at least to come to, and then depart from it – is Petrarch's precondition for knowing the city as well as he says he knows it. The fact that Petrarch has retreated from the city in order to write this letter is therefore significant.

English writers of the late sixteenth and seventeenth centuries could encounter this same counterintuitive insight in Montaigne's *De la vanité*. As it was in Bede, ancient Rome is, for all its historical distance from Montaigne, at once familiar and domestic. Rome is, to be more exact, a gift bestowed upon Montaigne by the father who had taken great pains to manage the circumstances under which his son acquired his facility in Latin. Wilson's attempts to work through the self's entanglement in Rome had already been printed when Montaigne published, and then repeatedly revised, his *Essais*:

[86] Petrarca, *Selected Letters*, vol. I.70–1. [87] Petrarca, *Selected Letters*, vol. I.68–71.

> Le soing des morts nous est en recommandation. Or j'ay esté nourry dès mon enfance, avec ceux icy: J'ay eu cognoissance des affaires de Rome, long temps avant que je l'aye eue de ceux de ma maison. Je sçavois le Capitolc et son plant, avant que je sceusse le Louvre: et le Tibre avant la Seine. J'ay eu plus en teste, les conditions et fortunes de Lucullus, Metellus, et Scipion, que je n'ay d'aucuns hommes des nostres. Ils sont trespassez: Si est bien mon pere: aussi entierement qu'eux: et s'est esloigné de moy, et de la vie, autant en dixhuict ans, que ceux-là ont faict en seize cens: duquel pourtant je ne laisse pas d'embrasser et practiquer la memoire, l'amitié et societé, d'une parfaicte union et très vive.[88]

I cite John Florio's 1613 translation:

> *The care and remembrance of evils is recommended unto us.* Now have I from my infancie beene bred and brought up with these: I have had knowledge of the affaires of *Rome*, long time before I had notice of those of my house. I knew the Capitoll, and it's platforme, before I knew *Louvre*, the pallace of our Kings in *Paris*; and the River *Tiber*, before *Seyne*. I have more remembred and thought upon the fortunes and conditions of *Lucullus, Metellus* and *Scipio*, then of any of our country-men. They are deceased, and so is my father, as fully as they: and is as distant from me and life in eighteene yeeres as they were in sixteene hundred: Whose memorie, amitie and societie, I notwithstanding omit not to continue, to embrace and converse withal, with a perfect and most lively union.[89]

Given that what Montaigne calls 'Le soing des morts' (the care of the dead) was a matter of great spiritual controversy in sixteenth- and seventeenth-century England, Florio has angled his focus to '*The care and remembrance of evils*'. The focus in Florio, then, is no longer, as it was in Montaigne, a synthesis of the care and remembrance of his dead father and ancient Rome. Instead, Florio's substitution has emphasized the 'evils' of the phenomenon of loss itself as he tries to negotiate Montaigne's fusion of father, son, and Rome in a 'parfaicte union'. A little deeper in the same essay he elaborates as follows:

> Les choses presentes mesmes, nous ne les tenons que par la fantaisie. Me trouvant inutile à ce siecle, je me rejecte à cet autre. Et en suis si

[88] Montaigne, *Essais*, ed. Jean Balsamo, Michel Magnien, and Catherine Magnien-Simonin (Paris: Gallimard, 2007), 1042. This reverses, consciously or not, Petrarch's despair in the face of the spectacle of Roman ignorance about Rome's glory.

[89] Montaigne (Michel Eyquem de Montaigne), *Essayes vvritten in French By Michael Lord of Montaigne, Knight of the Order of S. Michael, gentleman of the French Kings Chamber: done into English, according to the last French edition, by Iohn Florio reader of the Italian tongue vnto the Soueraigne Maiestie of Anna, Queene of England, Scotland, France and Ireland, &c. And one of the gentlemen of hir royall priuie chamber* (London, 1613), Ddd5^{v} [STC 18042].

embabouyné, que l'estat de ceste vieille Rome, libre, juste, et florissante (car je n'en ayme, ny la naissance, ny la vieillesse) m'interesse et me passionne.[90]

Even of present things wee have no other holde, but by our fantazie. Perceiving my selfe unfit and unprofitable for this age, I cast my selfe to that other; And am so besotted with it that the state of the said ancient, free, just and florishing *Rome*, (for I neither love the birth, nor like the old-age of the same) doth interest, concerne and passionate me.[91]

Rome, paternity, memory, friendship, and society are folded together in the search for an image of union between past, present, self, and other. This is, *par excellence*, a scene of absorption into a world that Montaigne and others understood as having been built by Rome. 'Interest', 'concern', and 'passion' are the hallmarks of that absorption. Montaigne is decisive: 'Et puis ceste mesme Rome que nous voyons, merite qu'on l'ayme'.[92]

These meditations on Rome's significance have as one of their vanishing points the corpus of set texts and disciplines studied and fostered in the schoolroom. A telling example can be discerned in a hugely influential set of sixteenth-century schoolboy colloquies or dialogues written by the Continental schoolmaster Maturin Cordier.[93] In a dialogue that falls towards the end of the volume, a pair of speakers named Phrygio and Stephanus are discussing the latter's travels to Italy. Stephanus spent a full year there, having resolved to visit 'Because of the fame of the country, touching which so many things are reported every where' ('Ob famam regionis, de quamtam multa multa ubique praecantur'). Stephanus confesses that his journey had been motivated by something that he has come to recognize as a form of quintessentially human perversity: 'you

[90] Montaigne, *Essais*, 1043. [91] Montaigne, *Essayes vvritten in French*, Ddd5^{v}-6^{r}.

[92] Montaigne, *Essais*, 1043. Florio: '*Rome* as it stands now, deserverth to be loved' (Montaigne, *Essayes vvritten in French*, Ddd6^{r}).

[93] Cordier had been John Calvin's schoolmaster at the Collège de la Marche, and it was at Calvin's request that he returned to Geneva to teach schoolboys after a career as master of rhetoric at Paris. Aside from essays by Elizabeth Hudson and others, not a lot is done with Cordier's Latin colloquies, but they were very widely used in Northern Europe and England: especially (though not exclusively) in reformed territories. The colloquies were in wide use in England by the 1590s if not earlier. Detailed 1607 instructions for probation-day exercises at the Merchant Taylors' School in London demand that students be able to translate and construe Cordier's dialogues and use them as models for their own productions. The statutes prescribe Corderius as an essential text for examinations in the second, third, and fourth forms. Later English translations by John Brinsley (first edition 1614) and Charles Hoole (1657) attest to the collection's continued popularity. Cordier's colloquies were first printed decades earlier at Geneva and Lyon in 1564, thereafter circulating widely in Northern European and English grammar schools. In 1576 John Harrison and George Bishop sought license to print Cordier's colloquies in England, but it is not clear that they actually produced an edition at this time. See Elizabeth K. Hudson, 'The Colloquies of Maturin Cordier: Images of Calvinist School Life and Thought', *The Sixteenth Century Journal*, 9.3 (1978), 61.

know well enough', he tells his friend, 'how greedy we are of novelties' ('Nec ignoras, quam simus rerum novarum cupidi'). 'O with what words', he is moved to ask when contemplating Rome's glories, 'or with what works, may we worthily enough glorifie thy name, O Lord!' ('O quibus verbis, quibus operibus satis digne glorificemus nomen tuum, Domine!').[94]

'With Latin words' must be one of the most obvious answers to this question, given the schoolbook context in which this question is asked. Exploring the implications of that potential answer will be one of the main projects of Chapter 3. Here, however, Stephanus can only lament that the thrill of his surroundings gradually dulled his commitment to acknowledging the thanks he owes to God. He tells his friend that he studied in and visited Genoa, Florence, and Venice. Finally, he visited 'last of all that *Rome*, which was called in times past the head of the world, but is now the fountain and original of all abominations' ('denique Romam illam, quae olim mundi caput dicebatur, nunc autem est omnium abominationum fons & origo').

To this last revelation that Stephanus visited Rome, Phrygio responds: 'Did you see that great beast?' ('Vidistine magnam illam bestiam?'). I have been citing here from the mid-seventeenth-century edition prepared by the London schoolmaster Charles Hoole, who does not comment upon this question concerning 'magnam illam bestiam'. However, earlier grammatical translations of Cordier by the schoolmaster John Brinsley offer the following terse marginal gloss: 'him, the Pope'.[95]

Throughout this exchange Stephanus emphasizes that 'all things almost did seem strange' or new to him in the cities in which he paused to study for three months at a time ('fere omnia mihi nova videbantur'). Scenes of study, novelty, and the bestial are mingling throughout this passage in suggestive ways, as Stephanus struggles to convey (for his own benefit as much as for that of his friend) the extent to which he became estranged from pursuits that are in a basic way quotidian, absolutely ordinary elements of his lot in life as a young scholar. The ultimate force of Stephanus' reflections is clear as he tacitly acknowledges that to be put through the paces of a humanist education during this period was to find

[94] All citations, Latin and English, are from Book 4, dialogue 34 of Maturin Cordier, *Maturini Corderii Colloquia scholastica, Anglo-Latina* (London, 1657), Cc1ᵛ–Cc3ᵛ [Wing C6292]. This edition includes both the original Latin text and translations by the seventeenth-century London schoolmaster Charles Hoole.

[95] Maturin Cordier, *Corderius dialogues translated grammatically; for the more speedy attaining to the knowledge of the Latine tongue, for writing and speaking Latine. Done chiefly for the good of schooles, to be vsed according to the direction set downe in the booke, called Ludus literarius, or The grammar-schoole* (London, 1614), Gg3ʳ [STC 5762].

himself living in the company of a relic of the past that had refused to loosen its hold on the present. It was, in short, a past that had become as monstrous as the Pope himself. Monstrous Rome, its Pope and the studies that bring Stephanus into their orbit are alluring and abominable precisely because they are inextricably tied both to one another and also to all the disciplines he has digested. He concludes the dialogue abruptly by saying that he doesn't have time to go into more detail concerning his travels because he has to get to his uncle's house for dinner. Schooling, and its connection with Rome itself, is another one of those things that won't fade from view even once the schoolboy has abandoned the schoolroom.[96]

The effort to come to terms with how Rome insinuates itself into the practice of education and the experience of learning ramifies outward into a number of sixteenth- and seventeenth-century texts. At a key moment in Book One of the 1605 first edition of *The Advancement of Learning*, Sir Francis Bacon pauses to take stock of 'those errours and vanities, which haue interueyned amongst the studies themselues of the learned'.[97] Though the *OED* cites 1615 as the first use of the verb, Bacon really does seem to mean 'interueyned' rather than 'intervened' – as though bloody networks of error and vanity were linking the studies of the learned. He divides this world of scholarly 'errours and vanities' into three classes: 'The first fantastical learning: The second contentious learning, & the last delicate learning, vaine Imaginations, vaine Altercations, & vaine affectations'.[98] That last category, marked as it is by both delicacy and vanity, subdivides and reproduces as Bacon works to find words to describe its composite threats to learning and the self. Note that in Bacon's final category the issue is not just learning but rather learning in conjunction with imaginations, altercations, and affectations: that is, with fantasies that organize the relationship between the self and its capabilities. It is there, within the last of his three categories, that Bacon begins. Like so many of the diagnoses and attacks ventured in the course of *The Advancement of Learning*, this particular one is immediately at risk of spiraling out of control.

The gods of grammar, historical sequence, and ideology seem almost to be toying with Bacon. He turns the history of humanist inquiry on its head, locating the origins of that complex and variegated set of intellectual,

96 This dialogue is regarded as a set of compliments to the great humanist printer Robertus Stephanus, or Estienne, a close personal friend of Cordier's.

97 Francis Bacon, *The Advancement of Learning*, ed. Michael Kiernan, The Oxford Francis Bacon 4 (Oxford: Clarendon Press, 2000), 21.

98 Bacon, *The Advancement of Learning*, 21.

pedagogical, and careerist programs not in centuries of Italian teaching, study, and collection, but rather in what he describes as the lone heroism of Martin Luther's attacks on Rome. Bacon thereby attempts to cast humanism as a specifically northern and essentially 'reformed' blast against Roman enormities. He is particularly interested in what he regards as Luther's efforts to awaken antiquity. He is fixated, finally, on waves of fashionable wrangling over standards of Latin prose, and concludes that those standards ran amuck in the wake of Luther's putative innovations:

> *Martin Luther* conducted (no doubt) by an higher prouidence, but in discourse of reason, finding what a Prouince he had vndertaken against the Bishop of *Rome*, and the degenerate traditions of the Church, and finding his own solitude, being no waies ayded by the opinions of his owne time, was enforced to awake all Antiquitie, and to call former times to his succors, to make a partie against the present time: so that the ancient Authors, both in Diuinitie, and in Humanitie, which had long time slept in Libraries, began generally to be read and reuolued.

Bacon's sense of Luther's supposed priority in awakening antiquity is surprising, as is his conviction that Luther was acting alone in his attempts to 'make a partie against the present time'. The language of factionalism pits the lone self and the dormant past against the present. Bacon's language is evocative, as those 'ancient Authors' are imagined sleeping away their days and nights in the libraries like overworked students. Nicely, he implicitly characterizes the Middle Ages not as a period during which those 'ancient Authors' are neglected, but rather as a period during which those authors had somehow needed to recharge, as though they had exhausted themselves during their own era through demands placed upon them by their cultural centrality.

Bacon soon turns his perspicacious eye towards fashions in Latin prose during the Middle Ages and beyond:

> This by consequence, did draw on a necessitie of a more exquisite trauaile in the languages originall, wherin those Authors did write: For the better vnderstanding of those Authors, and the better aduantage of pressing and applying their words: And thereof grew againe, a delight in their manner of Stile and Phrase, and an admiration of that kinde of writing; which was much furthered & precipitated by the enmity and opposition, that the propounders of those (primitiue, but seeming new opinions) had against the Schoole-men: who were generally of the contrarie part: and whose Writings were altogether in a differing Stile and fourme, taking libertie to coyne, and frame new tearms of Art, to expresse their owne sence, and to

> auoide circuite of speech, without regard to the purenesse, pleasantnesse, and (as I may call it) lawfulnesse of the Phrase or word.[99]

Bacon thereby praises the new attention to what he calls 'the Stile and Phrase' of antiquity, especially since this represented a rejection of what he regards as the perversities of Scholastic Latin. But he also emphasizes that these originally salutary developments, these welcome attacks on the terminological perversities of the schoolmen, had rotted and soured even in the course of ripening:

> This grew speedily to an excesse: for men began to hunt more after wordes, than matter, and more after the choisenesse of the Phrase, and the round and cleane composition of the sentence, and the sweet falling of the clauses, and the varying and illustration of their workes with tropes and figures: then after the weight of matter, worth of subject, soundnesse of argument, life of inuention, or depth of iudgement.[100]

And so the birth of preoccupations and projects that have come to be associated with humanist inquiry are first cast, strangely enough, as a reformed, Lutheran project that quickly fouled. Bacon studiously tracks that enterprise's rottenness through texts by Johannes Sturm on the continent, into the works of Nicholas Carr and Roger Ascham at Cambridge, and then back through Erasmus and beyond as he mounts his decisive criticism of these scholarly inquiries and stylistic disciplines: 'In summe', says Bacon, 'the whole inclination and bent of those times, was rather towards copie, than weight.'[101]

The most remarkable feature of all this is Bacon's insistence that Renaissance humanism is the child of a northern quarrel with Rome. One of Bacon's most recent editors, Michael Kiernan, calls this 'considerable rhetorical license' on Bacon's part.[102] After all, ancient Rome and its literary remains hardly needed to be reawakened for the first time in the 1510s, and far from being absolutely solitary and 'no waies ayded by the opinions of his owne time', scholars recognize that Luther was trained up into his interest in ancient texts by teachers and colleagues who were copartners in the enthusiasms Bacon wants to regard as Luther's innovations.[103] In light of these considerations, Bacon's quirky narrative of origins looks like something rather different from a strategic refusal to credit Rome with the developments ascribed to Luther. That, at least, is

[99] Bacon, *The Advancement of Learning*, 21–2. [100] Bacon, *The Advancement of Learning*, 22.
[101] Bacon, *The Advancement of Learning*, 23. [102] Bacon, *The Advancement of Learning*, 221.
[103] On this topic see Reinhard Schwarz, 'Beobachtungen zu Luthers Bekanntschaft mit antiken Dichtern und Geschichtsschreibern', *Lutherjahrbuch* 54 (1987), 7–22.

what Kiernan appears to be proposing when he speaks of Bacon's 'considerable rhetorical license'. Bacon's remarks, rather, read like tacit confessions that he simply cannot bear what the alternative might mean. That is, he cannot allow himself to see that one version of Rome had established a pattern for resisting and reforming another version of Rome, and that each version of Rome had continued to shape the educations, minds, and attainments of men like Bacon himself and of schoolboys across England and Europe.

Even in the midst of this, Bacon still has to face something when he speaks of Luther as having awakened 'all Antiquitie'. To propose that the Augustinian monk had induced in antiquity a renaissance, and then to track that reawakened beast as it slouches towards England, Carr, and Ascham, is to replay in a new key Rome's original military and administrative dominion over the island of Britain. The fact that Bacon's disquisition turns on matters of Latin prose style is all the more significant, given that ancient Rome's first hold over the island of Britain was secured in 55 and 54 BCE, when one of the late Republic's greatest and most distinctive prose stylists, a man who would come, in the wake of these military campaigns, to author some of the most enduring schoolbooks in European history, arrived on the shores of Britain with legions at his back demanding tribute from the Britons.

Scholars have long read these issues in terms of emergent discourses of nationalism. (I am thinking here of the enduring power of the idea of Julius Caesar, whose *Commentarii* became important schoolbooks during the late sixteenth century, or Renaissance England's deeply vexed relationship to its own histories of conquest by Rome, or century upon century of developments and fashions in Latin stylistics.) Alternatively, the discourse of civility has been a guide through this material, with scholars such as Richard Hingley taking their cue from John Milton's reluctant concession in *The History of Britain* that 'of the *Romans* we have cause not to say much worse, then that they beate us into some civilitie; likely else to have continu'd longer in a barbarous and savage manner of life'.[104] Camden, too, had already spoken in his *Britannia* of the complicated effects of Roman conquest.[105]

104 John Milton, *The History of Britain*, in *CPW*, vol. V.61. Norbert Elias cites the Abbé Gedoyn's essay 'De l'urbanité romaine' (1745), '*Urbanitas* signified that *politesse* of language, mind, and manners attached singularly to the city of Rome, which was called par excellence *Urbs*, the city' (Norbert Elias, *The Civilizing Process: Sociogenetic and Psychogenetic Investigations*, trans. Edmund Jephcott, rev. edn. (1939; London: Wiley-Blackwell, 2000), 88).

105 See the section 'Romani in Britannia', in William Camden, *Britannia, siue Florentissimorum regnorum Angliæ, Scotiæ, Hiberniæ, et insularum adiacentium ex intima antiquitate chorographica descriptio: nunc postremò recognita, plurimis locis magna accessione adaucta, & chartis chorographicis*

Bacon's unwillingness to credit Italy with the rise of humanist methods and preoccupations is obviously idiosyncratic. But it does help us to see that the fact of Rome, in all its threats, scandals, and abominations, insinuates itself into the schoolboy's, or former schoolboy's, relationship to himself. This is especially true where the schoolboy's reflections upon his own training-up by humanist tutors or schoolmasters are at stake. Matters of stylistic discipline and variation upon ancient models are regarded by Bacon as constitutive of Luther's personal, solitary project. They are even constitutive, it seems, of Bacon's sense that it really was a solitary project. Bacon, in any case, is every bit as committed to diagnosing personal stylistic perversities as he is to studying culture-wide failures or vanities.

All this establishes a proper reckoning of the stakes of Milton's decision to devote an important section of the *Defensio secunda* to the story of his 1638–9 Italian travels.[106] This is the story that Benet regards as the high-water mark of the 'escape from Rome' topos. Benet argues that the topos enables Milton 'to echo the public disapprobation of Italy, to remain true to his own esteem and affection for that country, to express his scorn for Roman Catholicism, and to present himself as utterly heroic'.[107] The *Defensio secunda* is a seminal treatise for any number of reasons, but my examination of it will focus somewhat narrowly on its efforts to fix the fact of Rome within Milton's understanding of the problem of the self.

At a famous moment in this treatise Milton turns his attention to what he is keen to depict as his unexpectedly early and expeditious return to England from Italy. The passage in question consolidates many of the issues surveyed to this point: from Spenser's negotiations with Du Bellay, to the intense self-consciousness with which Donne worked through his own connection to Rome, to the marks of self-division that run through the heart of Wilson's memories of the danger in which he found himself at

illustrata (London, 1607), D4^{v} [STC 4508]: 'Hoc Romanorum iugum quamuis graue, tamen salutare fuit. Salutare enim IHESU CHRISTI lumen Britannis una affulsit, de quo postea, & clarissimi illius imperii lux barbariem a Britannorum perinde ac reliquorum quos deuicerat, animis fugauit'; William Camden, *Britain, or A chorographicall description of the most flourishing kingdomes, England, Scotland, and Ireland, and the ilands adioyning, out of the depth of antiquitie: beautified vvith mappes of the severall shires of England*, trans. Philemon Holland (London, 1610), F1^{v} [STC 4509]: 'This yoke of the Romanes although it were grievous, yet confortable it proved and a saving health unto them: for that healthsome light of Iesus Christ shone withal upon the Britans, whereof more hereafter, and the brightnesse of that most glorious Empire, chased away all savage barbarisme from the Britans minds, like as from other nations whom it had subdued.'

106 For a recent point of entry into this topic see Filippo Falcone, 'Milton in Italy: A Survey of Scholarship, 1700–2014', *Milton Quarterly* 50 (2016), 172–88.

107 Benet, 'The Escape From Rome' (31). On the wider context see Catherine Gimelli Martin, *Milton's Italy: Anglo-Italian Literature, Travel, and Religion in Seventeenth-Century England* (New York: Routledge, 2017).

Rome, to the meditations of Petrarch and Montaigne. Milton can be said to have followed all these meditations and lines of inquiry to their ultimate source in the city itself. Given the charged confessional contexts in which Milton lived and wrote, the matter of Rome loomed at least as large for him as it had for either Spenser or Donne:

> Florentia Senas, inde Romam profectus, postquam illius urbis antiquitas & prisca fama me ad bimestre fere spatium tenuisset (ubi & Luca Holstenio, aliisque viris cum doctis tum ingeniosis, sum usus humanissimis) Neapolim perrexi: Illic per Eremitam quendam, quicum Roma iter feceram, ad Joannem Baptistam Mansum, Marchionem Villensem, virum nobillissimum atque gravissimum, (ad quem Torquatus Tassus insignis poeta Italus de amicitia scripsit) sum introductus; eodemque usus, quamdiu illic fui, sane amicissimo; qui & ipse me per urbis loca & Proregis aulam circumduxit, & visendi gratia haud semel ipse ad hospitium venit: discedenti serio excusavit se, tametsi multo plura detulisse mihi officia maxime cupiebat, non potuisse illa in urbe, propterea quod nolebam in religione esse tectior. In Siciliam quoque & Græciam trajicere volentem me, tristis ex Anglia belli civilis nuntius revocavit: turpe enim existimabam, dum mei cives domi de libertate dimicarent, me animi causa otiose peregrinari. Romam autem reversurum, monebant Mercatores se didicisse per literas parari mihi ab Jesuitis Anglis insidias, si Romam reverterem; eo quod de religione nimis libere loquutus essem. Sis enim mecum statueram, de religione quidem iis in locis sermones ultro non inferre; interrogatus de fide, quicquid essem passurus, nihil dissimulare. Romam itaque nihilo minus redii: quid essem, si quis interrogabat, neminem celavi; si quis adoriebatur, in ipsa urbe Pontificis, alteros prope duos menses, orthodoxam religionem, ut antea, liberrime tuebar: Deoque sic volente, incolumis Florentiam rursus perveni; haud minus mei cupientes revisens, ac si in patriam revertissem.[108]

> [From Florence I traveled to Siena and thence to Rome. When the antiquity and venerable repute of that city had detained me for almost two months and I had been graciously entertained there by Lukas Holste and other men endowed with both learning and wit, I proceeded to Naples. Here I was introduced by a certain Eremite Friar, with whom I had made the journey from Rome, to Giovanni Battista Manso, Marquis of Villa, a man of high rank and influence, to whom the famous Italian poet, Torquato Tasso, dedicated his work on friendship. As long as I was there I found him a very true friend. He personally conducted me through the various quarters of the city and the Viceregal Court, and more than once came to my lodgings to

[108] *Joannis Miltoni Angli Pro Populo Anglicano Defensio Secunda*, in John Milton, *The Works of John Milton* (*WJM*), ed. Frank Allen Patterson, 18 vols. (New York: Columbia University Press, 1931–38), vol. VIII.122–4.

call. When I was leaving he gravely apologized because even though he had especially wished to show me many more attentions, he could not do so in that city, since I was unwilling to be circumspect in regard to religion. Although I desired also to cross to Sicily and Greece, the sad tidings of civil war from England summoned me back. For I thought it base that I should travel abroad at my ease for the cultivation of my mind, while my fellow-citizens at home were fighting for liberty. As I was on the point of returning to Rome, I was warned by merchants that they had learned through letters of plots laid against me by the English Jesuits, should I return to Rome, because of the freedom with which I had spoken about religion. For I had determined within myself that in those parts I would not indeed begin a conversation about religion, but if questioned about my faith would hide nothing, whatever the consequences. And so, I nonetheless returned to Rome. What I was, if any man inquired, I concealed from no one. For almost two more months, in the very stronghold of the Pope, if anyone attacked the orthodox religion, I openly, as before, defended it. Thus, by the will of God, I returned again in safety to Florence, revisiting friends who were as anxious to see me as if it were my native land to which I had returned.][109]

Milton's careful, complicated work in this passage involves stitching together fictions in such a way as to answer charges levelled against him by the anonymous author of the *Regii sanguinis clamor ad Coelum adversus Parricidas Anglicanos* (1652).

Biographers have long recognized that Milton did not exactly rush home when he learned that his 'fellow-citizens at home were fighting for liberty'.[110] There is, after all, something like a confession lurking in Milton's assertion that he had been 'detained' or 'held' or maybe even 'embraced' (his Latin has the pluperfect subjunctive 'tenuisset', a verb with a wide semantic range) by 'the antiquity and venerable repute' of the city, as though Milton had only been half willing to acknowledge that Rome itself – its pleasures and splendours rather than its Catholic threats – had taken hold of him. A hint of passivity, moreover, is organizing his assertion that he 'experienced' ('sum usus') the humane courtesies of men of 'learning and wit', so that even in the midst of justifying his time in Italy Milton is already sliding in a provocative manner from detention to educated *otium* and the pleasures of sympathetic fellowship, confessing that news of what was presumably the First Bishop's War brings him face-to-face with

[109] John Milton, *Complete Prose Works of John Milton* (*CPW*), ed. Don M. Wolfe, 8 vols. (New Haven: Yale University Press, 1953–82), vol. IV.617–9.

[110] For a discussion of Milton's Italian journey and a detailed description of his itinerary see Gordon Campbell and Thomas N. Corns, *John Milton: Life, Work, and Thought* (Oxford University Press, 2008), 101–27.

the recognition that it would be 'base' to remain in Italy at 'ease for the cultivation' of his mind. Milton's remarks concerning his dashed plans to visit 'Sicily and Greece' briefly sketch, and then erase, the possibility of visiting one of two significant classical poles around which his education in ancient letters had revolved (here, Greece) only to see him forcibly, and as a result of what he describes as life-and-death deliberations, thrown back into the arms of the other: Rome. Milton thereby claims to have escaped not once but twice from Rome: first when he was 'detained' or 'held' ('tenuisset') by 'the antiquity and venerable repute of that city', and second, when he assures his readers that he narrowly escaped the clutches of English Jesuits with homicide on their minds.[111]

An analogous meditation on the desire to see Rome – and on the lack of wisdom that that desire betrays – can be located in Milton's elegy for his dear friend Charles Diodati in the *Epitaphium Damonis*, a poem written at the conclusion of his Italian travels. Milton laments that his journey had dragged him far from the scene of Diodati's death:

> Heu quis me ignotas traxit vagus error in oras
> Ire per aereas rupes, Alpemque nivosam!
> Ecquid erat tanti Romam vidisse sepultam?
> Quamvis illa foret, qualem dum viseret olim,
> Tityrus ipse suas et oves et rura reliquit.[112]

> [Alas, what wanderlust drove me to foreign shores, across the skyey summits of the snow-clad Alps? Was it so very important for me to see buried Rome? Would it have been, even if the city had looked as it once did when Tityrus himself left his flocks and fields to see it?][113]

These lines suggest that to seek Rome at buried Rome ('Romam ... sepultam')[114] is to fall into a version of the trap that Milton will later, in *Paradise Lost*, associate with 'Embryos and idiots, eremites, and friars', and with those pilgrims who have 'strayed so far to seek / In Golgotha him dead who lives in heaven'.[115] Milton's presence at 'Romam . . . sepultam', and his ignorance concerning his friend's death, entangle the poet's experiences of

[111] For wider context see Leo Miller, 'Milton Dines at the Jesuit College: Reconstructing the Evening of October 30, 1638', *Milton Quarterly* 13 (1979), 142–6. See also the useful caution by Campbell and Corns: 'It would not be safe to assume that something had gone terribly wrong when Milton had dined with the Jesuits in Rome' (*John Milton: Life, Work, and Thought*, 122).

[112] Milton, *Epitaphium Damonis* in *The Complete Shorter Poems*, ed. John Carey, 2nd edn. (Harlow: Pearson, 1997), lines 113–17.

[113] Milton, *The Complete Shorter Poems*, 284.

[114] Milton is perhaps echoing Vitalis' 'Roma . . . sepulta'.

[115] Milton, *Paradise Lost*, ed. Alastair Fowler, 2nd edn. (Harlow: Pearson, 2007), 3.474–7.

past, present, and future, and loosen his imaginative hold on the relationship between time and place:

> Et quae tum facili sperabam mente futura
> Arripui voto levis, et praesentia finxi,
> Heus bone numquid agis? nisi te quid forte retardat,
> Imus? et arguta paulum recubamus in umbra
> Aut ad aquas Colni, aut ubi iugera Cassibelauni?[116]

> [All unsuspecting, I was quick to seize upon the scenes which I hoped for so longingly in the future, and to imagine them as present: 'Hallo there! What are you up to? If there's nothing else you have to do let's go and lie down a bit in the rustling shade beside the streams of Colne or among the acres of Cassivelaunus'.][117]

Future dreams of resting by Diodati's side are now imagined as part of an impossible present, and they grade rapidly into Milton's poetic ambition to write on the subject of the matter of Britain. Future, past, and present collapse into each other once again via periphrasis as the region around his father's home at Horton is troped as 'iugera Cassibelauni'. Lamenting his travels to Rome at the time of Diodati's death, Milton imagines his own return to England under the rubric of Rome's earliest military encounters with the Britons. In effect, the Englishman will return home as a Caesar working his way into the territories of Cassivelaunus.

Throughout the wide range of examples collected in this section, we catch glimpses of Rome's doubleness. The city is, on the one hand, a repository of ancient virtues and works that have somehow managed to survive the ravages of time. This is, as the *Defensio secunda* has it, 'antiquity and venerable repute' of the kind that had left Milton glued to his seat in Rome. But Rome is also, as other popular expressions have it during the sixteenth and seventeenth centuries, a whore, a harlot, or the home of the Antichrist.[118] Even Montaigne had been moved to distinguish his interest in 'flourishing' Rome from his disinterest in the city's birth and senescence.

116 Milton, *Epitaphium Damonis*, in *The Complete Shorter Poems*, lines 145–9.

117 Milton, *The Complete Shorter Poems*, 284–5.

118 The classic source for these identifications is the Geneva Bible's marginal notes to the Book of Revelation. See also Thomas Nashe: 'Italy the paradice of the earth, and the Epicures heauen, how doth it forme our yong master?' The answer is grim: 'It makes him to kisse his hand like an ape, cringe his neck like a starueling, and play at hey passe repasse come aloft when he salutes a man. From thence he brings the art of atheisme, the art of epicurising, the art of whoring, the art of poysoning, the art of Sodomitrie. The onely probable good thing they haue to keepe us from utterly condemning it, is, that it maketh a man an excellent Courtier, a curious carpet knight: which it by interpretation, a fine close leacher, a glorious hypocrite. It is now a priuie note amongst the better

But there is more at work in these passages than a simple restatement of the city's conventional, if dangerous, doubleness. The texts and authors collected here help define the limits of rhetorical moves in which Rome anchors a series of metonymies. These metonymies designate perversities, abominations, and Popish impostures, but also learning, eloquence, and, even more broadly, powers of intellection, analysis, discipline, and interpretation.[119] It is crucial that these things are not simply understood as having derived from Roman traditions, but that they are actually susceptible to metonymically carrying the name Rome. In short, the word Rome designates things that are *out there*, but also things and faculties *in here*.

The effort to drive Wilson's and Milton's personal crises into the wider context of other literal and metaphorical encounters with the city suggests that what Benet calls the 'escape from Rome' is a metaphysical condition of the educated imagination, whether or not that imagination ever finds itself at Rome. It is the plight not only of intrepid Protestants who found themselves at, and then escaped from, Rome, but of anyone who has had their mind and body shaped by Rome and has recognized that they are living in the grips of that word's metaphorical registers. One more example drawn from Milton's work is the association between eloquence and 'Athens or free Rome' in *Paradise Lost*.[120] In *Paradise Regained*, too, Satan is made to confront the failures of 'the persuasive rhetoric / That sleeked his tongue' in lines that lead directly into the poem's vision of Rome.[121] That phrase, with its lovely transitive 'sleeked', provides an ideal image of Milton's self-consciousness concerning Rome's ability to remake the body in the course of nursing it into its attainments.

sort of men, when they would set a singular marke or brand on a notorious villaine, to say, he hath been in Italy' (*The vnfortunate traueller. Or, The life of Iacke Wilton* (London, 1594), L4[v] [STC 18380]). Roger Ascham complains that 'Italianated' Englishmen 'becum deuils in life and condition' as a result of their time at 'Circes Court' in Italy. See Ascham, *The scholemaster or plaine and perfite way of teachyng children, to vnderstand, write, and speake, the Latin tong, but specially purposed for the priuate brynging vp of youth in ientlemen and noble mens houses, and commodious also for all such, as haue forgot the Latin tonge, and would, by themselues, without à scholemaster, in short tyme, and with small paines, recouer à sufficient habilitie, to vnderstand, write, and speake Latin* (London, 1570), Iii[r] [STC 832].

119 See Alina Viaud, 'Rome et Montaigne dans Les Essais: le Transitoire et la Transition', Lurens [online], April 2011, www.lurens.ens.fr/travaux/literature-du-xvie-siecle/article/montaigne-et-rome. Rome is, on Viaud's account, 'par métonymie, une histoire animée par de grandes figures, une littérature et surtout une langue', and she calls attention to 'cette Rome intériorisée, édifice fait de savoirs, d'imaginaire et de mots'.

120 Milton, *Paradise Lost*, 9.671.

121 Milton, *Paradise Regained*, in *The Complete Shorter Poems*, 4.4–5.

Still in *Paradise Regained*, Milton describes the landscape around the plain of Latium as a protector and nourisher of the body, so that as the Saviour takes in his impossible view of Rome he sees 'a ridge of hills / That screened the fruits of the earth and seats of men / From cold Septentrion blasts'.[122] The view of Rome that Satan grants the Saviour, therefore, first pulls together in its urban geography sites that either display or care for the human body. The passage then throws into question the city's unaccountable hold on the human eye as the Saviour sees

> Porches and theatres, baths, aqueducts,
> Statues and trophies, and triumphal arcs,
> Gardens and groves presented to his eyes
> Above the height of mountains interposed.
> By what strange parallax or optic skill
> Of vision multiplied through air, or glass
> Of telescope, were curious to inquire.[123]

The principal backdrop here is an old scholastic debate concerning the question of how Satan could have shown the Saviour what he manages to show him during the temptation, but for my purposes here it is considerably more important to note that in *Paradise Regained* it is the vision of Rome *specifically* that brings Milton to the very verge of admitting that it might be pertinent to ask about the work of the Saviour's eyes in this scene. Milton has been pushed to the verge of asking this question by the theatres (or, as that word's etymology has it, 'seeing places') that crowd into view atop Rome's 'seven small hills' and amidst its 'palaces'. All this has been shaped, we are told, by 'the hand of famed artificers'.[124] Rome is a dangerous, tempting place, but Milton allows its name to stand for, and set before the mind as though they were an object of study, the labours of the hands that built it and of the eyes that take it in.

This passage makes an embodied Rome activate the hands and senses of the viewer (much as it activated tongue and mind in Petrarch), with the Capitol *and*, or rather *as*, its 'stately head'.[125] It treats Rome as a harbour for the body and offers a deft study of the city's capacity to 'sleek' and alter that body even as it throws into question the mechanisms by which the city is made available to the human eye. 'Cast round thine eye and see', urges Satan, sounding very much like Du Bellay in Spenser's translation.[126]

[122] Milton, *Paradise Regained*, in *The Complete Shorter Poems*, 4.29–31.
[123] Milton, *Paradise Regained*, in *The Complete Shorter Poems*, 4.36–42.
[124] Milton, *Paradise Regained*, in *The Complete Shorter Poems*, 4.35, 59.
[125] Milton, *Paradise Regained*, in *The Complete Shorter Poems*, 4.47–48.
[126] Milton, *Paradise Regained*, in *The Complete Shorter Poems*, 4.61.

Wilson and Milton appear to agree that the escape from Rome is as much a life-and-death negotiation with the self, the body, and one's own words, skills, and attainments as it is a flight from a dangerously Popish city, let alone a Satanic one, on the banks of the Tiber.

The Escape from the Self

I want to conclude with a few final glimpses at the remarkable plasticity of Milton's Rome. His material and imaginative encounters with the city and its plural legacies are shaped by several factors. After all, the city and its history combined all that an educated Englishman of distinctly neo-Roman political sympathies held dear, and all that a Puritan critic of Popish impostures found loathsome.[127] Milton, however, was unable to conclude that the city rested safely outside himself and that it could therefore be subjected only to the stark alternatives of disinterested study or polemical attack. A wider view of the issue helps us to come to terms with Milton's recognition that *both* versions of Rome had infiltrated his body and come to be associated even with the elusive shift and play of thought itself.

Milton's *Of Education* displays moments of simple appreciation for Roman discipline, as when the treatise suggests that mid-afternoon military exercises will be just the thing for schoolboys, asserting that they might 'by a sudden alarum or watchword ... be called out to their military motions, under skie or covert, according to the season, as was the Romane wont'.[128] In addition to this kind of conventional praise for Roman rigour, Milton also does much more penetrating work in the treatise. Note, for example, the following slide from a consideration of his program's overarching goals to an account of the past's grip on the present. From there, Milton tracks Rome's metaphorical troop movements inside the minds of his students:

> These are the studies wherein our noble and our gentle youth ought to bestow their time in a disciplinary way from twelve to one and twenty: unlesse they rely more upon their ancestors dead, then upon themselves living. In which methodicall course it is so suppos'd they must proceed by the steddy pace of learning onward, as at convenient times for memories sake to retire back into the middle ward, and sometimes into the rear of what

[127] On Milton and neo-Roman political theory see Quentin Skinner, *Liberty Before Liberalism* (Cambridge University Press, 1997).

[128] Milton, *CPW*, vol. II.411.

> they have been taught, untill they have confirm'd and solidly united the whole body of their perfected knowledge, like the last embattelling of a Romane legion.[129]

Thinking itself is troped here as an encircling force that marches methodically and inexorably under the banner of Rome. His imagined schoolboys are thereby inhabited by legionary troops fighting on behalf of the nation they have been exhorted to take as one of the chief objects of their study. Systematic thinking is, to put this another way, at once Roman and militant.

The troubles that assail this Roman encampment within the self are also perceptible in *Areopagitica*, where, in their effort to abrogate power 'into their owne hands', 'the Popes of *Rome*' are said to serve up daily evidence that they have successfully extended 'their dominion over mens eyes, as they had before over their judgments'.[130] This marks not so much an incursion into the self as it does the expansion of a power whose vestiges already lie within Milton's readers. As is often the case in Milton's poems and treatises, Rome always-already possesses that dominion, as interpretive and discursive faculties have come to be ruled by Rome – or at least susceptible to being explained as versions of Rome. This adds new force to the title of Richard J. DuRocher's study of Milton's curriculum, because it reformulates the question of what it might mean to imagine Milton not simply as living, teaching, and writing 'among the Romans', but as living with Rome and its Romans inside him.[131] This is surely part of Milton's goal in *Areopagitica*, where he works to compel Parliament to acknowledge the Inquisitorial origins of their licensing act. Parliament, like Milton himself, has thoroughly internalized Rome, but only one of these parties can see it.

These considerations, finally, supply a new perspective from which to assess Milton's characteristic depreciation of place. When Milton's attempts to determine what Rome might be regarded as 'meaning' require a turn inward towards the self, Rome is already there. This was the case in the passages cited from *Epitaphium Damonis*, where Milton imagines leaving Rome in order to return home to the island Rome had made its own. And when those attempts to determine what Rome might be regarded as 'meaning' involve asking what the present might owe the past, or what the past might want from the present, Rome's stirring and disorienting hold over time seems to be both the question and the answer.

[129] Milton, *CPW*, vol. II.406–7. [130] Milton, *CPW*, vol. II.501–2.

[131] See Richard J. DuRocher, *Milton Among the Romans: The Pedagogy and Influence of Milton's Latin Curriculum* (Pittsburgh: Duquesne University Press, 2001).

A final perspective on Rome is worth isolating here for its ability to establish Milton's understanding of sympathetic attachment. This view of the city and its possibilities is contained in a letter Milton wrote to Lukas Holste, a Protestant convert to Catholicism who had become librarian to Cardinal Francesco Barberini. Later, under Pope Innocent X, Holste would become Vatican librarian. Milton's letter was written in Florence and is dated March 30, 1639.[132] It sensitively commemorates Holste's generosity in admitting Milton to the Vatican Museum during his visit to Rome. He was, he says, a complete stranger, and he thanks Holste for having received him with the greatest politeness. He compares Holste's unpublished annotations on Greek writers to those souls who, in Virgil's *Aeneid* 6, await their journey back to the world of the living. His praise for this learned man is elaborate. The letter is most notable, however, for its depiction of the warmth and indulgence with which Milton says he was received by Cardinal Francesco Barberini – a great patron of the arts, a collector, and, indeed, a key figure of the Roman Inquisition: 'ipse me tanta in turba quæsitum ad fores expectans, & pene manu prehensum persane honorifice intro admiserit' ('he himself, seeking me in so great a crowd and awaiting me by the doors, practically taking me by the hand, admitted me within in a most honourable manner'). All this was performed, as Milton puts it, with truly Roman magnificence ('magnificentia vere Romana') that he was incapable of forgetting. To prevent forgetting is, after all, one of the great aspirations of Roman magnificence.

[132] For the full Latin text of the letter see Milton, *WJM*, vol. XII.38–45. See Campbell and Corns, *John Milton*, 122–3, for the wider context of the evening described.

CHAPTER 3

The Word

This chapter studies 'the word' by merging two fields of association: first, the agglomeration of human labours, social practices, cultural values, and codified grammatical systems that made possible and supported the acquisition of Latin; second, the inhuman order of the 'verbum Dei'. Each of these fields of association has, as its ultimate aim, the transformation of individual lives. It is under the rubric of this shared objective that I bring them together here.

Pressing these different constructions of 'the word' into conversation with each other can reveal something new about the work of Rome within language, the self, and salvation. The chapter, therefore, seeks to radicalize and redefine Chapter 2's treatment of the problem of the self. In that chapter, schooling, staring, and travel were used to study tensions between understandings of the self as being an immured condition of metaphysical finitude, on the one hand, and as being formed via the absorption of capabilities that arrive from the outside, on the other. Building upon that work, Chapter 3 argues that taking in (and learning to be altered by) the Latin word was the process by which Rome was experienced most intimately by the educated.

Because of the expansiveness and enduring significance of these issues, the chapter takes in a very wide historical range. The first half of the chapter explores aspects of the medieval Latin grammatical tradition and its early modern afterlives. My goal is to make some seventh-century wranglings on the subject of the Latin case system serve as a point of entry into later fashions of prose style, and into the pedagogical disciplines of systematic imitation that were developed to teach Ciceronian Latin to schoolboys. My chief interest is in the collection of implied understandings of the self that is being transformed via the Latin grammatical tradition, and in the extent to which grammar and exegesis could be understood as granting access to that self.

These concerns prepare the ground for the second half of the chapter, which opens with an anonymous seventeenth-century English translator's struggles to cope with some remarks ventured by Martin Luther at the conclusion of his 'Vorrede auff die Epistel S. Pauli an die Roemer' ('Preface to Paul's Epistle to the Romans'). In order to make sense of the translator's struggles, the chapter reconstructs the chain of texts (the New Testament's Luke-Acts nexus, Paul's Epistle to the Romans, and Augustine's *Confessions*) that underwrote Luther's remarks. Along this chain of texts Rome exerts a powerful but elusive conceptual force that Luther manages to harness even if it bucks his translator's efforts. Varied though these texts and topics may seem, they are united by their ability to show that minute grammatical and exegetical work enable Latin to provide a path to the world and a path to the self. These concerns bring into sharp focus the linguistic and spiritual stakes of medieval and early modern Britain's absorption into Rome.

Grammar, the Self, and the Vocative of *Ego*

Latin grammatical culture is one of Rome's most enduring and multiform legacies. Under the rubric of *Latinitas* ancient authorities constructed and debated standards of grammatical correctness. One special challenge for the Latin grammatical tradition's broad, trans-historical enterprise was to manage a pair of complex and destabilizing transitions away from the discipline's origins: from teaching Latin to its native speakers to teaching the language to foreigners in Spain, Africa, Gaul, Britannia, and Constantinople, and from teaching pagans to teaching within the dispensation of the Christian church and its civic and administrative cultures. Understandings of tradition and authority were constantly negotiated and renegotiated during the course of these transitions, from the pedagogical labours of the humblest teachers to the books produced by the most authoritative and influential late antique and medieval grammarians. The enduring emphasis on identifying and maintaining standards of correctness helps explain why grammatical and lexical oddities loomed so large in the tradition. It is relevant in this context that Latin grammatical inquiries are regarded as having originated in ancient Rome not as part of an objective and dispassionate analysis of the language and its structures, but rather in service of efforts to interpret stubborn religious and legal texts.[1]

[1] I am guided in these opening paragraphs by James E. G. Zetzel's invaluable *Critics, Compilers, and Commentators: An Introduction to Roman Philology, 200 BCE–800 CE* (Oxford University Press, 2018). On *Latinitas* as correctness see 52–6; on the shift from native to non-native speakers (94); on Isidore's role in transforming 'the categories of grammatical writing to accommodate a Christian world' (117); on the attraction to grammatical oddities (82–3, 92); on early laws and hymns (25). See also Robert

One of the more extreme forms of this fascination with grammatical oddities occurs in the work of a seventh-century grammarian who goes by the exceptionally unlikely name of Virgilius Maro Grammaticus. That name, of course, is a testament to this particular grammarian's eagerness to advertise the thoroughness of his absorption into the transnational and transhistorical grammatical cultures of Rome. Scholars now regard him as Irish. His works were widely read and cited by both Irish and English grammatical writers (for example, Aldhelm, Bede, and Alcuin) in Britain and on the Continent until the ninth century.[2]

Two works are associated with Virgilius: the *Epistolae* and the *Epitomae*. They are modeled on the hugely influential *Ars minor* and *Ars maior* of the fourth-century grammarian Aelius Donatus (teacher of Jerome). Virgilius, however, ranges out into ever more bizarre claims and presumably playful inquiries as he builds upon Donatus. He enumerates apparently invented forms of Latin, cites grammatical texts that seem never to have existed, compiles a catalogue of grammarians who appear to be fictitious, and creates for himself a fanciful vocational inheritance that connects him directly to ancient Troy in just a few generations. The original grammarian in this line, he claims, was one Donatus, who lived for a thousand years; this Donatus had a pupil named Virgil; this first Virgil taught a second Virgil; finally, a grammarian named Aeneas, discerning in his own pupil a renewal of the spirit of the ancient poet, bestowed the name Virgilius Maro upon our *grammaticus*. Several comic variations are being improvised on the subject of Donatus and Virgil's shared centrality in the ancient and medieval grammatical traditions.[3] As Rita Copeland and Ineke Sluiter observe, Virgilius appears to have set out to make the 'history of the world,

A. Kaster, *Guardians of Language: The Grammarian and Society in Late Antiquity* (Berkeley: University of California Press, 1988).

[2] For this characterization of his influence see Zetzel, *Critics, Compilers, and Commentators*, 354. For important work on Virgilius see Michael Herren, '*Bigero sermone clefabo*: Notes on the Life of Vergilius Maro Grammaticus', *Classica et Mediaevalia* 31 (1970), 253–7; Michael Herren, 'Some New Light on the Life of Vergilius Maro Grammaticus', *Proceedings of the Royal Irish Academy* 79.2 (1979), 27–71. The current consensus that Virgilius is 'clearly Irish' (Zetzel, *Critics, Compilers, and Commentators*, 354) comes in the wake of an earlier tradition that had judged him to have been a French grammarian writing in or around Toulouse. For an introductory discussion see Rita Copeland and Ineke Sluiter, 'Virgilius Maro Grammaticus, *Epistolae* and *Epitomae*, ca. 650', in Rita Copeland and Ineke Sluiter, *Medieval Grammar and Rhetoric: Language Arts and Literary Theory, AD 300–1475* (Oxford University Press, 2009), 248–54. For an extended treatment see Vivien Law, *Wisdom, Authority and Grammar in the Seventh Century: Decoding Virgilius Maro Grammaticus* (Cambridge University Press, 1995). Damian Bracken, 'Virgil the Grammarian and Bede: A Preliminary Study', *Anglo-Saxon England* 35 (2006), 7–21, offers a thoughtful assessment of the influence of Virgilius.

[3] On Donatus, Virgil, and the grammatical tradition see Wallace, *Virgil's Schoolboys*, 42–50.

of literature (if only evoked by the poet's name), and of grammar (Donatus) coincide'.[4] As this genealogy indicates, threads of play, parody, and serious inquiry weave in and out of the grammatical problems studied in the *Epistolae* and the *Epitomae*.

One of the more dizzying questions to absorb Virgilius concerns the Latin case system. Is there, he asks, a vocative of the word 'ego'?[5] A brief review may be useful here. 'Ego' is the Latin first-person pronoun as it appears in the nominative case (i.e., the case associated with the grammatical subject of a sentence). Ancient and modern grammarians distinguish the nominative (and sometimes the vocative) from the other cases, collectively referring to the others (namely, the genitive, dative, accusative, and ablative) as the 'oblique' cases. The word 'oblique' in this special grammatical sense shows that these cases were held to 'slant' or 'lean' or 'fall' (the latter explains the Latin term for grammatical case, 'casus') away from the grammatical subject, so that inflectional endings could be conceived of as spatializing the grammatical relations that inter-entangle individuals and the world. The process of coming to understand, even master, the case system's subtleties can be regarded as promising the individual a special kind of epistemological hold on the world. This involves a commitment to long hours of memory work and reading for the sake of learning to intuit the range of nuances that can be expressed by grammatical forms that compress within themselves a world of spatial, temporal, and ethical relations – all this as the relative freedom of Latin word order allows sentences to unspool themselves in unexpected directions.[6]

[4] Copeland and Sluiter, *Medieval Grammar and Rhetoric*, 249.

[5] Vivien Law notes that the question had already been tackled by the fifth-century grammarian Pompeius and others. See Law, *The History of Linguistics in Europe From Plato to 1600* (Cambridge University Press, 2003), 120. For other longstanding debates concerning the vocative case's numerous blind spots see John Rauk, 'The Vocative of Deus and Its Problems', *Classical Philology* 92 (1997), 138–49; Eleanor Dickey, 'O Egregie Grammatice: The Vocative Problems of Latin Words Ending in -ius', *The Classical Quarterly* 50 (2000), 548–62. Dickey notes that 'A long-lasting and sometimes acrimonious debate over the vocative form of second-declension Latin words in *-ius* began more than 800 years ago' (548).

[6] My description of these effects is influenced by Friedrich Nietzsche's account, in the *Götzen-Dämmerung*, of his earliest encounters with the Latin styles of Sallust and Horace. He recalls that a sudden and 'very serious ambition for *Roman* style' ('eine sehr ernsthafte Ambition nach *römischem* Stil') coincided with an unexpectedly decisive moment of self-recognition and self-possession: 'daran errieth ich mich' ('in that I knew myself'). Nietzsche discovers that he is intimate with what he (as a budding Hellenist and, as he puts it, his teacher's worst Latinist) had initially understood to be alien, and thereby teaches his readers how to re-experience as internal voices that might otherwise have remained stubbornly other. Nietzsche marvels: 'In certain languages what is achieved here is not even *desirable*. This mosaic of words in which every word, as sound, as locus, as concept, pours forth its power to left and right and over the whole, this minimum in the range and number of signs which

The singular and plural forms of the first-person pronoun are declined as follows:

Case	First-Person Pronoun	Translation
Nominative singular	Ego	I
Genitive singular	Mei	of me
Dative singular	Mihi	to me / for me
Accusative singular	Me	me (as direct object)
Ablative singular	Me	me (as object of a preposition)
Vocative singular	–	–
Nominative plural	Nos	We
Genitive plural	nostri (nostrum)	of us
Dative plural	Nobis	to us / for us
Accusative plural	Nos	us (direct object)
Ablative plural	Nobis	us (as object of a preposition)
Vocative plural	–	–

The vocative case governs direct address. Modern authorities agree that there is no vocative form for the first-person pronoun: i.e., no fixed form in which the first person can directly address the singular first person as a first person. J. C. McKeown concedes in his introductory textbook on classical Latin that, 'It may seem obvious that *ego* has no vocative (most people talk to themselves in the second person).' He is, however, keen to emphasize that some ancient and medieval grammarians and commentators were clearly puzzled by this blank.[7] McKeown notes that when, in Martianus Capella's *De nuptiis Philologiae et Mercurii*, the allegorical figure of Grammar begins listing irregular word forms, Minerva interrupts just as Grammar turns her attention to the first-person pronoun *ego*. McKeown interprets this as a sign that the author was orbiting a problem whose gravitational force he was keen to resist, as though perceiving the vexatious

achieves a maximum of energy of these signs – all this is Roman and, if one will believe me, *noble* par excellence.' ('In gewissen Sprachen ist Das, was hier erreicht ist, nicht einmal zu wollen. Dies Mosaik von Worten, wo jedes Wort als Klang, als Ort, als Begriff, nach rechts und links und über das Ganze hin seine Kraft ausströmt, dies minimum in Umfang und Zahl der Zeichen, dies damit erzielte meximum in der Energie der Zeichen – das Alles ist römisch und, wenn man mir glauben will, *vornehm* par excellence.') For the relevant passages from the chapter titled 'What I Owe to the Ancients' ('Was ich den Alten verdanke'), see *Twilight of the Idols / The Anti-Christ* (London: Penguin, 1990), 116–17. For the German see *Werke: Kritische Gesamtausgabe* (*KGW*), ed. Giorgio Colli and Mazzino Montinari, 9 vols. (Berlin: Walter de Gruyter, 1967–2015), vol. VI(3), 148–9.

[7] These observations appear in the augmented, online edition of J. C. McKeown, *Classical Latin: An Introductory Course* at www.jcmckeown.com. They do not appear in the 2010 print edition published by Hackett.

significance of an instability somewhere near the centre of an otherwise scrupulously mapped system.

If we are to believe Virgilius Maro Grammaticus, great minds simply could not get past this question about the vocative of *ego*:

> Verum Galbungus et Terrentius quattuordecim diebus totidemque noctibus in contentione mansisse referuntur tali, ut, si 'ego' uocatiuum casum haberet aut non haberet, ex omnibus doctorum ueterum traditionibus approbarent. Terrentius rennuebat uocatiuum casum 'ego' habere, qui casus uocatiuus secundae semper personae adiungi debet, 'ego' autem ad primam personam semper pertinebit. Galbungus etiam huic pronomini uocatiuum cassum accidere posse adfirmauit, in eo praecipue loco, ubi sub interrogationis modo uerbum primae personae haberetur, ut si dicas 'o egone recte feci?' uel 'dixi?'. Sed hic uocatiuus, id est ego, absque, 'o' et 'ne' adiumento circumpositorum stare non potest. Haec cum ad Aeneam quaestio me internuntio refferetur, ita eam uerissime euentilauit, ut, quia 'ego' primae personae pronomen est et uerbum primae personae imperatiuum modum non habet, cui uocatiuus casus semper annectitur, tunc tantummodo hoc pronomen uocatiuum casum retineret, cum sub interrogationis modo diceretur *o egone recte feci?* uel *locutus sum?*. Plurali tamen numero uocatiuum casum inueniri in dubium nulli uel contendentium parti uenire potest, ut nos o a nobis, praesertim cum imperatiuus modus etiam primae personae plurali numero flecti soleat; cum enim dicis 'nos dicamus', 'nos' hoc loco uocatiuus casus esse potest, licet et nominatiuus esse non negetur. Sed de hoc pronomine satis sit dictum.[8]
>
> [They say that Galbungus and Terrentius continued in debate for fourteen days and as many nights in an attempt to ascertain from the teachings of the ancients whether or not *ego* had a vocative case. Terrentius denied that *ego* could have a vocative, for the vocative must always be attached to the second person, whereas *ego* will always pertain to the first person. Galbungus claimed that the vocative case could be found in this pronoun, and particularly when a first-person verb in the interrogative mood was used, as when you say, 'O me (*ego*), have I done or spoken rightly?' But this vocative, that is, *ego*, cannot stand without the aid of the *o* and the *ne* on either side of it. When this question was referred to Aeneas with me acting as the intermediary, he held forth with utter veracity to the effect that since *ego* is a pronoun of the first person, and a verb of the first person does not have the imperative mood, which is the one with which the vocative is always associated, then this pronoun can only have a vocative case when 'O me (*ego*), have I done or spoken rightly?' is uttered in the interrogative mood. That the vocative case occurs in the plural number is doubted by no one,

[8] See the *Epistola de pronomine II* (70–97) in B. Löfstedt (ed.), *Virgilius Maro Grammaticus Opera Omnia* (Munich: K.G. Saur, 2003), 26–7.

> even on the part of the adversaries, i.e., *nos, o, a nobis* 'us, O us, by us,' especially since the imperative mood is routinely inflected in the first person plural. For when you say *nos dicamus* 'let us say', *nos* 'us' is here in the vocative case, even though it cannot be denied that it is also nominative. But let this suffice on this pronoun.][9]

Readers can be forgiven for failing, at first glance, to see the urgency of the question that kept the (surely fictitious) grammarians Galbungus and Terrentius awake for some three hundred hours. Given that Virgilius' *Epistolae* appear to ask to be read as, at least in part, a parody of grammatical culture, it is certainly possible that medieval grammarians would have been positioned to laugh along where modern readers are more likely to be baffled. Aldhelm, Bede, and Alcuin appear to have used him with caution.[10] It may be, too, that Galbungus, Terrentius, and Aeneas are nicknames designating a specific coterie of grammarians who were given to such play.[11] Finally, the entire production may be, as James Zetzel has proposed in a review of Vivien Law's study of Virgilius, a satirical *jeu d'esprit* of the kind that can remind us that the brilliant lunacy of texts such as Vladimir Nabokov's *Pale Fire* have lengthy prehistories.[12]

Whether he is bent on playfully amplifying certain perceived excesses in the preoccupations of the medieval grammatical tradition, or whether his principle goal is, as Law has argued, to embed grammar in the traditions of wisdom literature, Virgilius has located a problem that cuts to the heart of the ways in which ethical relations are mapped and constrained by prescriptive grammar.[13] The question here is whether Latin, which seemed to medieval grammarians (and, indeed, early modern authorities) to be capable of capturing, with clarity as well as subtlety, everything that was believed to be worth capturing, possessed distinct grammatical forms that

9 I cite the translation offered by Vivien Law in *Wisdom, Authority and Grammar*, 109–11.

10 See Rory Naismith, 'Antiquity, Authority, and Religion in the *Epitomae* and *Epistolae* of Virgilius Maro Grammaticus', *Peritia* 20 (2008), 59–85. Naismith observes that 'Aldhelm, Bede, and Alcuin seem to have been rather more cautious than most: for the bulk of early medieval readers, Virgilius and his companions could very easily blend into the classical and Late Antique background that was still standard fare in Latin grammars of the time' (72).

11 On learned nicknames in the period see M. Garrison, 'The Social World of Alcuin: Nicknames at York and at the Carolingian Court', in L. A. J. R. Houwen and A. MacDonald (eds.), *Alcuin of York: Scholar at the Carolingian Court*, Germania Latina 3 (Groningen: Forsten, 1998), 59–79. For a view of relevant contexts see Michael Herren, 'The Pseudonymous Tradition in Hiberno Latin: An Introduction', in J. J. O'Meara and B. Naumann (eds.), *Latin Script and Letters, AD 400–900: Festschrift Presented to Ludwig Bieler on the Occasion of his 70th Birthday* (Leiden: Brill, 1976), 121–31.

12 See Zetzel's review of Law, *Wisdom, Authority, and Grammar*, in *Bryn Mawr Classical Review*, 95.10.23.

13 On Virgilius and wisdom literature see Law, *Wisdom, Authority and Grammar.*

could govern situations in which speakers yearn to address themselves. This is not a matter of arcana and moldy paradigms, but rather of fundamental questions concerning how individuals might be understood to inhabit, experience, and relate to themselves in language. These are questions, even, about the unsettling arithmetic by which Latin grammar appears to compel the first person to address the self as a second person. Because Latin grammar's prescriptions are so systematic and so radically codified, and because its fundamental paradigms and exceptions had been in place for centuries by the time they reached Virgilius, apparent lacunae such as the vocative of *ego* called attention to themselves.

The question of what kind of access to the self Latin permits, and the related question of what the study of Latin demands of its novices, connect the nuts and bolts of grammar and grammatical culture to the larger machines of literary, political, pedagogical, philological, and cultural history. Though any number of dates might provide points of entry into these matters, the summer of 55 BCE serves as a case in point. This was the year in which one of the Late Republic's most rigorous prose stylists, the writer of *commentarii* (*De bello gallico* and *De bello civili*) that would become foundational schoolbooks across many centuries, arrived on the coast of Britain with thousands of legionary troops and cavalry forces at his back.[14] It is not possible to overstate the intensity of the connection between international power politics in the ancient world, on the one hand, and the spread of Latin, on the other.[15] Latin was one of the instruments by which Rome consolidated and normalized its authority over foreign lands and nations. It can also be regarded as one of the instruments by which individuals asserted empire over themselves.[16]

Virgilius, however, urges us to see that the analogy to empire mischaracterizes the nature of the relation to the self. His Terrentius addresses Aeneas in the decisive tones of a grammatical lawgiver ('Terrentius rennuebat uocatiuum casum "ego" habere, qui casus uocatiuus secundae semper

[14] On Caesar as stylist see Andreas Willi, 'Campaigning for *Utilitas*: Style, Grammar, and Philosophy in C. Iulius Caesar' in Eleanor Dickey and Anna Chahoud (eds.), *Colloquial and Literary Latin: In Honour of J. N. Adams* (Cambridge University Press, 2010), 229–42.

[15] On this topic see, for example, Bruno Rochette, 'Language Policies in the Roman Republic and Empire', trans. James Clackson, in James Clackson (ed.), *A Companion to the Latin Language* (Chichester: Wiley-Blackwell, 2011), 549–63; J. N. Adams, '*Romanitas* and the Latin Language', *Classical Quarterly* 53 (2003), 184–205; J. N. Adams, *The Regional Diversification of Latin, 200 BC–AD 600* (Cambridge University Press, 2007).

[16] On this subject in the context of early modern prose see, for example, John C. Leeds, *Renaissance Syntax and Subjectivity: Ideological Contents of Latin and the Vernacular in Scottish Prose Chronicles* (Farnham: Ashgate, 2010).

personae adiungi debet, "ego" autem ad primam personam semper pertinebit'). His outright rejection of the possibility that there is a vocative of *ego* is keyed to the assumption that the imperative mood would be the necessary vehicle for communication of this kind, and to the related conclusion that imperatives require the second person. Galbungus, by contrast, who is backed first by Aeneas and then finally by Virgilius himself, does manage to discern the stirrings of a vocative of *ego*. It lurks, as he puts is, 'sub interrogationis modo'. Galbungus, Aeneas, and Virgilius thereby agree to make room for this vocative under discursive conditions in which we are prepared to speak to ourselves in something other than the tones of a lawgiver. The speaker in this grammatical self-relation is to be imagined as harbouring misgivings about the solidity of the ground on which he or she stands, and as soliciting answers rather than thundering commands.

It is telling that the questions with which Galbungus illustrates his claim ('*o egone recte feci?* uel *locutus sum?*'; 'O me (*ego*), have I done or spoken rightly?') posit a self that is capable of deference, interest, modesty, courtesy, generosity, curiosity, and tact – especially towards itself. This amounts to an implied understanding of self-relation as involving an eager gentleness, as though we are not quite to understand our selves as being ours to command. We may want to command our selves, of course, and Virgilius appears to grant that Terrentius was on solid ground when he insisted that this discursive situation requires the imperative mood and, therefore, the second person. Galbungus, by contrast, reminds us that the imperative mode simply won't do in all circumstances, and that something more delicate and tentative is required to finesse the nuances of the *relation à soi*. The self is, after all, an unpredictable beast that should be approached with caution and care. Accordingly, it is only within the comparatively solicitous confines of the interrogative mood that Galbungus can imagine his way towards a vocative of *ego*.

In Virgilius, the structures of Latin grammar – which is to say, the phenomena that might seem least human, and therefore least congenial to our *ad hoc* understandings of selfhood – grant Rome, in its imperial spread, the power to make visible some of what is most elusive about the relation to the self and the grounds of our knowledge of the world. As he gropes his way towards what some linguists have come to call the 'epistemic mood' of the interrogative, Galbungus brings his readers to the brink of the deft play by which a much later Latinist, Montaigne, would replace the skeptic's positive (and therefore dogmatically self-defeating) assertion that humans have no grounds for certainty with the modest sleight-of-hand of a question – 'Que sçay-je?' We could do worse than to imagine Montaigne, who had grown up in a household in which he was addressed only in Latin, as speaking not to his contemporaries and readers when he posed this question, but rather to himself, and as having manufactured, as an epiphenomenon of his response to skepticism, a vocative of *je*.[17]

The opening paragraphs of Chapter 2 cited Kierkegaard's proposition that the self is 'a relation that relates itself to itself' ('Selvet er et Forhold, der forholder sig til sig selv'). This foundational tenet of Kierkegaard's understanding of the phenomenon of selfhood is deeply embedded in the philosopher's longstanding preoccupation with the relationship between 'inwardness' and grammatical moods. Kierkegaard is highly attuned to the force of grammar in his understanding of thinking, experience, and inquiry. One key measure of this preoccupation is his assertion, in *Enten-Eller* (*Either / Or*), that the 'Forførerens Dagbog' ('Seducer's Diary') section of that book is 'not indicative but subjunctive' ('ikke indikativisk, men conjunktivisk').[18] The assertion is not so much a description of the actual grammatical texture of the Danish text, but rather of the cast of mind in which the diary was composed by one 'Johannes'.[19] Kierkegaard emphasized that the study of Latin grammar had influenced his understanding of inwardness and selfhood.[20]

[17] The phrase was to be found not among the *Essais* but rather on a medallion that Montaigne had struck. It was accompanied by an image of scales and the Greek noun ἐποχή (i.e., a stoppage or suspension). On Montaigne's Latin education see especially Roger Trinquet, 'Les Origines de la Première Éducation de Montaigne et la Suprématie du Latin en France en 1530 et 1540', *Bulletin de la Société des Amis de Montaigne*, 4th ser. 16 (1968), 23–39; Philippe Desan, *Montaigne: Une Biographie Politique* (Paris: Odile Jacob, 2014), 58–75. 'Somme', writes Montaigne, 'nous nous latinizames' and he describes with pride the results of the process set in motion by his father: 'Quant à moy, j'avois plus de six ans, avant que j'entendisse non plus de François ou de Perigordin, que d'Arabesque: et sans art, sans livre, sans grammaire ou precepte, sans fouet, et sans larmes, j'avois appris du Latin, tout aussi pur que mon maistre d'escole le sçavoit: car je ne le pouvois avoir meslé ny alteré' (Montaigne, *Essais*, 180). See Florio's translation: 'And as for my selfe, I was about six yeares old, and could understand no more French or Perigordine, then Arabike, and that without arte, without books, rules, or gramer, without whipping or whining. I had gotten as pure a Latin tongue as my Master could speake; the rather because I could neither mingle or confound the same with other tongues' (Montaigne, *Essayes vvritten in French By Michael Lord of Montaigne*, H6^{v}).

[18] See Søren Kierkegaard, *Either/Or, Part I*, ed. and trans. Howard V. Hong and Edna H. Hong, Kierkegaard's Writings 3 (Princeton University Press, 1987), 304; *SKS*, vol. II.294.

[19] On this topic see Patrick Sheil, *Kierkegaard and Levinas: The Subjunctive Mood* (Farnham: Ashgate, 2010).

[20] See the essays collected in Jon Stewart (ed.), *Kierkegaard and the Roman World* (Farnham: Ashgate, 2009). Concerning Kierkegaard's education, Stewart notes that 'The strong emphasis on Latin grammar clearly made an impression on Kierkegaard, who frequently appeals to grammatical terms, often as metaphors, in his authorship' (x). Stewart instances a schoolroom epiphany concerning the phenomenon of inwardness as it is related in Kierkegaard's *Stadier paa Livets Vei*. Having asked a boy to explain the use of 'dum' with the subjunctive, the teacher offers a memorable account of the

Where grammar, by turns, enables and impedes access to the self, it operates like a Roman road through a wilderness that is at once unsettled and unsettling. Virgilius Maro Grammaticus and Kierkegaard help us to map this path. Hovering between those historical extremes is the broad spectacle of Renaissance humanism's protracted efforts to configure the relationship between self, language, authenticity, and self-discipline. The seductions of Latin style and artifice have their own peculiar histories, as do those individuals who found themselves born and trained up within a world that valued eloquence in the language of ancient Rome.

The Words of Others

Seventh-century explorations of Latin grammar by a figure as peculiar as Virgilius will, of course, differ in several respects from those of sixteenth- and seventeenth-century humanists. It would be easy to conclude that in this distinction we catch the difference between the history of a living language, on the one hand, and a dead or dying one, on the other. One early and still-trenchant version of this view can be found in C. S. Lewis' *English Literature in the Sixteenth Century, Excluding Drama*. In an introductory chapter provocatively titled 'New Learning and New Ignorance', Lewis insists that 'the classical spirit' that Renaissance humanism had helped inaugurate actually 'ended the history of the Latin tongue':

> This was not what the humanists intended. They had hoped to retain Latin as the living esperanto of Europe while putting back the great clock of linguistic change to the age of Cicero. From that point of view humanism is a great archaizing movement parallel to that which Latin had already undergone at the hands of authors like Apuleius and Fronto. But this time it was too thorough. They succeeded in killing the medieval Latin: but not in keeping alive the schoolroom severities of their restored Augustanism. Before they had ceased talking of a rebirth it became evident that they had really built a tomb.[21]

grammatical mood: 'the teacher . . . thereupon began to explain that we were not to regard the subjunctive mood in an external way as if it were the particle as such that took the subjunctive. It was the internal and the psychical that determined the mood, and in the case at hand it was the optative passion, the impatient longing, the soul's emotion of expectancy' (*Stages on Life's Way*, ed. and trans. Howard V. Hong and Edna H. Hong (Princeton University Press, 1988), 205; *SKS*, vol. VI.192: 'Det er rigtigt, svarede Læreren, men begyndte derpaa at forklare, at man ikke maatte betragte det Conjunctiviske paa en udvortes Maade, som var det Partiklen som saadan der styrede Conjunctiv. Det Indvortes og det Sjælelige var det, som bestemte Modus, og saaledes her den ønskende Lidenskab, Utaalmodighedens Længsel, Sjelens Bevægelighed i Forventning').

[21] C. S. Lewis, *English Literature in the Sixteenth Century, Excluding Drama* (Oxford: Clarendon Press, 1954), 21.

Lewis' remarks situate humanist labours among the necromantic fantasies that had animated Du Bellay's *Antiquitez* 5, where, in Spenser's translation, 'the shade of Rome' was likened to 'a corse drawne forth out of the tombe / By Magicke skill out of eternall night'.[22] What harrowing 'new thing' might stride from a tomb of the kind that Lewis sees humanism as having created?

Du Bellay and Spenser enable us to situate the linguistic matters that concern Lewis within the wider cultural phenomenon of encounters with the tenacity of the fact of Rome. What Du Bellay describes in *Antiquitez* 3 as a futile hunt for Rome at Rome (where the relationship between past and present is destabilized by the ancient city's persistence) drives its aftershocks into the history of Latin style. It was always thus; Lewis is right to acknowledge that the pattern for this effort can already be discerned in (but not by any means only in) Apuleius and Fronto.[23]

Lewis is equally animated on the subject of the contortions into which the humanists drove themselves:

> Elevation and gravity of language are admirable, or even tolerable, only when they grow from elevation and gravity of thought. To imitate them directly is to manufacture a symptom. The trouble is not that such manufacture is impossible. It is only too possible: even now any clever boy can be taught to write Ciceronian prose. The gestures and accents of magnanimity, laboriously reproduced by little men, clever, meticulous, primed with the *gradus* or the phrase-book, nervously avoiding what is 'low,' make an ugly spectacle. That was how the humanists came to create a new literary quality – vulgarity. It is hard to point to any medieval work that is vulgar. When medieval literature is bad, it is bad by honest, downright incompetence: dull, prolix, or incoherent. But the varnish and stucco of some neo-Latin work, the badness which no man could incur by sheer defect of talent but only by 'endless labour to be wrong' is a new thing.[24]

Making allowances for the stridency that emerges in Lewis's tone, these passages can still serve as a salutary critique of tendencies that have continued to shape some studies of the early modern period. Chapter 4 will argue, however, that it is possible to regard the tomb of humanistic

[22] Spenser, *Antiquitez*, 5.5–8.

[23] It could be argued that the classical Latin poetic dialect was already (specifically *because* it was the classical Latin poetic dialect) both a tomb and an experimental space. On the challenges that attend attempts to discriminate between old and new in Latin see J. H. W. Penney, 'Archaism and Innovation in Latin Poetic Syntax', in J. N. Adams and R. G. Mayer (eds.), *Aspects of the Language of Latin Poetry*, Proceedings of the British Academy 93 (Oxford University Press, 1999), 249–68.

[24] Lewis, *English Literature in the Sixteenth Century*, 24.

Latin not as humanism's narrow-minded betrayal of a living tradition, but rather as the logical progression of an insight that was already buried deep within medieval Latin: namely, that the living, vital language of learning and liturgy is by spiritual necessity the language of the dead.

In short, Latin was, like its speakers, all too mortal and human to be what churches and pedagogical authorities wanted their preeminent language to be. And although some humanist pedagogical writers were willing to celebrate the language as though it were *almost* timeless, Latin's longevity was also regarded as a hazard for students. According to the English humanist (and energetic champion of Greek studies) Roger Ascham, the language of Rome had rotted long before it managed to worm its way into England's sixteenth-century grammar schools:

> The Latin tong, concerning any part of purenesse of it, from the spring, to the decay of the same, did not endure moch longer, than is the life of a well aged man, scarse one hundred yeares from the tyme of the last Scipio Africanus and Lælius, to the Empire of Augustus. And it is notable, that Velleius Paterculus writeth of Tullie, how that the perfection of eloquence did so remayne onelie in him and in his time, as before him, were few, which might moch delight a man, or after him any, worthy admiration, but soch as Tullie might haue seene, and such as might haue seene Tullie. And good cause why: for no perfection is durable. Encrease hath a time, & decay likewise, but all perfit ripenesse remaineth but a moment.[25]

Far from being a stable singularity around which the educated could orbit, Latin eloquence is every bit as mortal and fragile as those who laboured to read, write, and speak it. Having established this one-hundred-year range of acceptable Latin, Ascham was ready to constrain it still further: 'Of this short tyme of any pureness of the Latin tong, for the first fortie yeare of it, and all the tyme before, we haue no peece of learning left, saue Plautus and Terence, with a little rude unperfit pamphlet of the elder Cato'.[26] According to Ascham, Latin provides readers not with a world of texts into which they can throw themselves with abandon, and certainly not with access to a vital, complex tradition of much more than one thousand five hundred years, but rather with a small coterie of specific authors among whom painstaking selections and discriminations must be made in order to establish the image of linguistic correctness – which is to say, the image of *Latinitas* – to which humanist pedagogical theorists had committed themselves. The best one could do, on Ascham's view, was to build up the educated self with texts and fragments selected for the purpose of

[25] Ascham, *The scholemaster*, Rii^{v}. [26] Ascham, *The scholemaster*, Rii^{v}.

reestablishing 'that purenesse of the Latin tong in Rome, whan Rome did most florish in well doing, and so thereby, in well speaking also'.[27] As far as Ascham is concerned, ripeness and flourishing are as essential to the life of a language as they are to the life of its speakers.

Latin is acquired under circumstances that bring before the eyes of its novices the fact of their humanity: the susceptibility to error, the attraction to difficulty that can somehow coexist with inveterate laziness, the spectre of the will. It is acquired (like any ancient language) via years of formal studies that ceaselessly test self-discipline as well as mental agility. The disciplined study of Latin, therefore, situates the student at once within the world and in relation to the self. It may be that this is one of the chief functions of language generally, but the self-conscious artificiality of classical, literary Latin (a language that was never really, not even in ancient Rome, anyone's mother tongue) plays a decisive role in these calculations.[28] Notwithstanding the claims of enthusiastic Renaissance title pages and dedicatory epistles, there has never been anything like a speedy way to acquire enough Latin to read the classical poetic texts that were among medieval and early modern pedagogy's most heralded goals. The Latin tongue's greatest ancient poetics texts, moreover, are written in a literary dialect that gives every appearance of having operated at arm's length from the spoken vulgate, and that seems, because of this, to have belonged to no one.[29] Forests of rules, exceptions, sanctioned variations, and omissions provided occasion for corporal punishment, celebrations of logical order, and even mystified speculation and meditation.

Latin eloquence could appear, in the eyes of medieval and early modern writers, to lift individuals out of their own age and, as though in violation of time's arrow, deposit them among the great stylists of antiquity. This is the function of the commonplace designation of so many individual writers, soldiers, and statesmen as *ultimus Romanorum* – 'last of the Romans'. Petrarch's Latin epistles to the ancient dead are one of the most spectacular testaments to this aspiration. Contacts with ancient authors are contacts with a self that has been made strange via the distinctiveness of the problematic that is Rome and its language. This self is at once housed in the body and estranged from the body's limits as it is built

[27] Ascham, *The scholemaster*, Rii^{v}.

[28] The foundational statement on the artificiality of Latin derives from Dante's *De vulgari eloquentia*. See Marianne Shapiro, *De Vulgari Eloquentia: Dante's Book of Exile* (Lincoln: University of Nebraska Press, 1990), 18–28.

[29] On this relationship see the essays collected in Dickey and Chahoud (eds.), *Colloquial and Literary Latin*.

up in the course of encounters with a vast network of grammatical, historical, and social phenomena.

Grammatical errors could see schoolboys punished with birch and palmer.[30] Poets could be mocked, and would-be authorities shamed, within the environment of Renaissance humanism's newly (and fiercely) constrained conceptions of eloquence. Poggio Bracciolini's attacks on Lorenzo Valla's *Elegantiae linguae latinae* offer a classic Continental instance of humanists feuding over Latin errors.[31] In Renaissance England these territories were contested in the so-called Grammarians' War.[32] The complex and even glorious artifice of the Latin grammatical system was in important ways a regulator of civic life throughout the Middle Ages and Renaissance. Understandings of selfhood, moreover, were forged and debated within the boundaries of prescriptive grammar. This, at least, is one of the lessons that Virgilius' work on the vocative of *ego* bequeathed to readers such as Aldhelm, Bede, and Alcuin during the Middle Ages. It also set a precedent for lessons that lurk within some influential humanist pedagogical practices.

A series of complex connections among the rigours of Latin grammar, the subtleties of Latin style, and conceptions of the self are perceptible in a 1528 Latin treatise by Erasmus. I noted in Chapter 2 that Erasmus was one of the targets of Bacon's criticisms on the subject of stylistic excesses and misplaced priorities, with Bacon complaining that 'the whole inclination and bent of those times, was rather towards copie, than weight'.[33] It is therefore fitting that Erasmus himself makes a series of thoughtful interventions into his own period's simultaneous valorization of both copiousness and concision, and into the stylistic excesses that humanist methods could breed. His *Dialogus, cui titulus Ciceronianus, sive, De optimo dicendi genere* advances a set of wry reflections on the cultural supremacy of a writer

[30] On birch, rod, palmer, and grammatical studies see Wallace, *Virgil's Schoolboys*, 209–213.

[31] On the ancient foundations of humanistic studies see Bloomer's *The School of Rome*. On Medieval Latin see F. A. C. Mantello and A. G. Rigg (eds.), *Medieval Latin: An Introduction and Bibliographical Guide* (Washington: Catholic University of America Press, 1996). For a wide-ranging discussion of Latin during the Renaissance see Ann Moss, *Renaissance Truth and the Latin Language Turn* (Oxford University Press, 2003). On feuds see S. I. Camporeale, 'Poggio Bracciolini versus Lorenzo Valla: The *Orationes in Laurentiam Valla*', in J. Marino and M. Schlitt (eds.), *Perspectives on Early Modern and Modern Intellectual History: Essays in Honor of Nancy S. Struever* (University of Rochester Press, 2001), 27–48.

[32] See David R. Carlson, 'The "Grammarians' War" 1519–1521: Humanist Careerism in Early Tudor England, and Printing', *Medievalia et Humanistica*, n.s. 18 (1992), 157–81; Rachel McGregor, '"Run Not Before the Laws": Lily's *Grammar*, the Oxford *Bellum grammaticale*, and the Rules of Concord', *Renaissance Studies* 29 (2015), 261–79.

[33] Bacon, *The Advancement of Learning*, 23.

whose prose had come to be regarded in many humanist circles as *the* model for eloquent, refined, and persuasive Latin.[34] Because of this, the sixteenth-century stylistic fashion that is called 'Ciceronianism' makes Cicero himself one of the dead whose rebirth was being pursued with the aid of the vivifying power of the language of Rome. Hyperbolic attention to Cicero's words is, to cite once again Spenser's translation of Du Bellay, the 'Magicke skill' that draws a living corpse from the tomb of 'eternall night' (5.5–8) and, unaccountably, strives to make that corpse take up residence within the self.

It is easy to see how rigorously programmatic imitation of a single model – for rigorously programmatic imitation was one of the chief educational disciplines fostered in early modern grammar schools – could be at once liberating and inhibiting. It was liberating because Cicero was venerated as one of the last great exemplars of the power of eloquence and the possibility of liberty under the ancient Republic of Rome. It was inhibiting because the logic of capture organized grammar-school exercises in translation, imitation, and composition. Erasmus shows that one of the many 'bipolar' views of new and old Rome can be made to revolve around the figure of 'Tully'.

Erasmus' dialogue satirizes extreme devotion to the ancient writer's words. As in Virgilius, parody leads directly to insights concerning the relationship between obsessive linguistic inquiries and access to the self. Parody, in this sense, might be regarded as a simulacrum of the questioning within which Virgilius roots the relation to the self, for parody and the interrogative mode can both work via subtle patterns of indirection.

In Erasmus' treatise a man named Nosoponus is encouraged to describe, and then compelled to face, the pernicious extremes to which he has been pursuing his passionate attachment to a narrow and excessively severe construction of eloquence. He is, to put the matter plainly, visibly ill as a result of his devotion. Ten years of disabling labour have left him at the

[34] On the Italian scene see Martin L. McLaughlin, *Literary Imitation in the Italian Renaissance: The Theory and Practice of Literary Imitation in Italy from Dante to Bembo* (Oxford: Clarendon Press, 1995). For a selection of relevant primary texts see JoAnn DellaNeva (ed.), *Ciceronian Controversies*, trans. Brian Duvick, The I Tatti Renaissance Library 26 (Cambridge, MA: Harvard University Press, 2007). For an overview of the English scene see Alvin Vos, '"Good Matter and Good Utterance": The Character of English Ciceronianism', *Studies in English Literature, 1500–1900* 19 (1979), 3–18. On the wider context within which Ciceronianism and its discontents must be understood see Peter Mack, *A History of Renaissance Rhetoric, 1380–1620* (Oxford University Press, 2011). For a salutary reminder that even Ciceronianism needs to be studied in a much longer historical range see George Hardin Brown, 'Ciceronianism in Bede and Alcuin', in Blanton and Scheck (eds.), *Intertext*, 319–29. See also Leeds, *Renaissance Syntax and Subjectivity*, 43–80.

mercy of 'diua quae Graece dicitur πειθώ' – which is to say, the goddess who is called 'persuasion' in Greek.[35] His acquaintance, Bulephorus, claims to know how to trace back to its origins in Latin stylistic excesses an illness that has produced all the visible signs of an erotic subjection. He confesses (though perhaps only as part of the satirical therapy he intends to minister to Nosoponus) that he has been vulnerable to the same condition: 'I know what a violent thing desire is and what it is to be νυμθόληπτον' ('Noui quam sit res violenta Cupido, et quid sit esse νυμθόληπτον'; the ancient Greek compound means 'captured by a nymph'). Thus far, the noun πειθώ has seemed to situate the illness of Nosoponus within the broad spectrum of an affective (and even erotic) attachment to rhetoric as such, so long as we recognize that the attachment in question is monogamous:

> NOSOP. Vt paucis dicam, mihi putet omnis eloquentia praeter Ciceronianam. Haec est illa nympha, cuius amore colliquesco.
> BUL. Nunc affectum intelligo tuum. Spetiosum illud et amabile Ciceroniani cognomen ambis.
> NOSOP. Adeo vt ni consequar, vitam mihi acerbam existimem.[36]

> [NO. – To put it in a few words, all eloquence revolts me, apart from the Ciceronian sort. That's the nymph for love of whom I'm melting away.
> BU. – Now I understand the state you're in. You're out to win that lovely, splendid title of 'Ciceronian'.
> NO. – Yes. I want it so much that if I don't achieve it, I shall consider my whole life bitter and wasted.][37]

By a submerged Epicurean logic, Ciceronian sweetness bestows so much (in this case, debilitating) pleasure that its absence is experienced as illness.[38] Accordingly, the quest for a clear, but rigorously narrow, conception of stylistic perfection conjures up a romance narrative involving love, imprisonment, and longing. This cluster of passions and predicaments is a longstanding marker of grammatical culture's attachment to the erotics of instruction that connects late antiquity and the Middle Ages to the Renaissance.[39]

Bulephorus and a third interlocutor, Hypologus, pretend to be in the grips of the same fervour as Nosoponus. This moves the latter to expound

[35] *ASD*, vol. I–2.607. [36] *ASD*, vol. I–2.607.
[37] Erasmus, *The Collected Works of Erasmus* (*CWE*) (University of Toronto Press, 1974–), vol. XXVIII.344.
[38] On Erasmus and Epicureanism see Peter Bietenholz, '*Felicitas* (Eudaimonia) ou les Promenades d'Érasme dans le Jardin d'Épicure', *Renaissance and Reformation* 30 (2006), 37–86.
[39] On this cluster see Wallace, *Virgil's Schoolboys*, 50–77.

upon practices that are at once scholarly disciplines and neurotic symptoms: 'And so,' he says, 'in the presence of initiates of the same god, I will reveal the mysteries. For seven whole years now I have touched no books but Ciceronian ones, abstaining from all the rest as religiously as a Carthusian from meat.'[40] This devotion imposes clear limits on his reading: 'there is absolutely no place in my library for anyone else at all but Cicero' ('nec vlli prorsus est locus in mea bibliotheca, praeterquam vni Ciceroni').[41] The devotion to one single model of eloquence shapes his surroundings, his possessions and even his dreams: 'I have a picture of him, nicely painted, not only in my private chapel and in my study, but on all the doors too; and I carry his portrait about with me, carved on gems, so that all the time he's present to my thoughts. I never see anything in my dreams but Cicero'.[42] This all-consuming discipline has been laboriously cultivated over a long period of time.

Nosoponus has spent seven years reading only the words of Cicero, and now projects another seven years (three of which have elapsed already) to be spent in laborious imitation of Cicero's texts. This time has been used to gather the raw materials of his devotion. First, he compiled a lexicon of all the words used by Cicero, then he pieced together an anthology of phrases peculiar to Cicero ('formulas loquendi M. Tullio peculiares').[43] Finally, he constructed a massive catalogue of the metrical rhythms employed by Cicero at the beginnings, middles, and ends of his sentences.

Still more extreme are the conditions in which Nosoponus needs to work in order to make possible this act of ventriloquism. Nosoponus boasts:

> Habeo Musaeum in intimis aedibus densis parietibus, geminis et foribus, et fenestris, rimis omnibus gypso piceque diligenter obturatis, ut vix interdiu lux aut sonitus ullus possit irrumpere, nis vehementior, qualis est foeminarum rixantium, aut fabrorum ferrariorum.[44]
>
> [I have a shrine of the Muses in the innermost part of the house, with thick walls and double doors and windows, and all the cracks carefully sealed up with plaster and pitch, so that hardly any light or sound can penetrate even

[40] *CWE*, vol. XXVIII.346; 'Ergo velut eidem initiatis deo, retegam mysteria. Iam annos septem totos nihil attingo praetor libros Ciceronianos, a caeteris non minore religione temperans, quam Cartusiani temperant a carnibus' (*ASD*, vol. I–2.609).

[41] *CWE*, vol. XXVIII.346; *ASD*, vol. I–2.609.

[42] *CWE*, vol. XXVIII.346; 'Non tantum in Larario Musaeoque, verum et in omnibus ostiis imaginem illius habeo belle depictam, quam et gemmis insculptam circumfero, ne vnquam non obuersetur animo. Nec aliud simulacrum in somnis occurrit praeterquam Ciceronis' (*ASD*, vol. I–2.609).

[43] *ASD*, vol. I–2.609. [44] *ASD*, vol. I–2.612.

> by day, unless it's a very loud one, like quarreling women or blacksmiths at work.][45]

Nosoponus' devotion is so extreme that he will not even employ a given word that *was* used by Cicero if none of Cicero's surviving texts contain it in the specific grammatical case required by Nosoponus' text. He emphasizes, too, that the strain of these labours is so intense that he can work only at night, when he can count on not being disturbed, and that he must consult an almanac so as to be certain that even this nighttime work will not be disturbed by storms. Finally, he says, 'Next, if I am projecting anything of this sort, I refrain from dinner in the evening, and have only a light lunch as well, to prevent any gross substance from invading the seat of the limpid mind, and to make sure no dampness steaming up from the stomach weighs down and "nails to earth the fragment of the breath of god"'.[46] He is willing to concede, however, that he does not *quite* starve himself: 'I take ten very small raisins, the Corinthian sort. They are not really food or drink, but yet they are in a way ... I add three sugared coriander seeds.'[47] It is remarkable that the effort to create a human voice should require ceaseless labour to get beyond the reach of human needs.

All this has the air of an extravagantly monkish renunciation of the self and the world to the exclusion of all but Cicero; there will be no wife, he says, and no children.[48] And yet, Nosoponus has repeatedly cast these disciplined contortions as the requirements of an attempt to attain a voice of his own. Rome's language lets these writers see, with absolute clarity, two things at once: first, that the self is bounded by a body that can learn, endure, and yearn; second, that the embodied self is entangled in, and

[45] *CWE*, vol. XXVIII.351.

[46] *CWE*, vol. XXVIII.352; 'Tum si quid huius rei paro, sub eam noctem a coena tempero, leuiter etiam pransus, ne quid crassae materiae, liquidioris animi sedem inuadat: neu qua nebula e stomacho exhalans, grauet *atque affigat humo diuinae particulam aurae*' (*ASD*, vol. I–2.613).

[47] *CWE*, vol. XXVIII.353; 'Sumo decem acinos vuae passae minutulae, quam Corinthiacam vocant. Hic neque cibus est, neque potus, et tamen vtrumque est ... Addo tria coriandri grana saccaro incrustata' (*ASD*, vol. I–2.613–4).

[48] Nosoponus sees emotional privation as necessary to his stylistic ambitions. Bulephorus offers his facetious support: 'Sapuisti Nosopone. Nam mea coniunx, si noctu parem ad istum modum operam dare Ciceroni, perrumperet ostium, laceraret indices, exureret schedas Ciceronem meditantes, et quod his etiam est intolerabilius, dum ego do operam Ciceroni, illa vicarium accerseret, qui ipsi pro me operam daret. Itaque fieret, vt dum ego meditor euadere Ciceroni similis, illa gigneret aliquem Bulephoro dissimilem' (*ASD*, vol. I–2.613); 'That was wise of you, Nosoponus. If I were to start giving that amount of attention at night to Cicero, my wife would break down the door, tear up my indexes, and burn all my papers with my Cicero exercises on them. Worse than that, while I was giving my attention to Cicero, she would invite in a substitute husband to give her a little attention in place of me. And so, while I was aiming to make myself the image of Cicero, she would produce a child who was anything but the image of Bulephorus' (*CWE*, vol. XXVIII.352).

pierced by, social practices, linguistic conventions, and celebrated authorities. Self-abnegation and self-affirmation are somehow coterminous here, so that if, on the one hand, Nosoponus is committed to erasing his own voice as part of his hyperbolic attention to the words of another man, he is also working to stand apart from his contemporaries and make himself singular in their eyes. He tries to achieve this in part by shutting himself off from the present and by refusing to speak Latin to those around him: 'speaking', he insists, 'makes us ready speakers; it certainly doesn't make us speak in a Ciceronian way' ('Dicendo fit vt dicamus expedite: vt Ciceroniano more, nequaquam').[49]

This is parody, of course, but excellent parody, and the history of sixteenth-century grammar-school education confirms the widespread support of at least some of the disciplines and goals that Nosoponus has embraced. Imitation was regarded as the basic condition of instruction. One of the most famous English formulations of this conviction can be found in *The scholemaster*, where Ascham describes the methods and pedagogical ambitions of exercises in double translation.[50] Full of his own fervour for Cicero, Ascham sets a scene in which a schoolmaster and schoolboy go to work on the ancient Roman's prose:

> First, let him teach the childe, cherefullie and plainlie, the cause, and matter of the letter: then, let him construe it into Englishe, so oft, as the childe may easilie carie awaie the understanding of it: Lastlie, parse it ouer perfitlie. This done thus, let the childe, by and by, both construe and parse it ouer againe: so, that it may appeare, that the childe doubteth in nothing, that his master taught him before. After this, the childe must take a paper booke, and sitting in some place, where no man shall prompe him, by him self, let him translate into Englishe his former lesson. Then shewing it to his master, let the master take from him his latin booke, and pausing an houre, at the least, than let the childe translate his own Englishe into latin againe, in an

[49] *CWE*, vol. XXVIII.355; *ASD*, vol. I–2.615. Other languages are suitable for everyday speech: 'And if I want to chatter about something or other unimportant, I'm quite content with French or Dutch' (*CWE*, vol. XXVIII.355); 'Ad garriendum quibuslibet nugis, sufficit mihi sermo Gallicus, aut Batauicus' (*ASD*, vol. I–2.615). The Latin Nosoponus protects by means of these contortions is 'the sacred tongue' ('sacram linguam'). By the time of Erasmus, Latin could be regarded as sacred to both Cicero and God. Strict Ciceronianism was one of the means by which Latin was lifted out of the ordinary.

[50] The technique predates Ascham but in England it is most commonly associated with him. See W. E. Miller, 'Double Translation in English Humanist Education', *Studies in the Renaissance* 10 (1963), 163–74; Dolven, *Scenes of Instruction*, 43–4, 55. On the relevance of double translation to understandings of the relationship between self and other see Andrew Wallace, '"What's Hecuba to him?": Pain, Privacy, and the Ancient Text', in Donald Beecher and Grant Williams (eds.), *Ars Reminiscendi: Mind and Memory in Renaissance Culture* (Toronto: Centre for Reformation and Renaissance Studies, 2009), 231–43.

> other paper booke. When the child bringeth it, turned into latin, the master must compare it with Tullies booke, and laie them both togither: and where the childe doth well, either in chosing, or true placing of Tullies wordes, let the master praise him, and saie here ye do well. For I assure you, there is no such whetstone, to sharpen a good witte and encourage a will to learninge, as is praise.[51]

The measure here of all that will be judged to be either right or wrong is Cicero's language. The passage as a whole suggests that this is not simply a lesson in grammar but rather something that should be understood as extending to wider lessons in discipline, submission, self-effacement, and self-constitution. 'Here ye do well' and here ye do not. Ascham's schoolboy is slotted into history as part of his careful and laborious efforts to master Latin.

He is slotted, that is, into a tradition that understood painstaking labour upon the words of others as a process of self-constitution. This process, which is negotiated via pedagogical encounters with Latin curriculum authors, begins to identify some of the routes by which Rome's language links individuals not simply to other traditions and generations, but also to themselves. This need not involve explorations of the role of language in helping to structure thinking and consciousness at their deepest cognitive levels. It is a matter, rather, of exploring the grammar and decorum of our attempts to reach ourselves, and of moving from the social networks and forms of praxis within which we constitute ourselves to the version of the self that we regard as nesting within the confines of the body.

One source of the pedagogical appeal of such an exercise is that there can be no confusion between what will count as understanding and failing to understand.[52] Ascham insists that only absolute precision can count as success, but he urges the master to patiently explain everything to his pupil:

> Tullie would haue used such a worde, not this: Tullie would haue placed this worde here, not there: would haue used this case, this number, this person, this degree, this gender: he would haue used this moode, this tens, this simple, rather than this compound: this aduerbe here, not there: he would haue ended the sentence with this verbe, not with that nowne or participle, &c.[53]

It should be noted that Ascham never suggests that the erring schoolboy who is to be corrected in this manner has written poor or even ungrammatical

[51] Ascham, *The scholemaster*, Ci^v^.
[52] See Dolven, *Scenes of Instruction*, 15–64, on the schoolmaster's search for proof.
[53] Ascham, *The scholemaster*, Cii^r^.

Latin, but rather only that he has not managed to find his way into Cicero's words and word order. By a paradox that runs through every dimension of humanist pedagogy's commitment to *imitatio*, to learn to move from Cicero's Latin to an accurate English translation of it, and then, after a modest interval of time, back again into Cicero's words in Cicero's word order, is regarded as an actualization of the educated self in its fullest intellectual maturity. The patience and gentleness of Ascham's hypothetical master are, in effect, versions of the interrogative solicitude that had helped Virgilius locate the object of his own grammatical quest.

Such industry can strike us as slavish, but its products were regarded by humanist teachers as radically new rather than derivative. A conventional gloss on these practices compared exercises in invention and imitation (finding and then gathering choice phrases, etc.) to the work of bees, for bees gather the best pollen that the flowers of the field can offer and then transform it, through labour and industry, into an astonishing new thing: honey.[54] The quintessential expression of this process – in France as well as England – occurs in Montaigne's *De l'institution des enfans*:

> Les abeilles pillotent deçà delà les fleurs, mais elles en font après le miel, qui est tout leur; ce n'est plus thin, ni marjolaine: Ainsi les pieces empruntées d'autruy, il les transformera et confondra, pour en faire un ouvrage tout sien: à sçavoir son jugement, son institution, son travail et estude ne vise qu'à le former.[55]

The process that makes a bee a bee, and that ensures that what bees make will be all their own ('tout leur'), establishes a pattern for the process by which a schoolboy encloses himself, as proof that he has learned his lesson, within the tomb of Cicero's words.

Strict Ciceronianism's complex blend of self-abnegation and self-affirmation sits at one extreme of a register that has as its other extreme Virgilius' efforts to search the foundational texts of the Roman grammatical tradition for traces of a vocative of *ego*. Each of these obsessive pursuits

[54] This was the solution of Nosoponus: 'Quod si qua res vrget, vt Latine dicendum sit, et pauca loquor, nec sine praemeditatione. Et in eum vsum habeo paratas aliquot formulas' (*ASD*, vol. I–2.615); 'If some pressing need arises so that I have to speak Latin, I say very little, and I don't do that without due forethought. I keep a number of ready-made phrases for that kind of situation' (*CWE*, vol. XXVIII.355).

[55] Montaigne, *Les Essais*, 157. See Florio's translation: 'The Bees do heer and there sucke this, and cull that flower, but afterward they produce the hony, which is peculiarly their owne, then is it no more Thyme or Marjoram. So of peeces borrowed of others, he may lawfully alter, transforme, and confound them, to shape out of them a perfect peece of worke, altogether his owne; alwaies provided, his judgement, his travell, studie, and institution tend to nothing, but to frame the same perfect' (Montaigne, *Essayes vvritten in French By Michael Lord of Montaigne*, G6ʳ).

marks an attempt to break a path, via Latin grammar, to the self. Each writer, moreover, understands the self as an entity that must be approached with patience and tact, and that can suddenly swing into view as a direct result of systematic encounters with Rome and its language. In Virgilius this is a matter of working, as he puts it, 'sub interrogationis modo', and of understanding the self-relation not under the logic of empire but as a phenomenon that requires courtesy and solicitude. Courtesy and solicitude, moreover, were the hallmarks of the scene of instruction described by Ascham, where the master is to work 'cherefullie and plainlie' in the course of explaining what 'Tullie' would have done. It is surely relevant in this context that Ascham was one of Renaissance England's foremost proponents of humanism's cherished figure of the loving master.[56]

The master's desire to see his schoolboy 'easilie carie awaie the understanding' of Cicero's epistle is a way of suggesting that the lesson will count as belonging to the child – i.e., count as being understood – when it becomes portable. The boy who passes back and forth from the master's company in the course of this lesson is, in turn, like the bee who travels, as Montaigne has it, 'deçà delà', and in the course of those travels transforms that which was quintessentially other ('autruy') into something that is utterly his ('tout sien'). These debates, passages, and scenes of instruction share a desire to wander amidst the thoroughly mapped territories of the texts of ancient writers. Even in Virgilius the objects of inquiry had been 'the teachings of the ancients', so that in each case the object of attention is specific, ancient, and constrained by the grammatical tradition's prescriptive conceptions of *Latinitas*. All this suggests, moreover, that any exploration of the possibilities and constraints of Latin grammar involves gazing outward and inward all at once, taking up and in the words of others, and locating the self via what Nosoponus called the 'sacred language' of Rome.

The tomb of humanist Latin, as Lewis has it, was therefore still, paradoxically, a giver of life and, as it had been since at least the time of Virgilius, a route to the self. It was also a vital connection between the living and the dead. Insofar as these linguistic matters reach into the heart of humanist pedagogy, and into the secret hopes and anxieties of individuals, they necessarily reach into the heart of medieval and early modern Christianity's conceptions of the Word, and into matters ranging from interpretation and salvation to the grounds of intelligibility as such. The

[56] On the figure of the loving master see Wallace, *Virgil's Schoolboys*, 50–77.

relation à soi thereby constitutes one of the points at which ancient texts, grammar, and salvation meet.[57]

The Word and the Road to Rome

Over the course of centuries, Christian grammarians laboured to bend the Latin grammatical tradition's authoritative texts – e.g., works associated with Donatus, Charisius, Servius, Diomedes, Pompeius, Priscian, and others – to the demands of their faith and, indeed, to the grammar and rhetoric of Biblical Latin. This involved, in the words of Catherine M. Chin, a web of efforts by which 'the discipline of grammar transformed linguistic work into incipient religious practice'.[58] These efforts, in turn, ranged from the outwardly humble replacement of traditional declensional paradigm words with Christian nouns, to much more ambitious recalibrations of the kind associated with Isidore of Seville. As Zetzel observes, 'Isidore, more than any other figure of the late antique church, has always been viewed at least in part within the tradition of Roman scholarship, as a kind of summary, conclusion, and transition to later forms of interpretation.'[59]

Western Christendom knew very well that 'the Word' had not been uttered in Latin, the language that had passed from ancient Rome to the Roman church, filling the Empire and then finally redefining the nature of that empire. Had the Word been Latin, medieval and Renaissance Europe, Britain, and Ireland would not have been compelled to live with the sting of knowing that even their most elevated and spiritualized cultures hovered at a considerable linguistic remove from divinity. Throughout the Middle Ages and Renaissance, Latin was viewed with reverence as western Europe's dominant language of pedagogy, liturgy, theology, administration, international diplomacy, and intellectual inquiry. By the early seventh century Isidore had already named it (with Hebrew and Greek) one of the *tres*

[57] This triad played a decisive role in the survival of ancient texts. See Zetzel, Critics, Compilers, and Commentators: 'It is a truism, but nevertheless true, that if Latin had not been adopted as the universal language of religion in the former western empire we would have precious little left of Latin literature, not to mention Roman scholarship' (202).

[58] See Catherine M. Chin, *Grammar and Christianity in the Late Roman World* (Philadelphia: University of Pennsylvania Press, 2008), 2.

[59] Zetzel, Critics, Compilers, and Commentators, 117. For a condensed overview of the range of efforts involved see Zetzel, *Critics, Compilers, and Commentators*, 214–17; on Isidore see 117–19. For the complementary linguistic move in the liturgy see Maura K. Lafferty, 'Translating Faith from Greek to Latin: *Romanitas* and *Christianitas* in Late Fourth-Century Rome and Milan', *Journal of Early Christian Studies* 11 (2003), 21–62.

linguae sacrae.[60] It was a treasured cultural possession of the elite. In the final analysis, however, Latin was damnably young.

The three sacred languages were subjected to intense comparison in the course of attempts to reflect on the origins and nature of the Word. The 1611 translators' Preface to the King James Bible establishes some telling distinctions: 'The Apostle excepteth no tongue; not Hebrewe the ancientest, not Greeke the most copious, not Latine the finest.'[61] Three distinct versions of preeminence are in play, but the formulation has the ultimate effect of making the refinement of Latin seem ornamental rather than fundamental. By contrast, 'the *Hebrew* text of the Olde Testament' and 'the *Greeke* of the New' are, as the Preface puts it, 'the two golden pipes, or rather conduits, where-through the oliue branches emptie themselues into the golde. Saint *Augustine* calleth them precedent, or originall tongues; Saint *Hierome*, fountaines'.[62] Throughout the Middle Ages and Renaissance a skilled Latinist could manoeuvre with authority within even the most elevated strata of European intellectual culture, but comparative grammar was already revealing that Latin would never be able to take anyone all the way *ad fontes*, let alone *ad fontem.*[63]

Joseph Farrell reminds us that several of ancient Rome's earliest authorities on Latin had already harboured similar misgivings that their language was in some basic way secondary to Greek – perhaps even simply one of its dialects. On Farrell's account, these insecurities were rooted in Rome's

60 Isidore had little knowledge of Greek or Hebrew. On his attempts to work through these thorny questions in relation to the latter, a language whose claims to priority were powerful, see Mark E. Amsler, *Etymology and Grammatical Discourse in Late Antiquity and the Early Middle Ages* (Amsterdam: John Benjamins, 1989): 'Isidore's ignorance of Hebrew in no way restricted his perception of what Jerome had called "Hebrew truth". Substituting Eden for the technographers' Golden Age of *latinitas* and using the concepts of the *tres linguae sacrae*, the economy of salvation, and the twin revelations of the Incarnation and the Bible, Isidore, like Augustine and others, believed that Latin contained within its verbal structure the spirit and essence of Hebrew truth. His etymological search for the Edenic purity of language, then, focused more on the spirit than the letter of language, on the motives for language rather than language itself' (150).

61 *The Holy Bible: 1611 Edition* (Nashville: Thomas Nelson, 1989), unnumbered.

62 *The Holy Bible: 1611 Edition*, *c2^{v}.

63 See especially Brian Cummings: 'The study of Greek and Hebrew raised a conflict in grammatical studies not because of the stylistic beauties or erotic paganism of classical Greek but because of the problem of comparative grammar. The ancient languages exposed an *aporia* in medieval grammatical theory by having a grammatical structure which could not be rationalized fully by the terminology developed in relation to Latin. This was particularly true of Hebrew, which had a radically different system of inflection and syntax. The study of Hebrew therefore forced some immediate revision in grammatical categories. However, it also cast commensurate doubt on how the older Latin categories could be held to be universal or authoritative. And since the issue of the meaning of the Hebrew text was still investigated largely in Latin, it raised a further and profoundly disturbing question of whether texts written in Hebrew and Latin could ever mean exactly the same thing' (*The Literary Culture of the Reformation*, 24).

complex relation to Greek culture and the Greek language: 'Again and again, when Latin culture confronts itself and inquires into its nature, it sees Greek.'[64] This helps explain why grammarians feasted on Greek forms and terminology in the course of devising systematic approaches to Latin grammar. Longing glances away from Latin are commonplace: the Roman Church would later look to Hebrew as the Word's 'ancientest' authority, and many humanist writers celebrated the sophistication and antiquity of Greek against that of Latin.[65] As a result, Latin – a language of power whose empire had encircled the entire Mediterranean – could seem to be, for all its marvellous compactness and elegant artifice (the features that made it 'finest' or 'golde' in the eyes of the translators of the King James Bible) much too clearly a product of historical forces and variable customs of usage.[66]

All this ensured that the stakes of translation would be urgently debated before, during, and after the Reformation. Close work upon Scripture in its original languages fed into Latin and vernacular texts; those texts fed, in turn, into further translations, commentaries, and paraphrases. An illuminating case in point is an anonymous 1632 translation into English of Luther's 'Preface to Paul's Epistle to the Romans'.[67] The volume's

64 Joseph Farrell, *Latin Language and Latin Culture: From Ancient to Modern Times*, Roman Literature and Its Contexts (Cambridge University Press, 2001), 28. On literary studies' bone-deep dependence on Greek see Andrew Ford, *The Origins of Criticism: Literary Culture and Poetic Theory in Classical Greece* (Princeton University Press, 2002): 'We speak Greek when we speak the language of literary criticism' (x).

65 On the revival of Hebrew studies see, for example, Luke Murray, 'Jesuit Hebrew Studies After Trent: Cornelius a Lapide (1567–1637)', *Journal of Jesuit Studies* 4 (2017), 76–97; David Price, 'Christian Humanism and the Representation of Judaism: Johannes Reuchlin and the Discovery of Hebrew', *Arthuriana* 19.3 (2009), 80–96; Ilona N. Rashkow, 'Hebrew Bible Translation and the Fear of Judaization', *The Sixteenth Century Journal* 21 (1990), 217–237. On Greek and Renaissance humanism see Micha Lazarus, 'Greek Literacy in Sixteenth-Century England', *Renaissance Studies* 29 (2015), 433–58; Paul Botley, *Learning Greek in Western Europe, 1396–1525: Grammars, Lexica, and Classroom Texts* (Philadelphia: American Philosophical Society, 2010). For an excellent example of the range of topics that could ramify outward from Greek studies in the context of the Reformation and post-Reformation see Jessica Wolfe, *Homer and the Question of Strife: From Erasmus to Hobbes* (University of Toronto Press, 2015).

66 On the wider cultural history of the language, see W. Martin Bloomer, *Latinity and Literary Society at Rome* (Philadelphia: University of Pennsylvania Press, 1997); Jürgen Leonhardt, *Latin: Story of a World Language*, trans. Kenneth Kronenberg (Cambridge, MA: Belknap Press, 2013); József Herman, *Vulgar Latin*, trans. Roger Wright (University Park, PA: Penn. State University Press, 2000).

67 The volume in question is Martin Luther, *A methodicall preface prefixed before the Epistle of S. Paul to the Romanes; verie necessarie and profitable for the better vnderstanding of it. Made by the right reuerend father and faithfull seruant of Christ Iesus, Martin Luther, now newly translated out of Latin into English, by W. W. student* (London: 1632) (STC 16986). Albert C. Outler notes that this is the volume that would have been read aloud during the so-called 'Aldersgate Experience' that John Wesley describes as having occasioned his own religious conversion on the evening of 24 May, 1738: 'In the

translator, one W. W. (possibly William Wilkinson, a religious writer and ecclesiastical lawyer, though the attribution is uncertain), provides a new vantage point from which to study the dynamic tracked in this chapter. The glory of 'that most fruitfull and profitable Epistle of S. Paul to the *Romans*', as W. W. puts it in his dedicatory epistle 'To the Cœlestiall Christian Reader', is that 'when thou canst well and wisely understand, first it will make thee ready armed, well furnished and instructed to withstand & answear all the popish Romanists (GODS greatest adversaries, and enemies to his Gospell)'.[68] W. W.'s 'popish Romanists' looks like an attempt to draw a firm distinction between contemporary Roman opponents and the ancient Roman community to which Paul had addressed his epistle.

W. W.'s fastidiousness is clearly influenced by his efforts to cope with what Luther had written about the final chapter of Paul's epistle. I cite W. W.'s translation of Luther's words:

> The last chap. containeth salutations or commendations: to which hee adjoyneth a verye good and most necessary admonition, namely that we should shunne & eschue (as the plague and extreame infection & poyson of faith) the doctrines and traditions of men where – with the Gospell and worde of God being contemned) the false Apostles do seduce & withdraw from Christ the hearts of the simple. For the Apost. foresaw in the Spirit, that there should arise and spring certaine Romanistes (for they are not worthie the name of Romans) out of Rome, and Romans: who by their wicked and blasphemous, most divilish and sathanical decretals, and their whole den of mans lawes and traditions, as by a most wast floude and huge deluge, wold labor to drowne, extinguish, and destroy not only this excellent Epistle, but even the whole body of Scripture: yea al the doctrine of faith and of the Spirit: insomuch that they should leaue vs nothing but this Idoll our belly, whose worshippers he doth call them heere and most plainely in the Epistle to the Philippians. For (saith he) there be many walke of whom I haue told you often, and now tell you weeping, they are the enemies of the Crosse of Christ whose God is their belly and their glory, to their shame, they are worldly minded. The GOD of all Peace brase and beate down Sathan and his kingdome vnder our feete. *Amen.*[69]

evening, I went very unwillingly to a society in Aldersgate Street, where one was reading Luther's Preface to the Epistle to the Romans. About a quarter before nine, while he was describing the change which God works in the heart through faith in Christ, I felt my heart strangely warmed. I felt I did trust in Christ, Christ alone for salvation; and an assurance was given me that he had taken away *my* sins, even *mine*, and saved *me* from the law of sin and death.' See Albert C. Outler (ed.), *John Wesley* (New York: Oxford University Press, 1964), 66.

68 Luther, *A methodicall preface*, A2^{v}.

69 Luther, *A methodicall preface*, D6^{r}-D6^{v}. A marginal gloss on 'this Idoll our belly' gives 'Papists belly gods'.

W. W. has been carried away by the topic at hand. His translation of this passage is considerably more copious, and several times more vehement, than Luther's German.[70] Even without knowing Luther's original, readers can likely perceive signs of a protracted struggle (at once spiritual and linguistic) in W. W.'s assertion that Paul 'foresaw in the Spirit, that there should arise and spring certaine Romanistes (for they are not worthie the name of Romans) out of Rome, and Romans'. Luther's original is a good deal simpler and more measured than this ('aus Rom vnd durch die Roemer'; 'out of Rome and through the Romans'), as is the original passage as a whole. W. W. draws a series of distinctions and repetitions (Romanistes / Romans, Rome, Romans) where Luther draws none.

W. W.'s efforts are doubly striking when juxtaposed with William Tyndale's free paraphrase of the 1522 text of Luther's 'Vorrhede auff die Epistel Sanct Paulus zu den Romern'.[71] It is clear that Tyndale wanted nothing to do with the notion that Rome and its Romans are, as it were, active ingredients in the mix of Paul's epistle, even though this is quite plainly what Luther wants his readers to acknowledge.[72] Nor does Tyndale want anything to do with Luther's sense that Paul had foreseen something

[70] The 1546 text runs as follows: 'Das letzte Cap. ist ein Gruscapittel. Aber darunter vermischet er gar eine edle warnung fur Menschenleren, die da neben der Euangelischen lere einfallen, vnd ergernis anrichten. Gerade als hette er gewislich ersehen, das aus Rom vnd durch die Roemer komen solten, die verfuerischen, ergerlichen Canones vnd Decretales, vnd das gantze geschwuerm vnd gewuerm menschlicher gesetzen vnd geboten, die jtzt alle Welt erseuffet, vnd diese Epistel vnd alle heilige Schrifft sampt dem Geist vnd Glauben vertilget haben, das nichts mehr da blieben ist, denn der Abgott, Bauch, des Diener sie hie S. Paulus schilt. Gott erloese vns von ihnen, AMEN.' See Luther's 'Vorrede auff die Epistel S. Pauli an die Roemer', in Martin Luther, *D. Martin Luthers Werke: die Deutsche Bibel* (*WA DB*), 12 vols. (Weimar: Herman Böhlaus Nachfolger, 1906–61), vol. VII.27. For the translation see Martin Luther, *Luther's Works* (*LW*), ed. Jaroslav Pelikan and Helmut T. Lehmann, 56 vols. (Philadelphia: Concordia Publishing House, 1955–1986), vol. XXXV.379–80: 'The last chapter is a chapter of greetings. But he mingles with them a noble warning against the doctrines of men, which break in alongside the teaching of the gospel and cause offense. It is as if he had certainly foreseen that out of Rome and through the Romans would come the seductive and offensive canons and decretals and the whole squirming mass of human laws and commandments, which have now drowned the whole world and wiped out this epistle and all the Holy Scriptures, along with the Spirit and faith itself; so that nothing remains anymore except the idol, Belly, whose servants St. Paul here rebukes. God save us from them. Amen.'

[71] William Tyndale, *A compendious introduccion, prologe or preface vn to the pistle off Paul to the Romayns* (London, 1526) [STC 24438]. The 1522 version of Luther's Preface already contains the phrase 'aus Rom vnd durch die Romer'. See the earlier text of the 'Vorrhede auff die Epistel Sanct Paulus zu den Romern' in *WA DB*, vol. VII.26. For interpretive context see Euan K. Cameron, 'Preface to the Epistle to the Romans 1522, and as Revised 1546', in Euan K. Cameron (ed.), *The Annotated Luther, Volume 6: The Interpretation of Scripture* (Minneapolis: Fortress Press, 2017), 457–63.

[72] Brian Cummings suggests (personal communication) that Luther would have worked with a keen sense of the significance of the epistle's declared audience: 'He is a good enough historian to know that the city of Paul's day is not to be confused with the church of Rome of his own day, but he is also a sophisticated reader who enjoys symbolic matching in words, and plays with them all the time.' Cummings adds that humanist exegetical procedures placed great emphasis on identifying

about the city's future. In Tyndale's paraphrase of Luther's text, the word 'Romans' is only ever used in order to refer to individual chapters of Paul's Epistle, and the word 'Rome' never occurs. The contrast with Tyndale's paraphrase reveals, therefore, that however much W. W. might strain the tone and sense of the final section of Luther's Preface, he is mounting a sustained effort to reckon with an aspect of Luther's text that Tyndale had not been able to bring himself to acknowledge. W. W.'s struggle to cope with Luther's remarks (for he is doing more than simply rendering them into English) points directly to the ways in which the fact of Rome is negotiated in Scripture and via encounters with the books of the New Testament.

At several points in this book I have referred to the persistence of the networks of roads that laced together the Roman world's far-flung regions. I have done so in an effort to foreground some of the material facts and conditions underlying Ernst Robert Curtius' metaphorical assertion that 'The Latin Middle Ages is the crumbling Roman road from the antique to the modern world.'[73] In Chapter 1, Roman roads provided one of several examples of the thoroughness with which Rome had established a conspicuous and enduring material order that survived well into the Middle Ages and Renaissance. Chapter 2 and the first half of Chapter 3 have metaphorically extended Roman roadwork in order to establish that Rome inhabits the self, especially where the relation to the self is to be understood as a path broken and mapped, at least in part, by the Latin language and its grammatical cultures.

The remaining sections of this chapter offer further metaphorical extensions of this roadwork by bringing together the city of Rome, the discourse of salvation, and the practice of scriptural exegesis. This involves studying Saint Augustine's and Martin Luther's encounters with Paul's Epistle to the Romans. Attention to the New Testament sequence that takes readers from the Gospels to the Acts of the Apostles to the Epistle to the Romans sees Rome itself generating a significant gravitational force within what is more commonly understood, in isolation, as Augustine's and Luther's transformative encounters with Pauline theology.[74] For this New

a text's addressees, and that Luther's unprinted 1515–16 'Lectures on Romans' had used Augustine's *De civitate Dei* as a model.

73 Ernst Robert Curtius, *European Literature and the Latin Middle Ages*, trans. Willard R. Trask (Princeton University Press, 1990), 19.

74 This is the order shared by the Vulgate, the Douay-Rheims, and King James bibles. My interest here is not in likely dates of composition, but rather in the logic of sequence as these texts are arranged in their canonical, biblical order.

Testament sequence is one of the roads by which the English reached Rome both before and after the Reformation.[75]

Paul's Epistle to the Romans became the key doctrinal text of Christian soteriology.[76] Relevant frames of reference for an inquiry into the letter's significance stretch across different disciplines and historical periods.[77] My goal is to establish the importance of the fact that (as Luther clearly saw) this vital doctrinal role should be played by a text addressed directly to Romans, and to argue that the epistle's wider setting in the New Testament provides yet another view of the fact of Rome as it surfaces in biblical narrative, critical exegesis, and the discourse of salvation. I have already cited Luther's suggestion, at the end of his 'Vorrede', that Paul had foreseen that the Rome to which he was addressing his letter would one day become a new and terrifying thing. The unmistakable implication is that Luther regarded the title of this epistle as a special dimension of its theological significance.

The Epistle to the Romans is the summit of a trajectory that is actually launched in the Acts of the Apostles, a book whose authorship is traditionally associated with Luke. Acts scrupulously establishes the importance of the city of Rome within the economies of salvation and the divine word, and thereby prepares the ground for Paul's epistle. This is the road Reformers walked as they worked through the New Testament. The plots of Acts cover the efforts by which the Word came to be preached to the Gentile nations. The book, however, is even more specifically designed, especially over the course of its final chapters, to show how the Word came to be preached at Rome by Paul.

This journey is initiated when Pentecostal fire make it possible for the apostles to speak to gentiles everywhere:

[75] On Augustine see Karla Pollman and Willemien Otten (eds.), *The Oxford Guide to the Historical Reception of Augustine*, 3 vols. (Oxford University Press, 2013). On Paul see, most recently, Stephen J. Chester, *Reading Paul With the Reformers: Reconciling Old and New Reformers* (Grand Rapids, MI: Eerdmans, 2017).

[76] Its significance is underscored by a modern phrase that is prominent in contemporary evangelical circles, where pastors and missionaries speak of a 'Roman Road' to salvation. This 'Roman Road' is a textual phenomenon, since the phrase groups together a series of key passages from Paul's Epistle to the Romans and treats them as something like a path to conversion and salvation. Lists of key passages are shifting, but they are commonly founded upon the so-called 'soul-winning' verses of Romans 3:10, 3:23, 5:12, 5:8, 6:23, 10:9–10, and 10:13.

[77] It has, for example, served as fertile ground for contemporary postcolonial theology. See Ian E. Rock, *Paul's Letter to the Romans and Roman Imperialism: An Ideological Analysis of the Exordium (Romans 1:1–17)* (Eugene, OR: Pickwick Publications, 2012). See also the essays collected in Kathy Ehrensperger and J. Brian Tucker (eds.), *Reading Paul in Context: Explorations in Identity Formation: Essays in Honour of William S. Campbell* (London: T&T Clark, 2010).

> [1] And when the day of Pentecost was fully come, they were all with one accord in one place. [2] And suddenly there came a sound from heauen as of a rushing mighty wind, and it filled all the house where they were sitting. [3] And there appeared unto them clouen tongues like as of fire, and it sate upon each of them. [4] And they were all filled with the holy Ghost, and began to speake with other tongues, as the spirit gave them vtterance. (Acts 2)

Parthians, Medes, and Elamites, along with the inhabitants of Mesopotamia, Judea, Cappadocia, Pontus, Asia, Phrygia, Pamphylia, Egypt, Libya, Cyrene, Jews, Proselites, Cretes, Arabians '& strangers of Rome' (Acts 2:9–11), all suddenly hear themselves addressed in their native tongues by the apostles. With this episode as one of its foundations, the Book of Acts gradually makes Rome its ultimate destination.[78]

The book's narratives are, for a time, as given to wandering as any Hellenistic romance,[79] but they gradually settle into a quasi-Virgilian teleological drive in which Rome stands as Paul's ultimate destination: 'After these things were ended, Paul purposed in the spirit, when hee had passed thorow Macedonia and Achaia, to go to Hierusalem, saying, After I haue bin there, I must also see Rome' (19:21). Acts, therefore, strives to explain, in retrospect, the incredible *translatio* by which a religion whose origins are in the Holy Land came to find itself at home in Rome.[80] Indeed, with the exception of the apocryphal books of Maccabees and one mention of 'Romans' in the Gospel of John, the word 'Rome' only begins to make its most important appearances in the Bible in Acts and in Paul's Epistle to the Romans. This fact helps draw attention to Paul's Epistle to the Romans, as does the sequence by which the New Testament moves from the Gospels to Acts to Romans, working from the fundamental concern with language that is on view throughout Acts to Paul's preaching at Rome. For it is by this route that the ministry of the Word in Acts will come, ultimately, to be associated with Latin words. The universalization of the Word among gentile nations is, as it must be, a road to Rome.

Even before Paul's pronouncement in Acts 19:21, the book is already emphatic that Rome is its destination and controlling frame of reference. In Acts 10, Cornelius the Centurion is the figure through whom the Word

[78] See, on this topic, Drew W. Billings, *Acts of the Apostles and the Rhetoric of Roman Imperialism* (Cambridge University Press, 2017).

[79] For a wide-ranging overview of debates on genre see Thomas E. Phillips, 'The Genre of Acts: Moving Toward a Consensus?', *Currents in Biblical Research* 4 (2006), 365–96.

[80] The literature on this topic is copious. See, for example, Paul W. Walaskay, *'And So We Came to Rome': The Political Perspective of St Luke* (Cambridge University Press, 1983).

begins to make inroads among the gentiles. In Acts 16, when Paul and Silas are imprisoned and beaten at Philippi, they are targeted for having taught that which was judged unfit to be taught to Romans. After their release, their guards are terrified to discover that the men whom they had beaten are Roman citizens. In Acts 17:7 it is emphasized that all this was performed 'contrary to the decrees of Cesar'. Acts 18 establishes, moreover, that the expulsion of the Jews from Rome is one of the backdrops against which this story is unfolding.

Though the historicity of the book's claim that Paul is a Roman citizen is less than firm, Acts 22 insists once more that this status has an unsettling effect on those around him: [81]

> [25] And as they bound him with thongs, Paul said unto the Centurion that stood by, Is it lawfull for you to scourge a man that is a Romane, and vncondemned? [26] When the centurion heard that, hee went and told the chiefe captaine, saying, Take heede what thou doest, for this man is a Romane. [27] Then the chiefe captaine came; and said vnto him, Tell me, art thou a Romane? He said, Yea. [28] And the chiefe captaine answered, With a great summe obteined I this freedome. And Paul said, But I was free borne. [29] Then straightway they departed from him which should haue examined him: and the chiefe captaine also was afraid, after he knew that he was a Romane, & because he had bound him. (Acts 22)

Following this arrest, Paul is reassured: 'And the night following, the Lord stood by him, and saide, Be of good cheere, Paul: for as thou hast testified of mee in Hierusalem, so must thou beare witnesse also at Rome' (23:11). Acts 25:12 sees Festus' famous response to Paul: 'Hast thou appealed vnto Caesar? vnto Caesar shalt thou go.' Paul's journey to Rome begins in Acts 27. Finally, across the last verses of Acts 28, he is conducted along the Via Appia to the Eternal City, where he will be Rome's prisoner and also its newest preacher.

The 'road' to Paul's Epistle to the Romans, therefore, runs through a book in which the city of Rome and its name become – chapter by chapter and verse by verse – increasingly resonant. The power of the city's name spills over from Acts into the first chapter of the Epistle itself. In effect, the Epistle takes its readers backwards into the Rome-bound plots of the Acts of the Apostles:

[81] The question of citizenship is perhaps to be regarded as one of the political fictions of Acts. See, on this topic, Paula Fredriksen, 'Paul and Augustine: Conversion Narratives, Orthodox Traditions, and the Retrospective Self', *Journal of Theological Studies*, n.s. 37 (1986): 'He may indeed have been a Roman citizen, but he nowhere mentions it; and this could be a plot device on Luke's part to get his hero to Rome' (17).

> [13] Now I would not haue you ignorant, brethren, that oftentimes I purposed to come vnto you, (but was let hitherto,) that I might haue some fruit among you also, euen as among other Gentiles. [14] I am debtor both to the Greeks, and to the Barbarians, both to the wise, and to the vnwise. [15] So, as much as in mee is, I am ready to preach the gospel to you that are at Rome also. (Romans 1)

Chapter 2 cited John Donne's attempts to work through the implications of Paul's wish. I emphasized there that Donne cites, glosses, and paraphrases Paul in such a way as to make his words sum up the spiritual condition of Donne's London parishioners:

> And in that sense, I may use the words of the Apostle, *As much as in me is, I am ready to preach the Gospel to them also that are at Rome:* at *Rome* in their hearts; at *Rome*, that is, of *Rome*, reconciled to *Rome*.[82]

Donne's embroidery upon the words of Paul conveys the metaphysical potency of the city's name. Donne sounds, moreover, much like W. W. will a decade later when Luther's Preface sends him spiraling down his own sequence of 'Romanistes', 'Romans', 'Rome', and 'Romans'. Donne and W. W. let us see, as though *in parvo*, how the fact of Rome explodes from these transformative encounters with New Testament texts. Donne's and W. W.'s clattering and copious responses to the word 'Rome' in and around Acts and Paul's Epistle belong to a tradition inaugurated by Augustine's famous account of his own conversion to Christianity.

To put this another way, the repetitions and revisions that mark Donne's and W. W.'s texts at these decisive moments are aftershocks of Luther's protracted dialogue with Augustine's *Confessions*. Augustine and Luther, of course, were both transformed (or, at different times in their careers, claimed to have been transformed) by their encounters with the Epistle to the Romans. Augustine and Luther tell their readers that they were remade in the course of their encounters with this cornerstone document of Pauline theology. But the New Testament's path from the conclusion of the Gospels to the first of the Pauline Epistles ensured that Augustine and Luther (and, for that matter, Donne and W. W.) would be compelled to read the Epistle not as a purely theological treatise but rather as part of a protracted negotiation with the pasts and futures of Rome itself.[83]

[82] Donne, *Sermons*, vol. IV.110.

[83] It is worth noting in this context that although the Geneva Bible's marginal glosses to the Book of Revelation are ready at almost every turn to identify individual verses as allegorical references to ancient Rome and its topography, the Roman Empire, the Church at Rome, the Pope, etc., actual references to Rome in, for example, Acts, elicit no allegorical moralizing. Somehow, threats and

The Fact of Romans

Bursting as it does from the aftermath of Alaric's sack of Rome in 410, *De civitate Dei contra paganos* is only the longest and most spectacular testament to Augustine's fixation on the Eternal City. His famous meditations, in Book One of the *Confessions*, on Dido and Christ are another. In Augustine, the matter of Rome is, all at once, the matter of self, speech, and salvation. This is most clear in the decisive eighth book of the *Confessions*, a meticulously constructed rhetorical set-piece in which Augustine makes readers see that the story of his conversion is to be understood as a chapter in the story of Rome. Looking back, Augustine tries to make sense of his own visceral attachment to Rome at a time when the city was in the grips of both paganism and Christianity. As is well known, the climax of this book is the moment when Augustine takes up a copy of Paul's Epistle to the Romans, but I want to spend some time establishing the care with which the entirety of Book Eight of the *Confessions* has been constructed to serve as a study of the self's entanglement in Rome.[84] In effect, this book is structured to mimic the New Testament's sequential progression from Acts to Romans.

The story catches Augustine at a moment when, having come to believe in the power of the story of Christ, he is nevertheless unable to commit himself steadfastly to his new beliefs. Seeking help, he turns to Simplicianus, a man esteemed for his devotion to the Christian God. Augustine has wrestled with anxieties about the vanity of his life, passions, and studies, but Simplicianus is able to nurse him to spiritual health in the course of an exchange that treats Rome as an urban network of competing traditions among which the correct path must be picked out with care and deliberation:

> Perrexi ergo ad Simplicianum, patrem in accipienda gratia tunc episcopi Ambrosii et quem vere ut patrem diligebat. narravi ei circuitus erroris mei. ubi autem commemoravi legisse me quosdam libros platonicorum, quos Victorinus, quondam rhetor urbis Romae, quem christianum defunctum esse audieram, in latinam linguam transtulisset, gratulatus est mihi quod non in aliorum philosophorum scripta incidissem plena fallaciarum et deceptionum secundum elementa huius mundi, in istis autem omnibus modis insinuari deum et eius verbum.

abominations in Revelation are said to 'mean' Rome (as does, for example, the Geneva Bible's gloss on the reference to Babylon at Revelation 18:2), but explicit references to the city are not allegorized or glossed.

[84] For an excellent overview of Augustine's protracted engagements with Paul see Fredriksen, 'Paul and Augustine'.

Deinde, ut me exhortaretur ad humilitatem Christi sapientibus absconditam et revelatam parvulis, Victorinum ipsum recordatus est, quem Romae cum esset familiarissime noverat, deque illo mihi narravit quod non silebo. habet enim magnam laudem gratiae tuae confitendam tibi, quemadmodum ille doctissimus senex et omnium liberalium doctrinarum peritissimus quique philosophorum tam multa legerat et diiudicaverat, doctor tot nobilium senatorum, qui etiam ob insigne praeclari magisterii, quod cives huius mundi eximium putant, statuam Romano foro meruerat et acceperat, usque ad illam aetatem venerator idolorum sacrorumque sacrilegorum particeps, quibus tunc tota fere Romana nobilitas inflata spirabat, popiliosiam et omnigenum deum monstra et Anubem latratorem, quae aliquando contra Neptunum et Venerem contraque Minervam tela tenuerant et a se victis iam Roma supplicabat, quae iste senex Victorinus tot annos ore terricrepo defensitaverat, non erubuerit esse puer Christi tui et infans fontis tui, subiecto collo ad humilitatis iugum et edomita fronte ad cruces opprobrium.[85]

[So I made my way to Simplicianus, who became father to the then bishop, Ambrose, who really did love him like a father, at the time when the latter received the grace of baptism. I told him how I had been going around in circles of sinfulness. But when I recounted how I had read certain Neoplatonist books that Victorinus, the former professor of rhetoric at Rome, who, so I hear, had died a Christian, had translated into the Latin language, he congratulated me for not having happened upon the writings of other philosophers, for they were full of falsehoods and deceits in accordance with the principles of this world, whereas God and his Word were intimately enmeshed in the Neoplatonist works in every way.

Next, when he urged me to accept the humility of Christ, which is hidden from the wise and revealed to babes, he recalled Victorinus himself, with whom he had been closely acquainted when he was at Rome, and he told me something of him that I will not fail to mention. Indeed it expresses great praise of your grace that I must confess to you. That most learned old man, an expert in all the liberal disciplines, who had read so much of the philosophers and had judged them against each other, a teacher, too, of so many high-ranking senators, because of his distinguished teaching record had earned the distinction of a statue in the forum at Rome, which the citizens of this world regard as a signal honor, and had agreed to it. Up to this moment in his life he had been a worshipper of idols and a participant in the blasphemous rituals that almost all the Roman aristocracy, in their arrogance, lived and breathed at that time: the gods of Numa Pompilius and the 'gods of every kind and Anubis the Barker; they all bore arms at one time against Neptune, Venus and Minerva,' and now Rome was on her knees before the gods she once had conquered. Over many years the old man

[85] Augustine, *Confessions* (*Conf.*), ed. and trans. Carolyn J.-B. Hammond, 2 vols., LCL 26–7 (Cambridge, MA: Harvard University Press, 2014), vol. I.358–61.

> Victorinus had often defended those monstrous creatures in thundering tones. Now he was not ashamed to be a child of your Christ and a baby baptized by you, bending his neck to the yoke of humility, his head submitting to the shame of the cross.]

Simplicianus' disquisition on Victorinus ensures that long before Augustine takes up and reads his friend's copy of Paul's Epistle to the Romans, the path to his conversion is already subsumed within meditations on Rome as place, idea, and fact. Indeed, the episode depicts the Latin language itself as having provided harbour to a pagan philosophical tradition in which 'God and his Word' have become 'intimately enmeshed'. Simplicianus' skillful teaching enables Augustine to perceive a logic submerged deep within his own training – a logic heretofore hidden from him – whereby a man produced by Rome can come to a new Rome by a quintessentially Roman route. This was the lesson to be learned from the story of Victorinus, who becomes a catechumen: 'mirante Roma, gaudente ecclesia' ('Rome was stunned, the Church was delighted').[86] These anthropomorphisms make Rome and the Church spectators rather than mere settings for Simplicianus' story of Victorinus. This episode thereby prepares the ground for the importance that Augustine will accord to the Epistle to the Romans in the story of his conversion.

Pedagogical diction and logic structure the entire episode: first, because Augustine admits that he was 'on fire to imitate' Victorinus ('exarsi ad imitandum');[87] second, because he is wise enough to know that it was for precisely this reason that Simplicianus had chosen the story of Victorinus. After all, Victorinus, like Augustine, had been a teacher of rhetoric, and when given the opportunity to make a private profession of faith he had chosen instead to do so publicly:

> non enim erat salus quam docebat in rhetorica, et tamen eam publice professus erat. quanto minus ergo vereri debuit mansuetum gregem tuum pronuntians verbum tuum, qui non verebatur in verbis suis turbas insanorum?[88]
>
> [After all, he had not usually taught salvation in rhetoric, and he had still professed that subject before the people. How much less, then, should he fear the reactions of your peaceable people when declaring your word, after he had no fear of raging crowds when relying only on words of his own?]

Rome, therefore, stages the collision between the Latin grammatical and rhetorical traditions, on the one hand, and the 'verbum Dei', on the other.

[86] *Conf.*, vol. I.362–3. [87] *Conf.*, vol. I.372. [88] *Conf.*, vol. I.364–5.

What is more, Augustine knows that Victorinus had been compelled, during the time of the Emperor Julian, to choose between teaching oratory and converting to Christianity: 'quam legem ille amplexus, loquacem scholam deserere maluit quam verbum tuum, quo linguas infantium facis disertas' ('Victorinus had accepted this law: he preferred to abandon a school of wordiness rather than your Word by whom you make eloquent the tongues of infants').[89] Augustine knows that in his own case a dilatory will, rather than the laws of imperial Rome, is the obstacle, but the example of Victorinus yokes grammatical and rhetorical studies to God's 'verbum' in a manner that helps Augustine to make sense of his own plight.

In the wake of this visit to Simplicianus, Augustine begins attending church with his friend Alypius, all the while continuing to ply his trade as a teacher of rhetoric: 'I was selling my talent for public speaking, if indeed teaching can impart such excellence' ('sicut ego vendebam dicendi facultatem, si qua docendo praestari potest').[90] He and Alypius are visited one day by Ponticianus, an African in imperial service. Ponticianus, a convert himself, rejoices to find that the book on the table before them is a copy of Paul ('invenit apostolum Paulum') rather than 'something from the books I was wearing myself down teaching' ('putaverat enim aliquid de libris quorum professio me conterebat').[91] Ponticianus speaks at length about his joy as a convert and offers news concerning monastic communities. The entire story twists Augustine into new and troubling forms of self-relation:

> Narrabat haec Ponticianus. tu autem, domine, inter verba eius retorquebas me ad me ipsum, auferens me a dorso meo, ubi me posueram dum nollem me attendere, et constituebas me ante faciem meam, ut viderem quam turpis essem, quam distortus et sordidud, maculosus et ulcerosus. et videbam et horrebam, et quo a me fugerem non erat. sed si conabar avertere a me aspectum, narrabat ille quod narrabat, et tu me rursus opponebas mihi et impingebas me in oculos meos, ut invenirem iniquitatem meam et odissem. noveram eam, sed dissimulabam et cohibebam et obliviscebar.[92]
>
> [Such was Ponticianus' story. But while he spoke, Lord, you were wrenching me back toward myself, taking me away from the place behind my back where I had set myself while I was refusing to look properly at myself. And you placed me before my very eyes so that I could see how vile I was, how deformed and filthy, how besmirched and full of sores. And I did see, and was horrified, and I had nowhere to run to away from myself. But if I tried to turn my gaze away from myself he kept on telling his tale, and once again

[89] *Conf.*, vol. I.372–3. [90] *Conf.*, vol. I.378–9. [91] *Conf.*, vol. I.380–1. [92] *Conf.*, vol. I.386–7.

> you set me against myself and impressed me upon my own eyes, so that I would find out my own sin and hate it. I knew it all right, but I was pretending I did not, and was suppressing and forgetting it.]

The spiraling in and out of view that characterizes this tortured self-relation encapsulates all that is 'Roman' about this chapter of Augustine's *Confessions*. Indeed, it sets before the eyes of readers the spectacle of rhetorical instruction at Rome, careers in the imperial service on the part of Africans who are also Romans, and, finally, the question of the metaphorical routes (reading, conversing with friends, epiphanies) by which individuals reach and constitute themselves. Augustine is, in effect, already mapping the self as a Kierkegaardian relation. He recalls that his reading of Cicero's *Hortensius* had first turned him towards wisdom and philosophy, but in his self-accusations over his inaction he perceives a contention in his soul. All this is an explicit meditation on what Paul says about the will in the Epistle to the Romans.[93] Augustine makes the whole scene pivot on a turn to the self ('ego ad me') as he beats a path through the thickets that entangle the teaching of Latin words within the life-altering power of the Word of God.[94]

In anger and desperation, he leaves Alypius and wanders alone, inwardly abusing himself and seeking to rise from the torpor that has settled over him. Weeping and disconsolate, he throws himself beneath a fig tree, agonizing over his sinfulness and unable to see how he might emerge from that condition. In the most famous section of Book Eight of the *Confessions*, Augustine recounts that he suddenly heard the voice of some unidentifiable child: 'et ecce audio vocem de vicina domo cum cantu dicentis et crebro repetentis, quasi pueri an puellae, nescio: "tolle lege, tolle lege"' ('And look! – from the house next door I hear a voice – I don't know whether it is a boy or a girl – singing some words over and over: "Pick it up and read it, pick it up and read it!"').[95] The phrase 'tolle lege, tolle lege' is a schoolroom locution, but Augustine's epiphany transfers to the child words that ought to belong to the teacher:

> statimque mutato vultu intentissimus cogitare coepi utrumnam solerent pueri in aliquo genere ludendi cantitare tale aliquid. nec occurrebat omnino audisse me uspiam, repressoque impetu lacrimarum surrexi, nihil aliud interpretans divinitus mihi iuberi nisi ut aperirem codicem et legerem quod primum caput invenissem.[96]

[93] It is no overstatement to say that Augustine's account of his suffering is haunted by Paul's teachings on the will. See Augustine, vol. I.392–5.

[94] *Conf.*, vol. I.390. [95] *Conf.*, vol. I.408–9. [96] *Conf.*, vol. I.408–9.

> [Immediately my expression transformed. I started to ask myself eagerly whether it was common for children to chant such words when they were playing a game of some kind. I could not recall ever having heard anything quite like it. I checked the flow of my tears and got up. I understood it as nothing short of divine providence that I was being ordered to open the book and read the first passage I came across.]

The child's voice takes Augustine backward and forward all at once: backward into his own schooldays and, presumably, into his life as a teacher; and forward into the new life that will burst from this process of divine tuition.

The episode's chief precedents are both Christian and Pagan. On the one hand, Augustine notes that he is remodeling for his own life an episode that he has heard concerning the life of St Anthony. On the other hand, though he does not mention the practice, he cannot have failed to know that this is how the book of Virgil's poems was sometimes consulted. As a Roman citizen born and educated in North Africa, trained up to great skill in Latin rhetoric, and then working as a grammarian at Rome before moving north to teach rhetoric at Milan, Augustine is 'of' Rome and yet not entirely 'at' Rome. His conversion turns on a sacred revision of the ancient practice of the *Sortes Virgilianae*, whereby Virgil's poems were opened at random and prophetic power was attributed to whatever passage first leapt to the seeker's eye.

Having interpreted the child's imperative verbs as a heaven-sent command to take up and read whatever was readiest to hand, Augustine returns to Alypius and to the book he had abandoned minutes earlier. Opening it, his eyes fall on the Latin of Paul's Epistle to the Romans, 13:13–14:

> [13] sicut in die honeste ambulemus non in comesationibus et ebrietatibus non in cubilibus et inpudicitiis non in contentione et aemulatione [14] sed induite Dominum Iesum Christum et carnis curam ne feceritis in desideriis.

> [13] not in rioting and drunkennesse, not in chambering and wantonnes, not in strife and enuying. [14] But put yee on the Lord Iesus Christ, and make not prouision for the flesh, to *fulfill* the lusts *thereof.*

Augustine affirms that he was forever changed by this encounter, and immediately tells Alypius what has happened: 'I neither wanted nor needed to read further. Immediately, the end of the sentence was like a light of sanctuary poured into my heart; every shadow of doubt melted away' ('nec ultra volui legere nec opus erat. statim quippe cum fine huiusce sententiae quasi luce securitatis infusa cordi meo omnes dubitationis tenebrae diffugerunt').[97] Inspired to imitate Augustine's method of self-discovery, Alypius reads on and applies to himself ('ille ad se rettulit') the opening words of Romans 14: 'infirmum autem in fide adsumite' ('Him that is weake in the faith receiue you.')[98]

These passages from Book Eight of the *Confessions* show that Augustine's encounter with the text of Romans 13:13–14 is the culmination of his effort to nurture a triangular relationship between Latin words, the self, and the Word. Augustine's account of his conversion is painstakingly constructed to show that Rome itself is the sum of those three angles. Book Eight of the *Confessions*, then, encloses within itself an encounter with the Acts / Romans nexus, so that Augustine is to be regarded as coming to terms with a Rome that belongs at once to pagans and Christians, and as seeing his way towards a new life that will demand of him something considerably more subtle than a simple rejection of the Eternal City. What he learns, via Simplicianus' account of the conversion of Victorinus, is that Rome already nurtures the life he is being called to live.

The encounter between Augustine-the-convert and Paul's Epistle was clearly intended as a deliberate echo of Paul's own conversion, which is narrated in the Book of Acts.[99] Augustine, in turn, will have been on Donne's mind as he pondered, in his 1622 sermon, what it would mean to live a life 'at *Rome*, that is, of *Rome*, reconciled to *Rome*'. For if Book Eight of the *Confessions* has an overarching story to tell, it is the story of Augustine's reconciliation to a new Rome by an unexpected route, and of the establishment of a literary tradition in which the Epistle to the Romans transforms its readers.

Martin Luther is the most famous aftershock of Augustine's encounter with Paul. Fittingly, Luther was an Augustinian monk, and his work on the Epistle to the Romans brings us into the gravitational centre of the linguistic and soteriological concerns that have been blending over the course of the chapter.[100] Luther quite precisely echoes the scenes of crisis described at length by Augustine. Painstaking linguistic work, in which grammatical and exegetical labours lead directly to a dramatic discovery,

[97] *Conf.*, vol. I.410–11. [98] *Conf.*, vol. I.410–11.

[99] See Fredriksen, 'Paul and Augustine', on the broad range of differences between the Lukan depiction of Paul in the narratives of Acts and Paul's self-presentation in the epistles.

[100] On the relevance of Luther's order see Scott Hendrix, 'Luther's Loyalties and the Augustinian Order', in Kenneth Hagen (ed.), *Augustine, the Harvest, and Theology (1300–1650), Essays Dedicated to Heiko Augustinus Oberman in Honor of his Sixtieth Birthday* (Leiden: Brill, 1990), 236–57. See also, in the same volume, David C. Steinmetz, 'Calvin and the Divided Self of Romans 7', 300–12. The Epistle to the Romans is a congenial home for this topic because the city of its addressees is, in the eyes of Reformers, itself a spectacular case of self-division.

enabled Luther to wield Paul's Romans against Rome's Church. The story, as told by Luther himself in the Latin Preface to his 1545 *Opera Omnia*, embeds a narrative of self-division and rebirth deep within the sort of slow, patient amassing of linguistic expertise that characterizes the experience of 'getting' Latin forms by heart and teaching complex texts. As Luther tells it, this is a story of crisis, patience, repetition, ardour, exegesis, and discovery:

> Interim eo anno iam redieram ad Psalterium denuo interpretandum, fretus eo, quod exercitatior essem, postquam S. Pauli Epistolas ad Romanos, ad Galatas, et eam, quae est ad Ebraeos, tractassem in scholis. Miro certe ardore captus fueram cognoscendi Pauli in epistola ad Rom., sed obstiterat hactenus non frigidus circum praecordia sanguis, sed unicum vocabulum, quod est Cap. 1: Iustitia Dei revelatur in illo. Oderam enim vocabulum istud 'Iustitia Dei', quod usu et consuetudine omnium doctorum doctus eram philosophice intelligere de iustitia (ut vocant) formali seu activa, qua Deus est iustus, et peccatores iniustosque punit.
>
> Ego autem, qui me, utcunque irreprehensibilis monachus vivebam, sentirem coram Deo esse peccatorem inquietissimae conscientiae, nec mea satisfactione placatum confidere possem, non amabam, imo odiebam iustum et punientem peccatores Deum, tacitaque si non blasphemia, certe ingenti murmuratione indignabar Deo, dicens: quasi vero non satis sit, miseros peccatores et aeternaliter perditos peccato originali omni genere calamitatis oppressos esse per legem decalogi, nisi Deus per euangelium dolorem dolori adderet, et etiam per euangelium nobis iustitiam et iram suam intentaret.[101]
>
> [Meanwhile, I had already during that year returned to interpret the Psalter anew. I had confidence in the fact that I was more skilful, after I had lectured in the university on St. Paul's epistles to the Romans, to the Galatians, and the one to the Hebrews. I had indeed been captivated with an extraordinary ardor for understanding Paul in the Epistle to the Romans. But up till then it was not the cold blood about the heart, but a single word in Chapter 1 [:17], 'In it the righteousness of God is revealed,' that had stood in my way. For I hated that word 'righteousness of God,' which, according to the use and custom of all the teachers, I had been taught to understand philosophically regarding the formal or active righteousness, as they call it, with which God is righteous and punishes the unrighteous sinner.
>
> Though I lived as a monk without reproach, I felt that I was a sinner before God with an extremely disturbed conscience. I could not believe that he was placated by my satisfaction. I did not love, yes, I hated the righteous God who punishes sinners, and secretly, if not blasphemously, certainly

[101] For Luther's Latin see *D. Martin Luthers Werke: Kritische Gesamtausgabe (WA)*, 68 vols. (Weimar: Herman Böhlaus Nachfolger, 1883–1999), vol. LIV.185. For the English translation see *LW*, vol. XXXIV.336–7.

murmuring greatly, I was angry with God, and said, 'As if, indeed, it is not enough, that miserable sinners, eternally lost through original sin, are crushed by every kind of calamity by the law of the decalogue, without having God add pain to pain by the gospel and also by the gospel threatening us with his righteousness and wrath!']

Through all this, the language of scholarly labour is surprisingly Catullan in its *odi et amo* bifurcation, and in its commitment to obsessive perseverance:

> Furebam ita saeva et perturbata conscientia, pulsabam tamen importunus eo loco Paulum, ardentissime sitiens scire, quid S. Paulus vellet.
>
> Donec miserente Deo meditabundus dies et noctes connexionem verborum attenderem, nempe: Iustitia Dei revelatur in illo, sicut scriptum est: Iustus ex fide vivit, ibi iustitiam Dei coepi intelligere eam, qua iustus dono Dei vivit, nempe ex fide, et esse hanc sententiam, revelari per eungeliam iustitiam Dei, scilicet passivam, qua nos Deus misericors iustificat per fidem, sicut scriptum est: Iustus ex fide vivit.
>
> Hic me prorsus renatum esse sensi, et apertis portis in ipsam paradisum intrasse. lbi continuo alia mihi facies totius scripturae apparuit. Discurrebam deinde per scripturas, ut habebat memoria, et colligebam etiam in aliis vocabulis analogiam, ut opus Dei, id est, quod operatur in nobis Deus, virtus Dei, qua nos potentes facit, sapientia Dei, qua nos sapientes facit, fortitudo Dei, salus Dei, gloria Dei.
>
> Iam quanto odio vocabulum 'iustitia Dei' oderam ante, tanto amore dulcissimum mihi vocabulum extollebam, ita mihi iste locus Pauli fuit vere porta paradisi.
>
> [Thus I raged with a fierce and troubled conscience. Nevertheless, I beat importunately upon Paul at that place, most ardently desiring to know what St. Paul wanted.
>
> At last, by the mercy of God, meditating day and night, I gave heed to the context of the words, namely, 'In it the righteousness of God is revealed, as it is written, "He who through faith is righteous shall live."' There I began to understand that the righteousness of God is that by which the righteous lives by a gift of God, namely by faith. And this is the meaning: the righteousness of God is revealed by the gospel, namely, the passive righteousness with which merciful God justifies us by faith, as it is written, 'He who through faith is righteous shall live.' Here I felt that I was altogether born again and had entered paradise itself through open gates. There a totally other face of the entire Scripture showed itself to me. Thereupon I ran through the Scripture from memory. I also found in other terms an analogy, as, the work of God, that is what God does in us, the power of God, with which he makes us strong, the wisdom of God, with which he makes us wise, the strength of God, the salvation of God, the glory of God.

> And I extolled my sweetest word with a love as great as the hatred with which I had before hated the word 'righteousness of God.' Thus that place in Paul was for me truly the gate to paradise.][102]

Luther's reminiscence, like that of Augustine, is predicated upon methodical self-exposure, meticulous interpretive labours, and then sudden transformation. The process recounted by Augustine, however, was socially anchored by his retreat from and then return to the side of his friend Alypius. Retreating from Alypius in desperation, Augustine hears the voice that sends him, via two imperatives (*tolle*, *lege*), back to a scene of instruction. He is, therefore, already marching under new orders when he returns to his friend's side and they engage in a corporate reading of Paul. Luther, by contrast, is alone: a scholar spiraling his way through a Catullan gyre of ardour and hate, beating again and again not at the door of a lover but upon Paul himself ('pulsabam tamen importunus eo loco Paulum'). Luther is playing a role that is familiar to readers of ancient Roman love poetry, but the *exclusus amator* who walks the streets of Rome in poems by Ovid, Catullus, and Tibullus has been transformed into a solitary scholar.[103]

Luther's account captures the labours – and especially the protracted frustrations that give way to sudden *éclaircissements* – that structure the experience of learning a new language, as he condenses into a few paragraphs a process that stretched across many years. In a genuinely thrilling discussion of these passages, and of Luther's wider career, Brian Cummings emphasizes that, 'In a remarkable way, Luther equates his religious anxiety with an anxiety over a semantic difficulty. Even more remarkably, he describes his dramatic change of heart as a μετάνοια about what this one word means'.[104] Cummings rightly emphasizes that this is a process of 'intense exegetical labour, developed over a series of years, examining and re-examining the meaning of critical texts in the Psalms, Paul, and Augustine'.[105] Cummings describes, more fully than anyone, how much of this transformation hangs on the linguistic conception of a shift from the active grammar of punishment to the passive grammar of grace.

[102] *WA*, vol. LIV.185–6; *LW*, vol. XXXIV.337.

[103] See Stephen Harrison: 'Latin love elegy is predominantly an urban genre; even Tibullus with his emphasis on the countryside sets only a small proportion of his poems in rural landscapes. The default location is the city of Rome, and within it often a private residence of some kind' ('Time, Place, and Political Background', in Thea S. Thorsen (ed.), *The Cambridge Companion to Latin Love Elegy* (Cambridge University Press, 2013), 144).

[104] Cummings, *The Literary Culture of the Reformation*, 64. For the entirety of Cummings' discussion of Luther and grammatical culture see 57–101.

[105] Cummings, *The Literary Culture of the Reformation*, 68.

Having squirmed through the jaws of this exegetical crisis, Luther insisted not simply on the value of the Epistle to the Romans but on the book's necessity. Where Du Bellay had proceeded in his Roman sequences by compelling his readers to stare, in hyperbolic attention, at Rome, Luther's 'Vorrede auff die Epistel S. Pauli an die Roemer' sees him urging his readers to ingest the book daily:

> Diese Epistel ist das rechte Heubstueck des newen Testaments, vnd das allerlauterste Euangelium, Welche wol wirdig vnd werd ist, das sie ein Christen mensch nicht allein von wort zu wort auswendig wisse, sondern teglich damit umbgehe, als mit teglichem brot der Seelen, Denn sie niemer kan zu viel vnd zu wol gelesen oder betrachtet werden, vnd je mehr sie gehandelt wird, je koestlicher sie wird, und das schmecket.[106]

> [This Epistle is really the chief part of the New Testament, and is truly the purest gospel. It is worthy not only that every Christian should know it word for word, by heart, but also that he should occupy himself with it every day, as the daily bread of the soul. We can never read it or ponder over it too much; for the more we deal with it, the more precious it becomes and the better it tastes.][107]

This obsessive commitment to reading and rereading what Paul had felt that the Christian community at Rome needed to hear ushers the city into the body by the eye and mouth. And like Du Bellay's Rome, which is a map of the world and its possibilities, Luther sees the Epistle to the Romans standing almost synecdochically for the New Testament.

In addition to being the text around which competing conceptions of punishment and grace revolved, Paul's Epistle to the Romans is the preeminent Christian expression of the will's self-division: 'For to will is present with me; but *how* to performe that which is good, I find not. For the good that I would, I do not: but the euill which I would not, that I doe' (Romans 7:18–19). Grammar at once instantiates and struggles to overcome such self-division. That was Luther's project as he beat ceaselessly and ardently against Paul's word, just as it was Virgilius' project in his ruminations on the vocative of ego. For the question of how one might reach, make, and remake the self is every bit as urgent as the question of how others might be reached, made, and remade by the Word.

Carried away in the course of his zealous efforts to render in English the final section of Luther's Preface to Paul's Epistle to the Romans, W. W. insisted that Paul had foreseen 'that there should arise and spring

106 'Vorrede auff die Epistel S. Pauli an die Roemer', in *WA DB*, vol. VII.3.
107 *LW*, vol. XXXV.365.

certaine Romanistes (for they are not worthie the name of Romans) out of Rome, and Romans'. As he proceeds, he amplifies at every turn the vehemence, and even simply the word count, of Luther's remarks. Those 'Romanistes' are products 'of Rome, and Romans'; I take that phrase to mean 'out of Rome, and [out of the Epistle to the] Romans'. This has the effect of making Paul's Epistle the creator of the 'Romanistes' W. W. abhors, and also of those who might somehow be 'worthie the name of Romans'. W. W.'s chosen rhetorical mode might be described as unbridled, heated copiousness. Here, one last time, we see the self entangled within what Rome has made, for the passage appears to associate its own surplus with the city's ability to pour forth 'most divilish and sathanical decretals, and their whole den of mans lawes and traditions, as by a most wast floude and huge deluge, wold labor to drowne, extinguish, and destroy not only this excellent Epistle, but even the whole body of Scripture'. Passages like this one serve as a reminder that although Milton, for example, could write with great power about the warrior hordes that had poured into the Roman empire from the north, Rome and its decretals were also a conquering horde.[108]

[108] When the rebel angels lift themselves from the burning lake in *Paradise Lost* Milton's epic voice asserts that they are 'A multitude, like which the populous North / Pour'd never from her frozen loins, to pass Rhene or the Danaw, when her barbarous sons / Came like a deluge on the south, and spread / Beneath Gibralter to the Lybian sands' (1:351–5). The poignant recursivity of this process helps explain Curtius' attraction to the argument of Arnold J. Toynbee, which Curtius summarizes as follows: 'the Germanic "barbarians" fall prey to the church, which had survived the universal-state end phase of antique culture. They thereby forego the possibility of bringing a positive intellectual contribution to the new historical entity. They fail in the situation which had gained the northern emigrants into the Balkan peninsula the victory over the Creto-Mycenean culture. The "Achaeans" forced their Greek tongue upon the conquered territory, whereas the Germans learned Latin. More precisely: the Franks gave up their language on the soil of Romanized Gaul' (Curtius, 5). Curtius is decisive: 'One is a European when one has become a *civis Romanus*' (12).

CHAPTER 4

The Dead

This chapter asks where and how Rome (and, by extension, polemics self-consciously characterized as reactions *against* Rome) figures in efforts to determine what the living owe to the dead, and what the dead can do for the living. Latin occupies a controlling position within this inquiry; so, too, do texts that cast the world of the living as the home of the dead; so, finally, will Reformation-era debates about the soteriological stakes of praying for the dead. Reformation England was a kingdom in which the official disavowal (and then, if only for a limited period of time under Queen Mary, the official recuperation) of late medieval ceremonies, and the development of waves of shifting prescriptions concerning the commemoration of the dead, reveal restless efforts to come to terms with the fractured afterlives of a longstanding social and spiritual economy. To couple Rome and the dead, as this chapter does, is to engage an area of concern that was central to Christian life and thought before, during, and after the Reformation.

To put the matter as decisively as possible, even at the risk of momentary oversimplification, one of the chief products of the English Reformation was an authorized theological economy in which the living and the dead were no longer vitally interdependent. Reformers worked, over the course of decades, to put the dead beyond the reach of the living.[1] The texts discussed in this chapter range from works by Augustine and Dante to Chaucer, Sir Thomas More's *Utopia*, and a small number of passages from Shakespeare, while also taking in Catholic books of hours and Protestant primers. These texts span a period of time in which Rome is the gravitational centre of a sequence of massive upheavals in vernacular piety and

[1] The most thorough guide to these changes is Peter Marshall, *Beliefs and the Dead in Reformation England* (Oxford University Press, 2002). Marshall emphasizes the inconsistencies, innovations, and reversals that riddle these serial changes, especially when they are measured against the backdrop of Catholic and Calvinist consistency. See also Sarah Tarlow, *Ritual, Belief and the Dead in Early Modern Britain and Ireland* (Cambridge University Press, 2011).

attendant debates about the relationship between the living and the dead.[2] The chapter argues that interpreting these debates as facets of the fact of Rome alerts us to the role that the human voice plays in probing the limits of mortality and the nature of the human as such.

'Non in caelo, sed in terra'

The background to an English poet such as Chaucer's engagements with these topics would have to include a teeming variety of texts, authors, and social practices ranging from antiquity to the Middle Ages. This is because medieval conceptions of *auctoritas* on any given subject were genuinely trans-historical, trans-national, and multilingual. For the sake of efficiency two authorities can be singled out. Augustine and Dante established many of the parameters within which later writers across Europe, Britain, and Ireland would broach these topics.

The tradition of regarding the Eternal City as a spectacle of death finds one of its most potent and influential expressions in the *De civitate Dei contra paganos*, a book conceived in the wake of the sack of Rome in 410 as a cornerstone of Augustine's effort to deny the charge that Christianity was to blame for the city's fate. Augustine measures the courage of those Christians who died at the hands of Alaric's armies against the courage of the great men of Roman antiquity. The Christian dead were martyrs, he says,

> qui Scaevolas et Curtios et Decios non sibi inferendo poenas, sed inlatas ferendo et virtute vera, quoniam vera pietate, et innumerabili multitudine superarunt. Sed cum illi essent in civitate terrena, quibus propositus erat omnium pro illa officiorum finis incolumitas eius et regnum non in caelo, sed in terra, non in vita aeterna, sed in decessione morientium et successione moriturorum, quid aliud amarent quam gloriam, qua volebant etiam post mortem tamquam vivere in ore laudantium?[3]

> [who surpassed men like Scaevola, Curtius and the Decii both in true courage, because they had true religion, and in their vast number. Their tortures were not self-inflicted, but they bore tortures that were inflicted by others. Those Roman heroes were citizens of an earthly city, and the goal of all their loyal service to it was its security and a kingdom not in heaven but

[2] For recent work whose reach is global see T. W. Laqueur, *The Work of the Dead: A Cultural History of Mortal Remains* (Princeton University Press, 2015); Paul Koudounaris, *Memento Mori: The Dead Among Us* (London: Thames and Hudson, 2015).

[3] Augustine, *The City of God*, ed. and trans. George E. McCracken et al, 7 vols., LCL 411–17 (Cambridge, MA: Harvard University Press, 1963), vol. II.214–15.

> on earth. Since there was no eternal life for them, but merely the passing away of the dying, who were succeeded by others soon to die, what else were they to love apart from glory, whereby they chose to find even after death a sort of life on the lips of those who sang their praises.]

This passage shows how speedily the earthly city of Rome acquires its metaphorical, explanatory power in Christian polemic, and how naturally the city fuels Augustine's efforts to distinguish between radically different conceptions of heroism. As a city located (as it must be) 'non in caelo, sed in terra', Rome is naturally positioned to teach lessons to mortals about the ways of the world, but its preeminence among earthly cities enables Augustine to depict it as *the* entity capable of teaching his readers that what is casually called life ought rather to be reinterpreted as death. The logic of the passage suggests that in the eyes of Augustine, life only counts as life if it is 'vita aeterna'. What unfolds on earth, by contrast, is to be understood not as life but rather as a grim dilation in which the dying can do little more than await their turn, hoping, at best, 'tamquam vivere' (so to speak, to live).

This perspective on life 'in terra' explains why the care of the dead looms so large in Augustine's understanding of Christian duties. It also explains why Augustine himself figures so prominently in medieval and Renaissance debates about proper comportment towards the dead. It explains, finally, why the care of the dead should be so urgently connected with Rome in his imagination. Rome is at once an earthly city and a spiritual condition that unremittingly brings before the eyes of believers the fact of death – which is to say, the experience of mortality as well as the social and devotional practices that encircle that experience. This, at any rate, was one of the lessons Augustine perceived in the sack of Rome. As he explains in the *De cura pro mortuis gerenda*, dead bodies had to be protected because they occupied a special position within God's providence. The dead were to be seen as corporate with the living in the mystical body of Christ.[4] In western Europe, pre-Reformation Christendom slotted believers into a genuinely international community of practices commemorating the dead under the imprimatur of Rome.

Rome, of course, has no actual monopoly on the phenomenon of mortality. Nevertheless, it was responsible for some of western Europe's

[4] See Paula J. Rose, *A Commentary on Augustine's De cura pro mortuis gerenda* (Leiden: Brill, 2013). Death, burial, and baptism raise a related group of issues in Augustine's writings. See J. Patout Burns, 'Baptism as Dying and Rising with Christ in the Teachings of Augustine', *Journal of Early Christian Studies*, 20 (2012), 407–38.

most conspicuous and lasting efforts to ensure that the living knew that they moved in a landscape that also belonged to the dead. One particularly evocative engagement with this aspiration occurs when Dante approaches the City of Dis and the circle of the heretics in Canto 9 of *Inferno*. Abandoning the inexpressibility topoi that dominate so much of the *Commedia*, Dante assures his readers that he knows precisely how to identify multiple earthly analogues to the astonishing place in which he finds himself:

> Sì come ad Arli, ove Rodano stagna,
> sì com' a Pola, presso del Carnaro
> ch'Italia chiude e suoi termini bagna,
>
> fanno i sepulcri tutt' il loco varo
> così facevan quivi d'ogne parte,
> salvo che 'l modo v'era più amaro.[5]
>
> [Even as at Arles, where the Rhone makes its delta,
> as at Pola, near the Carnaro
> that encloses Italy and bathes its boundaries,
>
> tombs variegate the place,
> so they did here on every side,
> except that the manner was more bitter.]

This slightly elliptical reference to sarcophagi at Arles and Pola may well have left some of Dante's early readers and commentators in the dark. The site at Arles is the surviving ancient Roman necropolis of Alyscamps (from *Elisii campi*). The site at Pola, in what is now Croatia, was a Roman necropolis that no longer survives. Sarcophagi at these sites made the ground uneven ('tutt' il loco varo') in both literal and metaphorical senses: literally, because they are inverted graves designed to assert the persistence of the dead above ground and amidst the living; metaphorically, because they thereby tested, even confused, the relationship between the living and the dead as these necropoles expanded through many centuries of use from antiquity to the Middle Ages and beyond. For although ancient Roman necropoles had been located, as a rule, outside cities, they remained a part of the daily lives of the residents of those cities. The populations of individual cities could both fall and rise during the Middle Ages and

[5] Dante, *The Divine Comedy*, ed. and trans. Robert M. Durling, 3 vols. (New York: Oxford University Press, 1997–2011), vol. I.9.112–17. References to Dante give volume, canto, and line numbers.

Renaissance, but the community of the dead could only grow.[6] As Dante's mind turns to what Rome had left behind at places like Arles and Pola, and to what the living traditions of the Middle Ages had taken up and enlarged, he finds multiple models for the terrain of his *Inferno*.

Rome occupies a special position within Dante's conception of the economy of the dead, but some of the contexts in which he invokes the city can nevertheless surprise.[7] In the *Purgatorio*, readers discover that it is from ancient Rome's city harbour, on the banks of the Tiber at Ostia ('dove l'acqua di Tevero s'insala'; 'where the Tiber becomes salt'[8]), that all the world's dead are conducted, by water, to the island mountain of purgatory. The point at which fresh- and salt-water mingle is a fitting expression of the complexity of the relationship between the living and the dead. The water that gives life is, as it were, salted by tears that both mourn and preserve. Dante is clearly writing against the background of Augustine's move to make the earthly city of Rome stand for earthly experience – and therefore mortality – as such. Rome's magnetic power gathers to itself all the dead who will make their way to Dante's purgatory. All roads and waterways lead from Rome.

Even within the *Purgatorio*, however, Rome can mark a rather different transitional point. From within the margins of the Earthly Paradise that sits on the uppermost peak of the mountain of purgatory, Beatrice makes Rome an ultimate destination rather than a sublunary city (let alone a metaphysics of carnality) that must be decisively abandoned by the Christian dead:

> Qui sarai tu poco tempo silvano;
> e sarai meco sanza fine cive
> di quella Roma onde Cristo è romano.[9]
>
> [Here you will be but briefly a dweller in the wood
> and with me, without end, you will be a citizen
> of that Rome of which Christ is a Roman.]

With the dead nested in rows of sarcophagi among which the living must pick their way, and with the risen Christ celebrated as the chief citizen of a genuinely, rather than rhetorically, Eternal City, Dante is studying Rome's ability to erase the lines that separate the living from the dead.

[6] On urban life and the dead see Vanessa Harding, *The Dead and the Living in Paris and London, 1500–1670* (Cambridge University Press, 2002).

[7] See especially Christopher Kleinhenz, 'The City of Rome in Dante's *Divine Comedy*', *Essays in Medieval Studies* 28 (2012), 51–68.

[8] Dante, *The Divine Comedy*, vol. II.2.101.

[9] Dante, *The Divine Comedy*, vol. II.32.100–2.

Once again, Paul's Epistle to the Romans may supply a helpful roadmap through, or at least set a precedent for, some of Christianity's counter-intuitive inversions of life and death: 'And if Christ be in you, the body is dead because of sinne' (Romans 8:10). Dante's miniature studies of the margin between life and death raise unsettling questions about the nature of what counts as 'human'. The beautiful condensation of thought in Dante's final formula ('quella Roma onde Cristo è romano') identifies the limits of conceptual territories that his inheritors will explore.

The Dead Boy's Latin

Chaucer's *Prioress's Tale* surveys those conceptual territories, with special emphasis on how Rome's language, along with the subtly interconnected texts of Rome's liturgy, cooperate to both constitute and defy the boundary between life and death. Pressing the *General Prologue*'s portrait of the Prioress into dialogue with her tale reveals that Chaucer channelled several linguistic and pedagogical concerns into a study of the power of Latin prayer and the living voice at the moment of death. In this tale, the boundary between life and death is demarcated by meditations on language, instruction, and the body. These meditations develop partly under the banner of Rome's dispersal to distant lands, and partly in relation to concerns that are set in motion by the *General Prologue*'s portrait of the Prioress.

The portrait's earliest moves return almost obsessively to minute attention to what comes from the Prioress' mouth. Attention is given to the delicacy of her speech ('Hire gretteste ooth was but by Seinte Loy'); the nasalization of her Latin vowels in liturgical contexts ('Ful weel she soong the service dyvyne, / Entuned in hir nose ful semely'); and the provenance of her possibly creaky French ('Frenssh she spak ful faire and fetisly / After the scole of Stratford atte Bowe, / For Frenssh of Parys was to hire unknowe').[10] Beyond this, the words and sounds that come from her mouth are, comically and as if by a natural extension, contrasted with

[10] Geoffrey Chaucer, *The Canterbury Tales* (*CT*), in *The Riverside Chaucer*, ed. Larry D. Benson, 3rd edn. (Boston: Houghton Mifflin, 1987), I(A).120, 122–3, 124–6. References to *The Canterbury Tales* are keyed to *The Riverside Chaucer's* fragment, group, and line numbers. For scholarship on the cultural and linguistic contexts from which the Prioress springs see the essays collected in Jocelyn Wogan-Browne (ed.) with Carolyn Collette, Maryanne Kowaleski, Linne Mooney, Ad Putter, and David Trotter, *Language and Culture in Medieval Britain: The French of England, c.1100–c.1500* (Martlesham: Boydell & Brewer, 2009); Thelma Fenster and Carolyn P. Collette (eds.), *The French of Medieval England: Essays in Honour of Jocelyn Wogan-Browne* (Martlesham: Boydell & Brewer, 2017).

extensive remarks on what does not come from her mouth. Readers are assured that 'At mete wel ytaught was she with alle; / She leet no morsel from hir lippes falle', and Chaucer's narrator tells us that she is an assiduous wiper of grease from her upper lip while at table.[11] The portrait concludes with a description of the Prioress' rosary, the brooch that hangs from it, and the brooch's Latin inscription:

> Of smal coral aboute hire arm she bar
> A peire of bedes, gauded al with grene,
> And theron heng a brooch of gold ful sheene,
> On which ther was first write a crowned A,
> And after *Amor vincit omnia*.[12]

The famous Latin tag is derived from the lament of the lover Gallus in Virgil's Tenth Eclogue. This potentially provocative choice can move in erotic as well as spiritual directions, or even, given the complex affective rhetoric of appeals to the Virgin, in both directions at once.[13] The Prioress' rosary plays a significant role within the tale's affirmations of the power of Latin prayer to connect the living to the dead under the name of Rome. It provides, moreover, an opportunity to revive and revise a mostly neglected explanation for an interpretive crux that has long attracted scholarly attention.

Like the *General Prologue*'s portrait of the Prioress, the *Prioress's Tale* treats the human body largely as a vehicle for words. This is initiated by the Prioress' opening remarks on the marvellous trajectory that has enabled praise of Christ and Mary to move, from mouth to mouth, throughout the world, and to emblematize Rome's reach in the process. Her Prologue is relatively brief, and citing it in its entirety will show that it is utterly dominated by what the Prioress calls the 'performance' of the Word:

> O Lord, oure Lord, thy name how merveillous
> Is in this large world ysprad – quod she –

[11] *CT*, I(A).127–35.

[12] *CT*, I(A).158–62. For bibliography and a guide to the Prioress's rosary see Laura Fulkerson Hodges, *Chaucer and Clothing: Clerical and Academic Costume in the General Prologue to the Canterbury Tales* (Cambridge University Press, 2005), 83–111. Noting that contemporary records preserve numerous accounts of nuns with precious rosaries, Fulkerson Hodges observes that 'her rosary cannot be classified as either curious or over curious; instead, it is ordinary' (82).

[13] On the tale's reception in relation to the cult of the Virgin see Heather Blurton and Hannah Johnson, 'Reading the *Prioress's Tale* in the Fifteenth Century: Lydgate, Hoccleve, and Marian Devotion', *Chaucer Review* 50 (2015), 134–58. For an overview of critical debates surrounding Chaucer's portrait of the Prioress see John V. Fleming, 'Madame Eglentyne: The Telling of the Beads', in Donka Minkova and Teresa Tinkle (eds.), *Chaucer and the Challenges of Medievalism: Studies in Honor of H.A. Kelly* (Frankfurt: Peter Lang, 2003), 205–33.

For noght oonly thy laude precious
Parfourned is by men of dignitee,
But by the mouth of children thy bountee
Parfourned is, for on the brest soukynge
Somtyme shewen they thyn heriynge.

Wherfore in laude, as I best kan or may,
Of thee and of the white lylye flour
Which that the bar, and is a mayde alway,
To telle a storie I wol do my labour;
Nat that I may encressen hir honour,
For she hirself is honour and the roote
Of bountee, next hir Sone, and soules boote.

O mooder Mayde! O mayde Mooder free!
O bussh unbrent, brennynge in Moyses sighte,
That ravyshedest doun fro the Deitee,
Thurgh thyn humblesse, the Goost that in th' alighte,
Of whos vertu, whan he thyn herte lighte,
Conceyved was the Fadres sapience,
Help me to telle it in thy reverence!

Lady, thy bountee, thy magnificence,
Thy vertu, and thy grete humylitee,
Ther may no tonge expresse in no science;
For somtyme, Lady, er men praye to thee,
Thou goost biforn of thy benyngnytee,
And getest us the lyght, of thy preyere,
To gyden us unto thy Sone so deere.

My konnyng is so wayk, O blisful Queene,
For to declare thy grete worthynesse
That I ne may the weighte nat susteene;
But as a child of twelf month oold, or lesse,
That kan unnethes any word expresse,
Right so fare I, and therfore I yow preye,
Gydeth my song that I shal of yow seye.[14]

[14] *CT*, VII.453–87. The transition from the *Shipman's Tale* to the Prologue to the *Prioress's Tale* is engineered by the Host's celebratory oath: 'Wel seyd, by *corpus dominus*' (VII.435). This is, in effect, the Host's oath about the eucharistic Host. It leads logically into the *Prioress's Prologue* and tale, and into questions about what gets put into mouths. I propose that the Host's second oath ('by Seint Austyn!' (VII.441)) be regarded not only as a merry response to the monk in the *Shipman's Tale* but as also paving a road towards the concern with the care of the dead that is on view in the *Prioress's Tale*. The oath has the power, therefore, simultaneously to invoke Augustine of Hippo (given the tale's concern with the care of the dead) and Augustine of Canterbury (given the destination of the pilgrimage).

These stanzas meditate the dispersal of the Roman Word and its spiritual scripts to the distant corners of the world. Over the course of decades scholars have reconstructed what appears to be the Prioress' special reliance in these stanzas on liturgical texts – particularly the Little Office of Our Lady. The first stanza, for example, tacitly slides material from the liturgy's Latin into Chaucer's Middle English as the Prioress translates and paraphrases the first verses of the opening psalm of the Matins service. The second stanza does the same with a Matins antiphon before venturing some more general words of praise for the Virgin.[15] Latin liturgical texts are collections of scripted speech acts that have been composed for the purpose of connecting individuals to each other, to their communities, to God, and to the Church at Rome. This multivalent feature of liturgical prayer is central to both the Prioress' Prologue and her tale.

The entirety of the *Prologue to the Prioress's Tale* is devoted to musings on linguistic and theological topics: the spread of Christ's name; the spiritual efficacy of praise and prayer; questions about how mouth and tongue might convey the nature of the Virgin's bounty, magnificence, virtue, and humility. The Prioress emphasizes that whatever manages to get itself spoken will have been made possible in advance by the Virgin. 'Help me to telle it in thy reverence!', she pleads, acknowledging that when believers pray it is Mary herself who goes 'biforn' those prayers. The Prioress begs, finally, for divine support of a kind that might lift her out of a condition that she likens to that of a child who has not yet learned how to speak.

This final stanza, which imitates Dante's remarks on Mary in *Paradiso* 33, must therefore be read as imposing a fully circular structure on the Prologue by reanimating the opening stanza's insistence that praise of the kind the Prioress envisions can be performed even 'by the mouth of children' who are 'on the brest soukynge'. The Prologue, that is, is structured as a formal poetic invocation in which the Virgin, as spiritual Muse, must speak liturgical texts directly into the mouth of one who is moved (and yet hardly able without help and training) to praise her. The Prioress is already imagining herself as a version of the dead boy whose tale she will tell, and whose mouth – both living and dead – will be filled with prayers by and for the Virgin Mother. Latin liturgical texts memorized by the Prioress breathe life into her Middle English poetry far west of Rome,

[15] For a recent engagement with this longstanding scholarly concern see Megan Murton, 'The *Prioress's Prologue*: Dante, Liturgy, and Ineffability', *Chaucer Review* 52 (2017), 318–40. Murton's essay is excellent on the rhetoric and decorum of prayer. She sees Chaucer's borrowings from the liturgy and Dante as having been designed 'to explore not a Prioress's personality, but a question about the capacity of human language as a medium of prayer' (323).

and the *Prioress's Tale* will see Madame Eglentyne sending that liturgical script far east of the Eternal City. The *Prologue*, therefore, reiterates and condenses its dominant preoccupations: it is concerned with the production of speech, but only with respect to speech acts that involve praise and prayer; it is interested in the conceptions of agency that underwrite the ability to speak, but relentlessly characterizes the speaker as a child capable of speaking only via the Virgin's intercession; it charts the spread of the Word, but chiefly as an epiphenomenon of the dispersal of Rome's language to distant lands. This Rome is the spiritual and verbal anchor of an international community of believers who convene, at far-flung sites, around the interlocked texts of a liturgy and Church calendar.

The *Prioress's Tale* takes readers into the heart of a series of vexatious topics. Foremost among these, as is well known, is its pronounced anti-Semitism.[16] The Prioress tells her co-travelers, for example, that 'the serpent Sathanas, / ... hath in Jues herte his waspes nest'.[17] The tale concludes with the Prioress's plea that another dead boy, 'yonge Hugh of Lyncoln, slayn also / With cursed Jewes', might pray for the living, thereby insisting upon the tale's relation to the blood-libel sagas of child murder that occupied such a prominent position in medieval anti-Semitism.[18]

One of the most striking aspects of the *Prioress's Tale* is its effort to establish how and why Latin song finds its way into the mouth of a dead boy.[19] The Prioress sets her tale 'in Asye, in a greet citee' that harbours both a Christian community and a Jewish ghetto.[20] The ghetto is situated along a busy thoroughfare: 'And thurgh the strete men myghte ride or wende, / For it was free and open at eyther ende'.[21] A Christian school operating on

[16] See Adrienne Williams Boyarin, *Miracles of the Virgin in Medieval England: Law and Jewishness in Marian Legends* (Martlesham: Boydell & Brewer, 2010). Boyarin shows that anti-Semitism is a significant element of medieval Miracles of the Virgin, as is attention to the Virgin's role in offering devotional instructions. See also Heather Blurton and Hannah Johnson, *The Critics and The Prioress: Antisemitism, Criticism, and Chaucer's* 'Prioress's Tale' (Ann Arbor: University of Michigan Press, 2017). See also the chapter 'Reprioritizing the Prioress's Tale' in Lisa Lampert, *Gender and Jewish Difference from Paul to Shakespeare* (Philadelphia: University of Pennsylvania Press, 2004), 58–100. A solid overview of older scholarship, including an assessment of the tale's sources and analogues, can be found in Beverly Boyd (ed.), *The Prioress's Tale: A Variorum Edition of the Works of Geoffrey Chaucer*, vol. II, in *The Canterbury Tales* Part 20 (Norman: University of Oklahoma Press, 1987).

[17] *CT*, VII.558–9.

[18] *CT*, VII.684–5. On this topic see Merrall Llewelyn Price, 'Sadism and Sentimentality: Absorbing Antisemitism in Chaucer's Prioress', *Chaucer Review* 43 (2008), 197–214.

[19] Boyd emphasizes that the clergeon tale told by the Prioress is 'old, widespread, and part of an international corpus of legends dealing with heroes (both historical and fictitious) of Christianity, their deeds, and their miracles' (14). There are dozens of analogues to the tale, several of which feature different Marian hymns.

[20] *CT*, VII.488. [21] *CT*, VII.493–4.

some sort of Roman model (the children study grammatical primers and books of antiphons) sits at one end of the ghetto, and the Prioress quickly narrows her narrative attention to one seven-year-old 'clergeon' (that is, a schoolboy or chorister) who is from the very beginning deeply attached to the Virgin Mary. School and devotion to Marian hymnology occupy equally prominent portions of his mind, heart, and mouth:

day by day to scole was his wone,
And eek also, where as he saugh th'ymage
Of Cristes mooder, hadde he in usage,
As hym was taught, to knele adoun and seye
His *Ave Maria*, as he goth by the weye.[22]

Because the tale is organized around a series of pedagogical scenes and their underlying vocabularies and logic, everything the boy does is characterized as something that he has been taught to do, so that education is cast as a condition of his existence and as the foundation of his connection to the Virgin. He is, at his very core, the product of the pedagogical and devotional cultures that flowed from Rome to distant 'Asye'. He is the creature, too, of an English prioress whose imagination has turned eastward in order to imagine – correctly – a world guided by the same texts and institutions that guide her own.

The entire scene can be read in part as Chaucer's attempt to reimagine the scope and central concerns of Augustine's account of his conversion in Book Eight of the *Confessions*. Like Augustine, the boy is transformed by Latin words spoken by children, even though (or perhaps in this case specifically because) the Latin that fills the mouths of those children is beyond the boy's reach:

This litel child, his litel book lernynge,
As he sat in the scole at his prymer,
He *Alma redemptoris* herde synge,
As children lerned hire antiphoner;
And as he dorste, he drough hym ner and ner,
And herkned ay the words and the noote,
Til he the firste vers koude al by rote.

Noght wiste he what this Latyn was to seye,
For he so yong and tendre was of age.[23]

The child, labouring over his grammatical primer, is glimpsed at one of the earliest stages of his education. As he works he hears boys of a more

[22] *CT*, VII.504–8. [23] *CT*, VII.516–24.

advanced age working through their books of antiphons.[24] He is unable to take it all in, and the fact that he is in the dark about the meaning of the words he has already started committing to memory helps prepare the ground for later humanist critiques of rote learning.[25] The world of the liturgy, however, reposes great faith in the power of memorized words, and Chaucer embeds the disciplines of memorization within an altogether more intimate pedagogical experience than we might expect to find. An older schoolboy comes to the clergeon's aid, expounding to him 'this song in his langage', sitting him on his knee, construing the hymn, and apparently making a protracted act of this instruction.[26]

The hymn to be learned, the *Alma redemptoris mater* is a liturgical antiphon:

> Alma redemptoris mater, quæ pervia cæli
> Porta manes et stella maris, succurre cadenti,
> Surgere qui curat populo, tu quæ genuisti
> Natura mirante tuum sanctum genitorem,
> Virgo prius ac posterius, Gabrielis ab ore
> Sumens illud Ave, peccatorum miserere.[27]

[24] Richard Taruskin's *Oxford History of Western Music* emphasizes that Western musical notation crossed the Alps from Italy into what is now France and beyond, in order to establish the tightest possible liturgical links between Rome and its satellite churches. This is one of the functions of the little chorister's antiphon as it brings Latin song, in Roman liturgical forms, to distant 'Asye', thereby moving eastward and reprising its historical move north and west under Charlemagne and his successors. See Richard Taruskin, *The Oxford History of Western Music*, 5 vols. (New York: Oxford University Press, 2005), vol. I.31–60.

[25] In *De recta latini graecique sermonis pronuntiatione*, Erasmus describes children as possessing 'a sort of innate, parrot-like desire, or rather delight, in copying and repeating what they have heard: indeed, their learning abilities are such that they recognize voices that are familiar to them quicker than they do faces' (*CWE*, vol. XXXVI.369–70); 'Et videmus in pueris recens natis, velut in psittacis, stadium quoddam natiuum ac voluptatem etiam aemulandi reddendique quod audierint tanta docilitate, vt prius auribus agnoscant consuetas voces, quam oculis dinoscant vultus' (*ASD*, vol. I–4.14). On the fear that such facility is alternately ennobling and debasing (and in some basic way inhuman), see Wallace, *Virgil's Schoolboys*, 78.

[26] *CT*, VII.526.

[27] For the text see F. J. E. Raby, *A History of Christian–Latin Poetry from the Beginnings to the Close of the Middle Ages*, 2nd edn. (Oxford: Clarendon Press, 1953), 226–7. The centrality of this hymn to the *Prioress's Tale* intensifies the teller's structural and conceptual debts to the liturgy. These are already on view in the Prologue to her tale. Audrey Ekdahl Davidson offers a useful reminder that Chaucer would have been most familiar with the version that was transmitted via Use of Sarum books, and that he may therefore have had in mind a fairly challenging musical setting for the hymn. A different musical setting was associated with the *Liber usualis*. For the Use of Sarum music see Audrey Ekdahl Davidson, *Substance and Manner: Studies in Music and the Other Arts* (Saint Paul, MN: Hiawatha Press, 1977), 24. The question of whether a Use of Sarum or Use of Rome musical setting of the hymn is to be imagined as the one that has made its way to some unnamed part of 'Asye' is tied chiefly to the question of whether the Childermass is one of the relevant liturgical contexts for the tale's origins. In any case, the text of the hymn remains the same. On the hymn see Boyd, *The Prioress's Tale*, 15–16.

This is the basic, unchanging text of the hymn, some indefinite portion of which ('the firste vers' can refer either to a single line or to some syntactic unit of it) the clergeon has managed get by heart without direct instruction. The hymn proper is followed by different versicles, responses, and collects, depending on the liturgical calendar. Chaucer, in any case, can rely on his audience's utter familiarity with the text of the hymn and does not cite it.

The *Prioress's Tale* emphasizes that the older boy takes pains to teach the seven-year-old what he has learned about the song. As it happens, this has nothing to do with the contents of the hymn's language (which he appears not to understand), and everything to do with its spiritual efficacy, and with the specific occasions on which it is to be sung:

> This song, I have herd seye,
> Was maked of our blisful Lady free,
> Hire to salue, and eek hire for to preye
> To been oure help and socour whan we deye.
> I kan namoore expounde in this mateere,
> I lerne song; I kan but small grammeere.[28]

Several related issues are in play here: first, the tongue that is being spoken when the older boy sets out 'T'expounden hym this song in his langage'[29] is never named by the Prioress; second, a Latin hymn is the text to be memorized; and third, the words and grammar of the hymn are beyond the reach of the boys who benefit by it, even though they are perfectly clear about (and eventually protected by) its spiritual function. The words of the hymn, and the process of internalizing those words, integrate the boys into the 'universal' network of Rome's Catholic Church. From the distance of this unnamed city in 'Asye', Latin words (including both the *Ave Maria* and the *Alma redemptoris mater*, along with the full contents of the book of antiphons and the grammatical primer from which the boys are working at school) organize the pedagogical and devotional lives of these boys and their schoolfellows.

Even without their being fully understood, the words of the hymn are efficacious since they allow Mary to intercede after death. She is, in the language of the hymn, 'pervia caeli porta' (the open gate of heaven). The older boy had set out to 'construe and declare', but he also admitted that the actual grammar of the Latin text is not in his command.[30] Instead, he has offered an account of the situational, spiritual value of the hymn to those who find themselves praying for 'help and socour whan we deye'.

[28] *CT*, VII.531–6. [29] *CT*, VII.526. [30] *CT*, VII.528.

The shape of the story lets us interpret that phrase in two ways. First, it can be interpreted as indicating that the hymn is to be sung by the living in order to secure, in advance, Mary's 'help and socour' when death one day comes unlooked for. Second, it can be interpreted as proposing that the hymn is to be sung by the dying – which is to say, at the very moment when Mary's 'help and socour' are genuinely essential. The territory that connects the words of the living to the fates of the dead is one of the provinces of Rome. The power of this hymn within that spiritual province becomes decisively clear as the tale proceeds.

Because the tale remains poised, as though standing vigil, on the border that connects the realms of life and death, it is worth emphasizing that the tale's murder plot occurs within the Jewish ghetto that separates (unless it is to be understood as connecting) the two halves of the city's Christian community. The Prioress has already implicitly associated the open thoroughfare of the ghetto with the anatomical route by which the boy's songs work their way through his body:

> His felawe taughte hym homeward prively,
> Fro day to day, til he koude it by rote,
> And thanne he song it wel and boldely,
> Fro word to word, acordynge with the note.
> Twies a day it passed thurgh his throte,
> To scoleward and homward whan he wente;
> On Cristes mooder set was his entente.[31]

This passage contributes to the tale's explicitly embodied description of song. Twice a day the boy passes through the ghetto's thoroughfare on his way to and from school; 'Twies a day' the hymn passes 'thurgh his throte' in the course of that journey. The unsettling effect of fusing throat and thoroughfare calls attention to the human body's openness from throat to mouth, just as the place of concealment of the boy's corpse focuses attention on the body's openness at the anus. The throat through which the hymn of praise has been passing is slashed, and his lifeless corpse is stashed in a privy.[32]

The boy's body rests in that privy, overcome by the silence of death, until his mother, in a submerged translation of the phrase 'Alma

[31] *CT*, VII.544–50.

[32] *CT*, VII.565–73. The *Second Nun's Tale* is relevant here. Its teller is a member of the Prioress' entourage. Her tale, which is set in Rome, sees Christian converts seeking the Pope in Rome's catacombs. The tale's central character, Cecilia, continues to preach even after her throat is cut. My decision to focus on the *Prioress's Tale* rather than the *Second Nun's Tale* is owing to the fact that the former studies the hold of Latin on life and death even far from Rome.

redemptoris mater', calls out for help from 'Cristes mooder meeke and kynde'.[33] When she finally searches for him 'Among the cursed Jues', his singing corpse retranslates his mother's phrase back into the title of the Latin hymn:[34]

> This gemme of chastite, this emeraude,
> And eek of martirdom the ruby bright,
> Ther he with throte ykorven lay upright,
> He *Alma redemptoris* gan to synge
> So loude that al the place gan to rynge.[35]

When his corpse is taken up it continues to sing all the way to its bier. The boy – or rather, the mysterious corpse that hangs, impossibly poised and full of Latin song, between life and death – explains the miracle of which he is a part:

> 'My throte is kut unto my nekke boon',
> Seyde this child, 'and, as by wey of kynde
> I sholde have dyed, ye, longe tyme agon.
> But Jesu Crist, as ye in bookes fynde,
> Wil that his glorie laste and be in mynde,
> And for the worship of his mooder deere
> Yet may I synge *O Alma* loude and cleere.'[36]

As he hovers here between life and death, no longer subject to what he calls 'wey of kynde', he describes the role that the Virgin has played in enabling the circumstances of his murder to emerge:

> This welle of mercy, Cristes mooder sweete,
> I loved alwey, as after my konnynge;
> And whan that I my lyf sholde forlete,
> To me she cam, and bad me for to synge
> This anthem verraily in my deyynge,
> As ye han herd, and whan that I hadde songe,
> Me thoughte she leyde a greyn upon my tonge.
>
> Wherfore I synge, and synge moot certeyn,
> In honour of that blisful Mayden free
> Til fro my tongue of taken is the greyn;
> And after that thus seyde she to me:
> 'My litel child, now wol I fecche thee,
> Whan that the greyn is fro thy tonge ytake,
> Be nat agast; I wol thee nat forsake'.[37]

[33] *CT*, VII.597. [34] *CT*, VII.599. [35] *CT*, VII.609–13. [36] *CT*, VII.649–55.
[37] *CT*, VII.658–69.

The Christian community's abbot eases the boy more fully into death, and as he removes the 'greyn' the boy 'yaf up the goost ful softely'.[38] Throughout the surprising turns of this tale, the Prioress has drawn attention to the life-giving force of Latin hymns and prayers, and to their capacity to open channels of communication between life and death, and between the mortal and the divine, via Mary, 'pervia cæli / Porta'.

A considerable amount of scholarly energy has been devoted to studying the 'greyn' that Mary placed in the boy's mouth, and to explaining its relation to the boy's Latin song.[39] It is, without question, a perplexing difficulty, and it is inextricably tied to the key concerns of the episode. Whatever it might be taken to 'mean' (Albert Friedman has argued that the quest for meaning is misplaced) the 'greyn' is playing a central role both in the ongoing training of the young clergeon and in confirming the efficacy of prayers to the Virgin when she is asked to be 'oure help and socour whan we deye'.[40]

All this is forcefully linked to the pedagogical context that has been explored in fits and starts since the beginning of the tale, where the Prioress brought together schoolboy and schoolbook in the course of describing 'This litel child, his litel book lernynge, / As he sat in the scole at his prymer'.[41] It was while enclosed within that schoolroom that the *Alma redemptoris mater* had first reached his ears. The boy's post-mortem account of the Virgin's intercession, and his gloss on its result, are therefore worth isolating:

> And whan that I my lyf sholde forlete,
> To me she cam, and bad me for to synge
> This anthem verraily in my deyynge,
> As ye han herd, and whan that I hadde songe,
> Me thoughte she leyde a greyn upon my tongue.

38 *CT*, VII.672.

39 For a collection of arguments and overviews of scholarship see, for example, Albert B. Friedman, 'The Mysterious Greyn in the "Prioress's Tale"', *Chaucer Review* 11 (1977), 328–33; Kathleen M. Oliver, 'Singing Bread, Manna, and the Clergeon's "Greyn"', *Chaucer Review* (1997), 357–64; Shannon Gayk, '"To wondre upon this thing": Chaucer's *Prioress's Tale*', *Exemplaria* 22 (2010), 138–56; Andrew Albin, 'The *Prioress's Tale*, Sonorous and Silent', *Chaucer Review* 48 (2013), 91–112; Sister Nicholas Maltman, 'The Divine Granary, or the End of the Prioress's "Greyn"', *Chaucer Review* 17 (1982), 163–70.

40 See Friedman: 'the grain which the Virgin places on the clergeon's tongue is simply a prop, an appropriate and necessary instrument of the action, however much the symbolic suggestiveness of "greyn" makes us overlook Chaucer's artistic logic in our straining to find something richer and more complex in the word' (332).

41 *CT*, VII.516–17.

Andrew Albin is right to emphasize that the miracle has *already* occurred (i.e., the throat-carved boy has just finished singing the *Alma redemptoris mater*) when the 'greyn' hits the clergeon's tongue. Because of this, I propose that the Virgin has come to him in the spirit of a schoolmaster or examiner, as though emerging from the logic of the tale's interest in scenes of instruction. The boy has mastered *Alma redemptoris mater* before the time at which he would have been taught the hymn at school, and so the moment of his death has been structured to ensure that his achievement can be confirmed not by his master but by the 'mater'.

With respect to the causal phrases that follow ('Wherefore I synge, and synge moot certeyn, / In honour of that blisful Mayden free / Til fro my tonge of taken is the greyn'), it is tempting simply to assume that the phrase 'synge moot certeyn' describes a magical compulsion whereby the boy sings and thereby 'discovers' his murder to the Christian community. But 'certeyn' can possess an adverbial force that reconnects the achievement to the pedagogical context in which the boy first encountered the song. The *Middle English Dictionary* glosses 'certeyn' in this adverbial sense as meaning 'definitely, with certainty' and 'unfailingly, unquestioningly'.[42] This reading of the word 'certeyn' enables the 'greyn' to confirm the boy's training in Marian devotion and, by extension, to help explain why the object placed upon the boy's tongue should be called a 'greyn' in the first place.

Several decades ago, Sister Mary Madeleva advanced an interpretation that has not had much staying power, even within the contours of her own argument.[43] She argued that the 'greyn' (in the sense of a 'particle' of something) was meant to be understood as the Host. In the course of outlining her argument, however, she conceded that 'greyn' was 'a common word for bead, prayer bead. As such beads were most commonly used to count Ave Marias upon, it seems evident that if the *greyn* was not the consecrated particle, it must have been the bead of the angelic salutation.'[44] I want to pursue here the implications of Sister Madeleva's mostly overlooked suggestion that 'greyn' – or, as Chaucer could have known from the Old French, 'grein' or 'grain' – can designate a singular rosary bead.[45]

[42] *MED*, 'certain, *adv.*', 1.b, 1.c.

[43] See Sister Mary Madeleva, 'Chaucer's Nuns', in *Chaucer's Nuns and Other Essays* (New York: D. Appleton and Company, 1925), 3–42. Friedman scornfully dismisses the interpretations proposed by 'the incorrigibly mysical Sister Madeleva' (328), but it is difficult to see why it should be regarded as having any element of mysticism in it.

[44] Madeleva, 'Chaucer's Nuns', 40.

[45] *MED* gives 'precious stone; small bits of gold or gems' ('grain, *n.*', 3.b), and offers the relevant lines from the *Prioress's Tale*. The *OED* ('grain, n.1') cites the Harley Lyrics on this transferred sense of the

It bears recalling that the *General Prologue*'s portrait of the Prioress was dominated by a detailed description of her prayer beads. Because of this, the spiritual function of the recitation of rosary prayers can be regarded as tying together, in a complex pattern of overlapping identifications, the Prioress, the young clergeon, and the Virgin.[46] The tale can therefore be read partly as the Prioress' effort to affirm the seriousness with which she carries her rosary, as though she had already anticipated the critical debates that have come to swirl around her portrait in the *General Prologue*. She has, in effect, driven a 'greyn' of the devotional object with which she herself is associated into the open mouth of her tale.

On this reading, the Virgin has responded to the boy's miraculous post-mortem singing of a Marian hymn by placing within the young singer's mouth a physical embodiment of Marian prayer.[47] This fits squarely with John Fleming's characterization of the Prioress's rosary as 'a decidedly material emblem of a presumably immaterial devotion'.[48] The 'greyn' performs its work on the threshold between life and death: 'in my deyynge' is the phrase with which the clergeon describes the moment of Mary's intercession. This is precisely the point at which the young clergeon's older schoolfellow had taught him that it was most important to honour Mary with the *Alma redemptoris mater*: 'Hire to salue, and eek hire for to preye / To been oure help and socour whan we deye'. And given that the clergeon

word: 'A bead, esp. one of the beads of a rosary (so French "grain"); also, a pearl' ('grain, n.1', II.6). See G. L. Brook (ed.), *The Harley Lyrics: The Middle English Lyrics of MS. Harley 2253* (Manchester University Press, 1948), 9.2 and glossary (100), comparing Old French 'grein'. The word is glossed as appearing in this sense in the lyric that opens 'A wayle whyt ase whalles bon / A grein in golde þat godly shon'.

46 Fleming speaks of the 'intimate self-identification with the Virgin that the regular recitation of the rosary is meant to induce' (223), and directs readers to Hardy Long Frank's 'Chaucer's Prioress and the Blessed Virgin', *Chaucer Review* 13 (1979), 346–62.

47 On Rome and the world of things see Sarah Stanbury, 'The *Man of Law's Tale* and Rome', *Exemplaria* 22 (2010), 119–37. For Stanbury, Rome is a 'fixed *omphalos* as well as mobile transhistorical ideogram' (121). A further context for my understanding of the clergeon's 'greyn' is to be found in medieval conceptions of the materiality of language. As Corey J. Marvin observes, 'medieval poets, philosophers, and other thinkers about language placed a great emphasis on the materiality of texts. For them language took place in the body. To the question where is language? the Middle Ages would have answered in part, along the lips, the tongue, the throat, and in the vocal apparatus and diaphragm' (*Word Outward: Medieval Perspectives on the Entry Into Language* (New York: Routledge, 2001), xvii). Marvin notes, further, that, 'In the area of music, words were long recognized to have a materiality all their own that was suitable for rhythm and melody', and he cites Geoffrey of Vinsauf, William of St. Thierry, and others on this subject: 'Such statements abound in medieval discussions of languages. They derive not only from the idea that literature ought to delight as well as instruct, but also from the commonplace notion of the deliciousness of words, their palpability in the mouth' (xviii). These concerns subtend Marvin's interpretation of the Prioress's Tale as 'the story of a painful entry into language'. See Marvin, *Word Outward*, 23–8.

48 Fleming, 'Madame Eglentyne', 207.

was passing through the ghetto when he was killed, the clergeon would have had Marian song in his throat. This 'greyn', as a rosary bead, is at once an embodiment of prayer and a testament to the answering of the boy's prayer. Mary's intercession allows the space between life and death to dilate and harbour the clergeon until the triple story of his murder, his piety, and Mary's miracle can be told.[49]

It is difficult to gauge whether the clergeon is to be regarded as living or dead in this part of the tale, and this helps us to see the urgency of understanding prayer as establishing a vital connection between these states. After all, even before learning the *Alma redemptoris mater* the clergeon had always had the *Ave Maria* in his mouth. It should not surprise, either, that rosaries sometimes featured beads in the form of skulls, so that the recitation of *Paters* and *Aves* could be regarded as involving systematic reflection on interactions between materialized prayers and the spectre of death.[50]

All through the *Prioress's Tale*, attention is given to the scene and nature of instruction: to the school itself, to the boy's status as a young clergeon just learning to wrestle with Latin grammar, to his reliance upon an older schoolfellow, to his learning liturgical song by rote. Attention is also devoted to the anatomical trajectory of song ('Twies a day' the song is said to have 'passed thurgh his throte'). The Virgin's 'greyn' gives material form to the Latin prayer that granted a living voice to the dead boy, and thereby materializes Rome's position within the practice of daily piety as far away as distant 'Asye'. Madame Eglentyne's Virgin is both the subject of *Alma redemptoris mater* and its final teacher. She is, moreover, a teacher whose ministrations reach beyond the barrier that ordinarily separates the living from the dead.

The 'greyn' does not make the dead boy's song possible. Rather, it confirms the young chorister's grasp of what Marian prayer does at the

[49] On the counterintuitive effort to perfect speech by placing an object in the mouth, Plutarch preserves the story that the ancient Athenian orator Demosthenes placed stones in his mouth to train himself to be both more clear and more precise as a speaker. Plutarch's biography of Demosthenes is in parallel with his treatment of Cicero. It is conceivable that Chaucer knew the anecdote. On the reception of Plutarch's *Lives* see Marianne Pade, 'The Reception of Plutarch from Antiquity to the Italian Renaissance', in Mark Beck (ed.), *A Companion to Plutarch* (Chichester: Wiley-Blackwell, 2014), 529–43. More practically, William Orme notes surviving pedagogical directives in which schoolboys are warned against speaking with food in their mouths (*Medieval Schools from Roman Britain to Renaissance England* (New Haven: Yale University Press, 2006), 102–3). On the training of choristers see Susan Boynton and Eric N. Rice (eds.), *Young Choristers, 650–1700* (Woodbridge: The Boydell Press, 2008).

[50] Several examples of such beads appear in Stephen Perkinson with Naomi Speakman, Katherine Baker, Elizabeth Morrison, and Emma Maggie Solberg, *The Ivory Mirror: The Art of Mortality in Renaissance Europe* (New Haven: Yale University Press, 2017).

threshold of life and death. It also confirms the strength of the clergeon's physical hold, as a species of non-cognitive *praxis* (he does not, after all, understand the prayer's Latin), on the words and things that Rome's authority had sent spiraling out into to distant lands. It also points directly to one of the trades that kept English merchants busy at Rome itself, since Sarah Stanbury has noted that English merchants at Rome 'were principally listed as Paternostrarii, makers or dealers in prayer beads, and that Rome's English Paternostrarii seem to have practiced a form of commerce that would have been consonant with Rome's signature as a site of Christian pilgrimage rather than luxury commerce'.[51] The hymn's Latin joins the boy to Christ's mother while also linking his unnamed 'greet citee' in distant 'Asye' to Rome and the centre of Western Christendom. The *Prioress's Tale*, then, is a spectacular narrative experiment in rooting prayer in the rhythms of daily life and then placing the prayers of the living in the mouths of the dead. As it happens, this was the foundational rhetorical conceit of the Roman Office of the Dead, in which prayer brought the faithful to a metaphysical limit and then enabled them to reach across that limit with the help of Rome's language.

Prayers for the Dead

The problems explored to this point are, to paraphrase a remark by Nietzsche's that was cited in Chapter 3, Roman *par excellence*. Before, during, and after the Reformation, Rome is the central node through which discourses and arguments pass in matters concerning the relationship between the living and the dead. Kelley Magill, for example, has recently shown that in post-Tridentine Rome, rediscovered ancient catacombs were regarded as having been places of worship and were promoted as models for devotional space grounded in Rome's potent intermingling of the living and the dead.[52] And insofar as the Eternal City is the site of this intermingling, we do well to recall that pagan antiquity had established its own complex decorum around the question of what the living owed to

51 Stanbury, *The Man of Law's Tale*, 129, citing Margaret Harvey, *The English in Rome, 1362–1420: Portrait of an Expatriate Community* (Cambridge University Press, 1999), 27.

52 See Kelley Magill, 'Reviving Martyrdom: Interpretations of the Catacombs in Cesare Baronio's Patronage', in John R. Decker and Mitzi Kirkland-Ives (eds.), *Death, Torture and the Broken Body in European Art, 1300–1650* (Farnham: Ashgate Press, 2015), 87–115: 'Pilgrims to SS. Nereo e Achilleo could imagine their veneration of the martyrs as a continuation of the devotional practices and piety of the early Church in the catacombs' (107).

the dead. The popularity of various forms of the Latin phrase 'De mortuis nihil nisi bonum' attests to this.[53]

A still more widespread and enduring image of Christian Rome's entanglement in these issues can be discerned in our modern habit of calling a mournful song a 'dirge'. The English noun is a corruption of the Latin imperative verb 'dirige' (direct, drive). The derivation makes sense only because 'dirige' is the opening word of the antiphon employed in the Matins liturgy of the Roman Office of the Dead: 'Dirige Domine Deus meus in conspectu tuo viam meam' ('Direct, O Lord, my God, my way in thy sight'). The antiphon's first word eventually became the familiar name of the Office itself. The modern word for mournful song, then, stands out not simply because of its unexpected etymology, but because it is part of the complex afterlife of a prayer cycle that probed connections and exchanges between the living and the dead.[54]

Peter Marshall's *Beliefs and the Dead in the Reformation* provides a clear reckoning of the cultural and soteriological stakes of those connections and exchanges. Taking as his focus the relationship between the doctrine of purgatory, on the one hand, and the practice of praying for the dead, on the other, Marshall argues that 'the ways in which late medieval Catholicism articulated its relationship with the dead may serve as a kind of synecdoche for that religious system as a whole'.[55] The bare outlines of this synecdoche are discernible in Chaucer's *Prioress's Tale*. To the extent that the religious and cultural upheavals that reached such intensity during the central decades of the sixteenth century were understood as demanding that one stand either with or against Rome, the relationship between the living and the dead constituted one of the most actively contested terrains in that dispute. The dissolution of the monasteries by Henry VIII testifies to that fact, since medieval monasteries had justified their existence partly in terms of the recitation of prayers on behalf of the dead in purgatory. Marshall stresses that the dissolution 'was an event of more than economic and social, or even religio-political significance. It represented an extra-ordinary repudiation of the hold of the past, and of past dead generations, on the present and the living'.[56]

[53] The phrase was ancient Greek in origin, but in western Europe it circulated in Latin.

[54] The *OED* indicates that the shift whereby 'dirge' moves from serving as shorthand for the Roman Office of the Dead to standing as a name for mournful song generally was occurring during the sixteenth century – that is, at a decisive stage in the Office's history in England.

[55] Marshall, *Beliefs and the Dead*, 7. On this topic see also P. Geary, *Living with the Dead in the Middle Ages* (Ithaca: Cornell University Press, 1994); C. Gittings, *Death, Burial and the Individual in Early Modern England* (New York: Routledge, 1984).

[56] Marshall, *Beliefs and the Dead*, 89–90.

What is frequently called 'the death of purgatory' under Protestantism is a complex process involving contestation, rejection, temporary revivification (under Queen Mary), and (under Elizabeth) renewed rejection. This process involves doctrinal changes advanced under the imprimatur of the Royal Supremacy, but it also involves arguments and shifts in cultural practices that continue to swirl indecisively across many decades. This is at least partly because polemics have a tendency to preserve within themselves, as though by necromantic power, the shape, allure, and urgency of the arguments and practices that they strive to destroy. The persistence of liturgical survivals and communal practices can be tracked with considerable precision via several forms of evidence (revisions to prayer books, articles for parish visitations, etc.).

Rather than set out fine distinctions among Catholic and reformed positions and practices concerning the commemoration of the dead, I want to emphasize the significance of a more fundamental point. The sometimes confused and unsystematic totality of the polemics swirling around the topic of the relation between the living and the dead is to be understood as yet another living component of the fact of Rome. The debate was understood, even during the period itself, as one in which 'Rome' served as a shorthand for an almost ungraspable range of practices, discourses, and cultural constructions.[57] This is preserved in a common periphrasis for the Reformation itself, where it remains common to speak simply of 'the break with Rome'. It is also latent in the programmatic efforts among reformers to speak not of the Pope but rather of 'the bishop of Rome'. Article Thirty Seven of the Thirty-Nine Articles, for example, insists that 'The Bishop of Rome hath no jurisdiction in this Realm of England'. The paradox, of course, is that the effort to diminish the Pope's authority by localizing it takes recourse to the name of a city whose reach has almost always exceeded its literal boundaries.

Because the dead figured so prominently in Reformation polemics, their status was, by logical necessity, among the issues most likely to be understood in direct relation to Rome. Reformation and post-Tridentine Counter-Reformation polemics ensured that debates concerning, for example, biblical authority for individual practices and ceremonies were always facets of the larger problem of Rome itself, and of the righteousness of one's position towards it. In the case of the commemoration of the dead,

[57] See, for example, Thomas Rist's assertion that in the eyes of sixteenth-century reformers the word "'Rome' equalled excess in post-mortem memorial' (*Revenge Tragedy and the Drama of Commemoration in Reforming England* (Farnham: Ashgate, 2008), 23).

theological debates of considerable nuance and sophistication ran up against equally urgent and subtle debates concerning custom, conformity, liberty of conscience, and charity.

To debate the question of what the living owed the dead was to work through the logic of a problem that was understood to have been constructed by Rome. The crux was this: medieval Christianity had, with increasing doctrinal complexity, and a measure of strategic indefinition, situated purgatory between heaven and hell.[58] One of the key early documents of the Henrician Reformation, the Ten Articles (1536), seems barely to know what it wants in its entry 'On Purgatory':

> FORASMUCH as due order of charity requireth, and the Book of Maccabees, and divers ancient doctors plainly shew, that it is a very good and charitable deed to pray for souls departed, and forasmuch also as such usage hath continued in the church so many years, even from the beginning, we will that all bishops and preachers shall instruct and teach our people committed by us unto their spiritual charge, that no man ought to be grieved with the continuance of the same, and that it standeth with the very due order of charity, a Christian man to pray for souls departed, and to commit them in our prayers to God's mercy, and also to cause others to pray for them in masses and exequies, and to give alms to others to pray for them, whereby they may be relieved and holpen of some part of their pain: but forasmuch as the place where they be, the name thereof, and kind of pains there, also be to us uncertain by scripture; therefore this with all other things we remit to Almighty God, unto whose mercy it is meet and convenient for us to commend them, trusting that God accepteth our prayers for them, referring the rest wholly to God, to whom is known their estate and condition; wherefore it is much necessary that such abuses be put clearly away, which under the name of purgatory hath been advanced, as to make men believe that through the bishop of Rome's pardons souls might clearly be delivered out of purgatory, and all the pains of it, or that masses said at *scala coeli*, or otherwise, in any place, or before any image, might likewise deliver them from all their pain, and send them straight to heaven: and other like abuses.[59]

[58] The classic study of this process is Jacques Le Goff, *The Birth of Purgatory*, trans. Arthur Goldhammer, rev. edn. (University of Chicago Press, 1986).

[59] *Articles Devised by The Kinges Highnes Majestie, To Stablyshe Christen Quietnes and Unitie Amonge Us, and To Avoyde Contentious Opinions* [1536], in Charles Lloyd (ed.), *Formularies of Faith Put Forth by Authority During the Reign of Henry VIII* (Oxford University Press, 1856), xxxi–xxxii. A revised and strategically augmented version of this article was reissued under the title 'Of Prayer for Souls Departed'. See *A Necessary Doctrine and Erudition for Any Christian Man; Set Forth by the King's Majesty of England* [1543], in Lloyd (ed.), *Formularies of Faith*, 375–6. Where, for example, the 1536 article urges 'a Christian man to pray for souls departed', the 1543 text speaks of praying 'for another, both quick and dead' (375). Perhaps surprisingly, the 1543 version asserts with respect to the dead

Henry, of course, wrestled with these questions and sponsored masses for the souls of his dead son and Jane Seymour. Funeral masses and prayers were to be offered on the grounds of Christian charity, but there are many signs that those prayers are still understood to be efficacious. They are offered so that the dead 'may be relieved and holpen of some part of their pain'. And when the living pray for the dead, they do so 'trusting that God accepteth our prayers for them'. Peter Marshall finds in the 1539 Six Articles (i.e., 'An Act Abolishing Diversity of Opinion', as it was called) increased uncertainty surrounding the condition and status of the dead, even if the dead were still to be regarded as participating, with the living, in the mystical body of Christ.[60] Marshall concludes that 'By the end of 1546, a hole had been cut clear through the web of customary connections regulating the relations of the living and the dead.'[61] This is presumably a reference to the 1545 authorized Henrician primer, where a revised Dirige has been framed primarily as a benefit to the living.

As the passage from the Ten Articles suggests, this was a debate in which the four-letter name of Rome could be invoked to epitomize a broad range of beliefs, cultural practices, and perceived errors on the subject of the relationship between the living and the dead.[62] As Tyndale memorably observed in his 1536 *Expositions and Notes on Sundry Portions of the Holy Scriptures*, the bare assertion that 'the bishop of Rome can deliver my conscience from fear of purgatory' simply begs the question, since this fear has its only source in what Tyndale dismisses as the 'poetry' of the bishop of Rome.[63] Thomas Wriothesley was equally forceful in a 1536 attempt to lay bare the stakes of belief in purgatory: 'thoppinion that there is a purgatory meynteyneth a favour to Rome for that opinion hath been maynteyned by the power of Rome'. The 1563 edition of the Thirty-Nine Articles denigrated purgatory as 'doctrina Romanensium', once again

that 'notwithstanding they be departed this present life, yet remain they still members of the same mystical body of Christ whereunto we pertain'. Prayers, masses, exequies, etc., are (on the account of the 1543 text) 'to be done for the universal congregation of Christian people, quick and dead' (376). In short, the 1543 text is newly insistent that the living and the dead are both objects of prayers formerly understood to have been for the benefit of souls in purgatory.

60 Marshall, *Beliefs of the Dead*, 78. 61 Marshall, *Beliefs of the Dead*, 92.

62 The 1543 text is more caustic and direct, demanding that 'all such abuses as heretofore have been brought in by supporters and maintainers of the papacy of Rome, and their complices, concerning this matter, be clearly put away' (*A Necessary Doctrine*, in Lloyd (ed.), *Formularies of Faith*, 376).

63 William Tyndale, *Expositions and Notes on Sundry Portions of the Holy Scriptures, Together With the Practice of Prelates*, ed. H. Walter (Cambridge University Press, 1849), 159. See Marshall, *Beliefs of the Dead*, 58. On the charge that purgatory was 'a vast piece of poetry', see Stephen J. Greenblatt, *Hamlet in Purgatory* (Princeton University Press, 2001).

localizing a doctrine that had been labeled 'doctrina scholasticorum' in the 1553 Forty-Two Articles.[64]

The point here is that this was not simply regarded as a suspect doctrine, but as a grand metonymic association with the city of Rome and its Church. To put this another way, purgatory was regarded as part of the semantic range of the proper noun 'Rome'. This doctrine held that the sins of the dead were purged in the middle space of purgatory, and that the souls of the dead could be aided in this process by the prayers of the living. This left the living and the dead radically connected and, given the ability of the latter to intercede on behalf of the former, interdependent in ways that decisively shaped doctrine and cultural practices throughout the Middle Ages. The issue is not that reformers had somehow discovered to their dismay that these matters were 'Roman'; rather, they were re-assessing, with newly polemical force, the stakes of an enduring association that had long been before the eyes of western Christendom. This is yet another echo of the sixteenth century's supposed 'discovery' of the material remains of Rome's dominion in Britain.

Augustine had argued in his *De cura pro mortuis gerenda* that funerals were to be understood as offering solace to the living rather than the dead, but the conviction that the prayers of the living were spiritually efficacious for the purgation of the dead came to dominate Catholic teachings and, by extension, expectations about how the relationship between the living and the dead was to be conceptualized and nurtured at the level of private prayer and quotidian commemorative practices. Recent work on both Catholic Books of Hours and Reformation-era primers provides another interpretative context within which to explore these questions.[65] Books of Hours underwrote devotional continuities between the early thirteenth century and the later sixteenth century, when Pope Pius V banned their use during the Counter-Reformation in 1571.

The texts gathered in Books of Hours and primers varied to a limited extent along sanctioned geographical lines. They advertised themselves as following the 'use' of Rome, use of Paris, use of Sarum or Salisbury and so on. The Dirige was always included in these books. This is as good a measure as any of the expectation that the dead would remain inescapably

[64] Quoted in Marshall, *Beliefs of the Dead*, 68, 126.

[65] For an introduction to primers, and especially to the ways in which people personalized and used them, see Eamon Duffy, *Marking the Hours: English People and Their Prayers, 1240–1570* (New Haven: Yale University Press, 2006). On habits of use see also Seth Lerer, 'Literary Prayer and Personal Possession in a Newly Discovered Tudor Book of Hours', *Studies in Philology* 109 (2012), 409–28.

present in the prayers of the laity. Primers were, to this extent, at least, designed to create the semblance of a connection between lay and monastic life. Detailed descriptions of the spiritual *praxes* associated with the nine canonical hours, the calendar of saints, excerpted gospel texts, groups of psalms (including the seven Penitential Psalms), and other prayers and offices were pulled together to give the laity a structured approach to daily piety after the pattern of the Roman liturgy.

Micheline White emphasizes that the Dirige played a vital role 'within an intercessory and sacramental economy of prayer that stressed man's cooperation with divine grace, the circulation of merit between the living and the dead, and the necessity of penitential contrition, confession and satisfaction'.[66] Because of this, texts of the Dirige insist on the tightest possible link between the living and the dead via the power of the human voice. In his seminal treatment of the tradition, Knud Ottosen emphasizes that the Roman Office of the Dead had developed against the backdrop of a series of shifts (between *circa* 800 and 1000) in understandings of the position of the dead within the economy of the Christian afterlife.[67] This tradition obviously became highly charged within Reformation polemics and debates, but it was exceptionally complex even within the pre-Reformation context.

The text of the Dirige was a sophisticated network of repurposed biblical texts that had been selected and recontextualized in order to create utterly new rhetorical circumstances. Ottosen's description of this process and its effects is illuminating:

> The readings from the Book of Job, when transferred from the wake at the deathbed to the organized office formed in accordance with the usual Hours of the Day and celebrated after the departure of the person or persons for whom it was meant, were not changed but given a new interpretation according to the liturgical setting. Job's complaints, fears and hope were no longer concerned with the immediate physical death, as when read during the wake for the dying, but relate to the sufferings of the souls in the afterlife before the Second Coming of Christ. In fact, the soul of the departed does not rest in peace. It suffers from its need of mercy from God, from his visitation, and it is a victim of fear as to what will happen on the Last Day.[68]

[66] Micheline White, 'Dismantling Catholic Primers and Reforming Private Prayer: Anne Lock, Hezekiah's Song and Psalm 50/51', in Alec Ryrie and Jessica Martin (eds.), *Private and Domestic Devotion in Early Modern Britain* (Farnham: Ashgate, 2012), 95.

[67] Knud Ottosen, *The Responsories and Versicles of the Latin Office of the Dead* (Aarhus University Press, 1993), 47.

[68] Ottosen, *The Responsories*, 47–8.

The liturgical setting of the Dirige, that is, recontextualizes psalm texts, for example, and words spoken by the living Job, as words spoken by the dead. These words are then spoken by the living as a kind of efficacious proxy for the dead. These biblical expressions of suffering are repositioned so as to conjure up, with psychological acuity and urgency, poignant images of suffering in which the living and the dead are rhetorically interchangeable. The Dirige, therefore, keeps active and continuous expressions of the suffering of the dead within the minds – and, more strikingly, within the mouths – of the living. To put matters as bluntly as possible, this is spectacular 're-use', in the linguistic sphere, of the kind that was on view in Chapter 1's treatment of Rome's material *uestigia*. Re-purposed and re-situated biblical texts blend self and other, living and dead. For the living speak, all at once, *as / for / with* the dead when they speak the Dirige. The Dirige is therefore an act of soteriological ventriloquism designed to push to its limits the self-other relation. The 'I' who speaks the Dirige's first-person psalms and scriptural extracts is simultaneously to be understood as a living, embodied speaker moved to prayer by love and charity, on the one hand, and as a disembodied soul suffering the terrors of the grave and the agonies of purgatory, on the other. The limits of the self and the limits of the human are mutually tested in the course of a complex soteriological gambit in which the living voice hurls itself into death in an attempt to speed dead souls through the pains of the afterlife.

In this pietistic dispensation the reader's attention was actively drawn, as it was in the *Prioress's Tale*, to the situational function of individual prayers, even where the language of the prayers themselves may have been unintelligible to those speaking them. A 1503 Latin Book of Hours, for example, introduces its Latin prayers by means of laconic English headnotes that were clearly intended to guide readers of uncertain (or perhaps non-existent) Latinity, thereby helping believers to embed prescribed prayer in their daily experiences of death and loss ('For thy fader and moder deed', 'For thy frende that is dede', 'For the lyuynge and dede').[69] We can discern here the bare outlines of the older boy's remarks to Chaucer's clergeon concerning his confident grasp of the situations in which the *Alma redemptoris mater* could most effectively do its work, irrespective of the boy's inability to make sense of the hymn's Latin.

The Dirige deliberately works to erase the distinction between the living and the dead by doing precisely what the *Prioress's Tale* had done: that is, by putting living voices in the mouths of the dead. This much remains clear

69 [*Horae ad usum Sarum*] (London, 1503), Cv^{v} [STC 15900].

in remarks on the Dirige that appear in an English primer printed in 1538. These remarks were published in the wake of Henry's formal break with Rome but years before a series of considerably more dramatic reactions against Roman doctrine under Edward. The note insists that the Dirige's origins are unknown and, indeed, insignificant. What matters, we are told, is the flexibility of its application:

> The makynge of this seruyce (that we call Dirige) some do ascribe to saynt Isodore and some to saynt Gregory but whether of them it was / forceth not moche / for certeyn it is / that al that is conteyned therin (the collettes except) may as well be applyed for the lyvyng / as for the dead.[70]

The remarkable interchangeability of the living and the dead (for what can be said on behalf of the former 'may as well be applyed for' the latter) is regarded as being somehow less in need of explanation than are the office's origins and, for that matter, even the basic spiritual propriety of offering prayers for the dead. Revealing tensions run through the following remarks:

> Palagius / bysshop of Rome dyd fyrst ordeyne the commemoracyon / of prayenge for the dead. Whiche thing (after the mynde of Isodore[)] was receyued as a tradityon of the apostles. Howbeit S. Ambrose affyrmeth that it was deryved of an olde custome had among the Hebrewes / which used longe lamentacyon for the dead after theyr departynge: as they dyd for Jacob the space of .xl. dayes / and for Moyses.xxx But we that are under the newe lawe / are taught of god by the mouthe of saynt Paule his apostle / not to mourne or be sory for them that be departed in the fayth of Chryst / but to reioyse / as in them that rest in the slepe of peace (for so is it dayly remembred in the Masse) untyll they shall be called unto the last judgment. Neverthelesse I thynke it very charytable / and to procede of a good & godly mynde / in that we use any worldely obsequies about the deade / or do pray for them / for saint Augustyn in his Enchiridion sayth. It is not to be denyed: but that the soules departed are greatly releued by prayer. Whiche use is very commendable for asmoche as it hath contynued in the chrysten churche evyn from the very infancy therof.[71]

This 1538 headnote to the Dirige is obviously a record of the struggle to balance Church traditions and patristic writings on the subject of prayers

[70] *Here after foloweth the prymer in Englysshe sette out alonge, after the vse of Sarum* (Rouen, 1538), Mviii^{v} [STC 16004].

[71] *Here after foloweth the prymer*, Mviii^{v}-Ni^{r} [STC 16004]. Ottosen observes that 'the celebration of the Office of the Dead as a service for the long departed rests on the tacit assumption that the souls after their separation from the body and before the Last Judgement experience an afterlife full of fear and trembling for which prayers and sacrifices from the living are the sole remedy' (48).

for the dead with the unquestioned authority of Paul, especially when the Epistle to the Romans is read in the context of the nascent break with Rome. The passage settles, as was common during the first years of the break, on charity as a proper justification for the Dirige, but it refuses to doubt that 'that the soules departed are greatly releued by prayer'. The headnote's final acceptance of the authority of Augustine's pronouncements seems to fudge, rather than solve, a problem that will only intensify in the following years.

What the volume does give us is an accompanying woodcut in which the living and the dead form a celebratory community; they dance hand-in-hand. (See Figure 4.1.) The image appears to strive to offer proof for the headnote's insistence that 'al that is conteyned therin . . . may as well be applyed for the lyvyng / as for the dead'. The woodcut's vivid intermingling of living and dead (operating as it does against the backdrop of the literary and visual traditions of the Dance of Death, with the living and the dead orbiting a central cross and bounded by a ring of bones) helps ease readers into the company of biblical texts that are re-set so as to appear to have been spoken not by the living on the subject of worldly suffering but rather by the dead on the agonies of the grave. The image is accompanied by a prayer that should be understood as an attempt to fuse the voices of the dead with those of the living. As in the Dirige itself, the living speak not just on behalf of the dead, but rather as though they were the dead:

> I have loved / for the lorde shall hear the voyce of my prayer. For he hath enclyned his eare unto me & all me lyfe I shall calle upon hym. The sorowes of deathe haue compassed me: and the perylles of hell have entangled me.[72]

Among the groups of prayers that precede the Dirige in this edition, the Prayers of St Bridget (also called 'The Fifteen Oos') call attention to the self-divisions of a primer printed in a period of active, if fitful and not entirely systematic, reformation:

> The .xv. prayers folowynge called commonly the .xv. oos are set forth in dyuers latyn prymers / with goodly paynted prefaces promisynge to the sayers therof many thynges both folyshe & false / as the delyuerance of .xv. soules out of purgatori with other lyke vanites: yet are the prayers selfe right good and vertuous / yf they be sayde without any suche superstycyons truste or blynde confydence. And therfore are they called the prayers of S Brygide / bycause that holy virgyn used dayly to say them (as many wryte) before the ymage of the Crosse in saynt Paules church at Rome.[73]

[72] *Here after foloweth the prymer*, Ni^{v} [STC 16004].

[73] *Here after foloweth the prymer*, Kiiii^{r} [STC 16004].

The Dirige.

¶ We haue ſomtyme abyde our chaūce.

But nowe ye muſt com a trace our daūce

I Haue loued/for the lorde ſhall hear the
voyce of my prayer.
For he hathe enclyned his eare vnto
me/& all me lyfe I ſhall calle vpon hym.
The ſorowes of deathe haue compaſſed me:and
the perylles of hell haue entangled me.
I haue frounde moche trouble and ſorowe: and
haue called vppon the name of the lorde.
O lorde delyuer my ſoule/for the lorde is pity:

Figure 4.1 From *Here after foloweth the prymer in Englysshe sette out alonge, after the vse of Sarum* (Rouen, 1538), Ni^{v} [STC 16004]. Reproduced by kind permission of the Syndics of Cambridge University Library.

This emphasis on the relationship between space, prayer, and daily routine is an important feature of primers both before and after the onset of reform. What is most notable here, in the early aftermath of the break with Rome, is the deliberate effort by which 'superstycyons' are to be banished from the mind during the recitation of these prayers, even as care is taken to establish that part of their spiritual authority derives from having been intoned, '(as many wryte) before the ymage of the Crosse in saynt Paules church at Rome'.

Catholic Books of Hours are considerably more systematic than are reformed primers with respect to their attempts to lay hold of every aspect of quotidian experience. Marian primers moralize the days of the week, and Rome's hold over the calendar is everywhere asserted, so that the laity can seek in their books guidance on every aspect of thought and pious conduct. Notable in this respect is a primer printed in 1555. This edition includes a translation of a preface by the late fourteenth-century French theologian Jean (Jehan) Quentin ('La manière de bien vivre devotement pour chascun jour'). Quentin's treatise sets out, in scrupulous detail, how every moment of the day is to be subsumed by the routines of faith. Good Christians are enjoined to: rise at six o'clock 'in all seasons' and thank God for the night that has passed; commend themselves to God, Mary, and the saint whose day is to be feasted; beseech God for deliverance from sin during that day and at all times; pray that God will accept works done by others on your behalf; dress; say 'matyns / pryme & houres yf ye may'; go to church before doing 'ony worldly werkes' and remain there for a low mass while thinking about God's might and virtue; think about the grace God has shown via baptism; think about offenses committed against God; make decisions about how to spend the time God has granted for penance; meditate Christ's sacrifice and the shame and violence he suffered in the world. The day, in short, is to be devoted to reflecting upon pains as well as benefits. For example, Christians are enjoined to 'Thynke on the horryble paynes of hell / & on the cruell company of deuylles: where without ende ye shall never / haue releas yf ye deye in deedly synne'; think of the saints; love Christ and 'hope yf ye lyue wel ye shall come to that glory'. 'And these ben the thoughtes that I wyll that ye haue in the chyrche', is the pithy conclusion to this section of the instructions.

Further instructions are elaborated for conduct, thought, and reflection throughout the rest of the day: 'Whan ye are come fro the chyrch take hede to your housholde or occupacyon tylle dyner tyme'; remind yourself that the pains of this world are nothing 'to the regarde of the infynite glory that ie shall haue yf ye take it mekely'; eat modestly and without excess; rest an hour after dinner while praying for God to favour your health; dispose of all business before supper. Time is to be reserved, finally, for the dead: 'And whan ye may / say Dyryge. and commendacyons for all chrysted soules at the leest way on the holy dayes and yf ye haue leaser say them on other dayes at the leest with thre lessons.' Further demands and instructions round out the day, making every inch of that day's territory an opportunity to bind the self to God's word and to the fullest understanding of human communion with the dead.[74]

The recto of the volume's second title page (see Figure 4.2) gives proto-phenomenological expression to the believer's entanglement in an understanding of time sponsored by Rome. The woodcut sees a human body pierced by the signs of the zodiac. Accompanying woodcuts and poems that had been reused over the course of decades read the months in relation to the stages of a believer's life. The days of the week are moralized. Twelve pages of Saint's Days consolidate this Marian primer's efforts to encircle all aspects of life and lived time.

In the face of the Catholic Church's successful establishment of all-encompassing devotional routines, reformers depicted themselves as striving to awaken their contemporaries from the unreflective everydayness of the believer's ties to Rome, and as labouring to make them see that these ties and routines are pernicious. A 1534 primer prepared by the printer and reformer William Marshall omitted both the Litany of the Saints and the Dirige, apparently at the instigation of Cromwell. His 1535 primer restored them to their traditional positions but added a scathing 'admonition or warning to the reader, necessary to be had and read for the true understanding and meaning of the Dirige hereafter following'.[75] Marshall complains that:

> Amongst all other works of darkness and deep ignorance, wherein we have blindly wandered, following a sort of blind guides, many days and years, I accompt not this one of the least, that we have rung and sung, mumbled, murmured, and piteously puled forth, a certain sort of psalms, hereafter ensuing, with response, versicles, and lessons to the same, for the souls of our Christian brethren and sisters that be departed out of this world.[76]

[74] *Here after foloweth the prymer in Englysshe and in Latin sette out alonge: after the vse of Sarum* (Rouen, 1555), Bvii^{v}-Bviii^{v} [STC 16070].

[75] *A goodly prymer in englyshe, newly corrected and printed, with certeyne godly meditations and prayers added to the same, very necessarie & profitable for all them that ryghte assuredly vnderstande not ye latine & greke tongues* (London, 1535) [STC 15988], in Edward Burton (ed.), *Three Primers Put Forth in The Reign of Henry VIII* (Oxford University Press, 1834), 232.

[76] *A goodly prymer in englyshe* [STC 15988], in Edward Burton (ed.), *Three Primers*, 232.

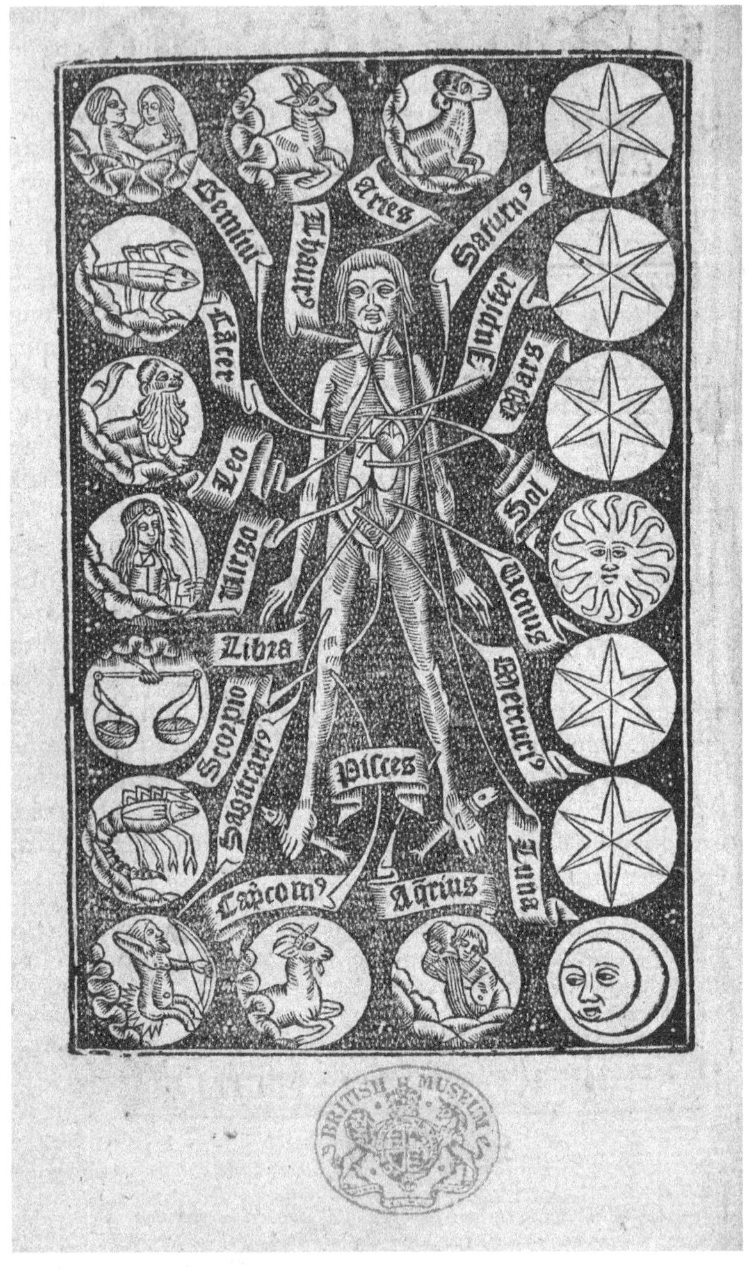

Figure 4.2 From *Here after foloweth the prymer in Englysshe and in Latin sette out alonge: after the vse of Sarum* (Rouen, 1555), unpaginated front matter [STC 16070]. Image courtesy of the British Library.

Marshall's scorn attaches itself to the work of the human voices that have become involved in what he regards as an empty charade. He sees the Dirige not as reasoned or hallowed speech, and not even as superstition or error, but rather as gibberish that is beyond the reach of sense: mere ringing, singing, mumbling, murmuring, and piteous puling. The Roman liturgy, on Marshall's account, has robbed Rome of its ancient association with eloquent and reasoned speech.

Marshall's primer adds a headnote to all of the individual psalms and biblical extracts that make up the Dirige, with the goal of forcing his readers to see the original context in which these texts occur in the Bible, and of compelling them to acknowledge the foolishness of the proposition that these could be taken to represent the words of the dead.[77] Regarding the Dirige's excerpts from the Book of Job, for example, Marshall asks:

> What an extreme fondness of fantasy is this, for men to be so brutish, and so far overseen, as to refer the complaint of that holy man Job, which he, being then in life, yea, and many days after, made unto God, in the midst of his misery and wretchedness, in the midst of his poverty, of his scabs and filthiness; to refer it, I say, to them that be gone, as though they should speak any such words as be in any of the said nine lessons included?[78]

Marshall's conclusion is withering:

> Job spake these words, as I have said before, then being in life, and in the great rage of his intolerable affliction; and must they now serve for the souls that be departed, and in the pains of I cannot tell what? Finally, there is nothing in the Dirige taken out of Scripture, that maketh any more mention of the souls departed than doth the tale of Robin Hood. But, Lord, such is the blindness of men.[79]

As these lines show, what Marshall finds most preposterous and objectionable is the Dirige's repurposing of biblical texts in such a way as to make believers who possess no Latin believe that they are projecting their own voices into the souls of the departed. This is, indeed, the Dirige's foundational conceit: that it should be taken as a record of the power of human speech beyond the outermost limits of mortal life.

[77] This approach ensures that Marshall's edition of the Dirige is consistently ironized by headnotes in which he insists that the text at hand does not represent the words of the dead. He notes, for example, on the subject of the first text of the Dirige (i.e., Psalm 114 / 116: 'Dilexi, quoniam exaudiet Dominus'), that 'This psalm is a thankful song for the help of the Lord, whereby David escaped, when he was now compassed in of Saul's host' (*A goodly prymer in englyshe* [STC 15988], in Edward Burton (ed.), *Three Primers*, 234).

[78] *A goodly prymer in englyshe* [STC 15988], in Edward Burton (ed.), *Three Primers*, 233.

[79] *A goodly prymer in englyshe* [STC 15988], in Edward Burton (ed.), *Three Primers*, 234.

Framing materials in reformed primers throughout this period are caustic in their rejections of Papal authority, but they nevertheless continue to vacillate on the question of what to do with Rome's cult of the dead.[80] The uneven process of reforming these primers ran in fits and starts for decades. Micheline White notes that Elizabeth's 1559 version of Henry's 1545 primer 'retained the Seven Psalms and a version of the Dirige that directed readers to pray for both the living and the dead', so that such prayers must have remained common.[81] The Reformation may have worked to put the dead beyond the reach of the living, but it did so in a desultory and unsystematic manner, surely recognizing the enormous stakes of the envisioned changes, along with their dramatic effect on understandings of the power of the living voice and of the nature of human community. Direct attacks on purgatorial doctrine succeeded in dislodging from its position 'the name of purgatory', but the imaginative legacy of the Dirige's promise that the living human voice could be projected into the souls of the departed managed to endure.[82] Echoes and distortions of that promise (unless it is to be understood as a threat) can be heard long after the Dirige itself was abandoned.

The fact that Henry VIII (along with figures such as John Fisher and Thomas More) had originally defended purgatorial doctrine against charges levelled at it by Luther, Tyndale, and others helps explain why the Henrician Church's eventual break with Rome did not immediately proscribe prayers for the dead. Henry thereby left in place devotional practices that clearly answered significant communal, as well as psychological needs.[83] Those practices also managed to generate a chain of further

[80] For further scholarship on sixteenth-century changes to Henrician primers see, for example, Richard Rex, *Henry VIII and the English Reformation* (New York: Palgrave, 2006), 102–5; Edgar Hoskins, *Horae Beatae Mariae Virginis or Sarum and York Primers* (London: Longmans, Green, 1901); Helen C. White, *The Tudor Books of Private Devotion* (Madison, University of Wisconsin Press, 1951); Charles C. Butterworth, *The English Primers (1529–1545): Their Publication and Connection with the English Bible and the Reformation in England* (New York: Octagon Books, 1971). Eamon Duffy notes that more than thirty editions of Catholic primers were printed during Mary's reign as a reaction against those produced under her father and brother (Duffy, *Fires of Faith*, 59).

[81] See White, 'Dismantling Catholic Primers', 96. Thereafter, changes are more decisive and systematic: 'In a series of visitation articles from 1560, we find questions asking whether any people used "Latin primers, or any other prayer books, than that be allowed by public authority", or whether any clergymen "sing any number of psalms, dirge-like, at the burial of the dead"' (White, 'Dismantling Catholic Primers', 113).

[82] 'Of Prayer for Souls Departed', in *A Necessary Doctrine and Erudition for Any Christian Man; Set Forth by the King's Majesty of England* [1543], in Lloyd (ed.), *Formularies of Faith*, 376.

[83] See Marshall, *Beliefs and the Dead*: 'In the process of regulating the dead, more perhaps than in any other aspect of the Reformation, theological absolutes met social and pastoral exigencies in an

meditations on the power of the human voice at the limits of human community.

The decisive change, or rather one of a sequence of decisive changes, came not under Henry, then, but rather via Edward VI's 1552 Book of Common Prayer. Among other significant liturgical revisions, the prayer book featured a reconceived burial rite from which the Eucharist, direct prayers for the dead, and accompanying psalms had all been removed. Each of these elements had been foundational to the Dirige's self-presentation. Eamon Duffy is decisive in his assessment of the enormity of these changes: 'There was nothing which could even be mistaken for a prayer for the dead in the 1552 funeral rite.' Duffy adds that, 'in the world of the 1552 book the dead were no longer with us. They could neither be spoken to nor even spoken about, in any way that affected their well-being. The dead had gone beyond the reach of human contact, even prayer.' Duffy emphasizes, finally, that a redefinition of the human as such was one of the ultimate products of the effort to come to terms with Roman doctrine: 'the dead person is spoken not to, but about, as one no longer here, but precisely as departed: the boundaries of human community have been redrawn'.[84]

Purgatory and intercessory prayer were reinstated by Mary (with religious effects that were more complex and enduring than they were long held to have been) and then banished once again under Elizabeth.[85] As Peter Marshall is keen to emphasize, the Elizabethan Church recognized that it needed 'to formulate its own distinctive and pastorally effective idioms of commemoration and remembrance'.[86] The result, he concludes, was the interweaving of two courses of action: one was punitive and focused on the Church hierarchy's efforts to ferret out talk of purgatory and traces of intercessory prayer; one was generative and committed to developing new liturgical engagements with the phenomenon of death.[87]

We are left, then, with a bipolar response to Rome's presence in these debates about the relationship between the living and the dead. On the one hand, an instinctive reaction against Rome breeds specific kinds of

unavoidable encounter. The conjoining was sometimes confrontational, sometimes creative, and the outcomes did much to give shape to the social experience of religious change as a whole' (187).

84 See Duffy, *The Stripping of the Altars*, 475.

85 For the revisionist account of Mary's rule see Duffy, *Fires of Faith.*

86 Marshall, *Beliefs and the Dead*, 124. This recalls a broad range of Elizabethan efforts to re-mythologize, if not quite re-sacramentalize, areas of human experience (marriage, for example) that had lost their sacramental status as a result of the Reformation.

87 Marshall, *Beliefs and the Dead*, 125.

monsters in the process of destabilizing traditional cultural practices.[88] On the other hand, Elizabethan and Jacobean England, in the intensity of humanism's continuing attachment to Roman antiquity, still find themselves within the body of Rome in some of their most public commemorative spectacles, and in Rome's shadow when they are resisting those spectacles.

I have already noted that the Dirige was transformed into the 'dirge'. The imperative verb's principal work had been to serve as shorthand for the entirety of the rite that promised the living that their prayers could count as the prayers of the dead. As the spiritually efficacious Dirige became a simple dirge, this aspiration would seem to have given way to associations that are mostly tonal and thematic rather than soteriologically prosopopoeic and efficacious. But as J. L. Austin memorably observed, words come to us 'trailing clouds of etymology', and it is still possible to hear, in mournful song, an effort to leap across seemingly insurmountable boundaries in order to share pain. [89]

All this is to suggest that the *Prioress's Tale*'s explorations of the efficacy of Latin prayers to Mary 'whan we deye' – that is, when we hover on the line that linked a single community that was both living and dead – subtend a set of longstanding debates that run from the Middle Ages and

[88] This is further complicated by the fact that contemporary texts attest to 'continued use of funeral and commemorative customs whose clear rationale was a belief in the ability of the living to ameliorate the condition of the dead' (Marshall, *Beliefs and the Dead*, 127). Preoccupations with commemorative practices of this kind are 'regularly reflected in episcopal visitation articles of the 1560s, 1570s, and 1580s' (127). Marshall notes that the authorized Elizabethan primer of 1559 appeared to sanction prayers for the dead (in any case, it resurrected Henry's 1545 primer and therefore marked a dramatic step away from key aspects of Edward's primer, which had done away with the Dirige). The Latin version of the BCP (authorized 1560) retained provisions for a 'celebratio coenae Domini in funeribus' (150).

[89] J. L. Austin, 'A Plea for Excuses' in *Philosophical Papers*, 3rd edn. (Oxford University Press, 1979), 201. I am proposing that the issues explored in this chapter bring us to the brink of what philosophy will eventually name 'the problem of privacy'. See Cavell's formulation of the stakes of this topic: 'I take the philosophical problem of privacy, therefore, not to be one of finding (or denying) a "sense" of "same" in which two persons can (or cannot) have the same experience, but one of learning why it is that something which from one point of view looks like a common occurrence (that we frequently have the same experience – say, looking together at a view of mountains, or diving into the same cold lake, or hearing a car horn stuck; and that we frequently do not have the same experiences – say at a movie, or learning the results of an election, or hearing your child cry) from another point of view looks impossible, almost inexpressible (that I have your experiences, that I *be* you). What is it I cannot do?' Cavell concludes: 'But I am filled with this feeling – of our separateness, let us say – and I want you to have it too. So I give voice to it. And then my powerlessness presents itself as ignorance – a metaphysical finitude as an intellectual lack. (Reverse Faust, I take the bargain of supernatural ignorance.)' (Cavell, 'Knowing and Acknowledging', in *Must We Mean What We Say?*, 262–3).

well into the Reformation and beyond, reconfiguring themselves several times along the way. The *Prioress's Tale* is instructive precisely because it already insists that these studies of limits and voices are legible as attempts to determine how life itself might be figured as presuming, in its very essence, a relation to Rome, even when a story is set in distant 'Asye'. The tale and its attendant complications also help us to regard the ordinary, the self, the word, and the dead as compass points by which individuals comprehend their orientations to, and against, Rome.

Under the Eyes of The Dead

These conflicted traditions and debates generate, among other cultural artefacts, a host of literary plots in which the living subsist under the eyes of the dead. Polemically entangled within the Dirige's afterlife, sixteenth-century reformers reconceptualized the mutual interdependence that characterized the Roman rite's view of the relationship between the living and the Christian dead as an *agon* in which the living are at the mercy of – even under surveillance by – the pagan dead.

Though the matters surveyed in the previous section make it possible to track with considerable clarity shifts in royal (i.e., 'authorized') attitudes towards the relationship between the living and the dead, it is safest to regard these shifts less as decisively altering the practice of private devotion than as repeatedly bringing to the fore new understandings of what is at stake in such practice. These stakes are, of course, formulated differently from author to author, from genre to genre, and even from year to year. Even a single text can activate quite different interpretive possibilities at different stages of its reception. The comparative freedom of the literary field (if only when compared to heated wrangling over the contents and editorial framing of primers) sees individual writers working adventurously with the devotional practices and commitments that surround the commemoration, and even the persistence, of the dead.

Thomas More's *Utopia* provides a telling instance of this phenomenon. In Book Two, the traveler Raphael Hythloday turns his attention to understandings of the relation between the living and the dead. *Utopia* is particularly interesting in this connection because its print history straddles some of the most decisive years of the Reformation. The work was first printed in Latin in 1516, the year before Luther's initial blast against Rome. Ralph Robinson translated it into English in 1551, the year before the publication of Edward VI's Book of Common Prayer, with its reconfigured 'Ordre for the Buriall of the Dead'. The period's protracted confessional conflicts had, of course, cost More his life, and they were still in the process of putting the living and the dead beyond each other's reach. Robinson published a revised translation during the reign of Mary, in 1556. I cite Robinson's 1551 English translation of the full passage:

> For all they beleue certeinly and sewerly, that mans blesse shall be so greate, that they doo morne and lamente euery mans sicknes, but no mans death; oneles it be one whom they see depart from his liffe carfully, and agaynst his will. For this they take for a very euell token, as though the sowle, beinge in dyspayre and vexed in conscience, through some preuy and secret forefeilyng of the punishment now at hande, were aferde to depart. And they thinke he shall not be welcome to God, whyche, when he ys called, runneth not to him gladly, but ys drawen by force and sore agaynste hys wyll. They therefore that see thys kynde of deathe doo abhorre it, and them that so die they burye wyth sorrow and silence. And when they have prayed God to be mercifull to the sowle, and mercifully to pardon the infirmities therof, they couer the dead coorpe with earthe. Contrarye wise all that depart merely and ful of good hoope, for them no man mournethe, but followethe the heerse with ioyfull synging, commending the soules to god with great affection. And at the last not with mourning sorrow, but with a great reuerence, they bourne the bodies; and in the same place they set vp a piller of stone, with the deade mans titles therin graued. When they be comme home they reherse his vertuouse maners and his good dedes. But no parte of his liffe is so oft or gladly talked of as his mery deathe. They thinke that this remembraunce of their vertue; and goodnes doth vehementely prouoke and enforce the quicke to vertue; and that nothing can be more pleasaunt and acceptable to the dead; whom they suppose to be present emong them when they talke of them, though to the dull and feoble eye sight of mortall men they be inuisibly. For it were an vnconuenient thinge, that the blessed shoulde not be at libertye to goo whether they wold. And it were a poynte of greate vnkyndnes in them, to haue vtterly caste awaye the desyer of vysytynge and seynge their frindes, to whome they were in theyr lyfe tyme ioined by mutuall loue and charytye; whych in good men after theyre deathe they cownte to be rather encreased then dymynyshede. They beleue therefore that the deade be presentlye conuersaunte emonge the quicke, as beholders and witnesses of all their woordes and deedes. Therefore they go more corragiously to their busines, as hauing a trust and affiaunce in such ouerseers. And this same belefe of the present conuersacion of their forefathers and auncetours emonge them fearethe them from all secrete dishonesty.[90]

[90] I cite the 1551 English and 1518 Latin as they are given in J. H. Lupton (ed.), *The Utopia of Sir Thomas More* (Oxford: Clarendon Press, 1895): 'hominum enim cuncti fere tam immensam fore beatitudinem pro certo atque explorato habent, ut morbum lamententur omnium, mortem uero nullius, nisi quem uident anxie e uita inuitumque diuelli. Nempe hoc pro pessimo habent augurio, tanquam

The belief that the dead are 'presentlye conuersaunte emonge the quicke, as beholders and witnesses of all their woordes and deedes' ('Mortuos ergo uersari inter uiuentes credunt, dictorum factorumque spectatores') pivots on both ancient Roman and Roman Catholic principles, as though oscillating between the Romes of Augustus and Augustine. To be sure, inhumation and cremation occupy different places in the imaginations of More's Utopians, so that a solemn burial executed 'wyth sorrow and silence' registers the misgivings of mourners, while cremation and a pillar registering names and titles hovers somewhere between a Christian headstone and a Roman monument offered 'Dis manibus sacrum' (to the gods of the underworld).[91] This is characteristic of More's habit of blending the alien and familiar in *Utopia*. Similarly, the understanding of death that keeps the dead at hand belongs to the mental world that was committed to the notion that the living and the dead were inextricably linked and capable of a kind of dialogue in which the words of the former were projected into

anima exspes ac male conscia occulto quopiam imminentis poenae praesagio reformidet exitum. Ad hoc haudquaquam gratum deo eius putant aduentum fore, qui quum sit accersitus non accurrit libens, sed inuitus ac detrectans pertrahitur. Hoc igitur mortis genus qui intuentur horrent, itaque defunctos moesti ac silentes efferunt, precatique propitium manibus deum, uti eorum clementer infirmitatibus ignoscat, terra cadauer obruunt.

Contra, quicunque alacriter ac pleni bona spe decesserint, hos nemo luget, sed cantu prosequuti funus, animas deo magno commendantes affectu, corpora tandem reuerenter magis quam dolenter concremant, columnamque loco insculptis defuncti titulis erigunt. domum reuersi, mores actaque eius recensent, nec ulla uitae pars aut saepius aut libentius quam laetus tractatur interitus. Hanc probitatis memoriam et uiuis efficacissima rentur incitamenta uirtutum, et gratissimum defunctis cultum putant; quos interesse quoque de se sermonibus opinantur, quanquam (ut est hebes mortalium acies) inuisibiles. Nam neque felicium sorti conueniat libertate carere migrandi quo uelint, et ingratorum fuerit prorsus abiecisse desyderium amicos inuisendi suos, quibus eos, dum uiuerent, mutuus amor charitasque deuinxerat; quanquam bonis uiris, ut caetera bona, auctam post fata potius quam imminutam coniectant. Mortuos ergo uersari inter uiuentes credunt, dictorum factorumque spectatores; eoque res agendas fidentius aggrediuntur, talibus uelut freti praesidibus, et ab inhonesto secreto deterret eos credita maiorum praesentia' (276–9). The 1556 English translation gives 'mutuall loue and amitie' in place of 'mutuall loue and charytye', even though the latter had translated more accurately the Latin 'mutuus amor charitasque' (*A frutefull pleasaunt, & wittie worke of the beste state of a publique weale, and of the newe yle, called Vtopia: written in Latine, by the right worthie and famous Syr Thomas More knyght, and translated into Englishe by Ralphe Robynson, sometime fellowe of Corpus Christi College in Oxford, and nowe by him at this seconde edition newlie perused and corrected, and also with diuers notes in the margent augmented* (London: 1556), Qvii^{r}). It is striking that the 1556 edition's marginal notes offer remarks upon modes of dying: 'A willing and a merye deathe not to be lamented' (Qvi^{v}); 'To die unwillingly an evel token' (Qvi^{r}). The text's reference to the 'present conuersation' of the living and the dead (Qvii^{r}), however, is passed over in silence.

91 This Roman formula, familiar from countless monuments, altars, and funerary markings all across the Roman world, had a complex history of crossing religious lines – possibly as a result of re-use. See, for example, Leonard Victor Rutgers' treatment of Jewish burial sites where the formula is employed: *The Jews in Late Ancient Rome: Evidence of Cultural Interaction in the Roman Diaspora* (Leiden: Brill, 1995), 269–72.

the mouths of the latter. The 1551 English 'conuersacion', by contrast, appears to operate in one of its obsolete meanings to signify presence or placement rather than speech ('The action of living or having one's being *in* a place or *among* persons').[92]

Robinson's translation of this passage sees More testing the foundations of mutuality and intelligibility within the full range of a population that includes (as Western Christendom did) both the living and the dead.[93] Here, in *Utopia*, the words of the former can only elicit the stares of the latter. The dead are 'beholders and witnesses' of words and deeds rather than interlocutors. Scholars have paid close attention to More's interest in surveillance in this episode. I want to emphasize, however, that the living and the dead are said to be yoked together by 'mutuall loue and charytye' ('mutuus amor charitasque') – the latter being one of the early grounds on which reformers had come to justify prayers for the dead. Perhaps most notably, the living regard commemorative speech itself as the phenomenon that makes this 'present conuersacion' possible. Living Utopians are said to suppose that the dead are present among them only 'when they talke of them'. Speech makes the dead present, but only insofar as they are the subject of that speech.

A further refinement of these issues can come by establishing a conversation between More's image of the relationship between the living and the dead in *Utopia*, on the one hand, and the visions framed in a short sequence of passages from Shakespeare, on the other. Shakespeare's own relation to Rome remains complex throughout his career.[94] He is responsible for images of Rome at risk, with barbarians either at or within the gates, as well as for speeches in which characters affirm that Rome is inexorable and beyond the reach of even modest resistance, let alone harm or danger.[95] These expressions tend to occur early enough in the

92 *OED* 1, 'conversation'. Italics in original.

93 See Peter Marshall: 'Thomas More's Utopians believed that the dead walked invisibly among them, witnessing their words and actions, and in this they may not have differed so greatly from the mentality of European peoples' (*Beliefs and the Dead*, 13).

94 This even without broaching the vexed topic of the testament of faith (now lost) that is said to have been written in his father's name. For a very selective point of entry into suggestive recent studies of the place of Rome in Shakespeare's imagination see, for example, Chernaik, *The Myth of Rome*; Gary Willis, *Rome and Rhetoric: Shakespeare's Julius Caesar* (New Haven: Yale University Press, 2011); Tom Muir, 'Without Remainder: Ruins and Tombs in Shakespeare's Sonnets', *Textual Practice* 24 (2010), 21–49; Maria Del Sapio Garbero (ed.), *Identity, Otherness and Empire in Shakespeare's Rome* (Farnham: Ashgate, 2009).

95 The quintessential expression of Rome's inexorability comes in the first scene of *Coriolanus*, where Menenius addresses the starving plebeians: 'For your wants, / Your suffering in this dearth, you may as well / Strike at the heaven with your staves as lift them / Against the Roman state, whose course

action of the plays in question to suggest that Shakespeare wants rapidly to epitomize the city so as to be able to treat Rome as possessing some form of macrocosmic control over the plots in hand.

In the opening scene of *Titus Andronicus*, for example, when Tamora, Queen of the Goths, is rapidly transformed from prisoner to Empress, she declares herself to have become 'incorporate in Rome' – this, tellingly, in a play in which scenes of mutilation and violent consumption are staged within the city's public spaces, its private homes, its adjacent rural landscape, its literature, and its legal history.[96] Tamora's 'incorporation' occurs in the wake of the sacrifice of her eldest son by the sons of Titus. The play's earliest and most generative disasters, therefore, are direct results of ritualistic efforts to reach and feed the dead. In this case, the rituals originate in ancient Rome:

> Give us the proudest prisoner of the Goths,
> That we may hew his limbs and on a pile
> *Ad manes fratrum* sacrifice his flesh
> Before this earthly prison of their bones,
> That so the shadows be not unappeas'd,
> Nor we disturb'd with prodigies on earth.[97]

Sacrifices, rather than prayers, provide the means by which the play's living seek to communicate with their dead brethren, and it is necessary to read these practices against the backdrop of decades of non-linear reformations and counterreformations of rites involving the commemoration of the dead. In this particular case, the living attempt to generate their 'conuersacion' (as the 1551 *Utopia* puts it) with the dead by means of a Latin tag and the ritualistic hewing of limbs. The Rome to which Titus has returned after so many years of warfare is, in essence, a tomb that is noisy with the voices of the dead. Titus is wrong, therefore, to believe (though perhaps he only hopes) that death is a condition of privation: 'No noise, but silence and eternal sleep.'[98] The voices of this Rome's dead, however, are both loud and unintelligible – in a sense, post-verbal. Titus had already justified the sacrifice of Alarbus on the grounds that only his death (and, presumably, his shrieks or groans) could 'appease their groaning shadows that are gone'.[99] Rome's dead can be as demanding and inexorable as the city itself, and although they are every bit as eager as the city itself to assert their power

will on / The way it takes, cracking ten thousand curbs / Of more strong link asunder than can ever / Appear in your impediment' (1.1.66–72).

[96] Shakespeare, *Titus Andronicus*, 1.1.462.
[97] Shakespeare, *Titus Andronicus*, 1.1.96–101.
[98] Shakespeare, *Titus Andronicus*, 1.1.155.
[99] Shakespeare, *Titus Andronicus*, 1.1.126.

over the living, their language is restricted to groans and thus liable, at every turn, to being misunderstood or even simply dismissed contemptuously. Their groaning resembles nothing so much as William Marshall's caustic remarks about the ringing, singing, mumbling murmuring, and 'puling forth' that the Dirige required of the living.[100]

The ancient Roman dead (though not, significantly, the ghost of the dead King of Denmark) speak a similarly unintelligible language in *Hamlet*. The play, as is well known, granted the doctrine of purgatory its own afterlife on London's public and private stages. And like *Titus Andronicus*, *Hamlet* turns its eye towards ancient Rome in support of an effort to survey disturbances along the border between life and death. The play drives these matters towards both modern and ancient Rome, as Danes with names like Barnardo and Horatio ponder the ghost of dead King Hamlet:

> BARNARDO Well may it sort that this portentous figure
> Comes armed through our watch so like the King
> That was and is the question of these wars.
> HORATIO A mote it is to trouble the mind's eye.
> In the most high and palmy state of Rome,
> A little ere the mightiest Julius fell,
> The graves stood tenantless and the sheeted dead
> Did squeak and gibber in the Roman streets;
> As stars with trains of fire, and dews of blood,
> Disasters in the sun; and the moist star,
> Upon whose influence Neptune's empire stands,
> Was sick almost to doomsday with eclipse.
> And even the like precurse of fear'd events,
> As harbingers preceding still the fates
> And prologue to the omen coming on,
> Have heaven and earth together demonstrated
> Unto our climatures and countrymen.[101]

Large sections of *Hamlet* can look like extended meditations on developments in literary styles, dramatic form, and performance practices during the decades in which Senecan tragedy had gradually moved into the heart of the English dramatic tradition's consciousness. The play is also a window on Reformation controversies that had radically unsettled conceptions of what was at stake (i.e., what could and could not be officially or

[100] *A goodly prymer in englyshe* [STC 15988], in Edward Burton (ed.), *Three Primers*, 232.
[101] Shakespeare, *Hamlet*, 1.1.109–25.

publicly countenanced, justified, etc.) in efforts to understand the relation between the living and the dead.[102]

Horatio has run, 'in the mind's eye', all the way to ancient Rome in order to fetch up emblematic examples of the notorious semi-intelligibility of portents. Stars with trains of fire, dews of blood, disasters in the sun: each of these falls short of sense. So, too, do the utterances of 'the sheeted dead'. It is one of this dark play's ironies that even though the ghost of the dead King Hamlet is every bit as loquacious as the living Player King, the Roman dead can only squeak and gibber. After all, the pedagogical dispensation within which Shakespeare had been trained up looked directly to 'the most high and palmy state of Rome' when selecting its most cherished models of eloquence. Squeaking and gibbering are unsettling testaments to the pagan dead's distance from the Christian Word to come. These lines, moreover, transfer to the dead the miserable ringing, singing, mumbling, murmuring, and piteous puling forth that William Marshall had associated with the outlandish speech acts forced upon the living by the Dirige. The Roman dead, unlike the dead King of Denmark, are beyond the reach of discourse and cannot answer our questions.

These passages from More and Shakespeare mount a series of efforts to test the limits of the category of 'the human'. I have already cited Duffy's suggestion that the 1552 Book of Common Prayer had decisively redrawn 'the boundaries of human community'. One inference to be drawn from this is that what counts as human has been redefined in direct relation to the break with Rome.[103] Chapter 1 cited Stanley Cavell's preoccupation with 'the fantastic in what human beings will accustom themselves to, call this the surrealism of the habitual – as if to be human is forever to be prey to turning your corner of the human race, hence perhaps all of it, into some new species of the genus of humanity, for the better or for the worst'.[104] This is one of the philosophical plots that organized the liturgical debates that bore on the dead.

'The Order for the Buriall of the Dead' in the Church of England's 1559 *Book of Common Prayer* opens by setting two biblical texts in apposition:

102 Though Rist argues that revenge tragedy typically endorses Catholic rituals, my own view is that the genre is (like a broad variety of other texts and literary kinds and modes) restlessly exploring different – and unstable – versions of Rome against the backdrop of profound changes to social and religious customs concerning the dead (Rist, *Revenge Tragedy*).

103 Duffy, *The Stripping of the Altars*, 475. For a recent collection of essays studying contested definitions of the human see the essays collected in Melissa Sanchez and Ayesha Ramachandran (eds.), *Spenser Studies: A Renaissance Poetry Annual* 30 (2016). The following paragraphs are condensed and adapted from 'Spenser's Dead', my contribution to the collection (255–70).

104 Cavell, 'The Uncanniness of the Ordinary', in *Quest of the Ordinary*, 84.

> I AM the resurrection and the life (saith the Lord) he that beleveth in me: yea, thoughe he were dead, yet shall he live. And whosoever liveth, and believeth in me, shall not dye for ever. *John* 11
>
> I KNOWE that my redemer lyveth, and that I shal rise out of the earth in the last daye, and shalbe covered agayne with my skinne, and shall se God in my flesh: yea, and I my selfe shall beholde hym, not with other, but with these same eyes. *Job* 19[105]

Elizabeth's 1559 'Order' is, in essence, identical to that of Edward's 1552 edition. One of the chief innovations of the latter had been to revise those places where the 1549 *Book of Common Prayer* had living parishioners speak directly to the corpse that was before their eyes. The 1549 script of direct address to the dead ('I commende thy soule to God the father almighty, and thy body to the grounde, earth to earth, asshes to asshes, dust to dust') is rephrased in both 1552 and 1559 as a communal statement ventured by the living on the subject of the dead ('Forasmuche as it hath pleased almightie God of his great mercy to take unto hym selfe the Soule of oure deare brother, here departed, we therefore committe hys bodye to the grounde, earthe to earthe, ashes to ashes, dust to dust.') [106]

By this and other revisions to the 1549 text (e.g., the omission of psalms, along with the deletion of prayers that referred to the day of judgment and to hopes of delivery from 'the gates of hell and paynes of eternall derkenes'), the 1552 and 1559 'Order' had made significant changes to the earlier text's account of the plight of the dead.[107] And yet, the rhetorical textures of the revised orders of 1552 and 1559 remain complex and perhaps even elusive in their handling of voice.

In spite of the quite significant disruptions occasioned by Edward's 1552 prayer book, the Church of England's fitful 'conuersacion' with the voluble spirits of the Dirige does seem to persist. The 1549, 1552, and 1559 texts all open with the same act of decontextualized ventriloquism: the voice and promise of Christ sits in apposition with the voice of an entity (call it Job) that speaks as though it had already been unlaced from what was once its body. Though all this material has been removed from the larger context of the Dirige's explicit emphasis on the spiritual efficacy of prayers for the dead, excerpted passages (even when tagged with their biblical book and chapter) continue to have the curious effect of making one wonder just who is to be imagined as speaking, and to whom.

105 *The Book of Common Prayer: The Texts of 1549, 1559, and 1662*, ed. Brian Cummings (Oxford University Press, 2011), 171.

106 *The Book of Common Prayer*, 82, 172.

107 *The Book of Common Prayer*, 88.

Indeed, by lacking explicit rhetorical framing and commentary on sources of the kind that William Marshall had employed as a systematic counternarrative to the Dirige in 1535, the 1552 and 1559 prayer books persist in making biblical excerpts sound like disembodied voices that reach us from beyond the grave. Asserting that it will one day 'be covered agayne' with its 'skinne', and that it will one day behold God 'not with other, but with the same eyes', the voice that is summoned into speech in the second of the two passages cited above hovers at some unknowable distance from 'the corps' around which 'The Order' revolves. The dead body is a spectacle upon which the ventriloquized voice comments. That voice, in turn, lets us see that surprising possibilities are latent in the scene: the dead body *was* human, the disembodied voice somehow *is* human, and the dead body will once again house a speaking voice 'in the last daye'.

For obvious reasons, the 1559 'Order' as a whole revolves around the body of the dead, with 'The priest metyng the corps at the Churche style', moving into speech and song, and then proceeding 'eyther unto the churche, or towardes the grave'. Metaphors are urged upon this corpse at the scene of interment. Man, we are told, 'cummeth up, and is cut downe lyke a floure, he flyeth as it were a shadow, and never continueth in one staye'. We die, of course, all the time: 'In the myddest of lyfe we be in death', and our only hope is that we may not be delivered 'into the bitter paynes of eternall death'.[108] The dead body that sits at the centre of 'The Order' mutely presses a claim of kinship on the living while also subsisting in an unnerving manner after death. It subsists, therefore, somewhere beyond the terms in which the human, as a category error in which body and soul roll together, was understood to reside. In this sense, the text of 'The Order' can be read as a rhetorical occasion in which the unsettling spectacle of a corpse prompts the believer's living voice to reassert its possession of, and find itself at home within, the living body that already harbours it.

What was this dead body imagined to be during the space of time in which it is separate from the first-person 'I' that knows it will, 'in the last daye', be covered once again with its skin and eyes? With this restoration of 'skinne' and 'eyes' still in the offing, the grave is understandably depicted as a locus of absolute sensory deprivation. The point may seem obvious, but preachers took pains to make worshippers bear the weight of the silence of the grave. In his sermon 'Preached upon Easter-day' (1622), John Donne draws distinctions among the sounds, voices, and sensations that dead

[108] *The Book of Common Prayer*, 171.

bodies do and do not hear or feel, and among the kinds of indignities those bodies may or may not suffer:

> The dead heare not Thunder, nor feele they an Earth-quake. If the Canon batter that Church walls, in which they lye buryed, it wakes not them, nor does it shake or affect them, if that dust, which they are, be thrown out, but yet there is a voyce, which the dead shall heare; *The dead shall heare the voyce of the Son of God,* (sayes the Son of God himself) *and they that heare shall live.*[109]

What they are not capable of hearing, however, in the wake of Church of England policy after the break with Rome, are the prayers of the living, and I propose that we should understand Donne's remarks as glancing back across the territories of his own break with Rome. This passage, and the ones that follow it, are characterized by a degree of elegiac intensity that suggests that Donne is actively working through – as he would have done time and again from the pulpit – the history of his own personal and family immersion in a vastly different understanding of the triangular relationship between the living, the dead, and the phenomenon of voice.

What is the status of the body between the moments of death and rebirth? Donne is clear that the apocalyptic voice will revivify 'that that was meerely nothing'. Even though,

> legions of Angels, millions of Angels shall be employed about the Resurrection, to recollect their scattered dust, and recompact their ruined bodies, yet those bodies so recompact, shall not be able to heare a voyce. They shall be then but such bodies, as they were when they were laid downe in the grave, when, though they were intire bodies, they could not heare the voice of the mourner.[110]

Removed, by sheer force of the Royal Supremacy and its aftermaths, from conversation – let alone dialogue – with the living, Donne's dead can only dream of being able to, as Shakespeare's Horatio put it, 'squeak and gibber in the Roman streets'.

[109] Donne, 'Preached Upon Easter-day. [1622]', in *Sermons*, vol. IV.69.
[110] Donne, 'Preached Upon Easter-day. [1622]', in *Sermons*, vol. IV.69–70.

Conclusion

Though Ovid has always been better known for the *Metamorphoses*, for his erotic poems in elegiac couplets, and for the ventriloquized female voices of the *Heroides*, the poems known as the *Tristia* (or, as the collection was commonly called, *de Tristibus*) were surprisingly common as curriculum texts in the grammar schools of early modern England.[1] Exiled to Tomis (the modern Romanian city of Constanța) by Augustus in 8 BCE, Ovid laments in this collection the disabling effects of his distance from Rome. A 1639 translation of the *Tristia* by one Zachary Catlin conveys a strong sense of how the process of Englishing the works of an ancient Roman poet could foster a quasi-nationalistic identification across time, space, and language. As Catlin remarks in his dedicatory epistle, 'to the meere *English* Reader, loe here *Ovid* is turn'd his own Countryman'.[2] Here, one final time, is an opportunity to regard the legacies of English humanism not as innovations or restorations, but rather as inflections of the persistence of Roman Britain: that is, as afterlives of the period when Britons and Romans *were* countrymen.

Restaging, as a grown man, what must have been his own early schoolroom encounters with Ovid's poems of exile, Catlin is clearly puzzled that the collection fell short of what he had once been taught could be achieved by eloquence. Marveling that Augustus never recalled Ovid from exile, Catlin can only conclude that 'me thinkes either *Augustus Cæsar* never read this Poem, or through selfe guiltinesse of some fault to which *Ovid* was conscious, (as *Actæon* to *Diana's* nakednesse) he was constrained to harden his heart against his charmes, like those deafe

[1] For indications of the popularity of the *Tristia* in grammar-school curricula see the index to T. W. Baldwin, *William Shakspere's Small Latine and Lesse Greek*. 2 vols. (Urbana, IL: University of Illinois Press, 1944).

[2] Ovid, *Publ Ovid. De tristibus: or Mournefull elegies, in five bookes: composed in his banishment, part at sea, and part at Tomos, a city of Pontus. Translated into English verse by Zachary Catlin, Mr. of Arts. Suffolke* (London, 1639), A3^{v} [STC 18981].

stones that killed *Orpheus*'.[3] This is one of those moments when former schoolboys appear to struggle to overcome their burgeoning suspicions that they were educated in bad faith concerning the power of eloquence.

A commendatory poem addressed to Catlin by a friend named Robert Pament insists that the translator's eloquence has generated some astonishing confusions between past and present, here and there, translator and poet. Pament asserts that

> Ovid weepes *English* now, nor doe we know
> From whither eye, the learn'der tear doth flow,
> The *Roman* or the *English*: whither *Rome*,
> Or your terse *English* more empearles his tombe.[4]

Reading his friend's translation, Pament adds that 'I had lost *Ovid*, and in Extasie, / Wept for your Exile, and thought you were he.' The confusions multiply: 'your lively sense / Transported me to thinke him banisht hence / Vnholily by us', so that the spectacle of the exercise of arbitrary power in seventeenth-century England is viewed from an exceptionally long historical perspective.[5]

These suggestive confusions and substitutions help account for the collection's popularity in England's grammar schools, since the poems would seem to have promoted a sense of kinship or even identification with the object of study. Another reason for this popularity (this time from the schoolmaster's perspective) is that the collection's poems repeatedly conjure up images of a Roman poet who is desperate not to lose his Latin. Ovid's schoolboys must have been able to recognize that even on the shores of the distant Black Sea the poet was well within the reach of the city that was keeping them glued to their seats in early modern England.

In *Tristia* 3.1 Ovid fears (or claims to fear) that his Latin fluency has fallen victim to his new life among barbarians. Later in the third book, he describes a scene in which a guard is manning walls and gates designed to keep out the hostile Getae. Ovid's emphasis on his distance from Rome leads directly to his confession that his Latin is beginning to slip through his fingers: 'saepe aliquod quaero verbum nomenque locumque, / nec quisquam est a quo certior esse queam' ('Often I am at a loss for a word, a name, a place, and there is none who can inform me.')[6] He fears, moreover, that the purity of his Latin has been compromised: 'crede mihi, timeo ne Sintia mixta Latinis / inque meis scriptis Pontica verba

[3] *Publ Ovid. De tristibus*, A3^{r}. [4] *Publ Ovid. De tristibus*, A5^{v}. [5] *Publ Ovid. De tristibus*, A5^{v}.

[6] Ovid, *Tristia, Ex Ponto*, ed. and trans. A. L. Wheeler, rev. G. P. Goold, Loeb Classical Library 151 (Cambridge University Press, 1988), 3.14.43–4.

legas' ('O believe me, I fear that Sintic and Pontic language may be mingled with the Latin in my writings.')[7] In 4.1 he makes himself an audience of one, asserting that no one can make sense of his Latin. In 5.2 he describes himself as being encompassed by barbarian tongues. In 5.7 he mourns his fate as a Roman poet who has been compelled to learn to speak a barbarian tongue. All he can do, he says, is address himself in half-forgotten Latin phrases. In 5.10 he declares that he has been reduced to speaking in gestures. Finally, in 5.12, Ovid asserts that he has, in an atmosphere filled with barbarism and the inhuman cries of beasts, been wholly absorbed into the linguistic order of this foreign place: 'ipse mihi videor iam dedidicisse Latine: / nam didici Getice Sarmaticeque loqui' ('I myself, I think, have already unlearned my Latin, for I have learned how to speak Getic and Sarmatian.')[8]

Ovid's increasingly intense and decisive assertions of his distance from Rome and its language would seem to tell a story that runs directly counter to the one that this book has tried to tell. The Rome that haunts the *Tristia* elegies and the *Epistulae ex Ponto* is not *répandue*, universal, inescapable, and eternal, but rather distant, unreachable, and fiercely specific in its situatedness. 'Quid melius Roma? Scythico quid frigore peius?' ('What is better than Rome? What worse than the cold of Scythia?') he asks in *Ex Ponto*, dividing the world between two poles that cannot meet.[9] Having known every inch of Rome, Ovid's experience of endlessly rewriting his relation to the city could not be that of the inhabitants of the land once known as Britannia.[10]

And yet, Ovid does give us a glimpse of the experience that could not otherwise be his when he turns his attention to the languages that he hears around him. By the fifth book of the *Tristia*, Ovid has learned to perceive the linguistic substratum of languages that had seemed to be mere noise, and he claims that he can hear the sound of Greek 'conquered' ('victa') within the Getic language. 5.7 extends this discovery, noting with respect to the locals that,[11]

[7] Ovid, *Tristia, Ex Ponto*, 3.14.49–50. [8] Ovid, *Tristia, Ex Ponto*, 5.12.57–8.

[9] Ovid, *Tristia, Ex Ponto*, 1.3.37.

[10] See Farrell on a paradox that is not often remarked upon: namely, that the ease with which we continue to speak confidently about 'Roman writers' is already a measure of our willingness to see Rome here, there, and almost everywhere. Farrell notes that Cicero's friend Atticus was 'that rarest of creatures in Latin culture: a native Roman, Roman by birth, or, as the phrase goes, "a Roman of Rome." None of Atticus' own literary works survives. If one were to appear, Cicero's friend would join Julius Caesar in a very select group, doubling the number of native Roman authors whose works still exist' (25).

[11] Ovid, *Tristia, Ex Ponto*, 5.2.68.

in paucis extant Graecae vestigia linguae,
haec quoque iam Getico barbara facta sono.
unus in hoc nemo est populo, qui forte Latine
quamlibet e medio reddere verba queat.
ille ego Romanus vates – ignoscite, Musae! –
Sarmatico cogor plurima more loqui.
et pudet et fateor, iam desuetudine longa
vix subeunt ipsi verba Latina mihi.
nec dubito quin sint et in hoc non pauca libello
barbara: non hominis culpa, sed ista loci.
ne tamen Ausoniae perdam commercia linguae,
et fiat patrio vox mea muta sono,
ipse loquor mecum desuetaque verba retracto,
et studii repeto signa sinistra mei.[12]

[A few retain traces of the Greek tongue, but even this is rendered barbarous by a Getic twang. There is not a single man among these people who perchance might express in Latin any words however common. I, the Roman bard – pardon, ye Muses! – am forced to utter most things in Sarmatian fashion. I admit it, though it shames me: now from long disuse Latin words with difficulty occur even to me! And I doubt not there are even in this book not a few barbarisms, not the fault of the man but of the place. Yet for fear of losing the use of the Ausonian tongue and lest my own voice grow dumb in its native sound, I talk to myself, dealing again with disused words and seeking again the ill-omened currency of my art.]

In these lines we encounter a version of the phenomenon that this book has set out to describe. On Ovid's account, the Getae are inhabited by Greek culture in something like the way I have tried to show that, for example, Bede and his contemporaries understood themselves to be inhabited by Rome. From the confines of what he depicts as a lonely outpost on the shores of the Black Sea, in what had once been an ancient Greek colony, Ovid, who is said to have studied for a time at Athens, may well be registering, and mourning, his own absorption into the fact of Greece.[13]

The writers, texts, and phenomena studied in this book were entangled in Rome in ways that they could not always perceive or comprehend. This much is certainly true of the complex aftermath of 'the break with

[12] Ovid, *Tristia, Ex Ponto*, 5.7.51–64.

[13] On tensions between Rome and Greece in Ovid see Ingo Gildenhard and Andrew Zissos, 'Ovid's "Hecale": Deconstructing Athens in the *Metamorphoses*', *The Journal of Roman Studies* 94 (2004), 47–72.

Rome' and its attendant debates about the relationship between the living and the dead. As place, idea, and fact, Rome is always 'Rome'. It was a multifaceted phenomenon whose plural legacies were always open to formal, explicit acceptance or resistance. But those legacies were also ceaselessly negotiated in countless – and nearly invisible – ways as the living settled their relation to a world mapped by Rome.

Bibliography

Adams, J. N., *The Regional Diversification of Latin, 200 BC–AD 600* (Cambridge University Press, 2007).

'*Romanitas* and the Latin Language', *Classical Quarterly* 53 (2003), 184–205.

Albin, Andrew, 'The *Prioress's Tale*, Sonorous and Silent', *Chaucer Review* 48 (2013), 91–112.

Allason-Jones, Lindsay (ed.), *Artefacts in Roman Britain: Their Purpose and Use* (Cambridge University Press, 2011).

Allen, Valerie and Ruth Evans (eds.), *Roadworks: Medieval Britain, Medieval Roads* (University of Manchester Press, 2016).

Alpers, Paul, *What is Pastoral?* (University of Chicago Press, 1996).

Amsler, Mark E., *Etymology and Grammatical Discourse in Late Antiquity and the Early Middle Ages* (Amsterdam: John Benjamins, 1989).

Aristotle, *Metaphysics*, ed. and trans. Hugh Tredennick, 2 vols., LCL 271, 287 (Cambridge, MA: Harvard University Press, 1933, 1935).

Armstrong, Richard H., *A Compulsion for Antiquity: Freud and the Ancient World* (Ithaca: Cornell University Press, 2005).

Ascham, Roger, *The scholemaster or plaine and perfite way of teachyng children, to vnderstand, write, and speake, the Latin tong, but specially purposed for the priuate bryngïng vp of youth in ientlemen and noble mens houses, and commodious also for all such, as haue forgot the Latin tonge, and would, by themselues, without à scholemaster, in short tyme, and with small paines, recouer à sufficient habilitie, to vnderstand, write, and speake Latin* (London, 1570) [STC 832].

Aston, Margaret, 'English Ruins and English History: The Dissolution and the Sense of the Past', *Journal of the Warburg and Courtauld Institutes* 36 (1973), 231–55.

Augustine, *The City of God*, ed. and trans. George E. McCracken et al, 7 vols., LCL 411–17 (Cambridge, MA: Harvard University Press, 1963).

Confessions (*Conf.*), ed. and trans. Carolyn J.-B. Hammond, 2 vols., LCL 26–7 (Cambridge, MA: Harvard University Press, 2014).

Austin, J. L., *Philosophical Papers*, 3rd edn. (Oxford University Press, 1979).

Avis, Paul, *Foundations of Modern Historical Thought: From Machiavelli to Vico* (New York: Routledge, 2016).

Bacon, Francis, *The Advancement of Learning*, ed. Michael Kiernan, The Oxford Francis Bacon 4 (Oxford: Clarendon Press, 2000).

Baldwin, T. W., *William Shakspere's Small Latine and Lesse Greek*. 2 vols. (Urbana, IL: University of Illinois Press, 1944).

Barkan, Leonard, 'Ruins and Visions: Spenser, Pictures, Rome', in Jennifer Klein Morrison and Matthew Greenfield (eds.), *Edmund Spenser: Essays on Culture and Allegory* (Aldershot: Ashgate, 2000), 9–36.

Unearthing the Past: Archaeology and Aesthetics in the Making of Renaissance Culture (New Haven: Yale University Press, 1999).

Beales, A. C. F., *Education Under Penalty: English Catholic Education from the Reformation to the Fall of James II* (London: Athlone Press, 1963).

Bede, *The Ecclesiastical History of the English People* (*HE*), ed. Bertram Colgrave and R. A. B. Mynors (Oxford University Press, 2007).

The History of the Church of Englande. Compiled by Venerable Bede, Englishman. Translated out of Latin in to English by Thomas Stapleton student in diuinite (Antwerp, 1565) [STC 1778].

Bell, Alexander (ed.), *An Anglo-Norman Brut*, Anglo-Norman Text Society XXI–XXII (Oxford: Blackwell, 1969).

Bell, Tyler, 'Churches on Roman Buildings: Christian Associations and Roman Masonry in Anglo-Saxon England', *Medieval Archaeology* 42 (1998), 1–18.

The Religious Reuse of Roman Structures in Early Medieval England (Oxford: Archaeopress, 2005).

Benet, Diana Treviño, 'The Escape From Rome: Milton's *Second Defense* and a Renaissance Genre', in Maria Di Cesare (ed.), *Milton in Italy: Contexts, Images, Contradictions* (Binghamton, NY: Medieval and Renaissance Texts and Studies, 1991), 29–49.

Biblia Sacra iuxta vulgatam versionem, 4th edn. (Stuttgart: Deutsche Bibelgesellschaft, 1994).

Bidwell, Paul, 'A Survey of the Anglo-Saxon Crypt at Hexham and its Reused Roman Stonework', *Archaeologia Aeliana: Miscellaneous Tracts Relating to Antiquity*, 5th ser., 39 (2010), 53–145.

Bietenholz, Peter, '*Felicitas* (Eudaimonia) ou les Promenades d'Érasme dans le Jardin d'Épicure', *Renaissance and Reformation* 30 (2006), 37–86.

Billings, Drew W., *Acts of the Apostles and the Rhetoric of Roman Imperialism* (Cambridge University Press, 2017).

Blanton, Virginia, *Signs of Devotion: The Cult of St. Æthelthryth in Medieval England, 695–1615* (University Park, PA: Penn State University Press, 2007).

Blanton, Virginia and Helene Scheck (eds.), *Intertexts: Studies in Anglo-Saxon Culture Presented to Paul E. Szarmach* (Tempe: Arizona Center for Medieval and Renaissance Studies, 2008).

Bloomer, W. Martin, *Latinity and Literary Society at Rome* (Philadelphia: University of Pennsylvania Press, 1997).

The School of Rome: Latin Studies and the Origins of Liberal Education (Berkeley: University of California Press, 2011).

Blurton, Heather and Hannah Johnson, *The Critics and The Prioress: Antisemitism, Criticism, and Chaucer's* 'Prioress's Tale' (Ann Arbor: University of Michigan Press, 2017).

'Reading the *Prioress's Tale* in the Fifteenth Century: Lydgate, Hoccleve, and Marian Devotion', *Chaucer Review* 50 (2015), 134–58.
Bodel, Jehan, *La Chanson des Saisnes*, ed. Annette Brasseur, 2 vols. (Geneva: Librairie Droz, 1989).
Bolgia, Claudia, Rosamond McKitterick, and John Osborne (eds.), *Rome Across Time and Space: Cultural Transmission and the Exchange of Ideas, c. 500–1400* (Cambridge University Press, 2011).
The Book of Common Prayer: The Texts of 1549, 1559, and 1662, ed. Brian Cummings (Oxford University Press, 2011).
Botley, Paul, *Learning Greek in Western Europe, 1396–1525: Grammars, Lexica, and Classroom Texts* (Philadelphia: American Philosophical Society, 2010).
Boyarin, Adrienne Williams, *Miracles of the Virgin in Medieval England: Law and Jewishness in Marian Legends* (Martlesham: Boydell & Brewer, 2010).
Boyd, Beverly (ed.), *The Prioress's Tale: A Variorum Edition of the Works of Geoffrey Chaucer*, vol. II, *The Canterbury Tales* Part 20 (Norman: University of Oklahoma Press, 1987).
Boynton, Susan and Eric N. Rice (eds.), *Young Choristers, 650–1700* (Woodbridge: The Boydell Press, 2008).
Bracken, Damian, 'Virgil the Grammarian and Bede: A Preliminary Study', *Anglo-Saxon England* 35 (2006), 7–21.
Braver, Lee, *Groundless Grounds: A Study of Wittgenstein and Heidegger* (Cambridge, MA: MIT Press, 2012).
Brook, G. L. (ed.), *The Harley Lyrics: The Middle English Lyrics of MS. Harley 2253* (Manchester University Press, 1948).
Brown, George Hardin, 'Ciceronianism in Bede and Alcuin', in Virginia Blanton and Helene Scheck (eds.), *Intertexts: Studies in Anglo-Saxon Culture Presented to Paul E. Szarmach* (Tempe: Arizona Center for Medieval and Renaissance Studies, 2008), 319–29.
Brown, Virginia, 'Latin Manuscripts of Caesar's *Gallic War*', in Giulio Battelli (ed.), *Paleographica Diplomatica et Archivistica: Studi in Onore di Giulio Battelli* (Rome: Edizioni di Storia e Letteratura, 1979), 105–58.
Browne, Sir Thomas, *The Major Works*, ed. C. A. Patrides (London: Penguin, 1977).
Burke, Kenneth, *Language as Symbolic Action: Essays on Life, Language, and Method* (Berkeley: University of California Press, 1968).
Burns, J. Patout, 'Baptism as Dying and Rising with Christ in the Teachings of Augustine', *Journal of Early Christian Studies*, 20 (2012), 407–38.
Burton, Edward (ed.), *Three Primers Put Forth in The Reign of Henry VIII* (Oxford University Press, 1834).
Butterworth, Charles C., *The English Primers (1529–1545): Their Publication and Connection with the English Bible and the Reformation in England* (New York: Octagon Books, 1971).
Caesar, Julius, *The Gallic War*, ed. H. J. Edwards, LCL 72 (Cambridge, MA: Harvard University Press, 1917).

Cambridge, Eric, 'The Architecture of the Augustinian Mission', in Richard Gameson (ed.), *St Augustine and the Conversion of England* (Stroud: Sutton, 1999), 202–36.

Camden, William, *Britain, or A chorographicall description of the most flourishing kingdomes, England, Scotland, and Ireland, and the ilands adioyning, out of the depth of antiquitie: beautified vvith mappes of the severall shires of England: vvritten first in Latine by William Camden Clarenceux K. of A. Translated newly into English by Philémon Holland Doctour in Physick: finally, revised, amended, and enlarged with sundry additions by the said author* (London, 1610) [STC 4509].

Britannia, siue Florentissimorum regnorum Angliæ, Scotiæ, Hiberniæ, et insularum adiacentium ex intima antiquitate chorographica descriptio: nunc postremò recognita, plurimis locis magna accessione adaucta, & chartis chorographicis illustrata. (London, 1607) [STC 4508].

Cameron, Euan K., 'Preface to the Epistle to the Romans 1522, and as Revised 1546', in Euan K. Cameron (ed.), *The Annotated Luther, Volume 6: The Interpretation of Scripture* (Minneapolis: Fortress Press, 2017), 457–63.

Campbell, Gordon and Thomas N. Corns, *John Milton: Life, Work, and Thought* (Oxford University Press, 2008).

Camporeale, S. I., 'Poggio Bracciolini Versus Lorenzo Valla: The *Orationes in Laurentiam Vallam*', in J. Marino and M. Schlitt (eds.), *Perspectives on Early Modern and Modern Intellectual History: Essays in Honor of Nancy S. Struever* (University of Rochester Press, 2001), 27–48.

Carley, James P., 'Polydore Vergil and John Leland on King Arthur: The Battle of the Books', in Edward Donald Kennedy (ed.), *King Arthur: A Casebook* (New York: Garland, 1996), 185–204.

Carlson, David R., 'The "Grammarians' War" 1519–1521: Humanist Careerism in Early Tudor England, and Printing', *Medievalia et Humanistica*, n.s. 18 (1992), 157–81.

Cavell, Stanley, *Disowning Knowledge in Six Plays of Shakespeare* (Cambridge University Press, 1987).

In Quest of the Ordinary: Lines of Skepticism and Romanticism (University of Chicago Press, 1988).

'Introductory Note to "The *Investigations*' Everyday Aesthetics of Itself"', in John Gibson and Wolfgang Huemer (eds.), *The Literary Wittgenstein* (London: Routledge, 2004), 17–20.

Must We Mean What We Say?, rev. edn. (Cambridge University Press, 2002).

Philosophical Passages: Wittgenstein, Emerson, Austin, Derrida (Cambridge, MA: Blackwell, 1995).

Themes out of School: Effects and Causes (University of Chicago Press, 1984).

This New Yet Unapproachable America: Lectures after Emerson after Wittgenstein (Albuquerque, NM: Living Batch Press, 1989).

Charles-Edwards, T. M., *Wales and the Britons, 350–1064* (Oxford University Press, 2013).

Chaucer, Geoffrey, *The Riverside Chaucer*, ed. Larry D. Benson, 3rd edn. (Boston: Houghton Mifflin, 1987).

Cheney, Patrick and Philip Hardie (eds.), *The Oxford History of Classical Reception in English Literature: Volume. II: 1558–1660* (Oxford University Press, 2015).

Chernaik, Warren, *The Myth of Rome in Shakespeare and His Contemporaries* (Cambridge University Press, 2011).

Chester, Stephen J., *Reading Paul With the Reformers: Reconciling Old and New Reformers* (Grand Rapids, MI: Eerdmans, 2017).

Chin, Catherine M., *Grammar and Christianity in the Late Roman World* (Philadelphia: University of Pennsylvania Press, 2008).

Cleary, A. S. Esmonde, *The Ending of Roman Britain* (Savage, MD: Barnes & Noble, 1990).

Coates-Stephens, Robert, 'Epigraphy as Spolia: The Reuse of Inscriptions in Early Medieval Buildings', *Papers of the British School at Rome* 70 (2002), 275–96.

Coldiron, A. E. B., 'How Spenser Excavates Du Bellay's *Antiquitez*; or, The Role of the Poet, Lyric Historiography, and the English Sonnet', *Journal of English and Germanic Philology* 101 (2002), 41–67.

Coleman, Dorothy Gabe, *The Gallo-Roman Muse: Aspects of Roman Literary Tradition in Sixteenth-Century France* (Cambridge University Press, 1979).

Colgrave, Bertram, 'Pilgrimages to Rome in the Seventh and Eighth Centuries', in E. Bagby Atwood and Archibald Hill (eds.), *Studies in Language, Literature, and Culture of the Middle Ages and Later* (Austin: University of Texas Press, 1969), 156–72.

(ed. and trans.), *Two Lives of Saint Cuthbert: A Life by an Anonymous Monk of Lindisfarne and Bede's Prose Life* (Cambridge University Press, 1985).

Cooper, Richard, *Roman Antiquities in Renaissance France, 1515–65* (Farnham: Ashgate, 2013).

Copeland, Rita (ed.), *The Oxford History of Classical Reception in English Literature: Volume I: 800–1558* (Oxford University Press, 2016).

Copeland, Rita and Ineke Sluiter, *Medieval Grammar and Rhetoric: Language Arts and Literary Theory, AD 300–1475* (Oxford University Press, 2009).

Cordier, Maturin, *Colloquiorum Scholasticorum libri quatuor. Auctore Maturino Corderio, ab ipso aucti, & recogniti, suis, quibúsque dictionibus, adiectis accentibus. Argumentum huius operis per Maturinum Corderium. Hîc tibi purus in est sermo, breuis atque Latinus: hîc bene viuendi sunt documenta simul* (London, 1608) [STC 5759.4].

Corderius dialogues translated grammatically; for the more speedy attaining to the knowledge of the Latine tongue, for writing and speaking Latine. Done chiefly for the good of schooles, to be vsed according to the direction set downe in the booke, called Ludus literarius, or The grammar-schoole (London, 1614) [STC 5762].

Maturini Corderii Colloquia scholastica Anglo-Latina, in varias clausulas distributa; observato utriusque linguæ idiomate, quò sc. ope vernaculi, in quotidiano sermone Latino pueri feliciùs exerceantur. Positi sunt insuper in utriusque confiniis numeri, quibus uniuscujúsqu vocabuli vel phraseos indicatur locus, &

usus genuinus. A Carolo Hoole A.Mio. è Col. Linc. Oxon. privatæ scholæ grammaticæ institutore inter Aurifabrorum diverticulum in Rubæ Crucis, & aream Virginei captis in Alneæ Portæ vicis, apud Londinates. Ipsum Latinè loqui, est illud quidem in magnâ laude ponendum, sed non tam suâ iponte, quàm quod est à plerísque neglectum. Non enim ram præclarum est scire Latinè, quam turpe nescire (London, 1657) [Wing C6292].

Corthell, Ronald, Frances E. Dolan, Christopher Highley, and Arthur F. Marotti (eds.), *Catholic Culture in Early Modern England* (University of Notre Dame Press, 2007).

Coz, Yann, 'The Image of Roman History in Anglo-Saxon England', in D. Rollason, C. Leyser, and H. Williams (eds.), *England and the Continent in the Tenth Century: Studies in Honour of Wilhelm Levison (1876–1947)*, Studies in the Early Middle Ages 37 (Turnhout, Belgium: Brepols, 2010), 545–58.

Cramp, R., 'The Anglo-Saxons and Rome', *Transactions of the Architectural and Archaeological Society of Durham and Northumberland*, n.s. 3 (1974), 27–37.

Crick, Julia, 'The British Past and the Welsh Future: Gerald of Wales, Geoffrey of Monmouth and Arthur of Britain', *Celtica* 23 (1999), 60–75.

Cummings, Brian, *The Literary Culture of the Reformation: Grammar and Grace* (Oxford University Press, 2002).

Cummings, Brian and James Simpson (eds.), *Cultural Reformations: Medieval and Renaissance in Literary History* (Oxford University Press, 2010).

Curran, John E., *Roman Invasions: The British History, Protestant Anti-Romanism, and the Historical Imagination in England, 1530–1660* (Newark: University of Delaware Press, 2002).

Curtius, Ernst Robert, *European Literature and the Latin Middle Ages*, trans. Willard R. Trask (Princeton University Press, 1990).

Dailey, Patricia, 'Questions of Dwelling in Anglo-Saxon Poetry and Medieval Mysticism: Inhabiting Landscape, Body, and Mind', *New Medieval Literatures* 8 (2006), 175–214.

Dante [Dante Alighieri], *The Divine Comedy*, ed. and trans. Robert M. Durling, 3 vols. (New York: Oxford University Press, 1997–2011).

Davidson, Audrey Ekdahl, *Substance and Manner: Studies in Music and the Other Arts* (Saint Paul, MN: Hiawatha Press, 1977).

Davies, Joshua, *Visions and Ruins: Cultural Memory and the Untimely Middle Ages* (Manchester University Press, 2018).

Davies, Sioned (ed. and trans.), *The Mabinogion* (Oxford University Press, 2007).

de Grazia, Margreta, 'The Modern Divide: From Either Side', *Journal of Medieval and Early Modern Studies* 37 (2007), 453–67.

DeGregorio, Scott (ed.), *The Cambridge Companion to Bede* (Cambridge University Press, 2010).

Del Sapio Garbero, Maria, *Identity, Otherness and Empire in Shakespeare's Rome* (Farnham: Ashgate, 2009).

DellaNeva, JoAnn (ed.), *Ciceronian Controversies*, trans. Brian Duvick, The I Tatti Renaissance Library 26 (Cambridge, MA: Harvard University Press, 2007).

Desan, Philippe, *Montaigne: Une Biographie Politique* (Paris: Odile Jacob, 2014).

Dickey, Eleanor, 'O Egregie Grammatice: The Vocative Problems of Latin Words Ending in -ius', *The Classical Quarterly* 50 (2000), 548–62.

Dickey, Eleanor and Anna Chahoud (eds.), *Colloquial and Literary Latin: In Honour of J.N. Adams* (Cambridge University Press, 2010).

Dio Cassius, *Roman History*, ed. and trans. Earnest Cary, 9 vols., LCL 32, 37, 53, 66, 82–3, 175–7 (Cambridge, MA: Harvard University Press, 1914–27).

Dolven, Jeff, *Scenes of Instruction in Renaissance Romance* (University of Chicago Press, 2007).

'When to Stop Reading *The Faerie Queene*', in Jennifer Lewin (ed.), *Never Again Would Birds' Song Be the Same: Essays on Early Modern and Modern Poetry in Honor of John Hollander* (New Haven: Beinecke Library, 2002), 35–54.

Donne, John, *The Complete Poems*, ed. Robin Robbins (Harlow: Pearson, 2010).

Pseudo-Martyr, ed. Anthony Raspa (Montreal and Kingston: McGill-Queen's University Press, 1993).

Sermons of John Donne, ed. Evelyn M. Simpson and George R. Potter, 10 vols. (Berkeley: University of California Press, 1953–62).

Doran, Susan and Jonathan Woolfson, 'Wilson, Thomas (1523/4–1581), Humanist and Administrator', *Oxford Dictionary of National Biography*. 23 September 2004, accessed 22 March 2020, www-oxforddnb-com.

Du Bellay, Joachim, *Œuvres Poétiques*, ed. D. Aris and F. Joukovsky, 2 vols. (Paris: Classiques Garnier, 1993).

Duffy, Eamon, *Fires of Faith: Catholic England Under Mary Tudor* (New Haven: Yale University Press, 2010).

Marking the Hours: English People and Their Prayers, 1240–1570 (New Haven: Yale University Press, 2006).

The Stripping of the Altars: Traditional Religion in England, 1400–1580, 2nd edn. rev. (New Haven: Yale University Press, 2005).

Dugdale, William, *Monasticon anglicanum, or, The history of the ancient abbies, and other monasteries, hospitals, cathedral and collegiate churches, in England and Wales. With divers French, Irish, and Scotch monasteries formerly relating to England. Collected, and published in Latin, by Sir William Dugdale, Knt. late Garter King of Arms. In three volums. And now epitomized in English, page by page. With sculptures of the several religious habits*, [trans. James Wright] (London, 1693) [Wing D2487].

DuRocher, Richard J., *Milton Among the Romans: The Pedagogy and Influence of Milton's Latin Curriculum* (Pittsburgh: Duquesne University Press, 2001).

Eaton, Tim, *Plundering the Past: Roman Stonework in Medieval Britain* (Stroud: Tempus, 2000).

Eckhardt, Caroline D., 'The Presence of Rome in the Middle English Chronicles of the Fourteenth Century', *Journal of English and Germanic Philology* 90 (1991), 187–207.

Ehrensperger, Kathy and J. Brian Tucker (eds.), *Reading Paul in Context: Explorations in Identity Formation: Essays in Honour of William S. Campbell* (London: T&T Clark, 2010).

Elias, Norbert, *The Civilizing Process: Sociogenetic and Psychogenetic Investigations*, trans. Edmund Jephcott, rev. edn. (1939; London: Wiley-Blackwell, 2000).

Eliot, T. S., *Selected Essays* (London: Faber and Faber, 1999).

Enterline, Lynn, *Shakespeare's Schoolroom: Rhetoric, Discipline, Emotion* (University of Pennsylvania Press, 2011).

Erasmus, Desiderius, *The Collected Works of Erasmus* (*CWE*) (University of Toronto Press, 1974–).

Opera Omnia Desiderii Erasmi Roterodami (*ASD*) (Amsterdam: North-Holland Publishing Company, 1969–).

Evans, Dylan Foster, 'Conquest, Roads and Resistance in Medieval Wales', in Valerie Allen and Evans, Ruth (eds.), *Roadworks: Medieval Britain, Medieval Roads* (University of Manchester Press, 2016), 277–302.

Falcone, Filippo, 'Milton in Italy: A Survey of Scholarship, 1700–2014', *Milton Quarterly* 50 (2016), 172–88.

Farrell, Joseph, *Latin Language and Latin Culture: From Ancient to Modern Times*, Roman Literature and Its Contexts (Cambridge University Press, 2001).

Fenster, Thelma and Carolyn P. Collette (eds.), *The French of Medieval England: Essays in Honour of Jocelyn Wogan-Browne* (Martlesham: Boydell & Brewer, 2017).

Ferguson, Margaret, '"The Afflatus of Ruin": Meditations on Rome by Du Bellay, Spenser, and Stevens', in Annabel Patterson (ed.), *Roman Images: Selected Papers from the English Institute* (Baltimore: Johns Hopkins University Press, 1984), 23–50.

Fleming, John V., 'Madame Eglentyne: The Telling of the Beads', in Donka Minkova and Teresa Tinkle (eds.), *Chaucer and the Challenges of Medievalism: Studies in Honor of H.A. Kelly* (Frankfurt: Peter Lang, 2003), 205–33.

Fletcher, Angus, 'Utopian History and the *Anatomy of Criticism*', in Murray Krieger (ed.), *Northrop Frye in Modern Criticism* (New York: Columbia University Press, 1966), 31–74.

Flynn, Dennis, 'Donne's Education', in Jeanne Shami, Dennis Flynn, and M. Thomas Hester (eds.), *The Oxford Handbook of John Donne* (Oxford University Press, 2011), 408–23.

Flynn, V. J., 'The Grammatical Writings of William Lily, ?1468–?1523', *Papers of the Bibliographical Society of America* 37 (1943), 85–113.

Ford, Andrew, *The Origins of Criticism: Literary Culture and Poetic Theory in Classical Greece* (Princeton University Press, 2002).

Frank, Hardy Long, 'Chaucer's Prioress and the Blessed Virgin', *Chaucer Review* 13 (1979), 346–62.

Frantzen, Allen J., 'The Englishness of Bede, From Then to Now', in Scott DeGregorio (ed.), *The Cambridge Companion to Bede* (Cambridge University Press, 2010), 229–40.

Fredriksen, Paula, 'Paul and Augustine: Conversion Narratives, Orthodox Traditions, and the Retrospective Self', *Journal of Theological Studies*, n.s. 37 (1986), 3–34.

Freud, Sigmund, *Civilization and Its Discontents*, trans. Joan Riviere, rev. James Strachey (London: Hogarth Press, 1969).

Sigmund Freud Studienausgabe, 10 vols. (Frankfurt: S. Fischer Verlag, 1969–1975).

Friedman, Albert B., 'The Mysterious Greyn in the "Prioress's Tale"', *Chaucer Review* 11 (1977), 328–33.

Frye, Northrop, *The Educated Imagination* (Toronto: Anansi Press, 2002).

Fulk, R. D., Robert E. Bjork, and John D. Niles (eds.), *Klaeber's Beowulf and the Fight at Finnsburg*, 4th edn. (University of Toronto Press, 2008).

Garrison, M., 'The Social World of Alcuin: Nicknames at York and at the Carolingian Court', in L. A. J. R. Houwen and A. MacDonald (eds.), *Alcuin of York: Scholar at the Carolingian Court*, Germania Latina 3 (Groningen: Forsten, 1998), 59–79.

Gayk, Shannon, '"To wondre upon this thyng": Chaucer's *Prioress's Tale*', *Exemplaria* 22 (2010), 138–56.

Geary, P., *Living with the Dead in the Middle Ages* (Ithaca: Cornell University Press, 1994).

The Geneva Bible: A Facsimile of the 1560 Edition (Madison: University of Wisconsin Press, 1969).

Geoffrey of Monmouth, *The Historia Regum Britannie of Geoffrey of Monmouth, I: A Single-Manuscript Edition from Bern, Burgerbibliothek, MS 568*, ed. Neil Wright (Cambridge: D. S. Brewer, 1984).

The Historia Regum Britannie of Geoffrey of Monmouth, II: The First Variant Version, A Critical Edition, ed. Neil Wright (Cambridge: D. S. Brewer, 1998).

The History of the Kings of Britain, ed. and trans. Michael A. Faletra (Peterborough: Broadview, 2008).

Gerrard, James, *The Ruin of Roman Britain: An Archaeological Perspective* (Cambridge University Press, 2013).

Gildas, *The epistle of Gildas, the most ancient British author: who flourished in the yeere of our Lord, 546. And who by his great erudition, sanctitie, and wisedome, acquired the name of sapiens. Faithfully translated out of the originall Latine.* (London, 1638) [STC 11895].

The Ruin of Britain and Other Works, ed. and trans. Michael Winterbottom (London: Phillimore, 1978).

Gildenhard, Ingo and Andrew Zissos, 'Ovid's "Hecale": Deconstructing Athens in the *Metamorphoses*', *The Journal of Roman Studies* 94 (2004), 47–72.

Gittings, C., *Death, Burial and the Individual in Early Modern England* (New York: Routledge, 1984).

A goodly prymer in englyshe, newly corrected and printed, with certeyne godly meditations and prayers added to the same, very necessarie & profitable for all them that ryghte assuredly vnderstande not ye latine & greke tongues (London, 1535) [STC 15988].

Gouwens, Kenneth, *Remembering the Renaissance: Humanist Narratives of the Sack of Rome* (Leiden: Brill, 1998).

Grane, Thomas, 'Did the Romans Really Know (or Care) About Southern Scandinavia? An Archaeological Perspective', in Thomas Grane (ed.), *Beyond the Roman Frontier: Roman Influences on the Northern Barbaricum* (Rome: Edizioni Quasar, 2007), 7–29.

Green, Archie, *Wobbles, Pile Butts, and Other Heroes: Laborlore Explorations* (Urbana: University of Illinois Press, 1993).

Green, Ian, *Humanism and Protestantism in Early Modern English Education* (Farnham: Ashgate, 2009).

Greenblatt, Stephen J., *Hamlet in Purgatory* (Princeton University Press, 2001).

Greene, Thomas M., *The Light in Troy: Imitation and Discovery in Renaissance Poetry* (New Haven: Yale University Press, 1982).

Greenhalgh, Michael, *Marble Past, Monumental Present: Building with Antiquities in the Mediaeval Mediterranean* (Leiden: Brill, 2009).

The Survival of Roman Antiquities in the Middle Ages (London: Duckworth, 1989).

Gwosdek, Hedwig (ed.), *Lily's Grammar of Latin in English: An Introduction of the Eyght Partes of Speche, and the Construction of the Same* (Oxford University Press, 2013).

Hadfield, Andrew, *Edmund Spenser: A Life* (Oxford University Press, 2012).

Hagen, Kenneth (ed.), *Augustine, the Harvest, and Theology (1300–1650): Essays Dedicated to Heiko Augustinus Oberman in Honor of his Sixtieth Birthday* (Leiden: Brill, 1990).

Harding, Vanessa, *The Dead and the Living in Paris and London, 1500–1670* (Cambridge University Press, 2002).

Hardwick, Lorna, *Reception Studies* (Cambridge University Press, 2003).

Harrison, Stephen, 'Time, Place, and Political Background', in Thea S. Thorsen (ed.), *The Cambridge Companion to Latin Love Elegy* (Cambridge University Press, 2013), 133–50.

Harvey, Margaret, *The English in Rome, 1362–1420: Portrait of an Expatriate Community* (Cambridge University Press, 1999).

Hawkes, Jane, '*Iuxta Morem Romanorum*: Stone and Sculpture in Anglo-Saxon England', in C. E. Karkov and G. H. Brown (eds.), *Anglo-Saxon Styles* (Albany: State University of New York Press, 2003), 69–99.

Heidegger, Martin, *Being and Time* (*BT*), trans. John Macquarrie and Edward Robinson (New York: Harper & Row, 1962).

Sein und Zeit (*ST*) (Tübingen: Max Niemeyer Verlag, 2006).

Helfer, Rebecca, *Spenser's Ruins and the Art of Recollection* (University of Toronto Press, 2012).

Hendrix, Scott, 'Luther's Loyalties and the Augustinian Order', in Kenneth Hagen (ed.), *Augustine, the Harvest, and Theology (1300–1650): Essays Dedicated to*

Heiko Augustinus Oberman in Honor of his Sixtieth Birthday (Leiden: Brill, 1990), 236–57.

Here after foloweth the prymer in Englysshe and in Latin sette out alonge: after the vse of Sarum (Rouen, 1555) [STC 16070].

Here after foloweth the prymer in Englysshe sette out alonge, after the vse of Sarum (Rouen, 1538) [STC 16004].

Herman, József, *Vulgar Latin*, trans. Roger Wright (University Park, PA: Penn State University Press, 2000).

Herren, Michael, '*Bigero sermone clefabo*: Notes on the Life of Vergilius Maro Grammaticus', *Classica et Mediaevalia* 31 (1970), 253–7.

'The Pseudonymous Tradition in Hiberno Latin: An Introduction', in J. J. O'Meara and B. Naumann (eds.), *Latin Script and Letters, AD 400–900: Festschrift Presented to Ludwig Bieler on the Occasion of his 70th Birthday* (Leiden: Brill, 1976), 121–31.

'Some New Light on the Life of Vergilius Maro Grammaticus', *Proceedings of the Royal Irish Academy* 79.2 (1979), 27–71.

Higgitt, J. C., 'The Roman Background to Medieval England', *Journal of the British Archaeological Association*, 3rd ser., 36 (1973), 1–15.

Higham, Nicholas John, 'Gildas, Roman Walls, and British Dykes', *Cambridge Medieval Celtic Studies* 22 (1991), 1–14.

Hilliard, Paul, 'Bede and the Changing Image of Rome and the Romans', in Elina Screen and Charles West (eds.), *Writing the Early Medieval West: Studies in Honour of Rosamond McKitterick* (Cambridge University Press, 2018), 33–48.

Hingley, Richard, *Hadrian's Wall: A Life* (Oxford University Press, 2012).

The Recovery of Roman Britain, 1586–1906: A Colony So Fertile (Oxford University Press, 2008).

Hodges, Laura Fulkerson, *Chaucer and Clothing: Clerical and Academic Costume in the General Prologue to the Canterbury Tales* (Cambridge University Press, 2005).

The Holy Bible: 1611 Edition (Nashville: Thomas Nelson, 1989).

Home, Gordon, *Roman London, A.D. 43–457*, rev. edn. (London: Eyre and Spottiswoode, 1948).

[*Horae ad usum Sarum*] (London, 1503). [STC 15900]

Hoskins, Edgar, *Horae Beatae Mariae Virginis or Sarum and York Primers* (London: Longmans, Green, 1901).

Howe, Nicholas, 'The Landscape of Anglo-Saxon England: Inherited, Invented, Imagined', in John Howe and Michael Wolfe (eds.), *Inventing Medieval Landscapes: Senses of Place in Western Europe* (Gainesville, FLA: University Press of Florida, 2002), 91–112.

Writing the Map of Anglo-Saxon England: Essays in Cultural Geography (New Haven: Yale University Press, 2008).

Hudson, Elizabeth K., 'The Colloquies of Maturin Cordier: Images of Calvinist School Life and Thought', *The Sixteenth Century Journal*, 9.3 (1978), 56–78.

Hui, Andrew, *The Poetics of Ruins in Renaissance Literature* (New York: Fordham University Press, 2017).

Jacks, Philip, *The Antiquarian and the Myth of Antiquity: The Origins of Rome in Renaissance Thought* (Cambridge University Press, 1993).

Jensen, Freyja Cox, *Reading the Roman Republic in Early Modern England* (Leiden: Brill, 2012).

Jones, Barri and David Mattingly, *An Atlas of Roman Britain* (Oxford: Blackwell, 1990).

Jones, Inigo, *The most notable antiquity of Great Britain, vulgarly called Stone-Heng on Salisbury plain. Restored by Inigo Jones Esquire, architect generall to the late King* (London, 1655) [Wing J954].

Jones, Michael E., *The End of Roman Britain* (Ithaca: Cornell University Press, 1996).

Kaster, Robert A., *Guardians of Language: The Grammarian and Society in Late Antiquity* (Berkeley: University of California Press, 1988).

Keilen, Sean, *Vulgar Eloquence: On the Renaissance Invention of English Literature* (New Haven: Yale University Press, 2006).

Kelleher, Richard, 'The Re-use of Coins in Medieval England and Wales c.1050–1550: An Introductory Survey', *Yorkshire Numismatist* 4 (2012), 183–200.

Kierkegaard, Søren, *Either/Or, Part I*, ed. and trans. Howard V. Hong and Edna H. Hong, Kierkegaard's Writings 3 (Princeton University Press, 1987).

The Sickness Unto Death: A Christian Psychological Exposition for Upbuilding and Awakening, ed. and trans. Howard V. Hong and Edna H. Hong, Kierkegaard's Writings 19 (Princeton University Press, 1983).

Søren Kierkegaards Skrifter (*SKS*), ed. Niels Jørgen Cappelørn, Joakim Garff, Jette Knudsen, Johnny Kondrup, Alastair McKinnon, and Finn Hauberg Mortensen (Copenhagen: Gads Forlag, 1997–).

Stages on Life's Way, ed. and trans. Howard V. Hong and Edna H. Hong, Kierkegaard's Writings 19 (Princeton University Press, 1988).

Kleinhenz, Christopher, 'The City of Rome in Dante's *Divine Comedy*', *Essays in Medieval Studies* 28 (2012), 51–68.

Koudounaris, Paul, *Memento Mori: The Dead Among Us* (London: Thames and Hudson, 2015).

Kynan-Wilson, William, 'Mira Romanorum Artifitia: William of Malmesbury and the Romano-British Remains at Carlisle', *Essays in Medieval Studies* 28 (2012), 35–49.

Lafferty, Maura K., 'Translating Faith from Greek to Latin: *Romanitas* and *Christianitas* in Late Fourth-Century Rome and Milan', *Journal of Early Christian Studies* 11 (2003), 21–62.

Laistner, M. L. W. and H. H. King, *A Hand-List of Bede Manuscripts* (Ithaca: Cornell University Press, 1943).

Lampert, Lisa, *Gender and Jewish Difference from Paul to Shakespeare* (Philadelphia: University of Pennsylvania Press, 2004).

Lapidge, Michael, 'Gildas's Education and the Latin Culture of Sub-Roman Britain', in Michael Lapidge and David Dumville (eds.), *Gildas: New Approaches* (Woodbridge: Boydell, 1984), 27–50.

Laqueur, T. W., *The Work of the Dead: A Cultural History of Mortal Remains* (Princeton University Press, 2015).

Lavezzo, Kathy, *Angels on the Edge of the World: Geography, Literature, and English Community, 1000–1534* (Ithaca: Cornell University Press, 2006).

Law, Vivien, *The History of Linguistics in Europe From Plato to 1600* (Cambridge University Press, 2003).

Wisdom, Authority and Grammar in the Seventh Century: Decoding Virgilius Maro Grammaticus (Cambridge University Press, 1995).

Lawrence-Mathers, Anne, 'William of Newburgh and the Northumbrian Construction of English History', *Journal of Medieval History* 33 (2007), 339–57.

Laȝamon, *Brut*, ed. G. L. Brook and R. F. Leslie, Early English Text Society 250, 257 (Oxford University Press, 1963).

Lazarus, Micha, 'Greek Literacy in Sixteenth-Century England', *Renaissance Studies* 29 (2015), 433–58.

Le Goff, Jacques, *The Birth of Purgatory*, trans. Arthur Goldhammer, rev. edn. (University of Chicago Press, 1986).

Faut-il Vraiment Découper l'Histoire en Tranches? (Paris: Éditions Seuil, 2014).

Leeds, John C., *Renaissance Syntax and Subjectivity: Ideological Contents of Latin and the Vernacular in Scottish Prose Chronicles* (Farnham: Ashgate, 2010).

Leonhardt, Jürgen, *Latin: Story of a World Language*, trans. Kenneth Kronenberg (Cambridge, MA: Belknap Press, 2013).

Lerer, Seth, 'Literary Prayer and Personal Possession in a Newly Discovered Tudor Book of Hours', *Studies in Philology* 109 (2012), 409–28.

'"On fagne flor": The Postcolonial *Beowulf*, From Heorot to Heaney', in Ananya Jahanara Kabir and Deanne Williams (eds.), *Postcolonial Approaches to the European Middle Ages: Translating Cultures* (Cambridge University Press, 2005), 77–102.

Levison, Wilhelm, *England and the Continent in the Eighth Century* (Oxford: Clarendon Press, 1946).

Lewis, C. S., *English Literature in the Sixteenth Century, Excluding Drama* (Oxford: Clarendon Press, 1954).

Liuzza, R. M. (ed. and trans.), *Beowulf*, 2nd edn. (Peterborough: Broadview Press, 2013).

Old English Poetry: An Anthology (Peterborough: Broadview Press, 2014).

Lloyd, Charles (ed.), *Formularies of Faith Put Forth by Authority During the Reign of Henry VIII* (Oxford University Press, 1856).

Löfstedt, B. (ed.), *Virgilius Maro Grammaticus Opera Omnia* (Munich: K.G. Saur, 2003).

Lupton, J. H. (ed.), *The Utopia of Sir Thomas More* (Oxford: Clarendon Press, 1895).

Luther, Martin, *D. Martin Luthers Werke: Kritische Gesamtausgabe* (*WA*), 68 vols. (Weimar: Herman Böhlaus Nachfolger, 1883–1999).

D. Martin Luthers Werke: die Deutsche Bibel (*WA DB*), 12 vols. (Weimar: Herman Böhlaus Nachfolger, 1906–61).

Luthers Vorreden zur Bibel, ed. Heinrich Bornkamm (Frankfurt: Insel, 1983).

Luther's Works (*LW*), ed. Jaroslav Pelikan and Helmut T. Lehmann, 56 vols. (Philadelphia: Concordia Publishing House, 1955–86).

A methodicall preface prefixed before the Epistle of S. Paul to the Romanes; verie necessarie and profitable for the better vnderstanding of it. Made by the right reuerend father and faithfull seruant of Christ Iesus, Martin Luther, now newly translated out of Latin into English, by W.W. student (London, 1632). (STC 16986).

MacColl, Alan, 'The Meaning of "Britain" in Medieval and Early Modern England', *Journal of British Studies* 45 (2006), 248–69.

Mack, Peter, *A History of Renaissance Rhetoric, 1380–1620* (Oxford University Press, 2011).

Madeleva, Sister Mary, *Chaucer's Nuns and Other Essays* (New York: D. Appleton and Company, 1925).

Magill, Kelley, 'Reviving Martyrdom: Interpretations of the Catacombs in Cesare Baronio's Patronage', in John R. Decker and Mitzi Kirkland-Ives (eds.), *Death, Torture and the Broken Body in European Art, 1300–1650* (Farnham: Ashgate Press, 2015), 87–115.

Maltman, Sister Nicholas, 'The Divine Granary, or the End of the Prioress's "Greyn"', *Chaucer Review* 17 (1982), 163–70.

Mann, J. C. and R. G. Penman (ed.), *Literary Sources for Roman Britain*, 3rd edn. (London: London Association of Classical Teachers, 1996).

Mantello, F. A. C. and A. G. Rigg (eds.), *Medieval Latin: An Introduction and Bibliographical Guide* (Washington: Catholic University of America Press, 1996).

Marno, David, 'Divine Poems', in Michael Schoenfeldt (ed.), *John Donne in Context* (Cambridge University Press, 2019), 85–93.

Marotti, Arthur F., 'John Donne's Conflicted Anti-Catholicism', *Journal of English and Germanic Philology* 101 (2002), 358–79.

Marshall, Peter, *Beliefs and the Dead in Reformation England* (Oxford University Press, 2002).

Martial, *Epigrams*, ed. and trans. D. R. Shackleton Bailey, 3 vols., LCL 94, 95, 480 (Cambridge, MA: Harvard University Press, 1993).

Martin, Catherine Gimelli, *Milton's Italy: Anglo-Italian Literature, Travel, and Religion in Seventeenth-Century England* (New York: Routledge, 2017).

Martindale, Charles, 'Reception – A New Humanism? Receptivity, Pedagogy, the Transhistorical', *Classical Receptions Journal* 5 (2013), 169–83.

Redeeming the Text: Latin Poetry and the Hermeneutics of Reception (Cambridge University Press, 1993).

Martindale, Charles and Richard F. Thomas (eds.), *Classics and the Uses of Reception* (Malden, MA: Blackwell, 2006).

Marvin, Corey J., *Word Outward: Medieval Perspectives on the Entry into Language* (New York: Routledge, 2001).

Marvin, Julia, *The Construction of Vernacular History in the Anglo-Norman Prose Brut Chronicle: The Manuscript Culture of Late Medieval England* (York Medieval Press, 2017).

Matthews, David, 'The Medieval Invasion of Early-Modern England', *New Medieval Literatures* 10 (2008), 223–44.

McGowan, Margaret M., *The Vision of Rome in Late Renaissance France* (New Haven: Yale University Press, 2000).

McKeown, J. C., *Classical Latin: An Introductory Course* (Indianapolis: Hackett, 2010).

McGregor, Rachel, '"Run not before the laws": Lily's *Grammar*, the Oxford *Bellum grammaticale*, and the Rules of Concord', *Renaissance Studies* 29 (2015), 261–79.

McLaughlin, Martin L., *Literary Imitation in the Italian Renaissance: The Theory and Practice of Literary Imitation in Italy from Dante to Bembo* (Oxford: Clarendon Press, 1995).

McManus, Denis, 'Rules, Regression and the "Background": Dreyfus, Heidegger and McDowell', *European Journal of Philosophy* 16 (2007), 432–58.

McMullen, A. Joseph, 'Rewriting History through the Landscape in *Breuddwyd Maxen Wledig*', *Proceedings of the Harvard Celtic Colloquium* 31 (2011), 225–41.

Merleau-Ponty, Maurice, *Phénoménologie de la Perception* (Paris: Gallimard, 2011).

Middle English Dictionary (*MED*), 20 vols. (Ann Arbor: University of Michigan Press, 1952–2001).

Miller, Anthony, *Roman Triumphs and Early Modern English Culture* (Houndmills, Basingstoke, Hampshire: Palgrave, 2001).

Miller, Leo, 'Milton Dines at the Jesuit College: Reconstructing the Evening of October 30, 1638', *Milton Quarterly* 13 (1979), 142–6.

Miller, W. E., 'Double Translation in English Humanist Education', *Studies in the Renaissance* 10 (1963), 163–74.

Milton, John, *Complete Prose Works of John Milton* (*CPW*), ed. Don M. Wolfe, 8 vols. (New Haven: Yale University Press, 1953–82).

The Complete Shorter Poems, ed. John Carey, 2nd edn. (Harlow: Pearson, 1997).

Paradise Lost, ed. Alastair Fowler, 2nd edn. (Harlow: Pearson, 2007).

The Works of John Milton (*WJM*), ed. Frank Allen Patterson, 18 vols. (New York: Columbia University Press, 1931–38).

Missuno, Filip, 'Glowing Paradoxes and Glimmers of Doom: A Re-evaluation of the Meaning of Old English *fāh* in Poetic Contexts', *Neophilologus* 99 (2015), 125–42.

Montaigne (Michel Eyquem de Montaigne), *Essais*, ed. Jean Balsamo, Michel Magnien, and Catherine Magnien-Simonin (Paris: Gallimard, 2007).

Essayes vvritten in French By Michael Lord of Montaigne, Knight of the Order of S. Michael, gentleman of the French Kings Chamber: done into English, according to the last French edition, by Iohn Florio reader of the Italian tongue vnto the Soueraigne Maiestie of Anna, Queene of England, Scotland, France and Ireland,

&c. And one of the gentlemen of hir royall priuie chamber (London, 1613) [STC 18042].

More, Thomas, *A fruteful, and pleasaunt worke of the beste state of a publyque weale, and of the newe yle called Vtopia: written in Latine by Syr Thomas More knyght, and translated into Englyshe by Raphe Robynson citizein and goldsmythe of London, at the procurement, and earnest request of George Tadlowe citezein & haberdassher of the same citie* (London, 1551) [STC 18094].

A frutefull pleasaunt, & wittie worke, of the beste state of a publique weale, and of the newe yle, called Vtopia: written in Latine, by the right worthie and famous Syr Thomas More knyght, and translated into Englishe by Raphe Robynson, sometime fellowe of Corpus Christi College in Oxford, and nowe by him at this seconde edition newlie perused and corrected, and also with diuers notes in the margent augmented (London, 1556) [STC 18095].

Morris, R. K. and Julia Roxan, 'Churches on Roman Buildings', in W. Rodwell (ed.), *Temples, Churches and Religion: Recent Research in Roman Britain*, BAR British Series 77 (1980), 175–209.

Moss, Ann, *Renaissance Truth and the Latin Language Turn* (Oxford University Press, 2003).

Muir, Bernard (ed.), *The Exeter Anthology of Old English Poetry: An Edition of Exeter Dean and Chapter MS 3501*, 2 vols., rev. 2nd edn. (University of Exeter Press, 2000).

Muir, Tom, 'Specters of Spenser: Translating the *Antiquitez*', *Spenser Studies*, 25 (2010), 327–61.

'Without Remainder: Ruins and Tombs in Shakespeare's Sonnets', *Textual Practice* 24 (2010), 21–49.

Murray, Luke, 'Jesuit Hebrew Studies After Trent: Cornelius a Lapide (1567–1637)', *Journal of Jesuit Studies* 4 (2017), 76–97.

Murton, Megan, 'The *Prioress's Prologue*: Dante, Liturgy, and Ineffability', *Chaucer Review* 52 (2017), 318–40.

Naismith, Rory, 'Antiquity, Authority, and Religion in the *Epitomae* and *Epistolae* of Virgilius Maro Grammaticus', *Peritia* 20 (2008), 59–85.

Nashe, Thomas, *The vnfortunate traueller. Or, The life of Iacke Wilton* (London, 1594) [STC 18380].

Nearing Jr., Homer, 'Julius Caesar and the Tower of London', *Modern Language Notes* 63 (1948), 228–33.

Nennius, [*Historia Brittonum*] *British History and The Welsh Annals*, ed. and trans. John Morris (London: Phillimore, 1980).

Nicholson, Catherine, *Uncommon Tongues: Eloquence and Eccentricity in the English Renaissance* (Philadelphia: University of Pennsylvania Press, 2014).

Nietzsche, Friedrich, *Twilight of the Idols / The Anti-Christ* (London: Penguin, 1990).

Werke: Kritische Gesamtausgabe (*KGW*), ed. Giorgio Colli and Mazzino Montinari, 9 vols. (Berlin: Walter de Gruyter, 1967–2015).

Noot, Jan van der, *A theatre wherein be represented as wel the miseries & calamities that follow the voluptuous worldlings as also the greate ioyes and plesures which the faithfull do enioy. An argument both profitable and delectable, to all that sincerely loue the word of God. Deuised by S. Iohn vander Noodt. Seene and allowed according to the order appointed* (London, 1569) [STC 18602].

O'Connell, Marvin R., *Thomas Stapleton and the Counter Reformation* (New Haven: Yale University Press, 1964).

OED Online (Oxford University Press, 2019).

Oliver, Kathleen M., 'Singing Bread, Manna, and the Clergeon's "Greyn"', *Chaucer Review* (1997), 357–64.

Orchard, Andy, 'Reconstructing "The Ruin"', in Virginia Blanton and Helene Scheck (eds.), *Intertexts: Studies in Anglo-Saxon Culture Presented to Paul E. Szarmach* (Tempe, ACMRS, 2008), 45–68.

Orlandi, Giovanni, '*Clausulae* in Gildas' *De Excidio Britanniae*', in Michael Lapidge and David Dumville (eds.), *Gildas: New Approaches* (Woodbridge: Boydell, 1984), 129–49.

Orme, William, *Medieval Schools from Roman Britain to Renaissance England* (New Haven: Yale University Press, 2006).

Ortenberg, Veronica, *The English Church and the Continent in the Tenth and Eleventh Centuries* (Oxford: Clarendon Press, 1992).

Osborn, Marijane, 'Laying the Roman Ghost of *Beowulf* 320 and 725', *Neuphilologische Mitteilungen* 70 (1989), 246–55.

Ottosen, Knud, *The Responsories and Versicles of the Latin Office of the Dead* (Aarhus University Press, 1993).

Outler, Albert C. (ed.), *John Wesley* (New York: Oxford University Press, 1964).

Ovid, *Publ Ovid. De tristibus: or Mournefull elegies, in five bookes: composed in his banishment, part at sea, and part at Tomos, a city of Pontus. Translated into English verse by Zachary Catlin, Mr. of Arts. Suffolke* (London, 1639) [STC 18981].

Tristia, Ex Ponto, ed. and trans. A. L. Wheeler, rev. G. P. Goold, LCL 151 (Cambridge, MA: Harvard University Press, 1988).

Pade, Marianne, 'The Reception of Plutarch from Antiquity to the Italian Renaissance', in Mark Beck (ed.), *A Companion to Plutarch* (Chichester: Wiley-Blackwell, 2014), 529–43.

Parry, Graham, 'Thomas Browne and the Uses of Antiquity', in Reid Barbour and Claire Preston (eds.), *Sir Thomas Browne: The World Proposed* (Oxford University Press, 2008), 63–79.

The Trophies of Time: English Antiquarians of the Seventeenth Century (Oxford University Press, 1995).

Penney, J. H. W., 'Archaism and Innovation in Latin Poetic Syntax', in J. N. Adams and R. G. Mayer (eds.), *Aspects of the Language of Latin Poetry*, Proceedings of the British Academy 93 (Oxford University Press, 1999), 249–68.

Perkinson, Stephen, with Naomi Speakman, Katherine Baker, Elizabeth Morrison, and Emma Maggie Solberg, *The Ivory Mirror: The Art of Mortality in Renaissance Europe* (New Haven: Yale University Press, 2017).

Petrarca, Francesco, *Selected Letters*, trans. Elaine Fantham, 2 vols. (Cambridge, MA: Harvard University Press, 2017).

Phillips, Thomas E., 'The Genre of Acts: Moving Toward a Consensus?', *Currents in Biblical Research* 4 (2006), 365–96.

Plato, *Theaetetus, Sophist,* ed. and trans. Harold North Fowler, LCL 123 (Cambridge, MA: Harvard University Press, 1921).

Pollard, A. W., and G. R. Redgrave, *A Short-Title Catalogue of Books Printed in England,* Scotland, *and Ireland, and of English Books Printed Abroad, 1475–1640,* 2nd edn., rev. W. A. Jackson, F. S. Ferguson, and Katharine F. Pantzer, 3 vols. (London: Bibliographical Society, 1976–1993).

Pollman, Karla and Willemien Otten (eds.), *The Oxford Guide to the Historical Reception of Augustine,* 3 vols. (Oxford University Press, 2013).

Potter, John F., 'The Occurrence of Roman Brick and Tile in Churches of the London Basin', *Britannia* 32 (2001), 119–42.

Prescott, Anne Lake, 'Spenser (Re)Reading Du Bellay: Chronology and Literary Response', in Judith H. Anderson, Donald Cheney, and David A. Richardson (eds.), *Spenser's Life and the Subject of Biography* (Amherst: University of Massachusetts Press, 1996), 131–45.

Price, David, 'Christian Humanism and the Representation of Judaism: Johannes Reuchlin and the Discovery of Hebrew', *Arthuriana* 19.3 (2009), 80–96.

Price, Merrall Llewelyn, 'Sadism and Sentimentality: Absorbing Antisemitism in Chaucer's Prioress', *Chaucer Review* 43 (2008), 197–214.

The primer, in Englishe and Latyn, set foorth by the Kynges maiestie and his clergie to be taught learned, and read: and none other to be vsed throughout all his dominions (London, 1545) [STC 16040].

The primer, set foorth by the Kynges maiestie and his clergie, to be taught lerned, & read: and none other to be vsed throughout all his dominions (London, 1545) [STC 16034].

Raby, F. J. E., *A History of Christian–Latin Poetry from the Beginnings to the Close of the Middle Ages,* 2nd edn. (Oxford: Clarendon Press, 1953).

Rashkow, Ilona N., 'Hebrew Bible Translation and the Fear of Judaization', *The Sixteenth Century Journal* 21 (1990), 217–37.

Rauk, John, 'The Vocative of Deus and Its Problems', *Classical Philology* 92 (1997), 138–49.

Rex, Richard, *Henry VIII and the English Reformation* (New York: Palgrave, 2006).

Rist, Thomas, *Revenge Tragedy and the Drama of Commemoration in Reforming England* (Farnham: Ashgate, 2008).

Roark, Ryan, '"Stonehenge in the Mind" and "Stonehenge on the Ground": Reader, Viewer, and Object in Inigo Jones' *Stone-Heng Restored* (1655)', *Journal of the Society of Architectural Historians* 77 (2018), 285–99.

Roberts, Brynley F. (ed.), *Breudwyt Maxen Wledic* (Dublin Institute for Advanced Studies, 2005).

Rochette, Bruno, 'Language Policies in the Roman Republic and Empire', trans. James Clackson, in James Clackson (ed.), *A Companion to the Latin Language* (Chichester: Wiley-Blackwell, 2011), 549–63.

Rock, Ian E., *Paul's Letter to the Romans and Roman Imperialism: An Ideological Analysis of the Exordium (Romans 1:1–17)* (Eugene, OR: Pickwick Publications, 2012).

Rose, Paula J., *A Commentary on Augustine's De cura pro mortuis gerenda* (Leiden: Brill, 2013).

Rouse, Robert, 'Arthurian Caerleon and the Untimely Architecture of History', *Arthuriana* 23 (2013), 40–51.

Rowley, Sharon M., 'Bede in Later Anglo-Saxon England', in Scott DeGregorio (ed.), *The Cambridge Companion to Bede* (Cambridge University Press, 2010), 216–28.

The Old English Version of Bede's Historia Ecclesiastica (Cambridge: D.S. Brewer, 2011).

Rutgers, Leonard Victor, *The Jews in Late Ancient Rome: Evidence of Cultural Interaction in the Roman Diaspora* (Leiden: Brill, 1995).

Sanchez, Melissa and Ayesha Ramachandran (eds.), *Spenser Studies: A Renaissance Poetry Annual* 30 (2016).

Schwarz, Reinhard, 'Beobachtungen zu Luthers Bekanntschaft mit antiken Dichtern und Geschichtsschreibern', *Lutherjahrbuch* 54 (1987), 7–22.

Schwyzer, Philip, *Archaeologies of English Renaissance Literature* (Oxford University Press, 2007).

Shakespeare, William, *The Riverside Shakespeare*, ed. G. Blakemore Evans and J. J. M. Tobin, 2nd edn. (Boston: Houghton Mifflin, 1997).

Shapiro, Marianne, *De Vulgari Eloquentia: Dante's Book of Exile* (Lincoln: University of Nebraska Press, 1990).

Shapland, Michael G., 'Meanings of Timber and Stone in Anglo-Saxon Building Practice', in Michael D. J. Bintley and Michael G. Shapland (eds.), *Trees and Timber in the Anglo-Saxon World* (Oxford University Press, 2013), 21–44.

Sheil, Patrick, *Kierkegaard and Levinas: The Subjunctive Mood* (Farnham: Ashgate, 2010).

Shirley, Victoria, 'The Galfridian Tradition(s) in England, Scotland, and Wales: Texts, Purpose, Context, 1138-1530', unpublished PhD thesis, Cardiff University, 2017.

Simon, Joan, *Education and Society in Tudor England* (Cambridge University Press, 1966).

Simpson, James, *Reform and Cultural Revolution, 1350–1547*, The Oxford Literary History vol. II (Oxford University Press, 2002).

Skinner, Quentin, *Liberty Before Liberalism* (Cambridge University Press, 1997).

Skyrme, Raymond, '"Buscas en Roma a Roma": Quevedo, Vitalis, and Janus Pannonius', *Bibliothèque d'Humanisme et Renaissance* 44 (1982), 363–7.

Smith, Lesley, *The Glossa Ordinaria: The Making of a Medieval Bible Commentary* (Leiden: Brill, 2009).

Sokolov, Danila, *Renaissance Texts, Medieval Subjectivities: Rethinking Petrarchan Desire from Wyatt to Shakespeare* (Pittsburgh: Duquesne University Press, 2017).

Spenser, Edmund, *Edmund Spenser: The Shorter Poems*, ed. Richard A. McCabe (Harmondsworth: Penguin, 1999).

The Faerie Queene, ed. A. C. Hamilton with text by Hiroshi Yamashita and Toshiyuki Suzuki, rev. 2nd edn. (Harlow: Pearson, 2007).

Stanbury, Sarah, '*The Man of Law's Tale and Rome*', *Exemplaria* 22 (2010), 119–37.

Stanley, Eric Gerald, *A Collection of Papers with Emphasis on Old English Literature* (Toronto: Pontifical Institute of Medieval Studies, 1987).

Stapleton, Paul J., 'Pope Gregory and the *Gens Anglorum*: Thomas Stapleton's Translation of Bede', *Renaissance Papers* (2008), 15–34.

Steinmetz, David C., 'Calvin and the Divided Self of Romans 7', in Kenneth Hagen (ed.), *Augustine, the Harvest, and Theology (1300–1650): Essays Dedicated to Heiko Augustinus Oberman in Honor of his Sixtieth Birthday* (Leiden: Brill, 1990), 300–12.

Stevens, Paul, 'Archipelagic Criticism and Its Limits: Milton, Geoffrey of Monmouth, and the Matter of England', *The European Legacy* 17 (2012), 151–64.

Stewart, Jon (ed.), *Kierkegaard and the Roman World* (Farnham: Ashgate, 2009).

Stocker, D. A. and P. Everson, 'Rubbish Recycled: A Study of the Re-use of Stone in Lincolnshire', in D. Parsons (ed.), *Stone Quarrying and Building in England*, A.D. *43–1525* (Chichester: Phillimore & Co.), 83–101.

Stocker, David, '*Fons et Origo*: The Symbolic Death, Burial and Resurrection of English Font Stones', *Church Archaeology* 1 (1997), 17–25.

Stow, John, *A Survey of London*, 2 vols. (Oxford: Clarendon Press, 1908).

Tarlow, Sarah, *Ritual, Belief and the Dead in Early Modern Britain and Ireland* (Cambridge University Press, 2011).

Taruskin, Richard, *Oxford History of Western Music*, 5 vols. (New York: Oxford University Press, 2005).

Thoreau, Henry David, *A Week, Walden, The Maine Woods, Cape Cod*, ed. Robert F. Sayre (New York: Library of America, 1985).

Trilling, Renée R., 'Ruins in the Realms of Thoughts: Reading as Constellation in Anglo-Saxon Poetry', *Journal of English and Germanic Philology* 108 (2009), 141–67.

Trinquet, Roger, 'Les Origines de la Première Éducation de Montaigne et la Suprématie du Latin en France en 1530 et 1540', *Bulletin de la Société des Amis de Montaigne*, 4th ser. 16 (1968), 23–39.

Tucker, G. H., *The Poet's Odyssey: Joachim Du Bellay and the 'Antiquitez de Rome'* (Oxford: Clarendon Press, 1990).

'*Roma Instaurata* en Dialogue Avec *Roma Prisca*: La Représentation néo-Latine de Rome Sous Jules III, 1553–55, chez Janus Vitalis, Joachim du Bellay et Lelio Capilupi (de l'Ekphrase à la Prosopopée)', *Camenae* 2 (2007).

'A Roman Dialogue with Virgil and Homer: Capilupi, the *Cento* and Rome', in Carlo Caruso and Andrew Laird (eds), *Italy and the Classical Tradition: Language, Thought and Poetry 1300–1600* (London: Bloomsbury, 2009), 204–37.

'*Roma Rediviva*: André de Resende, Joachim Du Bellay, and the Continuing Legacy of Janus Vitalis's Roman Diptych', *Bibliothèque d'Humanisme et Renaissance* 54 (1992), 731–6.

William Tyndale, *A compendious introduccion, prologe or preface vn to the pistle off Paul to the Romayns* (London, 1526) (STC 24438).

Expositions and Notes on Sundry Portions of the Holy Scriptures, Together With the Practice of Prelates, ed. H. Walter (Cambridge University Press, 1849).

Viaud, Alina, 'Rome et Montaigne dans *Les Essais*: le Transitoire et la Transition', Lurens [online], April 2011, www.lurens.ens.fr/travaux/literature-du-xvie-siecle/article/montaigne-et-rome.

Virgil, [Works], trans. H. R. Fairclough, rev. G. P. Goold, 2 vols., LCL 63–4 (Cambridge, MA: Harvard University Press, 1999).

Vitalis, Janus, *Iani Vitalis Panormitani Sacrosanctae Romanae Ecclesiae Elogia* (Rome, 1553).

Voltaire, *Essai sur les Mœurs et l'Esprit des Nations et sur les Principaux Faits de l'Histoire Depuis Charlemagne Jusqu'à Louis XIII*, ed. René Pomeau, 2 vols. (Paris: Garnier, 1963).

Vos, Alvin, '"Good Matter and Good Utterance": The Character of English Ciceronianism', *Studies in English Literature, 1500–1900* 19 (1979), 3–18.

Walaskay, Paul W., *'And So We Came to Rome': The Political Perspective of St Luke* (Cambridge University Press, 1983).

Walker, Greg, 'When did "the Medieval" End? Retrospection, Foresight, and the End(s) of the English Middle Ages', in Elaine Treharne and Greg Walker, with William Green (eds.), *The Oxford Handbook of Medieval Literature in English* (Oxford University Press, 2010), 725–38.

Wallace, Andrew, 'Education', in Michael Schoenfeldt (ed.), *John Donne in Context* (Cambridge University Press, 2019), 131–8.

'Pedagogy, Education, and Early Career', in *Edmund Spenser in Context*, ed. Andrew Escobedo (Cambridge University Press, 2016), 7–13.

'Spenser's Dead' in Melissa Sanchez and Ayesha Ramachandran (eds.) *Spenser Studies: A Renaissance Poetry Annual* 30 (2016), 255–70.

Virgil's Schoolboys: The Poetics of Pedagogy in Renaissance England (Oxford University Press, 2010).

'"What's Hecuba to him?": Pain, Privacy, and the Ancient Text', in Donald Beecher and Grant Williams (eds.), *Ars Reminiscendi: Mind and Memory in Renaissance Culture* (Toronto: Centre for Reformation and Renaissance Studies, 2009), 231–43.

Walsham, Alexandra, *Catholic Reformation in Protestant Britain* (Farnham: Ashgate, 2014).

The Reformation of the Landscape: Religion, Identity, and Memory in Early Modern Britain and Ireland (Oxford University Press, 2011).

Walton, Izaak, *The Lives of John Donne, Sir Henry Wotton, Richard Hooker, George Herbert and Robert Sanderson* (Oxford University Press, 1936).

White, Helen C., *The Tudor Books of Private Devotion* (Madison: University of Wisconsin Press, 1951).

White, Micheline, 'Dismantling Catholic Primers and Reforming Private Prayer: Anne Lock, Hezekiah's Song and Psalm 50/51', in Alec Ryrie and

Jessica Martin (eds.) *Private and Domestic Devotion in Early Modern Britain* (Farnham: Ashgate, 2012), 93–113.

Whitehead, Maurice, *English Jesuit Education: Expulsion, Suppression, Survival and Restoration, 1762–1803* (Farnham: Ashgate, 2013).

Willi, Andreas, 'Campaigning for *Utilitas*: Style, Grammar, and Philosophy in C. Iulius Caesar', in Eleanor Dickey and Anna Chahoud (eds.), *Colloquial and Literary Latin* (Cambridge University Press, 2010), 229–42.

Williams, Howard, 'Ancient Landscapes and the Dead: The Reuse of Prehistoric and Roman Monuments as Early Anglo-Saxon Burial Sites', *Medieval Archaeology* 41 (1997), 1–32.

Williams, Kelsey Jackson, *The Antiquary: John Aubrey's Historical Scholarship* (Oxford University Press, 2016).

Willis, Gary, *Rome and Rhetoric: Shakespeare's Julius Caesar* (New Haven: Yale University Press, 2011).

Wilson, Thomas, *Arte of Rhetorique*, ed. Thomas J. Derrick (New York: Garland, 1982).

The arte of rhetorique, for the vse of all soche as are studious of eloquence, set forthe in Englishe (London, 1560) [STC 25800].

Wing, D. G., *A Short-Title Catalogue of Books Printed in England, Scotland, Ireland, Wales, and British America, and of English Books Printed in Other Countries, 1641–1700*, 2nd edn., rev., 4 vols. (New York: Modern Language Association of America, 1972–1998).

Witcher, R. E., Divya P. Tolia-Kelly, and Richard Hingley, 'Archaeologies of Landscape: Excavating the Materialities of Hadrian's Wall', *Journal of Material Culture* 15 (2010), 105–28.

Witcher, Robert, 'Roman Roads: Phenomenological Perspectives on Roads in the Landscape', in Colin Forcey, John Hawthorne, and Robert Witcher (eds.), *TRAC 97: Proceedings of the Seventh Annual Theoretical Roman Archaeology Conference* (Oxford: Oxbow, 1998), 60–70.

Wittgenstein, Ludwig, *Culture and Value*, ed. G. H. von Wright with Heikki Nyman, trans. Peter Winch, rev. 2nd edn. (Oxford: Basil Blackwell, 1980).

Philosophical Investigations, trans. G. E. M. Anscombe, rev. P. M. S. Hacker and Joachim Schulte, 4th edn. rev. (Chichester: Wiley-Blackwell, 2009).

Remarks on the Philosophy of Psychology, ed. G. H. von Wright and Heikki Nyman, trans. C. G. Luckhardt and M. A. E. Aue, 2 vols. (Oxford: Basil Blackwell, 1980).

Zettel, ed. G. E. M. Anscombe and G. H. von Wright, trans. G. E. M. Anscombe (Oxford: Basil Blackwell, 1967).

Wogan-Browne, Jocelyn (ed.), with Carolyn Collette, Maryanne Kowaleski, Linne Mooney, Ad Putter, and David Trotter, *Language and Culture in Medieval Britain: The French of England, c.1100-c.1500* (Martlesham: Boydell & Brewer, 2009).

Wolfe, Jessica, *Homer and the Question of Strife: From Erasmus to Hobbes* (University of Toronto Press, 2015).

Wood, Ian, 'The End of Roman Britain: Continental Evidence and Parallels', in Michael Lapidge and David Dumville (eds.), *Gildas: New Approaches* (Woodbridge, Suffolk: Boydell, 1984), 1–25.

Woolf, D. R., *The Social Circulation of the Past: English Historical Culture, 1500–1730* (Oxford University Press, 2003).

Wrenn, C. L., *Beowulf with the Finnesburg Fragment* (London: Allen & Unwin, 1953).

Wright, Neil, 'Gildas' Prose Style and Its Origins', in Michael Lapidge and David Dumville (eds.), *Gildas: New Approaches* (Woodbridge: Boydell, 1984), 107–28.

'The Place of Henry of Huntingdon's *Epistola ad Warinumin* in the Text-History of Geoffrey of Monmouth's *Historia regum Britannie*: A Preliminary Investigation', in Gillian Jondorf and David N. Dumville (eds.), *France and the British Isles in the Middle Ages* (Woodbridge: Boydell & Brewer, 1991), 77–113 (91).

Young, R. V., 'Donne and Bellarmine', *John Donne Journal: Studies in the Age of Donne* 19 (2000), 223–34.

Zetzel, James E.G., *Critics, Compilers, and Commentators: An Introduction to Roman Philology, 200 BCE–800 CE* (Oxford University Press, 2018).

Index

Printed in the United States
by Baker & Taylor Publisher Services